MW00635268

US Tax and SAP®

SAP PRESS

SAP PRESS is a joint initiative of SAP and Galileo Press. The know-how offered by SAP specialists combined with the expertise of the publishing house Galileo Press offers the reader expert books in the field. SAP PRESS features first-hand information and expert advice, and provides useful skills for professional decision-making.

SAP PRESS offers a variety of books on technical and business related topics for the SAP user. For further information, please visit our website: *www.sap-press.com*.

Satish M. Badgi
Practical SAP US Payroll
2007, app. 324 pp.
978-1-59229-132-8

Thomas Michael
Reporting for Asset Accanting
2007, app. 96 pp.
978-59229-4

Kumar Srinivasan and Sridhar Srinivasan
SAP NetWeaver BI Integrated Planning For Finance
2007, 314 pp.
978-1-59229-129-8

Sachin Sethi
Enhanching Supplier Relationship Management Using SAP SRM
2007, 694 pp.
978-1-59229-068-0

Michael Scott

US Tax and SAP®

Galileo Press

Bonn • Boston

ISBN 978-1-59229-155-7

1st edition 2007

Acquisitions Editor Jawahara Saidullah
Developmental Editor Jutta VanStean
Copy Editor Julie McNamee
Cover Design Silke Braun
Layout Design Vera Brauner
Production Vera Brauner
Typesetting SatzPro, Krefeld
Printed and bound in Germany

Contents at a Glance

Contents

Acknowledgments

This book is dedicated to my parents, James F. and Jacqueline Scott, who taught me to work hard and encouraged me to never stop learning. For that, I will forever be grateful.

I also would like to express thanks to the professionals at IBM, PricewaterhouseCoopers, and Accenture who, through countless hours of consulting work on often challenging projects, have added to the knowledgebase of SAP and taxes; and also to the tax professionals in the many corporations I have worked with over the years who have given me the opportunity to assist them with their SAP projects.

Foreword

SAP implementations present unique United States tax issues. Unfortunately, many SAP implementation teams do not have the necessary tax expertise or the understanding that an SAP implementation may create significant issues for a corporate tax department and that these need to be addressed during the implementation. For example, one issue related to SAP and tax is that the mandatory detailed data that was once available to corporate tax departments may no longer be accessible after an SAP implementation, unless special attention is paid to the tax requirements during the SAP implementation.

Many groups will benefit by reading this book, which addresses SAP-related tax issues. SAP implementation teams will increase their knowledge of tax requirements and techniques available to solve the SAP-related tax issues. Corporate tax departments will gain a better understanding of SAP and its strengths and limitations. IRS auditors will gain a better understanding of SAP's DART tool and finally financial auditors will increase their understanding of tax issues and controls offered by SAP.

The author of this book, Michael Scott, is a long time friend and former colleague of mine. We worked together at PricewaterhouseCoopers on a special team that helped corporations during and after an SAP implementation to identify and address tax issues. Michael has the skill set of being an expert on SAP, while also having a very strong tax background, making him uniquely qualified to have written a book on SAP and US tax. Within our firm, his blended skill set placed him in high demand to consult with our largest clients on SAP-related tax issues. While we worked together, Michael also led training classes for the IRS' computer audit specialists, as well as for SAP teams at many Fortune 100 companies.

Nina O'Connor
Tax Partner
PricewaterhouseCoopers
July 2007

Preface

For the SAP professional, a collage of feelings is usually at play in any SAP implementation. Often, in the area of taxes, a feeling of frustration is part of the mix. This is generally a result of a lack of knowledge and understanding of the inherent capabilities of SAP software. Common protocol is to provide a liasion between the tax department and the SAP team, whose job it is to make sure all necessary tax functions are included in the final implementation. Unfortunately, if the liasion chosen does not have enough experience with the implementation process or doesn't have a solid understanding of the basic do's and don'ts of SAP software, tax issues can be bypassed because of implementation deadlines, and, ultimately, result in an implementation that does not fully satisfy the client's needs.

With basic skills and knowledge of tax issues as they relate to SAP implementations, frustrations can be kept to a minimum, and fruitful communication between the tax department and the SAP team will be maximized. This results in an implementation that fulfills the requirements of the company and meets the requirements of tax professionals. As a result, large amounts of time are saved, which ultimately results in dollars saved.

The intent of this book is to provide the basic skills and knowledge necessary for tax professionals to confidently address and engage an SAP team in the tax implementation area. It is absolutely possible for even a novice to learn the basics of SAP and be successful in assisting in its implementation.

My Own Experience

Ten years ago, I rigorously pursued learning everything I could about SAP software with the goal of joining an SAP implementation team. At the time, I was working in the tax department of a large computer services corporation. When the corporation began implementing SAP, I was chosen to be the tax liaison on the implementation team. The company had successfully implemented SAP software in many of its international areas but was struggling with the United States. U.S. taxation was one of the stumbling blocks. The organizational structure chosen included legal entities being defined as company codes, but things went haywire from there.

Only one plant was planned, and cost objects were being defined on a responsibility basis instead of jurisdictionally. At the same time, the tax department did not want manual intervention in tax decisions. I did not have enough experience with R/3 at the time to understand how the system was designed to work and was unable to offer the quality assistance I could otherwise have. If I had the information contained in this book, it would have been a tremendous help to the implementation.

This book is intended to be a guide for tax professionals and Financials (FI) configuration teams in approaching tax compliance and planning requirements. This book will be helpful to tax professionals and SAP team members dealing with various tax-related issues. This book is not, however, intended to replace experienced tax integration professionals, as no book is capable of doing that.

How This book Is Structured

Chapter 1: In this chapter, you will learn about tax integration and how it fits into an SAP implementation. You will learn the phases of an SAP project, how the work is divided by teams, how SAP projects are managed, and how the project teams are measured.

Chapter 2: This chapter gives you an overview of U.S. taxation, covering topics such as income tax, sales and use tax, property tax, and payroll taxes. The discussion is designed to give a tax overview for SAP project team members not immersed on a daily basis in tax issues.

Chapter 3: This chapter discusses the importance of setting up structural elements within the SAP system in a way that facilitates tax analysis, planning, and compliance. It discusses the proper use of company codes and revenue and cost objects.

Chapter 4: Specific federal income tax issues are discussed in this chapter, including the chart of accounts, fixed assets, intercompany transactions, and international tax issues.

Chapter 5: In this chapter, withholding tax issues are addressed, including those for 1099 backup withholding and 1042 NRA withholding. Both classic and extended SAP withholding functionality are discussed.

Chapter 6: This chapter discusses IRS rules for retention of tax related documents and how the SAP Data Retention Tool (DART) satisfies IRS requirements. Configuration of DART extracts and views is also discussed.

Chapter 7: Payroll taxes and the role they play in corporate taxation are discussed in this chapter. You will also learn about Tax Reporter, the payroll tax tool that is included in the HR module.

Chapter 8: In this chapter, you will learn about SAP master data and master data fields required by a corporate tax department to effectively handle tax analysis, planning, compliance, and audits.

Chapter 9: Tax reporting and how to work with tax departments on reporting issues is covered in this chapter. SAP standard reports and ad hoc reporting tools such as SAP Query, Report Painter, and Report Writer are discussed as possible tax reporting tools.

Chapter 10: This chapter covers a variety of important tax topics, such as the domestic production activities deduction, the R&D tax credit, third-party income tax software, apportionment, and other topics.

Chapter 11: Property tax and property tax systems are addressed in this chapter. You will learn about asset cost buildup and how to segregate asset cost layers in the SAP system to save on property tax.

Chapter 12: We begin our discussion of sales and use tax in this chapter and specifically talk about tools available to assist with the tax calculation process. You will also learn about the three U.S. tax procedures with the SAP internal jurisdictional procedure being discussed in detail.

Chapter 13: Sales and use tax processing using an external tax software system is discussed in this chapter with emphasis on the configuration link between the SAP system and the external tax software using the SAP Tax Interface System.

Chapter 14: This chapter discusses sales and use tax configuration and master data settings for all three of the U.S. tax procedures.

Chapter 15: Franchise tax is addressed in this chapter followed by a discussion of "green" taxes. Beverage taxes and bottle and can deposit fees are discussed in detail as are the various kinds of waste taxes.

Chapter 16: In this final chapter, you will learn about how transfer pricing is handled in an SAP system. A discussion of operational transfer pricing versus transfer pricing for tax is presented along with new developments in the ECC releases that assist with transfer pricing.

With this summary in mind, turn to Chapter 1, where you will learn more about tax integration and how tax professionals approach integrating tax into the implementation process while serving as members of the implementation team.

Understanding tax integration and how SAP project teams approach implementations is helpful for tax personnel responsible for solving tax issues. Chapter 1 defines tax integration, describes the steps in the tax integration process, and explains how SAP projects are managed.

1 Introduction

Many tax professionals are not familiar with SAP; thus, this chapter includes a brief history about the company. SAP was founded in Walldorf, Germany in 1972 by a group of former IBM programmers. The firm's name is a source of some confusion in the United States. Although the acronym SAP originally stood for three German words, it now stands for Systems, Applications, and Products in data processing and should be pronounced S...A...P.

SAP successfully marketed R/1 (R stands for real-time data processing) in Germany until the late 1970s. In the late 1970s, SAP developed the R/2 system, which still used mainframe technology. The creation of R/2 resulted in expansion of sales efforts within Germany and expansion into Austria around 1985.

The firm continued marketing and development efforts through the 1980s and introduced R/3 in the early 1990s. By that time, the company had expanded throughout Europe and into the United States. By the end of 1992, over half of SAP revenues were generated outside of Germany. R/3 was based on client-server architecture and was a huge success around the globe.

Today, SAP has a large U.S. presence, but during much of SAP's development efforts over the past 40 years that have led to today's systems, SAP has been solely a German company. When it comes to SAP and U.S. tax departments, this is a very important point to make and grasp. The early developers at SAP were not German tax experts, and most certainly, they were not U.S. tax experts. Thus, SAP does not have a tax solution that automatically delivers a U.S. corporate tax return. This is not that unusal, however; many other ERP (Enterprise Resource Planning) systems, even if they are U.S.-based, do not have tax solutions either.

U.S. tax department needs span the entire SAP system, and it would take a massive effort to develop a tax module to handle all U.S. taxes and continue to handle them each year with the multitude of changes that occur to the U.S. tax code on a yearly basis. However, if implemented properly, SAP systems can supply a major part of the granular data that U.S.-based tax departments need for tax compliance, tax planning and analysis, tax reporting, and tax audit defense. Proper implementation of the system from a tax point of view is the key. Proper implementation should include tax-integration strategies during the blueprint and configuration stages of the project to assure that tax needs are met later on.

1.1 What Is Tax Integration?

Tax integration involves considering and addressing tax department needs during the implementation process to the greatest extent possible. Tax integration is best done by individuals who have extensive knowledge of SAP systems and of taxation. Unfortunately, individuals with both SAP and tax knowledge are difficult to find. Even the most experienced consultants with good knowledge of both SAP and taxation cannot solve all tax issues that might come up, however, they can assist with solutions for many of these issues. Tax integration provides a huge return on investment when you consider the alternative of doing tax analysis manually over the life of the system. One of the benefits you will get from reading this book is the knowledge required to take advantage of the benefits of tax integration.

Many tax departments fail to get involved in the implementation process and then find out that they have less information available after the new SAP system is installed than they had with their legacy systems. SAP implementation teams follow standard procedures and are under deadlines to finish the implementation. Addressing tax issues can slow progress, so while most implementation teams will talk to tax departments and attempt to address some tax issues, tax issues are often not the first priority. Therefore, tax departments must be proactive in being involved in the SAP implementation project and devote resources to the implementation. Otherwise, they risk not only losing improvements that can be made but also possibly losing existing functionality. The bottom line is that tax department involvement is crucial to SAP implementations, and tax departments are responsible for making sure their needs are known.

Team Structure

Some tax departments assign a good tax resource person to the SAP team who starts out with very little SAP knowledge. Tax departments that follow this practice are to be applauded because of their effort to contribute to the implementation. This approach works successfully most of the time; in some cases, however, the tax resource person that assisted with the implementation might look back at the end of the project wishing he knew then what he knows now, realizing that he didn't really have the necessary knowledge at the outset of the project. Further, the approach of assigning a tax resource person to the SAP team is sometimes taken with the hope of retaining the SAP knowledge in the tax department after implementation; however, often that resource is more valuable with the SAP experience gained and leaves the company or transfers to the internal SAP team.

Thus, the best team structure for tax integration involves at least one resource person from the tax department and one or more resource persons who are already well steeped in tax integration experience and techniques. The risk of losing the tax resource persons lent to the SAP project is still there, but the SAP knowledge is available at the beginning of the project, when it is most needed. Most companies will have to search carefully for resource persons with combined SAP and tax knowledge but will usually be able to find someone at one of the major consulting firms.

Note

We'll look at different types of implementation teams in more detail later in this chapter.

1.2 The Tax Integration Process

Tax integration is an art that takes a variety of routes depending on the needs of the client. Different clients have different tax demands, and tax departments often need help in specific tax areas. Although all implementations differ, tax integration projects generally follow these steps:

1. **Reviewing implementation plans**
   Tax integration is best introduced during the blueprint phase of the project. Otherwise, implementation teams might have to rewrite plans because the tax department comes to the table late, which is not a good use of time and resources. Some decisions may also have already been made

that are irreversible and negatively affect tax issues. Thus, tax departments or their representative(s) must get involved early in the project.

2. **Identifying tax needs at the data element level**
   Good tax integration involves identifying every piece of information the tax departments will need to get out of the SAP system. This is commonly done by preparing a *tax data matrix* that includes the type of tax and the elements needed to calculate and defend a number on a tax line during future audits. Tax numbers are audited at the transaction level, and each type of transaction needs to be looked at to determine what elements are needed. Master data also needs to be identified.

3. **Deciding which data elements can be obtained from SAP**
   Many data elements do not lend themselves to inclusion in an ERP system. It is therefore helpful before preparing tax-related wish lists and requesting functionality to sit down with a tax integration specialist to understand what the SAP system is capable of and what kind of data it will house. Data elements that will not be housed in the SAP system need to be identified early and not placed before the SAP project team.

4. **Expressing needs in SAP terms**
   Attempting to roll out all of the detailed tax data elements to SAP project teams and then following up on them usually does not work well. Data elements are too detailed and too tax-centric to be meaningful to SAP configuration teams. Preparing a tax data matrix is therefore useful to assure that all areas of tax are reviewed before being converted into language SAP personnel can understand.

   For example, it means much more to an SAP configuration specialist dealing with fixed assets if you tell him you want a depreciation area for states not adopting federal bonus rules as opposed to telling him that you want asset historical cost, useful life, mid-year convention, depreciation method, and so on. SAP systems already include all of those items, and it helps if the tax representative already knows that. One of the purposes of this book is to assist tax professionals in dealing with and communicating effectively with SAP project teams. As you become more familiar with SAP systems and continue to study the concepts in this book, you will develop the skills necessary to summarize the detail and explain tax data elements in SAP configuration terms.

5. **Assigning tax needs to specific project teams**
   SAP project teams follow very methodical steps to complete an implementation. In most cases, the consulting team has done this many times before and has a software tool for tracking the assignment of detailed processes.

Tax representatives need to understand how SAP project teams work and the tools that are in place to assign tasks to various teams. Trying to work outside the team's procedures and policies does not endear tax representatives to the project management office (PMO).

Tax representatives also need to be prepared to work with SAP team leaders and members to explain what needs to be done and why. SAP teams are usually under pressure, working long hours under tight deadlines, and are not prepared to accept additional work unless they are convinced of a legitimate business need. Assignment of tax needs becomes a negotiating process and requires flexibility as to what team can best perform the functions and what impact the work may have on other parts of the system. Again, having experience working with both tax needs and SAP avoids many common pitfalls in this area.

6. **Working with project teams to provide assistance with solutions**
   Team members representing tax departments rarely do configuration work, but they require an in-depth understanding of how configuration works and what is possible in the system. Tax people are sometimes told that something cannot be done because it takes additional time or budgetary resources, when in reality the system, if tweaked properly, is capable of accomplishing the task. Tax integration specialists, when placed in these situations, must be experienced enough to offer viable solutions that accomplish the task without requiring significant time or budgetary resources. There are other situations when the effort required to accomplish the task does not merit the end result, and integration specialists need to understand these situations as well. When occurrences of this type arise, the tax specialists must present the facts to SAP team leaders and to the tax department and let them decide how to pursue the issue. If integration specialists are well versed in SAP and taxation, they can prove invaluable by assisting with tax solutions.
7. **Testing and verifying tax solutions**
   Most SAP projects take years to implement, and many times tax integration specialists are not present for the entire project. It is important that testing of tax solutions be done and that processes set out during blueprinting be completed. If tax integration specialists are leaving the project, it is imperative that they create a test and validation plan prior to their departure that can be executed by tax department personnel closer to the time of the project's completion.

1.3 Understanding Your SAP Team

SAP project teams use more acronyms than you can imagine. In addition to acronyms, terms often have been created and others used in ways inconsistent with established usage elsewhere. Thus, to work effectively with your SAP project team, you need to know how to communicate with them and the format in which they need data. Tax integration specialists who have actual implementation experience on large SAP projects know how to work with SAP project teams. The ability to put tax requirements in a format that SAP configuration specialists can understand is vital to achieving good integration.

From My Experience

When I represented the tax department on my first SAP implementation, I was sure the SAP team was speaking a different language. The conversation went a little like this:

"We understand exactly what you need for tax, but you will need to complete a PDD and then break it down into BPPs. A COE will have to be done for configuration work, and aWRICEF will have to be completed for any new items. Once the DR is completed and you have EDD numbers, the work will be forwarded to India for development and testing using the UTP that you will need to complete. We will start in DEV, then progress to QA, and then to PROD. You will need access to all those environments, so talk to Security and have them set you up in RD1, RQ1, and RP1. You may need to get onto the RD2, RQ2, and RP2 boxes as well."

"By the way, you should have told us all this in the blueprint phase because now we are in Realization, and this will be a big GAP. We are not sure whether to assign it to ATR, OTC, or PTP. The PMO is not going to like this. Where have you been anyway?"

Looking at this conversation, you can easily see why you need to learn how to communicate effectively with SAP project implementation teams.

Formatting Tax-Related Requirements

As mentioned earlier, the tax data element level is appropriate during the analysis phase to assure that all required tax processes are identified, but it is too detailed for SAP project teams to deal with. If a tax integrator understands SAP systems, the detail can be summarized into concise requirements that configurators can understand. Let's explore in more detail how to format your requirements by looking at the fixed asset example outlined earlier. The following list shows several fixed asset data elements identified on an SAP implementation project for the tax area Depreciation Expense:

- Useful Life
- Depreciation Method
- Depreciation Convention
- Historical Cost
- Accumulated Depreciation
- Current Year Depreciation Expense
- Depreciation Area
- Asset Class or Category
- Bonus Depreciation Taken
- Section 179 Depreciation Taken

All of the data elements can be condensed by telling the fixed asset configurers that the tax department needs depreciation areas for the financial books, federal income tax, alternative minimum tax (AMT), and adjusted current earnings (ACE) depreciation. Elements such as asset number, depreciation period, and depreciation methods are standard in the software. Elements such as methods, useful lifes, and G/L (General Ledger) accounts can be taken care of when asset classes are discussed. Several requirements summarized at an appropriate level can replace hundreds of lines of detail.

1.4 Implementation Teams

SAP implementation projects typically span several years and consist of tens of thousands of tasks. Successful implementers have developed implementation methodologies that help them control and methodically complete the implementation on a step-by-step basis. The work is divided between many teams and broken down into detailed tasks within those teams. It is important that tax integrators understand the functions that each team performs so they can approach the proper team with the proper question. Unfortunately, team names vary between implementations, but a few commonly used names and their responsibilities include the following:

- **Project Management Office (PMO) Team**
  The PMO team develops the overall workplan, documentation standards, progress reports, and whatever else is needed to manage the implementation process.

The PMO team is responsible for overall project management, which includes choosing and operating a project management solution such as Solution Manager discussed later. The PMO is also responsible for establishing testing and documentation requirements and guidelines. Each step of an SAP implementation is documented, and the PMO supplies the documentation templates and enforces deadlines through reporting to upper management. Tax integration specialists are generally required to comply with these documentation and testing standards.

- **Basis Team**
  The *Basis* team is home to the SAP software and hardware specialists. They are responsible for setting up the system environments and assuring system performance and hardware needs are met.
- **Development Team**
  The *Development* team is responsible for creating solutions to WRICEF items (Workflows, Reports, Interfaces, Conversions, Enhancements, and Forms) presented to them by the process teams. To do so, the team uses ABAP4 programming and other software tools.
- **Order to Cash (OTC) Team**
  The *Order to Cash* (OTC) team is a process team responsible for identifing and implementing processes from the time a customer places an order to the time the payment is received. This includes accounts receivable.
- **Procure to Pay (PTP) Team**
  The *Procure to Pay* (PTP) team is involved with processes and implementation ranging from the purchase or procurement of goods to the payment for those goods. This includes accounts payable.
- **Record to Report (RTR) Team**
  The *Record to Report* (RTR) team is concerned with financial items such as the G/L, the accounting close, financial and management reporting, and usually fixed assets. In asset intensive businesses, you might find a separate team set up for just asset accounting. This team is usually called *Acquire to Retire* (ATR).
- **Material to Inventory (MTI) Team**
  Manufacturing intensive organizations often include special teams called *Material to Inventory* (MTI) teams to handle plant accounting and the cost build-up of inventory. These teams play a significant role in product costing and intercompany transactions and work with the RTR team on these issues.

You might find that the team names used in your implementation differ, but the required tasks will be similar from implementation to implementation. To accomplish the work required, a division of tasks into teams similar to those listed previously is needed. Becoming quickly familiar with team names and responsibilities will help you know who to approach for assistance. It will also be helpful if you familiarize yourself with the stages in an implementation. As you continue into the next section, you will learn more about implementation phases.

1.5 Phases of an SAP Implementation

SAP implementation teams work in phases to complete different steps in the implementation process. The earlier the tax department can get involved in this process, the better. The typical phases include the following:

- **Proof of Concept**
  The early look at an SAP project to determine feasibility from financial and technical angles.
- **Cross Functional Blueprint**
  This stage of the project involves spending time with subject matter experts (SMEs) and other users to understand existing processes and how necessary processes will be re-created in the new system. This stage is at a high level and is also intended to identify relationships impacting other processes and teams.
- **Initiative Blueprint**
  The initiative blueprint is completed in much more detail and identifies the values and methods that will be used to actually configure the system. During this stage, a detailed plan is developed that provides the "blueprint" for building the system.
- **Realization**
  In this phase, configuration and development work are completed, which tells the system to activate the processes identified in the preceding steps. Realization brings the system to life.
- **Testing**
  Realization results in a viable working system. Testing tells you how effectively the system runs and whether it is ready for prime time.

- **Training**
  As the system nears completion, training documents and scripts will be created and rolled out to users across the organization.
- **Go-Live**
  The Go-Live phase involves flipping the switch and making the SAP system the official book of record. By this time, the system has been tested, users are trained, and all impending issues have been addressed. This is the final phase of the implementation process. Go-Live can be as wild as a cat fight or as calm as a summer morning, depending on the success of planning and execution.

1.6 SAP Solution Manager and Its Role in Project Management

In addition to becoming familiar with each of the project teams and the implementation methodology, understanding project management and the way tasks are assigned to the teams is vital. SAP has recently released version 4.0 of its project methodology called Solution Manager. *Solution Manager* is an application that assists project managers with controlling and monitoring the progress of the implementation. Many other management tools are available as well. All tend to create a bureaucracy that is needed but also adds red tape and overhead to an already monumental project. Solution Manager and other management software divide the work into various steps, easing the process. Solution Manager uses the following terminology:

- **Scenarios**
  Statements describing high-level processes needing to be accomplished during the implementation.
- **Processes**
  Statements describing a collection of activities that need to be done to complete the scenario.
- **Process Steps**
  Lower-level tasks that have to be completed to accomplish the level two process.

The following illustrates an example of this:

Scenario: Perform tax accounting.
Process: Account for sales and use tax.

Process Steps: Calculate tax amount.
Accrue tax liability.
Pay tax jurisdiction.

Process steps are then further broken down into specific *business process procedures* (BPPs). BPPs relate to transaction codes in SAP software. Transaction codes relate to screens or processes within SAP. Good tax integration specialists not only understand SAP terminology but can also relate tax requirements to processes or transaction codes within SAP. They can also assist with which team is best capable of handling the requirement.

Solution Manager Breakdown Structures

Figure 1.1 shows the **Configuration** tab from Solution Manager, identifying the breakdown structures for the various scenarios. You will note that this is for the configuration phase of the project and lists the scenarios, processes, and process steps on the left side of the screen. On the right side of the screen, the process **Perform Tax Accounting** shows a configuration step required to assign a tax procedure and set up a tax code. Each of the configuration steps are defined in Solution Manager.

Note

When Solution Manager is fully in place, the old transaction code SPRO will no longer be used to reach the Implementation Guide (IMG). Instead, all configuration will be done by accessing R/3 or ECC (ERP Central Component) through Solution Manager. Tax integrators need to be familiar with this new process, which is currently being used in at least one implementation in the United States.

The team's PMO monitors the progress of teams and team members by the number of steps completed at any one time. Tax requirements must be assigned to a team and specific team members; they have an impact on the team's workload and performance analysis.

Solution Manager is also used to pull in transaction codes under the **Transactions** tab to document what transactions are to be used for a given process step on the application side of the SAP system. In addition, tasks can be assigned to teams and team members tracked through Solution Manager reports.

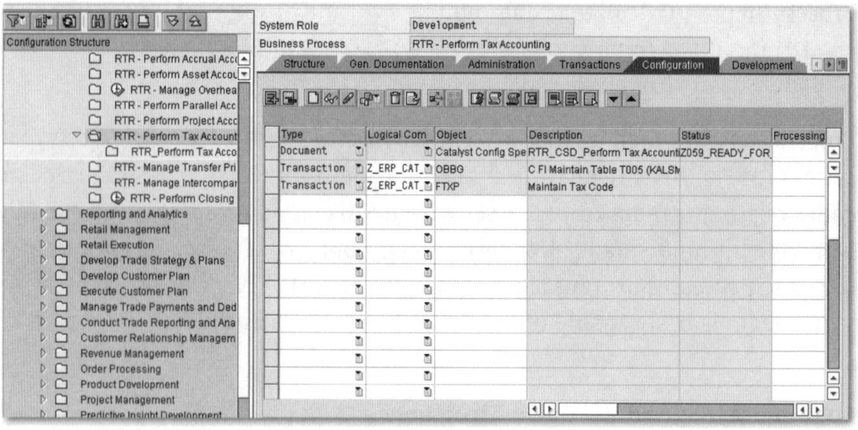

Figure 1.1 The Configuration Tab in Solution Manager

1.7 Summary

The overall objective of tax integration is to assist tax departments in getting the most functionality out of their new SAP system. Tax integration can also be accomplished on existing systems but is much easier and more readily accepted during new implementations. SAP releases such as R/3 and ECC can assist with tax requirements if configured appropriately during implementation. Tax integration specialists can assist with meeting tax objectives during the implementation process, leading to results that often pay for integration fees many times over. You should remember that tax integration specialists and tax integration itself are most successful when the following is accomplished:

- Tax integrators must come to the table at the beginning of the blueprint phase.
- Tax integrators must understand SAP project team and implementation terminology.
- Tax integrators must understand the functions of each SAP project team.
- Tax integrators must be able to relate tax requirements to SAP processes or transaction codes.
- Tax integrators must understand how SAP teams are measured and how work is allocated.

- Tax integrators must be able to work within the PMO's framework of tools (Solution Manager) and meet SAP team documentation and testing standards.
- Tax integrators must help the implementation team meet their goals and deadlines.

Chapter 2 will provide an overview of different areas of U.S. taxation and will address some of the challenges you're likely to encounter with reference to U.S. taxes and the SAP system.

A basic understanding of the different types of taxes levied within the United States is crucial to an understanding of how to integrate tax into an SAP system. Chapter 2 discusses the basic taxes with which large corporate tax departments have to comply and some of the challenges encountered within the SAP system.

2 Overview of Taxation in the United States

U.S. taxation is a very complicated affair due to the myriad of taxes and multitude of jurisdictions involved. Unlike many foreign countries, the United States has attempted to follow the old adage of "No taxation without representation." This means that many taxes are levied at the local level where people have the most say in how much is collected and what the money is used for. Although this is an equitable way of imposing taxes, it creates problems for companies doing business in the United States.

Many international companies that have SAP systems installed in Europe or other foreign countries feel they can simply roll their template out to the United States. This does not work, however, at least not without many changes. Most companies end up deciding to install a separate U.S. instance instead, rather than making the changes required to a foreign template to facilitate U.S. activities. It is also much easier to use a U.S. template and adopt it for foreign use.

In this section, you will gain an understanding of U.S.-based taxes and the challenges encountered by tax departments using SAP and configuration specialists dealing with SAP-related tax issues. It will be helpful for SAP configuration teams to understand the burdens that corporate tax departments are under to meet tax authority requirements while paying the least amount of tax legally acceptable. In doing so, many tax departments are actually revenue generators for the corporation.

Note

Tax people usually love tax but tend to avoid information technology. Their motto often is "If you can't do it in Excel, it cannot be done." Further, the mantra of many tax professionals is "Achieve consistency with as little manual intervention as possible." That is, if logic can be used to populate a field, that's much preferred to a person populating it. I have certainly come to agree with the latter philosophy as a result of years of experience and aim for that objective when approaching a tax integration project.

We'll now look at the different types of U.S. taxes, which include the following:

- Federal income taxes
- State and local income taxes
- Sales and use taxes
- Property taxes
- Payroll and benefits taxes

In addition, we'll briefly look at other taxes to be taken into consideration, international taxation issues and record retention.

2.1 Federal Income Taxes

The U.S. Treasury Department and more specifically, the Internal Revenue Service (IRS), has responsibility for collecting taxes at the national level in the United States. Although the IRS collects more types of taxes than just federal income tax, the discussion in this book will be limited to just income taxes because that is what is most pertinent to tax professionals with regard to SAP.

Note

Corporations, partnerships, trusts, cooperatives, and individuals doing business in the United States are all required to file a U.S. income tax return. The majority of U.S. companies have adopted a corporate entity as their form of doing business and often use an ERP system such as SAP R/3 or SAP ERP Central Component (ECC). The remaining business entities are generally too small to need an ERP system, although some partnerships do run on SAP. The discussions in this book are limited, therefore, to the corporate form of business entity.

2.1.1 Defining Income Tax

Income taxes are often referred to as *direct taxes* because they are paid directly to the taxing jurisdiction by the taxpayer making the money. This is opposed to *indirect taxes*, such as sales and use taxes, which are most often collected by the seller of goods from the purchaser and then remitted to the taxing authority. The remitter in an indirect taxing relationship technically does not bear the tax liability but bears the burden of collecting the tax from others. Once collected, the remitter then acquires a liability and responsibility to remit the tax to the appropriate tax jurisdiction. As mentioned earlier, income tax is a direct tax on income, in this case of a corporation, and the taxpayer (the corporation) is therefore required to pay tax on income produced during the taxable period.

2.1.2 IRS Form 1120

IRS Form 1120, shown in Figure 2.1 is used to report taxable income and tax due for corporations doing business in the United States. Form 1120 is a form filed annually at the corporation's year end, but the IRS may also require estimated tax payments to be made on a quarterly basis. Form 1120 consists of an income statement and balance sheet but can have a variety of other IRS forms attached to it as supporting detail. The final income tax return can often fill several banker's boxes when filed with the IRS.

The federal government has opted to differ from generally accepted accounting principles (GAAP) in many cases, which results in differences between financial income and taxable income. The basis of the 1120 form is the annual report or financial income of the corporation, but for tax purposes, the income statement and balance sheet are adjusted due to statutory requirements. These adjustments and the difference in treatment between IRS rules and GAAP result in challenges for tax professionals using SAP or any other ERP software. Some differences require calculations that SAP cannot reasonably perform, whereas others can be done if configuration has been completed appropriately.

Form **1120** — Department of the Treasury, Internal Revenue Service

U.S. Corporation Income Tax Return

For calendar year 2006 or tax year beginning ...., 2006, ending ...., 20 ....

► See separate instructions.

OMB No. 1545-0123

2006

A Check if:
1 Consolidated return (attach Form 851) . ☐
2 Personal holding co. (attach Sch. PH) . ☐
3 Personal service corp. (see instructions) . . ☐
4 Schedule M-3 required (attach Sch. M-3) . ☐

Use IRS label. Otherwise, print or type.

Name

Number, street, and room or suite no. If a P.O. box, see instructions.

City or town, state, and ZIP code

B Employer identification number

C Date incorporated

D Total assets (see instructions)
$

E Check if: (1) ☐ Initial return (2) ☐ Final return (3) ☐ Name change (4) ☐ Address change

Income

1a	Gross receipts or sales ___ b Less returns and allowances ___ c Bal ►	1c
2	Cost of goods sold (Schedule A, line 8)	2
3	Gross profit. Subtract line 2 from line 1c	3
4	Dividends (Schedule C, line 19)	4
5	Interest	5
6	Gross rents	6
7	Gross royalties	7
8	Capital gain net income (attach Schedule D (Form 1120))	8
9	Net gain or (loss) from Form 4797, Part II, line 17 (attach Form 4797)	9
10	Other income (see instructions—attach schedule)	10
11	**Total income.** Add lines 3 through 10 ►	11

Deductions (See instructions for limitations on deductions.)

12	Compensation of officers (Schedule E, line 4)	12
13	Salaries and wages (less employment credits)	13
14	Repairs and maintenance	14
15	Bad debts	15
16	Rents	16
17	Taxes and licenses	17
18	Interest	18
19	Charitable contributions	19
20	Depreciation from Form 4562 not claimed on Schedule A or elsewhere on return (attach Form 4562)	20
21	Depletion	21
22	Advertising	22
23	Pension, profit-sharing, etc., plans	23
24	Employee benefit programs	24
25	Domestic production activities deduction (attach Form 8903)	25
26	Other deductions (attach schedule)	26
27	**Total deductions.** Add lines 12 through 26 ►	27
28	Taxable income before net operating loss deduction and special deductions. Subtract line 27 from line 11	28
29	**Less:** a Net operating loss deduction (see instructions) . . . 29a	
	b Special deductions (Schedule C, line 20) . . . 29b	29c

Tax and Payments

30	**Taxable income.** Subtract line 29c from line 28 (see instructions)	30
31	**Total tax** (Schedule J, line 10)	31
32a	2005 overpayment credited to 2006 . 32a	
b	2006 estimated tax payments . . . 32b	
c	2006 refund applied for on Form 4466 . 32c ( ) d Bal ► 32d	
e	Tax deposited with Form 7004 . . . 32e	
f	Credits: (1) Form 2439 ___ (2) Form 4136 ___ 32f	
g	Credit for federal telephone excise tax paid (attach Form 8913) . . . 32g	32h
33	Estimated tax penalty (see instructions). Check if Form 2220 is attached ► ☐	33
34	**Amount owed.** If line 32h is smaller than the total of lines 31 and 33, enter amount owed	34
35	**Overpayment.** If line 32h is larger than the total of lines 31 and 33, enter amount overpaid	35
36	Enter amount from line 35 you want: **Credited to 2007 estimated tax** ► ___ **Refunded** ►	36

Sign Here

Under penalties of perjury, I declare that I have examined this return, including accompanying schedules and statements, and to the best of my knowledge and belief, it is true, correct, and complete. Declaration of preparer (other than taxpayer) is based on all information of which preparer has any knowledge.

Signature of officer ▶ Date ▶ Title

May the IRS discuss this return with the preparer shown below (see instructions)? ☐ Yes ☐ No

Paid Preparer's Use Only

Preparer's signature ▶ Date | Check if self-employed ☐ | Preparer's SSN or PTIN

Firm's name (or yours if self-employed), address, and ZIP code ▶ | EIN | Phone no. ( )

For Privacy Act and Paperwork Reduction Act Notice, see separate instructions. Cat. No. 11450Q Form **1120** (2006)

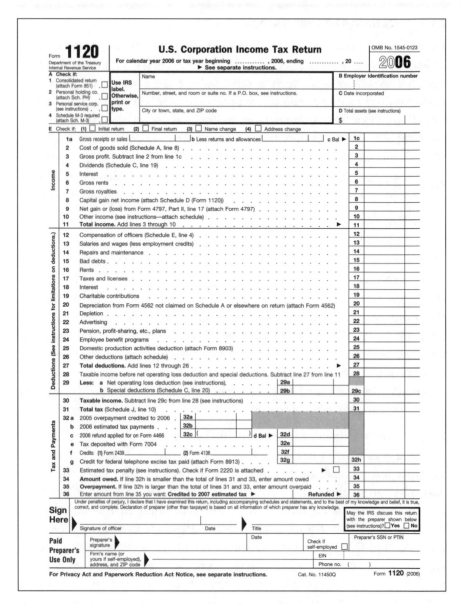

Figure 2.1 IRS Form 1120 (Source: IRS website http://www.irs.gov/formspubs/lists/0,,id=97817,00.html)

2.1.3 Income and SAP Modules

Income is comprised of a simple formula of *revenues minus expenses for the period*. This means that a tax return is prepared using data from all modules of an SAP system, including the Financials (FI) portion of the system, as well as the Controlling (CO), Materials Management (MM), Sales and Distribution (SD), Project System (PS), Human Resources (HR), and other system modules, to assure that income tax needs are being met.

2.1.4 Tax Classification

The IRS looks at some revenues and expenses with more scrutiny than it does others, requiring some types of income and expenses to be classified in the system so that they are easily identifiable. Tax professionals often ask for additions to the chart of accounts to facilitate these requirements. Sometimes the additional account can be facilitated through the use of a cost object, but often it cannot. For example, meals and entertainment expenses are handled much differently for tax purposes than they are for financial purposes. If only one account is set up called *Travel Expense* for all travel, meals, and entertainment expenses, the tax department will be faced with analyzing that account over the life of the system. Thus, good tax classification is required to easily meet IRS requirements.

2.1.5 Tracing Income

In addition to the income calculation itself, income sourcing is also required for income and other types of U.S. taxes. Tracing the jurisdiction the money came from and the jurisdiction the money flowed to is an IRS requirement to assure that corporations are not shifting income from jurisdictions with high tax rates to those with low taxes. SAP software effectively creates an audit trail for these types of activities if the system is configured properly from a tax standpoint.

2.1.6 International Tax Concerns

Federal income taxation has an international aspect in that U.S. corporations are responsible for reporting transactions in foreign countries and between foreign countries and the United States. The sourcing spoken of in the previous section is helpful in this regard, but intercompany transactions also need to be scrutinized for pricing appropriateness (Transfer Pricing) and for withholding issues. Even though a corporation may not be rolling out SAP to its foreign possessions, company codes need to be set up for foreign affiliates to satisfy U.S. requirements.

2.1.7 Audit Requirements

Nearly all tax authorities require corporations to produce data at a transaction level upon audit. SAP software adheres to a document approach, which means it creates a document for nearly everything entered into the system and maintains a linkage and audit trail between documents. The document feature of SAP enables tax auditors to trace transactions through the system, which is a valuable tool for tax departments.

> **Note**
>
> Legacy systems that pass data to SAP software through an interface at a summary level remain the system of record, and the IRS has the authority to request data from the legacy system in addition to the SAP system.

2.1.8 Legal Entity Accounting

Legal entity accounting is also required by the IRS and other taxing authorities. Each corporation in the United States is considered a legal entity and must have a federal tax identification number. Each must file a tax return or be part of a consolidated tax return annually. SAP has designed the system so that each legal entity is assigned a company code. Assignment of a company code is the easiest way to meet the legal entity requirement. Other attempts will be discussed later in this book.

In this section, we've discussed several important concepts about federal income taxation:

- Taxable income differs from GAAP income.
- Revenue and expense classification is very important for tax departments.
- Revenue and expense tracing from source to destination is necessary to meet tax requirements.
- Federal income taxation has an international aspect.
- Tax data is required at a transaction level.
- Tax authorities require legal entity reporting and master data concerning the legal entity.

- If logic can be used to populate a field, this method is much preferred to a person populating it.

These topics will be discussed in depth as we explore tax integration and configuration in more detail in Chapter 4.

2.2 State and Local Income Taxes

State and local income taxing authorities often follow the lead of the IRS by adopting many federal statutes. States sometimes resist following federal laws, however, when it impacts their revenue streams adversely. This can easily be seen with the current division over the state acceptance of federal bonus depreciation rules. Differences of this kind prevent corporations from simply filing a corporate return and then quickly dividing it by 50 and sending a copy to each of the states. Corporations are responsible for reporting revenues produced in the state and matching them against expenses incurred in the state as closely as possible. The same principles exist for cities with income tax laws.

The concept of tax sourcing mentioned earlier is extremely important for state and local income taxation. Tax departments not only need to know the country but the state, county, and city where the revenue was produced and the expenses incurred. Both R/3 and ECC versions of SAP are equipped to capture and supply this information on a consistent basis, if configured as designed.

2.2.1 Apportionment

State and local income tax compliance cannot be done without some degree of allocation for services or assets that benefit all jurisdictions. This leads to what is known as apportionment. *Apportionment*, in basic terms, involves the determination as to which state gets what portion of revenue and expenses that are not clearly assigned elsewhere. Apportionment will be discussed in detail in Chapter 10.

2.2.2 Differences Between State and Local Tax Laws and Federal Government Tax Laws

State and local governments do not always follow the lead of the federal government when they are adversely affected by IRS laws. When configuring fixed assets, for example, it is good to know that many states opted out of adopting federal bonus depreciation rules because of the negative revenue impact. When tax professionals ask for an additional depreciation area for depreciation without bonus, it is for this reason.

Other differences also exist. The state of California, for example, has different useful lives on many of its asset groupings than the federal government. If the company has substantial business in California, an additional depreciation area for California may also be required. An addition of a depreciation area such as one for California is not very difficult but may take some negotiation nonetheless.

Note

Keep in mind that tax professionals usually ask for functionality they have not had before or for items that they still need and that will save time if provided. Some implementation teams, unfortunately, take the stance that they will provide existing functionality but not improved functionality as part of the implementation. Thus, an SAP implementation is an excellent time for tax departments to catch up on the technology curve by replacing manual processes with automated ones and convincing implementation teams of the need for new functionality.

To summarize, here is a list of the main concepts discussed in this section.

- State and local taxation follows federal rules in most areas, but significant differences do exist.
- Tracing revenue and expense from source to destination is extremely important and must be done down to the county and city level.
- Apportionment presents challenges for tax professionals that must be addressed.

2.3 Sales and Use Taxes

Sales and use taxes generally get the most attention during SAP implementations. Tax integration in the sales and use tax area requires attention to facilitate as little manual effort as possible. Sales and use tax is an indirect tax as opposed to the taxes discussed earlier in this chapter, which are direct taxes. During the blueprint phase of the project, it is important to address how sales and use tax is approached. Sales and use tax is a transaction-based tax, and SAP software can be configured to handle the tax calculation and consider exceptions when coupled with third-party bolt-on software or even a client's custom system. However, SAP software without bolt-on software typically doesn't perform as well unless the company does business in very few tax jurisdictions.

Important Considerations

Remember from our earlier discussion that determining the source and destination of the transaction is very important to tax departments. And nowhere is it more important than in the area of sales and use tax. Accurate calculation of sales and use tax requires knowledge of the shipping point and the shipping destination. SAP certified bolt-on software exists in the marketplace that can consistently identify the shipping point and the shipping destination to the ZIP code level if SAP is configured correctly.

While sourcing information is required for accurate sales and use tax calculations, how the product will be ultimately used is equally as important. Tax exemptions exist in some jurisdictions for some products. Information concerning the product and its use must be captured in the SAP system if an accurate tax rate is to be applied.

As with other taxes, sales and use tax authorities require legal entity reporting. Income statements and balance sheets are not necessary for sales and use tax compliance, but tax entities are still registered, and compliance is completed on a legal entity basis. Information about the legal entity is also required for accurate reporting. Master data needs to be captured and maintained concerning the legal entity. This includes the corporate name, tax ID number, address, and other pertinent information. The R/3 or ECC company code master file along with configuration settings under company code global parameters will meet this requirement.

A final element to consider is the multitude of jurisdictions that large corporations must deal with. Many corporations have tens of thousands of jurisdictions, each using different report forms and rules with which to comply. Getting sales and use tax right in the implementation can significantly reduce the compliance and audit effort.

The following list summarizes sales and use tax:

- Tracing source and destination to the ZIP code level is required and is possible with bolt-on software.
- Using SAP tax functionality without bolt-on software is not recommended.

- The ultimate use of the product or service is required for accurate tax calculations.
- Tax authorities require reporting by legal entity and master data concerning the legal entity.
- Large corporations must report to tens of thousands of tax jurisdictions.

2.4 Property Taxes

Property taxes are often not addressed during SAP implementations, but if approached correctly, can pay for the tax integration project many times over! The property tax calculation differs depending on jurisdiction, but generally, it is based on the asset cost and the property tax rate for the given jurisdiction. Property tax therefore has all of the sourcing needs required by other taxes but needs it driven down to the street address level to accurately compute the tax. Many property tax bolt-on systems rely on the five-digit ZIP code that does not get down to the street address level. The tendency is to move to the nine-digit ZIP code that goes to a much lower level.

The buildup of the asset cost provides opportunities for tax savings and will be discussed in more detail in Chapter 11. If items such as sales tax, embedded software, installation fees, and freight can be separated out of the asset cost, considerable savings can be obtained in certain jurisdictions.

Note

Most assets subject to property tax are also subject to depreciation. Unfortunately, property tax depreciation differs by tax jurisdiction. Many companies have made adjustments to the property tax depreciation area supplied by SAP, but there is not much benefit when useful lives, depreciation methods, and asset buildup differ from jurisdiction to jurisdiction.

Low-value assets that are expensed for financial purposes but that need to be captured for property tax purposes also present a challenge for tax professionals. SAP approached this challenge by setting up an asset class for low-value assets. However, these assets need to be classified by the type of asset for correct property tax reporting. At the least, this asset class is a catchall that might be preferable to using G/L accounts as many companies have in the past.

To summarize, some property tax integration challenges to consider include the following:

- Location or jurisdiction of the asset
- Cost buildup of the asset
- Asset depreciation
- Low-value assets

2.5 Payroll and Benefit Taxes

Many payroll and benefit issues impact tax professionals besides filing tax returns. Payroll modules are often implemented on a different instance of SAP or even a different software program. Some corporations have payroll functions outsourced to providers such as ADP or Hewitt. In very few cases does the corporate tax department actually prepare and file payroll and benefit tax returns. These tasks are instead usually handled by the payroll department. However, tax departments do have to face and be knowleadgable with IRS auditors when the time comes for an audit. In addition, tax departments rely on payroll numbers for many other tax calculations. Consider these examples:

- Payroll numbers are an integral part of jurisdiction tax returns. When payroll numbers exist in other software systems or on different instances of SAP, tax integration professionals assist with the decisions regarding how and at what level payroll data will be brought into the financial SAP instance.
- Former employees often end up as independent contractors in the same year, which invites an IRS Information Document Request (IDR) as to why.

As you can see, tax departments require information concerning payroll for many purposes other than just filing payroll and benefit tax forms. Some of the payroll issues that can confront tax professionals during SAP implementations include the following:

- Assuring that information is available for payroll and benefit tax returns
- Replying to jurisdictional document requests on audit
- Obtaining proper payroll data for income tax calculations, especially when data is not on the same SAP instance or the same software

2.6 Other Taxes

Many other taxes exist in the United States that may have to be considered by tax integration specialists and SAP configuration specialists during an SAP implementation:

- Customs and duties
- Franchise taxes
- Bottling tax
- Waste tax

Some of these taxes will be addressed in more detail in Chapter 15.

2.7 International Taxation

As mentioned before, the IRS requires reporting of international affiliates and company codes to handle intercompany transactions and other tax matters. Corporations also have local tax requirements for foreign countries that require compliance. This book is limited to taxation within the United States, however, and therefore does not address local country tax requirements. If the implementation involves local country taxes, considerable effort needs to be given to addressing Value-added Tax (VAT) taxes. Bolt-on software now exists for VAT taxes and is becoming more capable of accurate tax calculations on a global basis.

2.8 Record Retention Issues

IT Professionals often ask how long tax data has to be retained. The answer is that tax departments do not know. Ten years might be a good rule of thumb but that is not long enough in all cases. Tax data has to be kept until the tax department says it can be destroyed. IRS regulations state that tax data must be retained for three years from the due data of the return, including extensions. While this seems easy enough, large corporations are constantly under audit, and audits extend the rule just mentioned.

Example

I have worked with some companies that have state audits still going on from the 1980s. Unfortunately, this means that electronic books and records must be retained for many years and that IT professionals have to prepare for that.

SAP software produces a high volume of information because of its document approach. Although the document approach is a blessing because it provides excellent audit trails, the large amounts of information it creates can impact system performance in a short period of time. For this reason, SAP created an archive system that removes data from the system as needed.

Archiving-Related Issues and the Data Retention Tool (DART)

Although SAP archiving helps with system performance, it also presents tax professionals with the following challenges:

- Archiving removes data from the live system so it can no longer be easily accessed by tax professionals.
- Archiving does not maintain the integrity of the accounting period.
- Archived files are not easily queried.

The challenges just outlined led the *America's SAP User Group* (ASUG) to work with SAP to develop the *Data Retention Tool (DART)* in the late 1990s. DART allows information to be copied from SAP tables and fields prior to archiving, so it is retained for tax audits. DART and archiving will be covered in much more detail in Chapter 6.

Besides, record retention is a legal requirement. See Table 2.1 for a brief list of IRS record retention requirements.

IRS Item	Description
Internal Revenue Code Section 6001	Requires retention of records supporting federal tax returns
Revenue Procedure 98–25	Governs records created by automatic data processing systems
Revenue Procedure 97–22	Governs scanned images

Table 2.1 IRS Rules Regarding Record Retention for Tax

All of these regulations have specific retention requirements regarding tax departments, and SAP tax professionals should be familiar with them. In addition, Revenue Procedure 98–25 will be addressed in detail in Chapter 6. In summary, SAP tax professionals dealing with record retention issues need to address the following issues:

- The absence of clear retention guidelines as far as length of time
- Challenges presented by SAP archiving
- Proper implementation of DART or some other retention tool

2.9 Summary

In this chapter, we briefly covered many U.S. taxes that need to be addressed by tax professionals during an SAP implementation. The remainder of this book will cover these taxes in more detail and delve deeper into specific tax calculations that should be addressed during SAP implementations. You also learned in this chapter that U.S. taxation is complex and consists of multiple jurisdictions that have created many layers of tax requirements. Some of these requirements can be categorized into the following areas:

- Federal income tax
- State and local income tax
- Sales and use tax
- Property tax
- Payroll and benefits tax
- Other taxes
- International income tax issues
- Record retention for tax

Chapter 3 will explore the importance of the implementation approach and organization structure as it pertains to tax integration. It also discusses the important role that cost objects play in achieving good tax integration.

The way a company chooses to implement R/3 or ECC can have a dramatic impact on the ability to calculate and retrieve tax information. The organizational structure in SAP software is the basis of an implementation and is the most important concern when striving for good tax integration.

3 Impact of Organizational Structure on Tax

Nothing is more important to the adequate flow of good tax information than the way the SAP system is structured. Unfortunately, companies often spend millions on SAP systems and then install them in a way other than intended. Or, they buy an SAP system and then work for years to make it look just like the legacy systems they are retiring. However, changing a system like SAP to work in a way other than designed only creates implementation challenges far beyond the already existing complexities and challenges that usually arise during a normal implementation, and unnecessary challenges continue to surface during maintenance and upon upgrade.

In this chapter, we will discuss the way an SAP system should be designed for the best flow of tax information. Structural options employed by some companies in an attempt to create savings in other parts of the business will also be discussed.

Note

The SAP system as designed is the optimal approach for tax departments. If deviations from this design are undertaken, they should produce substantial savings that are detailed and explained, and the impact on tax departments considered in the budgeting process over the life of the system.

3.1 The Use of Company Codes in SAP

The IRS has designed its system of collecting and monitoring tax by assigning federal tax ID numbers by legal entity, which means that tax returns are completed on a legal entity basis and tax is remitted on the same basis. Corporate tax departments therefore are required to report and remit to the IRS – and all other taxing authorities – on a legal entity basis. This is a legal requirement.

SAP systems are designed in the SAP Financials (FI) module with a company code that is intended to represent a legal entity. The FI company code is integrated into the system so that a complete set of financial statements can be generated at that level. It is also a required field on every transaction flowing through the system. The way in which SAP has designed the FI company code satisfies tax legal entity reporting, as long as every legal entity comprising the corporation is assigned a company code. Advantages of using the SAP company code for legal entity reporting includes the following:

- A complete set of financial statements can be produced at the company code level, which is a requirement for IRS legal entity reporting.
- A company code is required on every transaction flowing through the system. This means that every transaction is assigned to a legal entity and captured as part of a financial statement.
- The company code is described by master data contained in the company code master, an example of which is shown in Figure 3.1, which lists the corporate name, city, country, language, and currency. Without descriptive master data concerning the company code, the system will not populate address information and tax ID numbers on invoices, tax returns, and other documents used for external purposes.

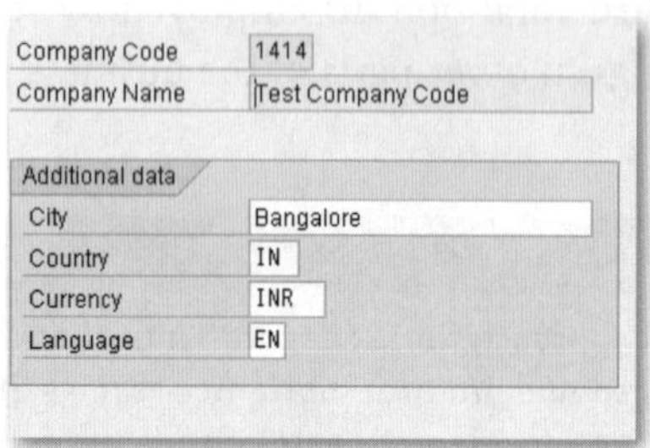

Figure 3.1 The Company Code Master

- The company code has been used as a key for third-party software programs that assist with tax compliance.
- Internal programs such as those tracking and generating tax forms 1099 and 1042 rely on the company code for the computation.

- The DART module relies on the company code for completing DART extracts.
- Standard SAP reporting is designed to work on a company code basis. Many legal entity reports can be obtained using standard reporting if the system is configured using a one-to-one relationship between the legal entity and the company code.
- Intercompany transactions and transfer pricing issues are more easily handled if an SAP company code is assigned on a one-toone relationship to legal entities.

Each of these advantages will be discussed in more detail in this chapter to help you understand why tax departments should insist on legal entity accounting and an SAP company code representing each legal entity comprising the corporation. Figures 3.2 through 3.4 illustrate master data retained in the system regarding the company code. These figures contain fields for the complete address information and for structural assignments such as the chart of accounts, the credit control area, the fiscal year variant, and more.

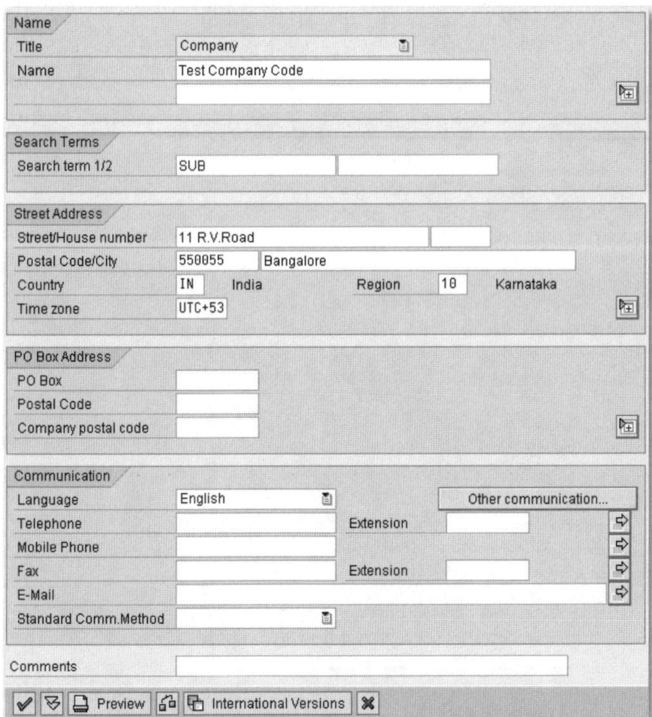

Figure 3.2 Company Code Address Data

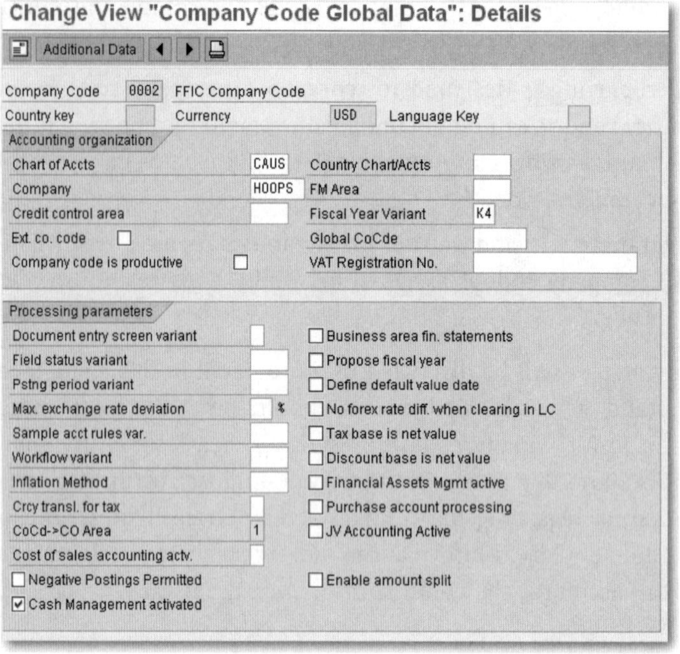

Change View "Company Code Global Data": Details

Additional Data

Company Code 0002 FFIC Company Code
Country key Currency USD Language Key

Accounting organization
Chart of Accts CAUS Country Chart/Accts
Company HOOPS FM Area
Credit control area Fiscal Year Variant K4
Ext. co. code Global CoCde
Company code is productive VAT Registration No.

Processing parameters
Document entry screen variant
Business area fin. statements
Field status variant
Propose fiscal year
Pstng period variant
Define default value date
Max. exchange rate deviation %
No forex rate diff. when clearing in LC
Sample acct rules var.
Tax base is net value
Workflow variant
Discount base is net value
Inflation Method
Financial Assets Mgmt active
Crcy transl. for tax
Purchase account processing
CoCd->CO Area 1
JV Accounting Active
Cost of sales accounting actv.
Negative Postings Permitted
Enable amount split
Cash Management activated

Figure 3.3 Company Code Global Data

Maintenance of Additional Data for Company Code 0002

Name	Parameter value
Company Number	
Place of Jurisdiction	
LSV Key CHF	
ISR Subscriber Number CHF	
LSV Key EUR	
ISR Subscriber Number EUR	
NIT Number	
Detail Tax Entry with MIRO	
Invoice Summary Factory Calen.	
DGI office	
Delivery character	
Foundation date of company	
Tax type	
Gross income tax no.Buenos Air	
Gross income tax number	
Identification number	
Tax number type	
Authorization Check Nota Fisc.	
CNPJ Business Place	

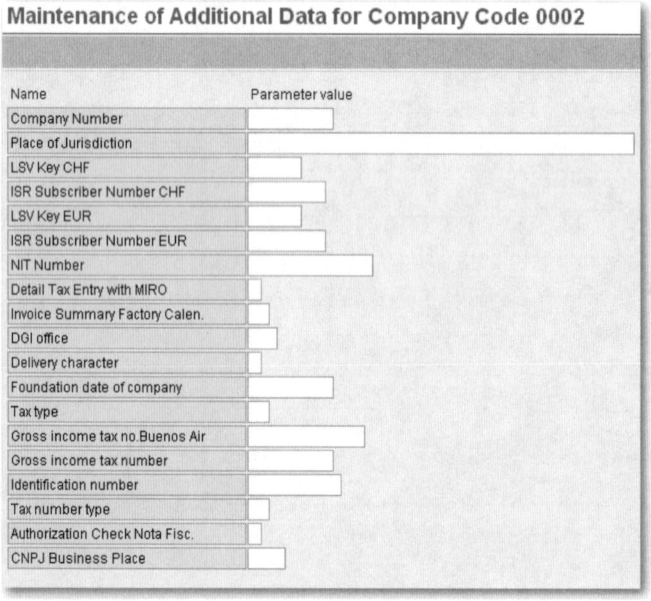

Figure 3.4 Additional Company Code Global Data

3.1.1 The Importance of a One-To-One Legal Entity to Company Code Relationship

Income tax returns are based on financial statements. IRS form 1120 is basically an income statement and balance sheet reported according to tax accounting guidelines. Page 1 of form 1120 is illustrated in Figure 2.1 of Chapter 2. The entire form is included in Appendix H under Tax Forms for Chapter 1. Differences between financial income and taxable income do exist, but the basis is always the financial books of the legal entity. As mentioned earlier, SAP has designed the FI module to produce a complete set of financial statements based on the SAP company code field. SAP systems configured with a one-to-one relationship between legal entity and company code meet this requirement easily. Systems configured differently have a more difficult time. Therefore, a one-to-one relationship between legal entity and company code is very important for tax considerations. No other way exists that can meet this requirement without difficulty.

Let's look at several differing approaches that attempt to solve the legal entity accounting issue: the single company code approach, the business area approach, and the profit center approach.

3.1.2 The Single Company Code Approach

Companies often fear the number of entries that an SAP system produces and feel that field personnel cannot be trained to select the right company code for each transaction. As a result, they often opt for less functionality by using only one company code for their entire business. However, a one-company code concept adversely affects all of the previously mentioned advantages of the general SAP company code concept because it ignores the role the company code plays in legal entity accounting. Further, it doesn't take into consideration much of the functionality in the SAP system. Tax departments who have to work with this type of implementation might need twice the staff to research which transactions belong to which legal entity.

The New General Ledger (G/L) and Document Splitter

In the past, the company code has been the only way to produce a GAAP financial statement for a legal entity. Now, the new general ledger (G/L), when coupled with the document splitter, also can conceptually be used to produce GAAP financial statements. The *document splitter*, if configured properly, allows every document coming through the system to be split out to a profit center and a balance sheet account. In theory, therefore, it is possible to produce GAAP financial statements without some kind of allocation in the equity section of the balance sheet. Instead, profit centers can be assigned to legal entities to accomplish tax accounting, thereby negating the need for numerous or more than one company code.

Although this sounds fine on paper, you still lose many of the advantages of using a company code per legal entity. Some of the bigger challenges include splitting the current balance sheet down to a profit center level, splitting every document that comes through the system, and finding a place to keep the related legal entity master data needed to file tax returns. Using profit center for legal entity is discussed in more detail later in this chapter.

Note

This approach may work well and may be widely accepted in the future, but it currently requires a great deal of customization and is not a viable alternative yet.

3.1.3 The Business Area Approach

Another approach that was fairly popular six or seven years ago was to set up one company code and then have the business area represent legal entity. Several problems exist with this approach, as follows:

Note

SAP has advised against using the business area approach.

- Business area is seldom required for every transaction flowing through the system, and using it to represent legal entity may result in large numbers of unassigned entries, which is not good for tax reporting.
- The FI module does not have the capability to create a complete set of GAAP financial statements by business area. Although you can produce financial statement by business area, they will be inaccurate. Financial statements produced by business area are prone to unassigned entries and the balance sheet cannot be completed without allocation.
- Business area does not have a related master file with descriptive master data needed for tax purposes. If a corporation is comprised of several large legal entities having popular brand names, they will either be forced to customize the system or send communications under one name because they only have one company code master file. Some corporations employing a one company code concept have been forced to maintain a company code master outside of the SAP system to meet the need for legal entity master data.

- Business area is designed for the operations of the business to assist with internal cost reporting. Business areas often cross legal entity lines, which results in tax professionals having to manually split a business area into two or more legal entities.

> **Note**
>
> I have worked with one of the largest corporations in the world and witnessed their tax department having to put in this type of manual effort because the SAP system was not set up as designed.

- Internal and third-party tax software do not communicate with business area codes. Vertex, Taxware, and Sabrix are all sales and use tax bolt-on solutions designed to use company code for legal entity. Fortunately, these third-party software packages have become more flexible and can be adapted to work with the different scenarios but still work best with SAP systems that are configured as designed. SAP internal programs such as the 1099 program, the 1042 program, and DART are not as flexible and require custom coding to react to business area.
- Intercompany transactions requiring documentation for transfer pricing and other tax requirements are not easily tracked.

3.1.4 The Profit Center Approach

With the new SAP G/L and the release of ERP Central Component (ECC) versions 5.0 and 6.0, some companies are using profit center for legal entity in place of company code. Some concerns with this approach include the following:

- Profit center does not have a master file with master data information needed for tax purposes. This scenario results in a one-company code concept with the profit center code being used to break out legal entities. Conceptually, this works with the new G/L and debit and credit balancing by profit center, but master data still needs to be maintained on a legal entity basis either inside or outside the system.
- Profit center does not enjoy the same hierarchy advantages that company code does. The FI module is designed with many standard reports based on company code. Many system master files can link to company code but not necessarily to profit center. Period closing procedures are designed on a company code basis and not on profit center. Using profit center to represent legal entity forces you to start all over in the reporting and account-

ing close arena. You will have to have a can-do attitude and a large customization budget for the initial implementation and for subsequent upgrades as well.

In theory, the profit center approach when coupled with the document splitter should be capable of producing financial statements that are up to GAAP standards, but it has not been done in practice. The functionality is new and untested and will result in companies customizing SAP to build financial statements and closing procedures on this basis rather than using predefined functionality available on a company code basis.

- Tax software does not communicate with profit center codes. As mentioned earlier, the bolt-on software designed for sales and use tax is more flexible than it once was but still must be passed proper information to make correct tax decisions. These software programs look for information from predefined SAP fields, and SAP software has to be redesigned to pass legal entity information that is not in the company code field. As with the other single-company code solutions, 1099 and 1042 programs also have to be redesigned to accept legal entity information that is not contained in the company code field. Single-company code solutions also do not allow DART to run by individual legal entities, which results in huge DART extracts that take hours to run, if they run at all with existing hardware.
- Profit centers are not necessarily included on all transactions. They can be traced to a cost center that may be required on all transactions, but the link is not direct. Additional programming is required to generate queries or reports by legal entity.
- Intercompany transaction functionality within SAP is not keyed to profit center. SAP has created transfer pricing functionality in ECC 5.0 and ECC 6.0 that can be done on a profit center or a legal entity basis, but it has not been widely tested.

Note

The profit center approach is very new with only one company implementing a scenario of this kind as of the middle of 2006. Tax professionals will likely prefer the traditional method of a one-to-one relationship between a legal entity and a company code. If savings using profit center are substantiated, and the current implementation is completed on a satisfactory basis, other companies will follow the lead. Tax departments may need to follow but should do so with eyes wide open and a firm commitment from corporate leaders to address tax challenges created by this type of implementation.

Although the organization structure has the biggest impact on tax functionality, the way cost objects are defined is a very close second so we'll look at this challenge next.

3.2 The Role of SAP Revenue and Cost Objects

SAP software equips users with many more ways of capturing revenue and cost than traditional legacy systems. In the next discussion, we will look at the objects in the following list and how they can best be leveraged for tax purposes:

- Cost Centers
- Profit Centers
- Internal Orders
- Projects
- Work Breakdown Structures (WBS Elements)
- Plants
- Storage Locations
- Business Area Codes
- Functional Area Codes

3.2.1 Cost Centers

The implementation design for the use of SAP cost objects is critical to tax purposes. As mentioned earlier, tax departments need the source of the transaction and the destination captured for every type of tax. Appropriate use of cost centers goes a long way toward solving source or destination challenges. Failure to use cost centers results in inaccuracy and inconsistency from manual input. Companies assign cost centers in two different ways, either based on responsibility or based on jurisdiction. From a tax standpoint, only the former is acceptable. Let's look at both in detail.

Responsibility-Based Cost Center Assignment

To IT personnel, it usually doesn't matter how cost centers are used in the system, as long as there are as few of them as possible. They are tasked with having a system that responds quickly while hopefully getting the best information possible. Everyone, regardless of their background, wants a good mix of both. The idea of responsibility centers is usually raised by the accounting department because functional financial analysts are tasked with the responsibility of reporting accurate costs to department heads on a periodic basis. Assigning cost centers to departments is a very logical way of helping cost center managers track costs associated with their organization.

Example

Let's look at an example. An engineering department based in Los Angeles is assigned a cost center to track spending. This sounds simple enough, but what happens if the same department has personnel based in Ventura as well? Most people would conclude that because the personnel in Ventura are still engineers and report to someone in Los Angeles, it makes sense to include them in the Los Angeles cost center.

However, difficulties arise because SAP designed the cost center master to carry a jurisdiction code, and there is only room for one code on the master. In the preceding example, if the people in Ventura are assigned to the Los Angeles cost center, everything they buy will be taxed at a Los Angeles rate instead of at a Ventura rate, and tax on those purchases and sales if applicable will be remitted to Los Angeles. When Ventura auditors come in later, they realize that Los Angeles got all their money and force the corporation to pay again.

Some would suggest leaving the jurisdiction code field blank and allowing accounting clerks to populate it. However, you will remember that one goal of tax integration is to have as much of the process as possible automated. Automated field population leads to consistency and eventually accuracy. The jurisdiction code can be effectively defaulted into the transaction on a consistent basis from the cost center but not under a pure responsibility accounting arrangement.

Overall, it is not advisable to have accounting clerks in shared service centers entering jurisdiction codes for thousands of locations with which they are not familiar. Tax integration specialists therefore recommend a geographical or jurisdictional solution to cost center assignment.

Jurisdictional-Based Cost Center Assignment

To facilitate tax department needs, cost centers should be assigned on a geographical or jurisdictional basis. Figure 3.5 shows the **Address** tab of the cost center master, which has room for the complete address of the cost center location along with the jurisdiction code. Cost centers must be used in the system in this manner if source or destination challenges are to be solved. This tab should be completed for every cost center in the system, and care taken that the cost center does not capture cost for activity other than for the defined location.

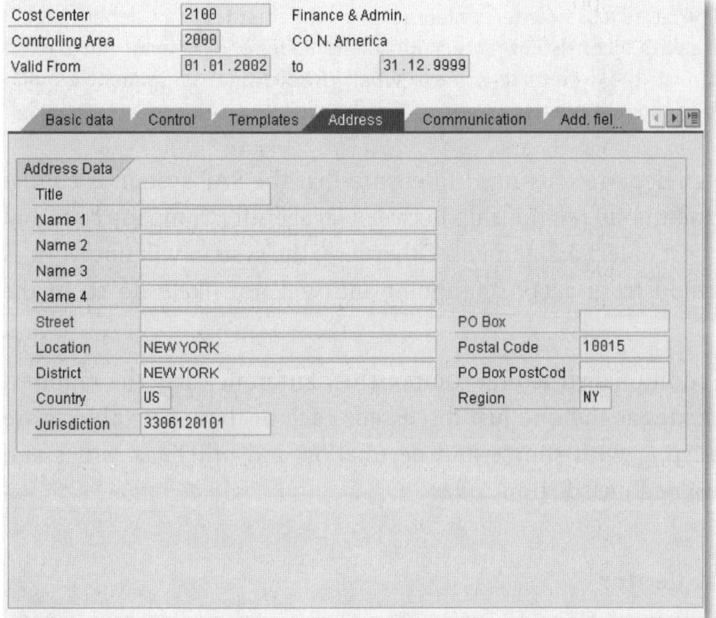

Figure 3.5 Cost Center Master — Address Tab

Responsibility accounting in the example introduced earlier can be facilitated by jurisdictional-based cost center assignment by assigning a cost center to Los Angeles and a cost center to Ventura and then rolling those two cost centers up into the engineering department. This approach actually breaks the cost down to a lower level for better cost-control purposes and solves source and destination challenges at the same time.

Note

Some argue that a jurisdictional approach creates too many cost centers and will eventually choke the system. In my experience, however, systems configured in this manner handle tax matters far more efficiently than those that are not.

Case Study

I worked on an implementation where the tax department had agreed to responsibility-based cost center assignment but continued to want the jurisdiction code defaulted into the transaction. The company has still not successfully implemented in the United States and has been trying for seven years. Jurisdictional cost center assignment is a necessity if source or destination challenges are to be handled on an accurate and consistent basis.

If responsibility-based cost center assignment is implemented, tax departments must either live with inconsistent manual jurisdictional input or convince management to customize the system to achieve what jurisdictional assignment would have achieved in the first place.

To reiterate, tax departments need to ensure that the SAP system is configured using a one-to-one relationship between legal entity/company code and jurisdictional cost object assignment. Otherwise, the system will not work as fluidly as it could from a tax standpoint and will not likely do so in the future.

We'll look at additional structural components, but none carry the ramifications for tax issues as the one just discussed. Each of these cost objects are capable of assisting with source and destination and other tax issues and need to be assigned jurisdiction codes.

3.2.2 Profit Center

As mentioned earlier, the primary role of the SAP profit center is not for legal entity accounting but to capture revenue for targeted parts of the business and then match expenses against the revenue. It is a tracking tool for internal cost accounting more than financial accounting. Profit centers can be linked to cost centers to accomplish the revenue and expense matching concept and play a role in tax computations by defining in what jurisdictions revenues are earned.

If a profit center representing a sales office is defined with an appropriate jurisdiction code, tax departments can reliably report those sales on tax returns for that jurisdiction. Profit centers are used in a variety of ways in the system, but again, they best assist tax departments when defined on a jurisdictional basis. Figure 3.6 shows the profit center master. With ECC 6.0 and the document splitter, profit centers have become an even more powerful tool because more complete financial statements can be obtained at the profit center level.

Figure 3.7 illustrates how cost centers are linked to profit centers for matching revenue and expense. Each cost center can carry a profit center code that will link expenses for that cost center to revenue captured by the profit center. Complete financial statements on a profit center basis are available in ECC 6.0 due to the creation of the document splitter but will not result in a GAAP financial statement unless the pre-SAP balance sheet is accurately broken down to the profit center level when initially loaded in SAP.

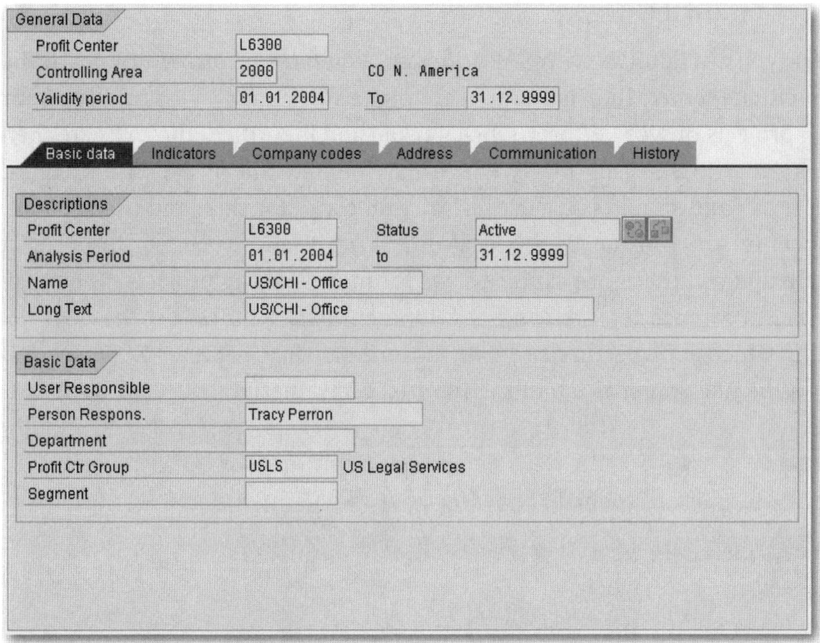

Figure 3.6 Profit Center Master

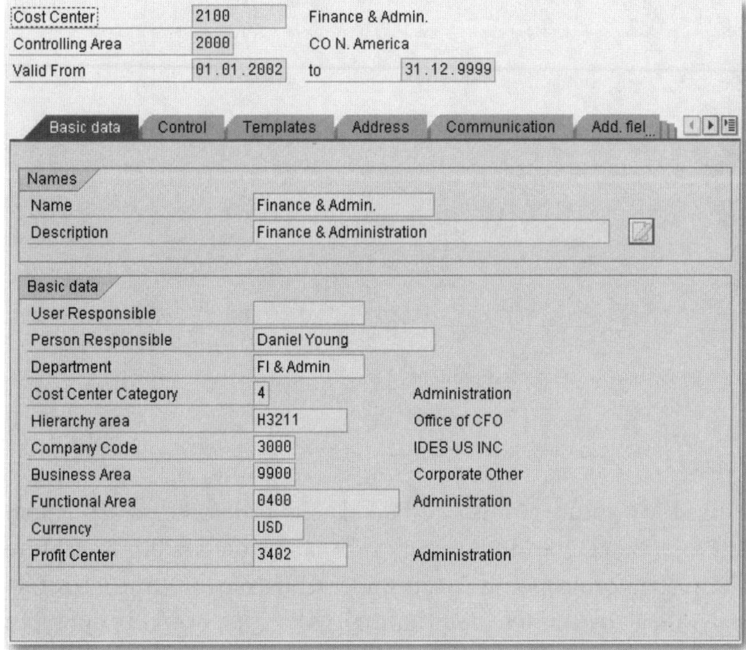

Figure 3.7 Cost Center Master — Basic Data Tab

3.2.3 Internal Orders

Unless you are familiar with SAP software, you have probably not heard the term *internal order*. Internal orders are objects designed to capture costs for small projects or work efforts. Once tracked and identified, the costs are then settled to a final resting place, which may be an asset or expense account. Orders can and should carry tax jurisdiction codes for sales and use tax compliance. In some instances, internal orders are used in place of the project system and can therefore capture costs for more lengthy projects. They may be used to capture research and development expenditures for the R&D tax credit, which will be discussed in more detail in Chapter 10. Figure 3.8 shows the **Assignments** tab of the internal order master.

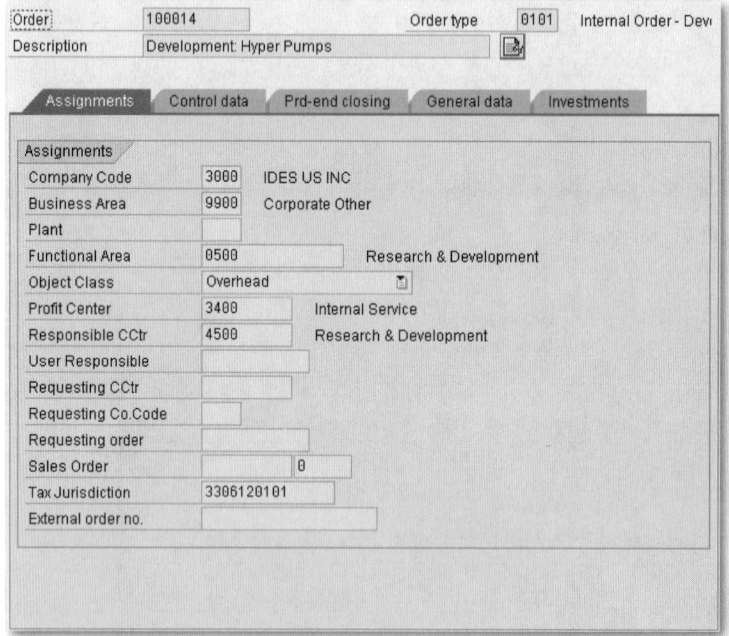

Figure 3.8 Internal Order Master — Assignments Tab

3.2.4 Projects

Projects are used to capture project costs and, like orders, have settlement procedures. Projects are used in a variety of ways in the system to capture the cost of long-term projects and Assets under Construction (AuC). If structured properly, they are useful in determining R&D costs, breaking out types of cost for property tax, and tracking expenses involved in major corporate efforts.

3.2.5 Work Breakdown Structure (WBS) Elements

Work Breakdown Structure (WBS) elements are components of projects and are set up for different types of expenses that will compose the project. A WBS element has master data that describes the element and gives the tax jurisdiction code for the expenses charged to the element. Figure 3.9 shows some of the master data for a WBS element, on the **Assignments** tab.

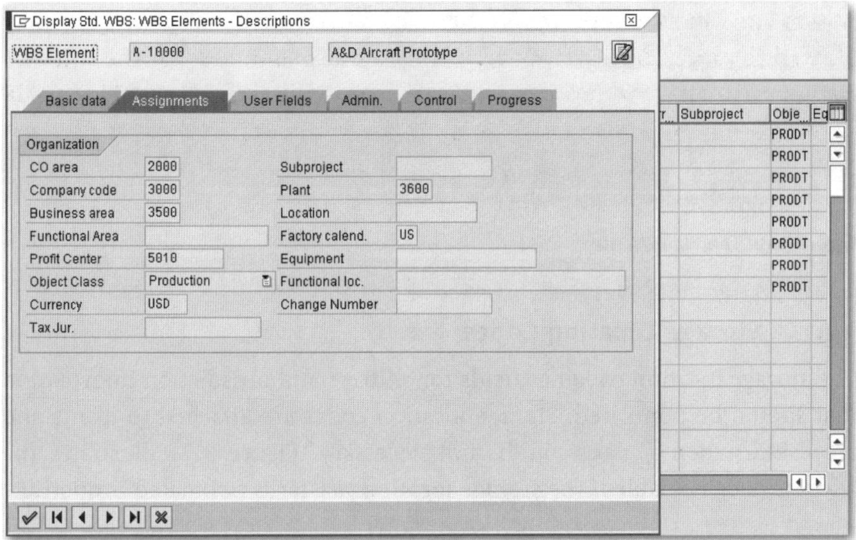

Figure 3.9 WBS Element Master — Assignments Tab

3.2.6 Plant Codes

Plant codes are an additional cost object in SAP and can represent actual plants, administrative offices, shipping and storage locations, warehouses, and other facilities. Plants carry jurisdiction codes and should therefore not cross jurisdictional boundaries. Plants can be maintained independent of company codes so they can process products for more than one legal entity; however, the assets associated with a given plant have to be owned by a single legal entity or divided in some rational way between legal entities.

The plant code often represents the shipping point for goods sold by the company but may have SAP storage locations coupled with it. Plants codes with jurisdictional information are useful in determining the shipping point of goods produced at the plant and the destination point for goods purchased for plant consumption. Detailed plant accounting is also useful for computing the domestic manufacturing deduction, which is of great advantage to domestic manufacturers. The plant master is populated in the IMG (Implementation Guide) and is shown in Figure 3.10.

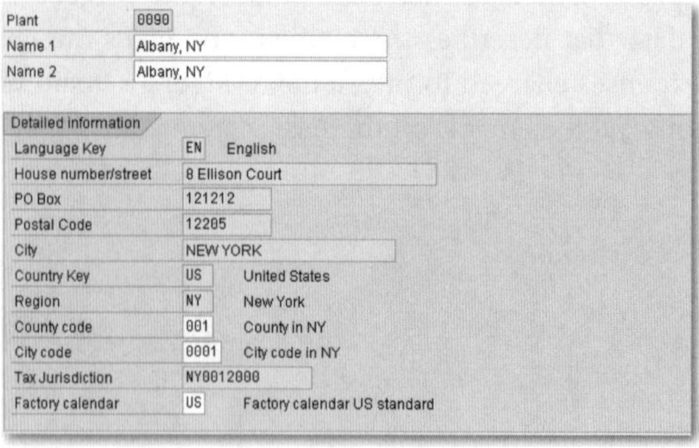

Figure 3.10 The Plant Master

3.2.7 Storage Location Codes

The storage location code has fields for address and jurisdiction information that should be populated. Storage location codes are attached to plants and are useful when a plant code is not necessary. Figure 3.11 illustrates the address data available if the storage location master is populated properly.

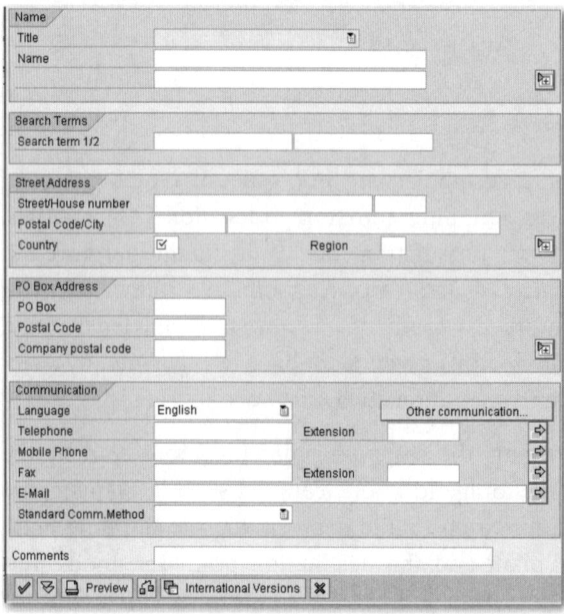

Figure 3.11 Storage Location Master — Address Tab

3.2.8 Business Area Codes

Business area codes were covered earlier in the legal entity and company code discussion. You can use these codes to capture cost for certain segments of the business, and they are useful for internal cost control. Financial statements are standard for business areas but are not appropriate for financial reporting. The business area is a useful tool when used properly. There are not any ramifications for tax departments when used appropriately.

3.2.9 Functional Area Codes

Functional area codes are used to separate different functions of the business such as sales versus accounting, engineering versus research, development versus human resources, and so on. Functional areas, such as business areas, are defined during configuration, which gives companies the flexibility to set up as many functional areas as needed. They differ from business areas because they are designed to represent functional parts of a business as opposed to divisions, brands, or other areas of the operation. In reality, the codes can be used for just about anything a company desires. Functional area is usually an internal cost accounting tool but can prove useful for capturing cost for the R&D tax credit if all R&D is done in one area of the company. Functional areas are generally set up on master records resulting in segregating master records into functional groupings. Records can be grouped on several different bases depending on what makes sense for your organization. G/L accounts, cost elements, and cost centers can all be divided into functional areas for reporting. Like business areas, functional areas do not have a related master file and therefore cannot be associated with tax jurisdiction codes.

3.3 Summary

In this chapter, we briefly discussed different ways to implement an SAP system as well as various revenue and cost objects used in the system. Although new G/L functionality when coupled with the document splitter may, in time, possibly result in a capable method for legal entity accounting, assigning one company code to one legal entity still seems preferable at this point. To provide good source and destination information for tax purposes, cost objects and profit centers should all carry complete address information and accurate jurisdiction codes and be set up on a jurisdictional basis as opposed to a responsibility basis.

In Chapter 4, we will discuss income taxes in more detail and concentrate on areas such as the chart of accounts, fixed assets, and intercompany transactions. Our goal will be to discuss how taxes can be worked into the configuration plans to improve the quality of life for tax professionals.

Income tax is impacted by activities and transactions that originate in all areas of SAP systems, and effective tax integration in the income tax area can result in lasting efficiencies and savings. In this chapter, we will discuss issues affecting different aspects of income tax and what can be done in SAP systems to facilitate the handling of these issues.

4 Federal, State, and Local Income Tax Integration

Income tax is a many faceted tax that spans all areas of a corporation's business. In this chapter, we'll discuss several aspects of corporate income tax in detail, including the following:

- Chart of accounts
- Fixed assets
- Intercompany transactions
- International tax issues

4.1 Chart of Accounts

In Chapter 3, we discussed the importance of legal entity accounting to tax professionals and explained how a one-to-one relationship between legal entity and company code can solve legal entity accounting challenges. Nearly as important to tax professionals is the concept of identifying the source and destination for each transaction. We previously discussed how jurisdictional cost center assignment provides a solution to this tax need. Another tool that assists in proper classification of revenue and expenses for tax is the chart of accounts. Proper classification is essential if tax professionals are going to avoid doing account analysis on a monthly basis over the life of the system.

4.1.1 Classifying Costs

The chart of accounts is the common tool that allows accounting systems to classify costs into meaningful areas for reporting in general ledger (G/L) and financial statement format. Many companies installing SAP software have more than 20,000 accounts and subaccounts currently used in legacy systems. The fact that the new SAP system will only have a couple thousand accounts at most and that there will not be subaccounts usually comes as a surprise. SAP software has many more cost objects that serve to capture costs than just G/L accounts and therefore does not need nearly as big a chart of accounts. It is important to recognize when an account is needed versus when the information can be captured some other way. The SAP team in charge of the chart of accounts is usually tasked with controlling the number of accounts set up and therefore requests justification and a description for each account added to the chart. This makes good business sense because information that can be captured easier using a different cost object does not need a G/L account. A tax integration specialist is experienced in deciding when to ask for an additional account and when not to. We will look at this in more detail next.

4.1.2 When to Create New Accounts

With chart of accounts minimization and control in mind, there are still situations where tax departments need new accounts and need to be able to justify this need to the SAP project team. Also, the U.S. side of international taxation has a heavy need for additional accounts to capture the different cost buckets required for compliance. The number of new accounts needed by tax departments is primarily dependent on how old charts of accounts are mapped to the new SAP chart of accounts and which accounts are deleted and which are retained.

> **Note**
>
> In Appendix A, you will find tax accounts I have added during implementations I have been part of. These accounts may help you by serving as examples of accounts added by other multinational corporations, but they need to be reviewed carefully. Your situation may call for something very different.

Tax sensitization of the chart of accounts, however, is only one tool used during tax integration to make the system more tax friendly. The chart of accounts is a product of the G/L Master, and G/L Master data must therefore be addressed. Few things on the G/L Master affect tax other than setting up the account correctly in the first place. Fields that impact tax on the G/L Master are listed in Chapter 8 "Master Data."

Many other accounts on the G/L Master should be populated as part of the accounting system, but the accounts in Chapter 8 are especially pertinent to tax and need to be populated and reviewed by tax departments for accuracy. The tax department should be part of the governance process early on so that new codes being set up (company codes, G/L accounts, cost centers, etc.) are circulated to the tax department prior to finalization.

4.2 Fixed Assets

The SAP fixed asset system is flexible and works well for tax purposes when configured properly, but it is configuration intensive. Objections to requests for fixed asset configuration may stem from the amount of configuration required or the precedent set during a global implementation.

Example

Unfortunately, some implementers are determined to put in a standard SAP system, regardless of what the client needs. For example, I worked on an implementation where the tax department was refused the asset classes and depreciation areas they needed in the United States, for not entirely clear reasons. Be aware that if you're a tax professionals you need to ask for, and sometimes repeatedly, what you need, even if you encounter resistance. Also, if your first approach doesn't work, you can try to find a different solution but pursue the best solution for as long as is feasible.

Fixed assets have a far-reaching impact on tax departments. There are several areas that affect tax departments most heavily. These deal with the chart of depreciation, depreciation areas, and asset classes. If these areas of the application are configured properly, tax departments will breathe much easier. Let's take a closer look.

4.2.1 Chart of Depreciation

The *chart of depreciation* is a collection of depreciation areas that generally meets the regulations of a particular country. SAP supplies a chart of depreciation for a number of larger countries. The United States has its own chart of depreciation that serves as a starting point for custom configuration to meet tax needs. In any given implementation, the chart of depreciation will be assigned to a country, and within that country numerous company codes may be assigned to the chart of depreciation. Each chart of depreciation will then have several depreciation areas assigned to it to handle specific depreciation needs within that country.

4.2.2 Depreciation Areas

Depreciation areas are generally referred to as *depreciation books* by tax departments. SAP software is capable of computing depreciation under a number of different scenarios. This is accomplished through the use of depreciations areas. A *depreciation area* is an independent computation structure within R/3 and ECC that allows depreciation to be calculated using different depreciation conventions. Depreciation areas fall under the umbrella of a chart of depreciation and can only be used with one chart of depreciation.

Scenarios for Creating Additional Depreciation Areas

Most people are familiar with the concept of financial depreciation that is used for external financial reporting. The IRS has issued depreciation rules that allow assets to be written off or depreciated more rapidly than what most companies use for financial reporting. IRS rules have changed over the years with changing tax legislation. Depreciation rules can be used to stimulate investment, so they change periodically. When the IRS changes depreciation rules, the states often follow with similar changes, but depending on financial condition and various state objectives, states can elect not to adopt federal rules. This was the case, for example, with the federal bonus rules issued in 2002. A portion of the states elected to adopt the rules, but many others did not. International depreciation rules are also often not the same as those used in the United States. These types of differences led to the need for additional depreciation areas, set up as part of a tax integration project. Examples of commonly added depreciation areas include the following:

- Financial or book depreciation
- Tax depreciation (ACRS/MACRS)
- Alternative Minimum Tax (AMT) depreciation
- Adjusted Current Earnings (ACE) depreciation
- States (ACRS/MACRS) without bonus
- Corporate earnings and profits
- California state depreciation

Further, additional areas are needed at the state level for AMT and ACE depreciation for states not adopting federal bonus rules. The California depreciation area is added for firms with many California-based assets. Other states differ from federal rules in more ways than just bonus depreciation and may need separate areas set up if the firm has a large asset base within the state. Figure 4.1 shows standard depreciation areas in an SAP system.

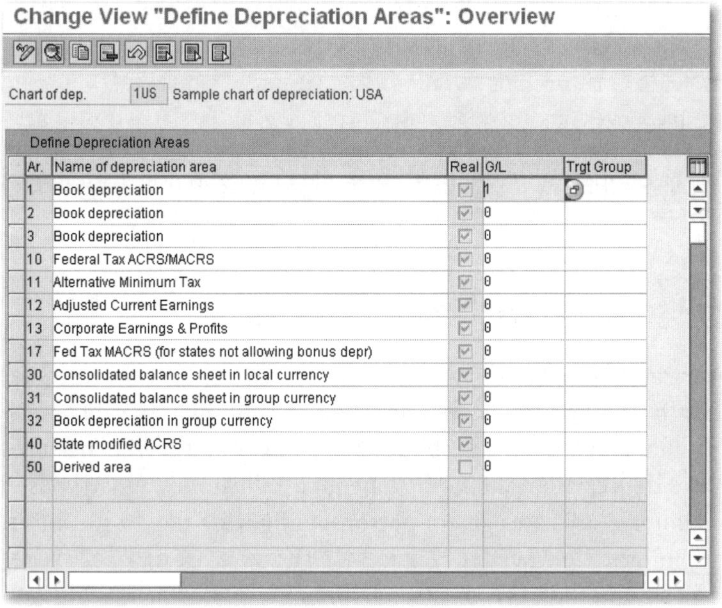

Change View "Define Depreciation Areas": Overview

Chart of dep. 1US Sample chart of depreciation: USA

Define Depreciation Areas

Ar.	Name of depreciation area	Real	G/L	Trgt Group
1	Book depreciation	☑	1	
2	Book depreciation	☑	0	
3	Book depreciation	☑	0	
10	Federal Tax ACRS/MACRS	☑	0	
11	Alternative Minimum Tax	☑	0	
12	Adjusted Current Earnings	☑	0	
13	Corporate Earnings & Profits	☑	0	
17	Fed Tax MACRS (for states not allowing bonus depr)	☑	0	
30	Consolidated balance sheet in local currency	☑	0	
31	Consolidated balance sheet in group currency	☑	0	
32	Book depreciation in group currency	☑	0	
40	State modified ACRS	☑	0	
50	Derived area	☐	0	

Figure 4.1 Depreciation Areas

Property Tax Depreciation Area

SAP software also includes a property tax depreciation area in an attempt to assist with property tax depreciation rules. Although it may benefit some users, it is not used a great deal in practice. There are so many property tax jurisdictions with differences in useful lives and depreciation methods that a property tax depreciation area does not seem to offer much. Situations where a class of common assets, such as automobiles, are depreciated using different useful lives and depreciation methods over a multitude of property tax jurisdictions are not easily addressed by the SAP depreciation system.

However, independent asset classes can be assigned to depreciation areas, thereby providing the ability to select different useful lives, depreciation methods, and G/L account code assignments. This leads to the next topic: asset classes.

4.2.3 Asset Classes

Asset classes within the SAP asset accounting module are templates that determine default accounting practices for the *useful life*, the *depreciation method*, and the *G/L account assignment* of assets assigned to a particular asset class. The tax department therefore needs a separate asset class for every situation where the IRS dictates a different useful life and depreciation method for an asset.

Example

If, for example, passenger cars are depreciated over five years but large tractor rigs are depreciated over three years (which happens to be the case), a separate asset class must be set up for both categories. New additions placed in these asset classes will have depreciation information defaulted into the depreciation calculation, and depreciation for the asset class will be consistent and accurate. Asset classes are the key ingredients in each depreciation area and can be assigned to more than one area and one chart of depreciation.

A depreciation area or chart of depreciation that has a category with similar characteristics can use the same asset class used by multiple other depreciation areas. It is vital that asset classes be set up to satisfy all specific instances of useful life and depreciation method. Appendix B illustrates a matrix used by tax integration specialists to give a person configuring fixed asset information the tax information needed. Figure 4.2 shows a list of asset classes that have been configured in this particular system.

Change View "Asset classes": Overview

New Entries

Class	Short Text	Asset class description
11019901	Land	Land
21019901	Land Improvements	Land Improvements
22019901	Railroad sidings	Railroad sidings
31013301	Building Improvement	Building Improvements
31013302	Building Imp. non	Building Improvements in non ownded land
31013401	Bldg Installations	Building Installations
31013901	Light B'dings	Light Buildings
31019901	Buildings	Buildings
32019901	Spec. Purpose Build.	Special Purpose Buildings
39019901	Buildings - Cap. Int	Buildings - Capitalised Interest
41019901	Leashold Improvement	Leashold Improvements
49019901	Leaseh. Impr. C. Int	Leashold Improvements - Capitalised Interest
51013301	Mach. & Equipmt. Imp	Machinery and Equipment Improvements
51013901	Mach Specific	Specific Machinery and Equipment
51013902	Petty equipment	Petty Equipment
51019901	Machinery & Equipmt.	Machinery and Equipment
52019901	Milk C. & Cheese H.	Milk Cans and Cheese Hoops

Figure 4.2 Asset Classes

Figure 4.3 shows some of the details of an asset class. It would take several figures to show the complete asset class functionality. Some of the functionality of the asset class is listed here:

- The asset class provides an area to enter the G/L account number for account determination.
- The asset class provides an area that determines if the account is used with an AuC account and how settlement will be done.
- The asset class provides an indicator that tells whether the asset class should be included in inventory figures.

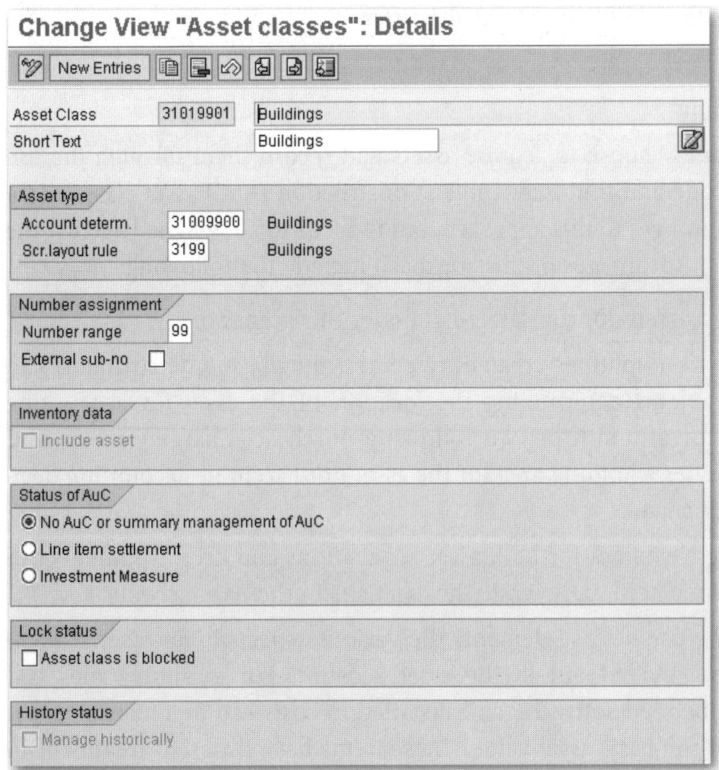

Figure 4.3 Asset Class Details

Asset classes have a multitiered structure and are used to accomplish two additional processes not mentioned in the preceding list:

- They house and control the useful life of the assets assigned to them.
- They are assigned a depreciation method that is pertinent to all assets assigned to them.

You can assign any number of charts of depreciation to each asset class. In this way, you can have country-specific depreciation terms for each combination of asset class and chart of depreciation. These depreciation terms are the default values in the given chart of depreciation.

4.2.4 Asset Capitalization

The acquisition and capitalization of assets has an impact on taxation. The IRS requires asset depreciation to start when the asset is placed in service and not necessarily when it is purchased. In many cases, the two dates are the same, but attention should be given to capturing the placed-in-service data within the system when the two dates differ.

Asset Recording

Some companies choose to acquire assets and record them through the use of a project code and the Asset Under Construction (AuC) asset class. There are many advantages to this approach, but it needs to be weighed against the disadvantages. Advantages of this approach include the following:

- Constructed assets appropriately fall under this scenario.
- The acquisition volumes created by central purchasing departments can lead to problems determining the location of the asset for accounting treatment for a month or two following purchase. Charging to an AuC account creates a holding area for the asset until accurate accounting decisions can be made.
- Accounting treatment for bulk asset acquisitions and drop shipments can be determined accurately while the asset sits in the AUC account.
- Through the use of cost elements the various aspects of an asset acquisition can be divided out in the asset account. For example, sales tax, freight, embedded software, and installation costs can be recorded separately from the basic asset value. These items have different treatment in many property tax jurisdictions and can lead to huge savings for asset-intensive organizations.

Disadvantages include the following:

- Depreciation does not start until the asset is transferred out of the AuC account. It is important that assets be cleared out of the account on a timely basis so that depreciation can begin.

- The AuC account requires constant monitoring so that items aren't indefinitely suspended and the account grows into a dumping ground.
- Using an AuC account for all asset purchases requires double booking of all acquisitions as opposed to booking the correct entry in the first place.

If your organization is not asset-intensive, it may be easier to record the asset directly to its final account and location. If you have numerous asset purchases and construction projects, consider going through a project code and an AuC account until the final account and accounting treatment is determined and then settle the assets to the proper asset class.

Asset Tracking

Do organizations know at any given time where all of their assets are physically located? Probably not, and this is not easily addressed. In an SAP system, an asset is recorded, and pertinent location facts are populated in the asset and equipment master files. After an asset is moved, the SAP system (like any other accounting system) does not have any secret method of figuring out that an asset was relocated and to where. As GPS technology improves, it will be possible to tag assets and detect their location automatically, but that time has not quite yet arrived.

For now, the equipment master is designed and used as the tracking master file in SAP, and the jurisdiction code on both the equipment master and the asset master should be kept in sync. This is easier done with newer versions of SAP software but still not entirely accurate. The equipment master requires updating on each equipment move, which involves a manual tracking procedure. If this is done properly, property tax compliance will be assured. If it is not done properly, you may have problems on audit. It is therefore important to physically audit the equipment condition and location on at least an annual basis. Unfortunately, sometimes budgets do not allow for annual audits, and the accuracy of the asset location information may be unknown until a jurisdictional audit.

4.2.5 Low Value Assets

Low value assets are expensed for financial purposes but require tracking and capitalization for property tax purposes. SAP set up a low value asset class to assist property tax professionals with capturing these types of assets. This asset class serves as a catchall for low value assets and as such does not classify the assets by asset type, useful life, and depreciation method as asset classes are designed to do. Placing all of your assets into a single asset class, just like setting up a G/L account to place your assets into, captures the majority of these purchases for later analysis but does not serve as a complete solution. Manual effort is required to account for them correctly from a property tax standpoint. Although perhaps more than needed, a better solution might be to set up an asset subclass for each asset class where assets can be classified and tracked correctly.

Note

Most tax departments either use the low value asset class or the G/L account, or they don't address the issue at all.

4.2.6 The Asset Master

The asset master holds the descriptive information used for accounting. It is a large master file with multiple tabs, including the **General**, **Time-dependent**, **Origin**, and **Deprec. Areas** tabs. An example of this file for an asset with the **General** and **Time-dependent** tabs selected is shown in Figures 4.4 and 4.5, respectively. For new asset purchases, the information in this file is entered manually. For legacy assets, the information is uploaded electronically prior to R/3 or ECC production startup.

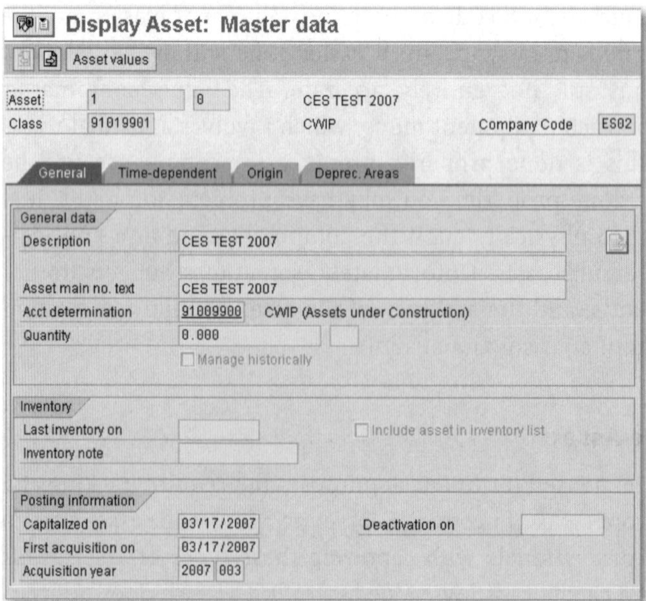

Figure 4.4 The Asset Master — General Tab

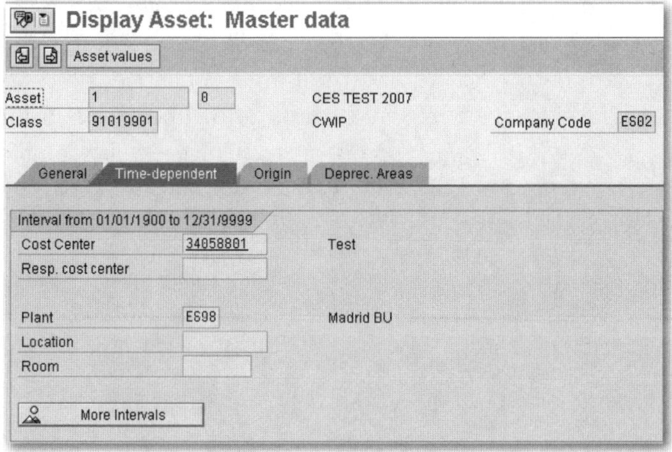

Figure 4.5 The Asset Master — Time-Dependent Tab

4.2.7 Asset Migration from Legacy Systems

Asset migration from legacy systems to the new SAP system is a big project and may require tax assistance in addition to tax review. Many times, assets are being migrated from different depreciation systems with different formats, and it is necessary to determine which fields are going to be populated in the new SAP system master file so that migration teams can determine which legacy field goes into which SAP field. Some fields in the legacy systems require conversion to SAP nomenclature. For example, a three-digit GEO code used in your old asset master needs to be converted to the jurisdiction code format and naming convention in SAP. If it is not converted, you will have proverbial apples and oranges in your file, and reports from the asset master will be meaningless.

In addition, you may want to populate some fields on the new SAP master file that did not exist in the legacy systems. If this is required, tax departments will have to decide what data is desired in the field and supply the values to the fixed asset team member so it can be uploaded.

Figure 4.6 shows the **NetWorth Tax** tab of the asset master which contains information related to property tax. For example, it has fields for tax office, assessment notice, and land registration information.

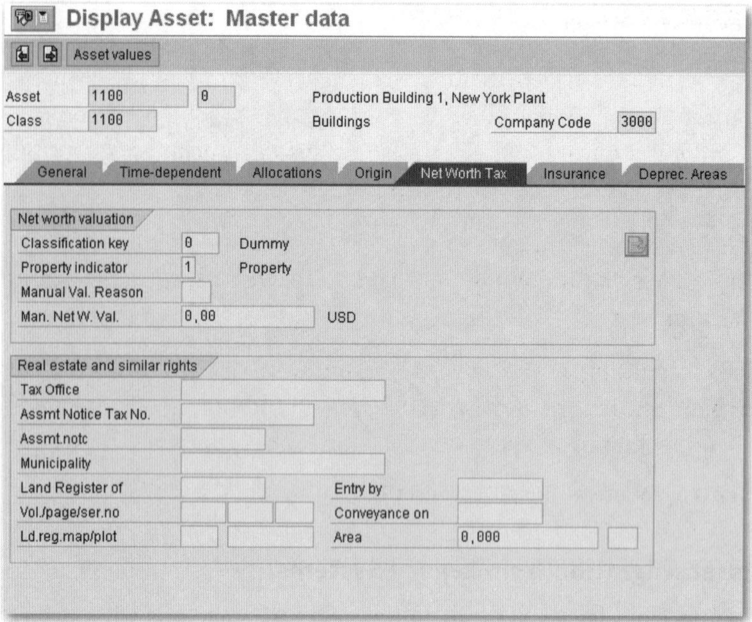

Figure 4.6 The Asset Master — Net Worth Tax Tab

4.2.8 Further Considerations

Adding new depreciation areas, asset classes, and master data fields can create work that the tax department did not realize it had when it asked for the additional data. A good tax integration specialist can identify issues such as this one and inform the tax department in advance so they have no last-minute surprises.

Loading historical asset data also needs consideration. Many companies load assets net of depreciation or at the tax basis and then load accumulated depreciation and current year depreciation so that they arrive at the full original acquisition cost. Again, if depreciation areas have not existed in the past, values will have to be computed for each asset and loaded to have the information in the future. Some companies also load initial cost information into the SAP system and then recalculate depreciation to the current period. Although this cleans up any past depreciation problems, it leaves the question as to how you handle the difference if one occurs. Differences of this sort are not easily written off, so the first method is generally used.

As you can see, much can be done in the asset management area to integrate tax processes into SAP systems. Another important area that deserves attention from tax professionals is the subject of intercompany transactions.

4.3 Intercompany Transactions

Intercompany transactions represent a challenge for most tax departments due to legal requirements involving transfer pricing and the need for accurate legal entity accounting. Also, most legacy systems included accounting that did not allow a clear vision of the entire transaction.

SAP systems handle intercompany transactions in a variety of ways. Tax integrators should keep the following points in mind when approaching intercompany accounting:

- Complete accounting entries should result from the transaction. This means that FI entries are created in the system and not just inventory-to-inventory movements that result from an SAP stock transfer.
- Both sides of the entry should be visible in the system. This is not generally a problem with a highly integrated system such as R/3 or ECC, but it has been a big problem in many legacy systems.
- Cross-border intercompany transactions are subject to transfer pricing rules and should reflect an arms length markup. SAP stock transport orders should be done with billing whenever possible.
- Some companies treat intercompany transactions similar to transactions with external vendors or customers, and this may be an option worth considering.
- SAP systems have improved intercompany transactions through the power of integration by delivering a more complete audit trail of the transaction.

Next, we'll look at transfer pricing.

Note

Transfer pricing was briefly mentioned in Chapter 2, and SAP's new transfer pricing functionality will be discussed in detail in Chapter 16. The discussion in the next section only serves as an introduction to the requierements to facilitate our discussion of intercompany transactions.

4.3.1 Transfer Pricing

With transfer pricing in an SAP system, it is not possible to see the markup or profit margin on intercompany transactions. Companies with transfer pricing issues must convince the IRS that they are not trying to shift revenue to low-tax jurisdictions and therefore must be able to substantiate the markup used and justify that the markup is equal to that used in a third-party transaction. The inability to break out the markup in intercompany transactions has led most companies to put manual procedures in place or to build in fixed markups in product pricing procedures in an attempt to satisfy IRS requirements.

Example

One company actually sweeps the SAP system for cross-border intercompany transactions on a monthly basis and then adjusts the margin between companies to a predetermined agreed rate. They then re-enter the corrected information, and bills are produced by SAP for the proper amount. Manual effort is involved monthly, but the result is good compliance with transfer pricing requirements. Others attempt to build much more functionality into the system to assist with rate determination in the first place. Whichever solution you decide on, the point is that the SAP system often requires some customization or manual intervention.

Transfer pricing confronts tax professionals with several challenges stemming from the need to illustrate the arms length transaction requirement. The issues are outlined in the list that follows:

- Justification of the transfer pricing rate.
- Development of the transfer pricing rate.
- Isolation of the profit margin in the SAP system.
- Identification of transfer pricing entries in the SAP system.
- Control of the transfer pricing procedures for a multinational corporation.
- Newer transfer pricing functionality within ECC 6.0 is based on profit center accounting and requires the use of the material ledger. The material ledger can store valuation approaches for group, profit center, and legal entity.

The functionality provides several pricing strategies such as cost plus, fixed values, receiver-specific prices, and time-related prices. And the price can be dependent on material, material type, valuation type, material group, plant, and a variety of other factors. This area is new and viritually untested in SAP and deserves and requires examination as an option to handle transfer pricing.

4.3.2 Intercompany Balances

In addition to transfer pricing issues, intercompany transactions usually result in intercompany balances. Balances between legal entities have tax implications because of imputed interest rules and sometimes play a role in 263A calculations for construction period interest and taxes. While tracking the transaction is a must, good accounting for balances between legal entities and interest rates imposed is also important.

4.4 International Tax Considerations

U.S. corporations with international operations are required to comply with internal revenue procedures regarding those operations. They may be responsible for attaching international forms to the 1120 tax return, some of which are listed here:

- Form 1118 Foreign tax credit calculation
- Form 5471 Information Return of U.S. Persons with Respect to Certain Foreign Corporations
- Form 8865 Return of U.S. Persons with Respect to Certain Foreign Partnerships
- Proposed Form 8858 Information Return of U.S. Persons with Respect to Foreign Disregarded Entities
- Form 5713 International Boycott Report
- Form 8873 ETI Calculation

To meet the requirements in this list, operations in foreign countries must be reflected in a U.S. GAAP set of books in both U.S. and local currency. This means that a company code should be set up to capture revenue and expense for these entities. Under applicable local law, a legal entity may be defined as an office, branch, distribution center, corporation, partnership, or joint venture.

To facilitate multinational operations, a single global chart of accounts should be maintained to aid in data conversion and downloads into different tax software. As mentioned earlier in the chapter, tax accounting for international operations requires many additions to the chart of accounts to assist with capturing costs related to foreign tax credit calculations and the subpart F calculation. These accounts are listed in the chart of accounts as recommended additions in the appendix.

4.5 Summary

In this chapter, we have discussed ways to improve the flow of tax information from the SAP system to enhance legal entity accounting and income tax compliance. The discussion centered on the following areas:

- The chart of accounts
- Fixed asset accounting
- Intercompany accounting
- Transfer pricing issues
- International accounting

In Chapter 5, we will talk about additional federal and state issues regarding withholding on payments. SAP provides two applications for withholding, and we will look at the advantages to each of them.

When the topic of tax withholding comes up, most think of 1099 backup withholding. But an SAP system also has the power to assist accounts payable and tax departments with Non-Resident Alien (NRA) withholding. NRA withholding presents challenges to most corporations but can be dealt with effectively using SAP enhanced withholding.

5 Tax Withholding and Reporting

U.S. Code Section 1441 and others require money to be withheld on certain payments and remited to the IRS. Most U.S. companies are familiar with the rules governing 1099 backup withholding and related W-9 requirements. However, 1042 Non-Resident Alien (NRA) withholding is possibly more important to many companies and has a plethora of W-8 requirements. As you continue to read, you will learn about the two withholding tools within R/3 and ECC and which one is best for your company.

5.1 Classic Withholding versus Extended Withholding

The accounts payable department, in most corporations, handles 1099 and NRA withholding and reporting. For this reason, tax departments are not as concerned with these issues until an audit arises, but withholding needs to be addressed and handled properly. Implementation of an SAP system is a good time to improve procedures in areas that may have been neglected in the past. SAP R/3 and ECC have two types of withholding programs shipped with the software:

- Classic Withholding (also called standard withholding)
- Extended Withholding

Probably more than 95 % of companies use the classic or standard withholding application. The widespread use of the standard withholding application does not, however, mean that it is the best choice or that companies are necessarily in compliance that use it. Extended withholding functionality has been slow to catch on among implementers and can take considerably more time to configure. Very few consultants are well versed in the principles of both 1099 and NRA withholding or familiar with the configuration required to adequately install extended withholding. For these reasons, extended withholding has often been avoided in the marketplace.

However, SAP help literature actually stated nearly five years ago that the company no longer recommends the use of standard withholding. SAP recommends the use of extended reporting programs going forward. The extended withholding application has the following advantages:

- Extended reporting is flexible enough to be activated by company code, which means that you need only use it for legal entities having difficult withholding problems.
- Activating extended withholding adds an additional screen to the customer and vendor masters allowing withholding rate and type information to be added.
- Extended withholding allows a corporation to withhold from both the customer and vendor sides of the transaction.
- Extended withholding allows a company code to have several different withholding types.
- Extended withholding has added reporting features.

Extended withholding has many advantages, with most concerning NRA withholding. The 1099 program is similar in both applications. A company that has very few foreign transactions is probably safe using classic withholding, but for multinational corporations, extended withholding deserves a closer examination than it has received so far in the marketplace. Figures 5.1 and 5.2 illustrate the effect on the customer and vendor master files of activating extended withholding.

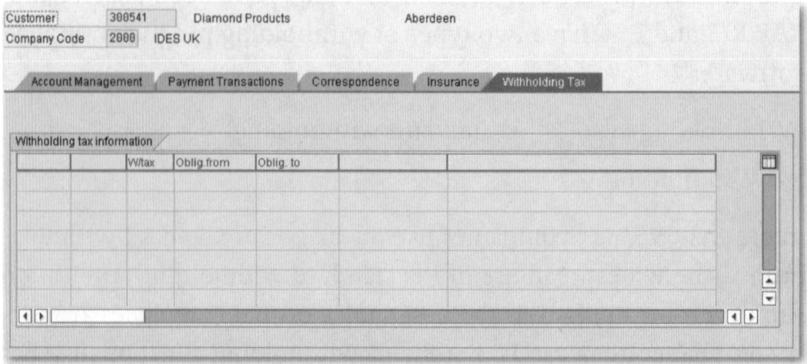

Figure 5.1 Customer Master — Withholding Tax Tab

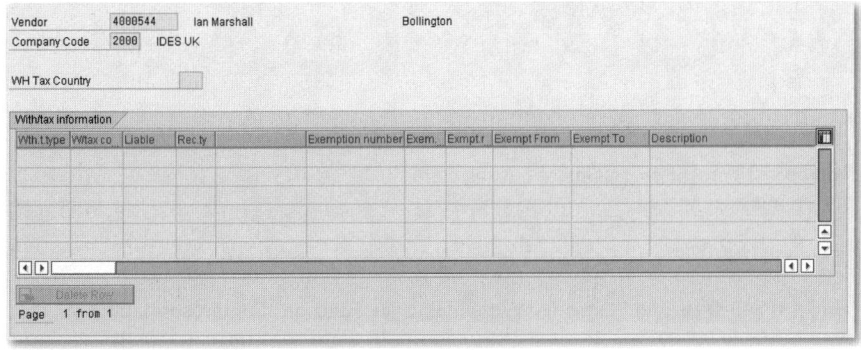

Figure 5.2 Vendor Master — Extended Withholding

Table 5.1 is a comparison table prepared by SAP to illustrate the differences between the two applications.

Individual Functions	Classic Withholding Tax	Extended Withholding Tax
Withholding tax on outgoing payment	X	X
Withholding tax on incoming payment		X
Withholding tax posting at time of payment	X	X
Withholding tax posting at time of invoice		X
Withholding tax posting on partial payment		X
Number of withholding taxes for each document	Max. 1	Several
Withholding tax base:	Net amount	X
	Modified net amount	X
	Gross amount	X
	Tax amount	X
	Modified tax amount	X
Rounding Rule		X
Cash discount considered		X
Accumulation		X

Table 5.1 SAP Classic and Extended Withholding Tax Functions Comparison Table (Source: SAP AG)

Individual Functions	Classic Withholding Tax	Extended Withholding Tax
Minimum/maximum amounts and exemption limits		X
Number assignment on document posting (certificate numbering)		X
Calculation formulas	X	X

Table 5.1 SAP Classic and Extended Withholding Tax Functions Comparison Table (Source: SAP AG) (cont.)

Before we look more closely at the configuration of extended withholding, let's briefly examine 1099 and 1042 withholding and reporting in more detail.

5.2 1099 Withholding and Reporting

U.S. 1099 reporting is required at both the federal and state level. Either of the SAP programs examined previously will handle 1099 compliance. SAP has made needed improvements to their 1099 programs over the past eight years to add more functionality. The 1099 programs within R/3 and ECC require interaction with the system at basically three different times and in three different places, as we'll discuss next.

5.2.1 Vendor Setup

As vendors are set up, a decision needs to be made concerning the type of entity the vendor is and whether the vendor needs to receive a 1099 at year end. Based on this decision, master data fields on the vendor master must be populated. Two areas exist for tax ID numbers: one for the social security number and another for the federal tax ID number. Individuals with only a social security number will usually receive 1099s and need to be tracked in the system. Entities with federal ID numbers may need to be tracked depending on their business form and type of business. To facilitate tracking, a 1099 code must be entered on the vendor master. To facilitate backup withholding, SAP uses the same field but has adopted different codes.

5.2.2 Configuration

1099 codes are adopted in the configuration phase of the implementation. 1099 configuration is relatively straightforward and needs to be done if ECC is to be used for 1099 tracking and reporting.

5.2.3 Vendor Master

The Accounts Payable application within the Financials (FI) module contains the reporting selection for 1099s. Year end IRS reporting requires a hard copy to be sent to the 1099 receiver and an electronic copy to be filed with the IRS. 1099 reporting also has reports for use during the year to secure social security numbers and help in maintenance activities. Reporting at the state level can also be kicked off here. Figure 5.3 shows the 1099 configuration page in classic withholding.

Configuration in classic withholding allows several options for designing how backup withholding will work. The percentage rate of withholding is controlled here as is the base amount the rate is applied against. You will note that you can also control whether withholding is done at the time of invoice or at the time of payment. For 1099-MISC withholding, codes exist that determine what type of payments have been made to the vendor. This is required because multiple types of payments are reported using form 1099-MISC.

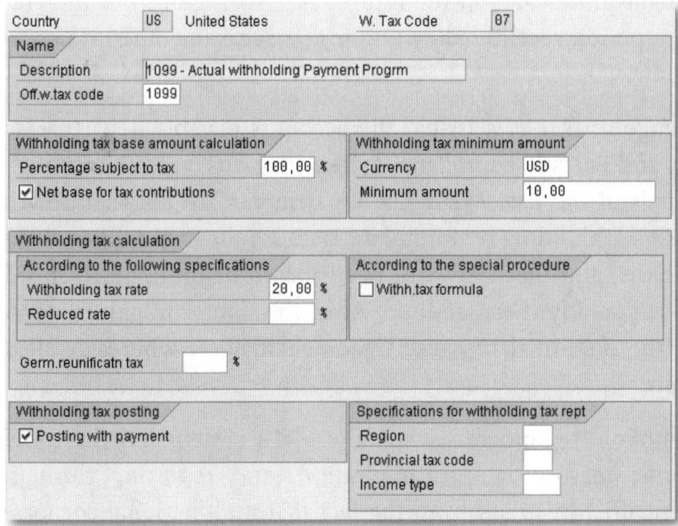

Figure 5.3 Classic Withholding 1099 Configuration Page

Figures 5.4 and 5.5 illustrate the reports available from the system.

Withholding Tax
General
S_P00_07000134 - Generic Withholding Tax Reporting
S_PL0_09000447 - Withholding Tax Report for the Vendor

Figure 5.4 Classic Withholding — General Reports

USA
S_ALR_87012142 - Postcard Printout of 1099 Vendor Addresses for Tax Code
S_ALR_87012143 - 1099 Listings
S_PL0_09000314 - 1099-Misc
S_ALR_87012145 - 1042 Reporting (USA)

Figure 5.5 Classic Withholding 1099 — USA Reporting

5.3 1042 (NRA) Withholding and Reporting

The IRS requires withholding and reporting on certain transactions between foreign countries either internal to a company or between third parties. Monies withheld from these transactions must be deposited with the IRS on an ongoing basis, and 1042s must be filed by March 15 of each year. Often, corporations have a hard time administratively keeping up with the effort created by NRA withholding. The IRS has also had a difficult time auditing this area but has made gestures in the past year or two that indicate that they will be more vigilant in this area in the future. One such gesture is the voluntary compliance period recently allowed for taxpayers to come into compliance with the law.

Part of the challenge in this area is that the accounts payable departments have to interpret and enforce compliance when they are typically not well versed in the details of the law. Many tax departments are not themselves well versed in NRA withholding requirements because they are not involved on a day to day basis, and they have not been forced to come up to speed because the area has seldom been audited. Also, for some companies, NRA withholding has the potiential to cause major challenges, whereas others have little exposure.

As with 1099 withholding and reporting, the 1042 system has the same three touch points: master data, configuration, and reporting through accounts payable. Difficulty arises from the fact that multinational corporations become withholding agents for payments of U.S. source income to foreign affiliates or third parties from U.S. entities. They may also become withholding agents due to the actions of foreign affiliates using U.S. source income to pay outside vendors in other foreign countries. The rules and forms required are numerous in this area, and extended withholding is best used to handle difficult tax situations.

Configuration for NRA withholding requires knowledge of income, recipient types, and withholding types in foreign countries. Tax treaty information is also required. Not many consultants have the experience in this area to configure ECC and supply the tax information as well. An extended withholding project requires a consultant with some knowledge of SAP withholding procedures and client tax and accounts payable departments willing to do the research needed to supply data for configuration.

5.4 Configuration of Extended Withholding

Extended withholding has merit and should be used more widely than it is currently. With that in mind, the following discussion will examine functionality and configuration requirements of extended withholding, including the **Basic Settings**, **Calculation**, **Company Code** and **Posting**, and **Reporting** nodes of the **Extended Withholding Tax** configuration tree from the Implementation Guide (IMG).

5.4.1 Basic settings

Figure 5.6 shows the **Basic Settings** node. Let's look at each of the settings contained in this node in more detail.

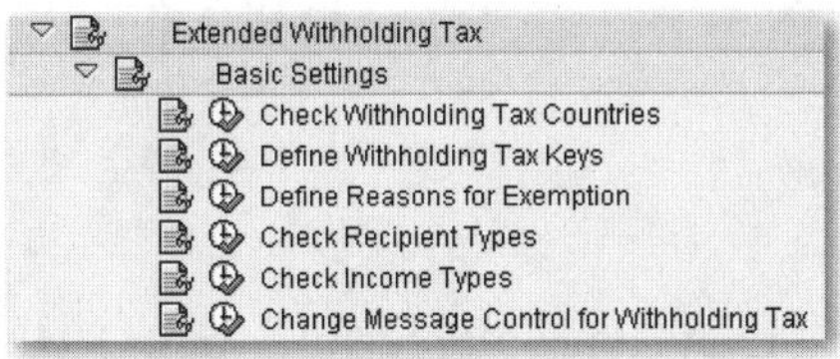

Figure 5.6 Basic Settings Configuration Items in the IMG

Check Withholding Tax Countries

Extended withholding is a global program, so the first step in configuration is to activate your withholding tax countries. SAP software is shipped with values for these fields, but the official list of country keys should be substituted for the shipped values. All countries expected to have NRA transactions should be activated here. Because individuals doing configuration seldom know this information, AP or tax personnel are responsible for collecting this data and other data needed for configuration.

Define Withholding Tax Keys

Withholding tax keys may need to be set up for some countries to identify specific withholding types mandated by those jurisdictions. These keys are later assigned to withholding tax codes and represent the official code specified by the tax jurisdiction for the withholding tax type. The values shipped with R/3 or ECC may have to be deleted and the official codes set up for complete compliance.

Define Reasons for Exemption

Exemption reasons are set by some jurisdictions and need to be defined in this basic area of the configuration tree. In the absence of country requirements, a firm can configure its own reasons in this area. The 1042 requires the use of official reason codes.

Check Recipient Types

Recipient types also must be identified for reporting purposes. In the United States, codes point to the income type and the legal entity type. For example, interest, corporate; interest, individual; and so on, identify the type of recipient for 1042 reporting in the United States (for example, corporation, individual, partnership, artist, athlete, etc). The US 1042 form requires official codes to be used for each recipient type, and these should be used in the system.

Check Income Types

The income type allows for classification by type of revenue. U.S. 1042 requires an income code to be entered for the type of income reported on the 1042. Official codes are supplied by the IRS. These codes need to be set up during configuration for automatic inclusion on the tax form.

Change Message Control for Withholding Tax

The **Basic Settings** node also allows you to control messages sent back from the system. This configuration table is blank unless you provide some messages. Messages can be either warnings or hard errors that stop the program. The message area is completely customizable.

5.4.2 The Withholding Calculation

You can see from Figure 5.7 that the withholding calculation itself is governed by three keys. Let's look at each in more detail.

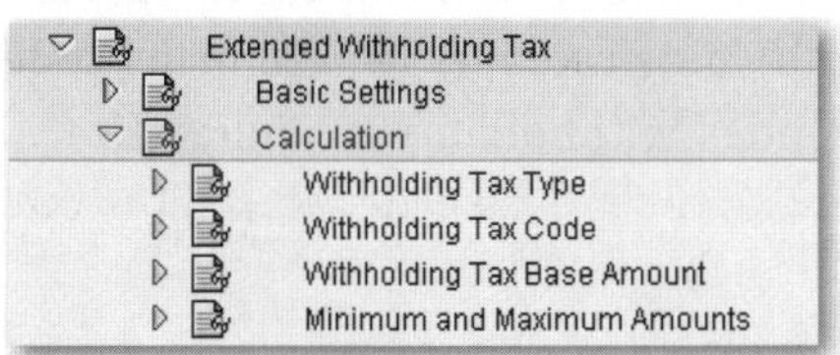

Figure 5.7 The Calculation Configuration Node

Withholding Tax Type

The **Withholding Tax Type** key represents the various types of withholding tax in a corporation. For example, most corporations will have some 1099 backup withholding and some NRA withholding. Some countries may have other withholding tax laws as well.

Withholding Tax Code

The **Withholding Tax Code** key is used to control the rate or percentage for the tax calculation. The code can be made to point to whatever rate is necessary for the withholding tax type.

Withholding Tax Base Amount

The **Withholding Tax Base Amount** key instructs the calculation to apply the percentage just described to either a gross or discounted amount.

Minimum or Maximum Amounts

The program allows the user to select minimum and maximum amounts to which the withholding percentage will be applied. The minimum amount is especially useful to prevent administrative work on very small dollar transactions. Minimum and maximum amounts can be maintained at either the Withholding Tax Type level or the Withholding Tax Code level depending on what is preferred. These settings are not required and do not make complete sense for U.S. withholding compliance because the IRS does not allow corporations not to withhold under a minimum amount or to stop withholding over a maximum amount.

5.4.3 Activation by Company Code

As mentioned earlier, extended withholding can be activated by company code. Figure 5.8 shows the **Company Code** node, which enables the person in charge of configuration to assign withholding tax types to a company code and to activate a company code for extended withholding.

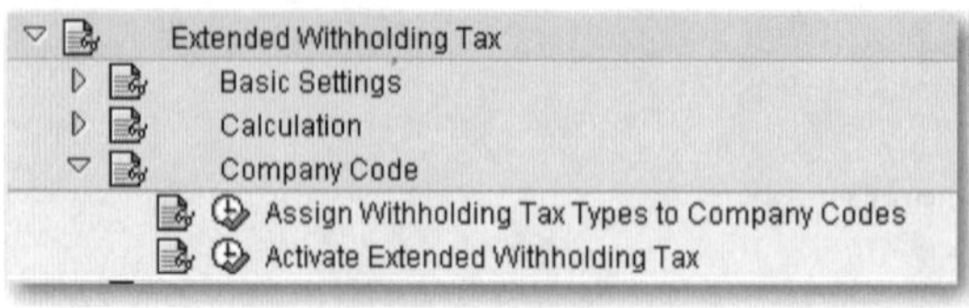

Figure 5.8 The Company Code Node

5.4.4 Posting

Figure 5.9 shows the **Posting** node, which is used for two functions. It enables general ledger (G/L) accounts to be entered for account determination for extended withholding accounting entries, and it lets you set numbering for withholding certificates

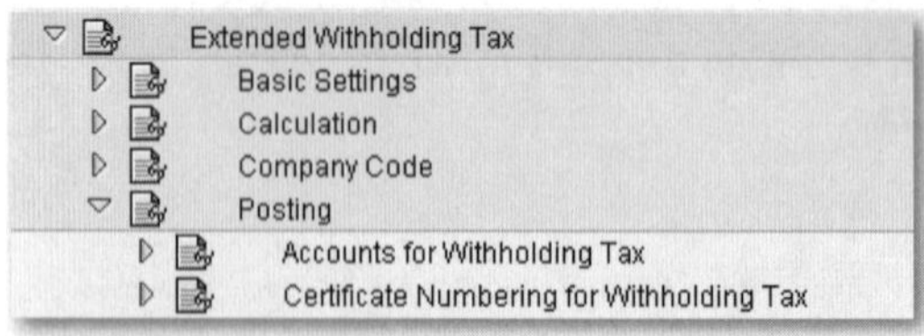

Figure 5.9 The Posting Node

5.4.5 Reporting

Figure 5.10 shows the **Report** node. As with classic withholding, extended withholding has standard reports as well. Options located under this node give users some flexibility in determining standard report layouts.

Extended withholding projects take considerable time to implement due to the amount of reseach required before NRA configuration can be done. Don't take this effort lightly when doing the work plan for a project. Investing the added time to comply with NRA withholding will pay dividends at the time of an IRS audit.

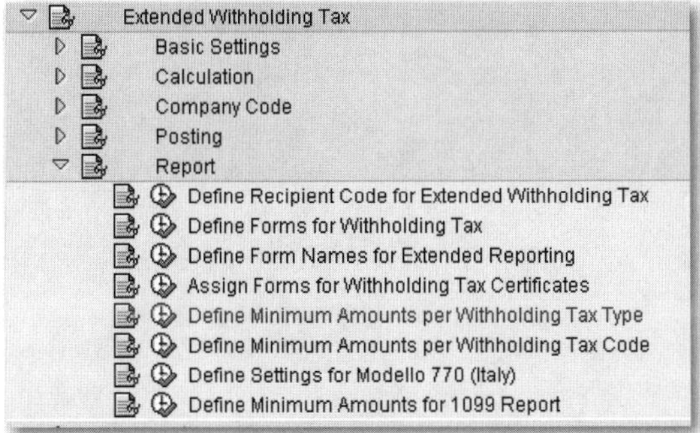

Figure 5.10 The Reporting Node

5.5 Summary

SAP R/3 and ECC systems contain two withholding programs: classic withholding and extended withholding. While classic withholding is currently the most widely used, extended withholding has more functionality and is the SAP recommended application. Extended withholding projects require research and are configuration intensive but when done properly can increase a firm's compliance with withholding tax statutes.

Chapter 6 discusses requirements for maintaining tax data after tax returns have been filed. The IRS and other jurisdictions require that data used to prepare the tax return be retained until they have either had a chance to audit the information or to pass on the opportunity. DART is the primary tool used for SAP data retention and will be discussed in detail.

Retention of tax data is required by law. SAP created the Data Retention Tool (DART) to help comply with this requirement. This chapter discusses DART implementations and configuration and explores the creation of DART views. It also discusses SAP's approach to content management for unstructured documents.

6 DART and Record Retention for Tax Departments

Record retention for tax departments can be categorized into two major areas, as outlined in the following list. Both types of documentation are required by law:

- Electronic books and records in the ECC system
- Unstructured records such as spreadsheets, contracts, and so on that provide support for the data from the system and the tax return

Internal Revenue Code (IRC) Section 6001 governs documentation needed to support the tax return and is broad enough to include any documents used in return preparation. Revenue Procedure 98–25 states that if records are in an electronic format, they must be provided to the IRS in a similar format. SAP software was running into difficulty meeting the requirements of 98–25 in the late 1990s and teamed with America's SAP User Group (ASUG) to develop the Data Retention Tool (DART). We will talk about DART in more detail later in this section. DART, if implemented properly, meets the needs of the IRS and is also available for the use of other jurisdictional auditors such as sales and use tax and property tax auditors.

SAP did not offer a solution for unstructured records until it released the NetWeaver suite of products. The acceptance of NetWeaver functionality is gaining momentum and will continue to do so as companies upgrade to ECC releases. NetWeaver functionality is broad, and some applications are being used much more than others. For example, the NetWeaver Knowledge Management (KM) tool is still in its infancy, but it is the SAP response to many of the content management systems currently in the marketplace. KM should at some point in the future be a viable tool for tax storage and management of unstructured documents, given SAP's history of aggressively marketing and improving its software to maintain its position in the marketplace. We will discuss the NetWeaver KM tool in more detail later in this chapter.

6.1 DART

In the mid 1990s, U.S.-based companies using SAP started their first round of audits with the IRS. Many companies had archived data and faced challenges responding to IRS Information Document Requests (IDRs) when audited. As a result, the ASUG tax special interest group worked together with SAP to develop DART. Archived data still presents challenges to tax users stemming from the following facts:

- Archived files do not maintain the integrity of the accounting period.
- Archived files are not easily queried to bring back large amounts of period-oriented transaction data.
- Transaction documents are unlinked from related master data as a result of fragmentation between multiple archiving runs.
- Multiple archiving runs for the same accounting period destroy audit trail links between one transaction document and another.

After DART was created, companies typically held off on archiving until DART extracts were run because archiving purges data from SAP tables and fields, whereas DART copies data for later use. Archived files preserve the transaction record, which can be retrieved at a later time, but the retrieval process is usually one record at a time. Revenue Procedure 98–25 requires companies to provide hundreds of thousands of records in flat file format. This is not easily done from archived files even with specific query software. DART was designed to fill this need and has served as a satisfactory data extraction and query tool for the past seven years.

DART has both strengths and limitations, which we'll explore in this section. You need to understand them when considering a DART implementation.

6.1.1 Advantages of DART

Although DART is not the only tool used by the IRS, it serves as the most widely used tool for extracting data from SAP tables and responding to IRS inquiries. Advantages of the tool include the following:

- DART is a good extraction tool that typically has very few extraction errors.
- DART has two user exits that allow it to be customized. This includes adding fields and segments to the extract.
- DART comes with standard views (reports), and additional views can be written by users.
- DART creates a text file, which is an acceptable format for the IRS. Once created, the extract cannot be altered without recreating the entire extract.
- DART is at a transaction level so files are huge, but no drilldown is needed.
- DART extracts master data as well as transaction data. Master data is extracted based on what is in the master files when the DART extract is run. As long as DART is run consistently close to when transactions are recorded, the master data and transaction data remain relatively in sync. If you wait several years before running DART extracts, however, this will likely not be the case.

Note

Between the years 2000 and 2004, I instructed IRS computer audit specialists (CAS) on many occasions on the workings of DART and other SAP software. The inroads made during that time assisted with the acceptance of DART by IRS auditors.

6.1.2 Disadvantages of DART

Although DART extracts are accurate and, with customization, satisfactory for audit needs, some disadvantages exist:

- The DART query tool is not equipped with functionality to perform rapid data selection through the use of catalogues or universes as are modern data mining tools. This is important considering the number of tables across which DART data is spread. Building queries through drag-and-drop functionality is also not possible.
- Linked with the data mining weakness of the DART view tool is the lack of ability to format, total, and subtotal reports in a manner generally expected by today's business professionals. DART reports are functional, but they are not as comprehensive as those produced by third-party software currently in the marketplace.

- DART has not been updated to include many of the newer SAP modules and does not extract data from customer defined "Z" and "Y" tables without customization.
- DART is not a real-time extraction system. It is limited (without modification) to no less than a monthly interval.
- DART was created and designed for federal tax audits. It must be customized to safely handle audits in other tax areas.

6.2 Implementing DART

DART implementations are best handled well before the need to archive. Many tax and IT professionals confuse the SAP DART and the SAP archiving tool. Implementation of the two can be done independently and are basically separate projects. The only point of contact is that both tools create large files that can be stored in the same storage solution. As mentioned earlier, DART extracts should be run before any financial archiving is done. DART implementations can best be broken down into three phases, as follows:

- **Phase 1:** Tax analysis.
- **Phase 2:** Construction.
- **Phase 3:** Training and production.

Note

My extensive experience with DART includes managing around 40 DART implementations and talking to hundreds of companies about how to best use the tool. The tool works very well for data extraction and is accepted by the IRS. The software comes with your SAP license and implementation is relatively inexpensive. I recommend DART unless you require a multi-million dollar tax warehouse.

6.2.1 Tax Analysis Phase

The tax analysis phase is the most important phase of a DART project and should be performed by professionals experienced with R/3 and ECC, DART, and tax issues. Many vendors offer quick DART implementations by omitting the majority of the work in this area. Standard DART can be put in very quickly and so can R/3 or ECC, but this is usually not the right approach.

Identifying Tax-Related Tables and Fields

Large corporations have tables and fields that are pertinent to taxes but are not picked up in standard DART. The tax analysis phase of the project reveals the tables and fields needed for taxes that are not selected by standard DART. Compliance with Revenue Procedure 98–25 requires a DART extract containing all the data pertinent to the tax return; therefore, you should invest the necessary resources in the tax analysis phase. If data is not in the extract, it is difficult to get later and usually not practical. The tax analysis phase generally takes a couple of weeks, and tax integration specialists approach it by looking at the following items:

- Custom development in the system impacting tax
- Employed modules not selected by DART
- Current reports used by tax departments
- IRS audit history
- Fields needed for various tax returns

From My Experience

During my work experience, DART teams rigorously mapped all of the fields on various tax returns into R/3 or ECC and then into the DART module to see which data was actually picked up in DART. It was an exercise that resulted in a great deal of knowledge concerning the SAP data dictionary. Once this was done for one client, the information was leveraged for others with the need for only incremental mapping for any new tax forms. This methodology is called the *top down approach* to tax analysis because we were looking at line items on the tax return and then drilling down to the supporting detail comprising the return line, similar to an IRS auditor.

To offer a more complete analytical service, we also researched all of the SAP source tables for DART and looked at the fields selected from each of the tables. We then examined those that were not selected by DART and termed them *Non-Selected Fields*. Each DART engagement went through a process of examining which of these fields were populated with data and then which were tax relevant.

In addition to a top down approach, DART teams I worked with also used a *bottom up approach*. This approach consists of examining a client's audit history and tax reports. The resulting analysis is used to identify items used to prepare the tax return or respond to audits that are mapped to fields that are not selected by standard DART. Part of the bottom up approach also includes the examination of custom fields and tables. Often, tax departments have no knowledge of custom tables that have tax relevance.

In instances where a custom tax solution has been developed, the tables definitely need to be added to the extract. All client-defined tables need to be examined as part of the analysis phase to assure that tax-relevant data is added to the extract.

Tax relevance is an objective issue, but through conversations with tax departments and based on prior experience with the DART tool and IRS examination teams, a reasonable number of fields can be added to the extract. The process discussed here illustrates a reasonable effort to comply with Revenue Procedure 98–25.

Records Retention Limitation Agreement

The only way to get complete assurance that all information requested on audit is included in the extract is to have the IRS participate in the DART project and have them sign a Records Retention Limitation Agreement (RRLA). This can be difficult to accomplish, however.

From My Experience

To give you an idea, from 2001 to 2003, I was able to negotiate 5 RRLAs with the IRS. Each of these were negotiated with good results for both the client and the IRS. In 2004, however, changes were made that made it very difficult to obtain an RRLA as allowed by Section 11 of Revenue Procedure 98–25. The RRLAs negotiated in the early 2000s were the first ones in the United States and the only ones I am aware of to this date.

Involving the IRS

Around 10 of the engagements I managed involved the IRS in some form or other, and their participation added to the quality of the deliverable. We found IRS teams easy to work with and considerate of the implementation deadlines. I encourage companies under the Large and Mid Sized Business(LMSB) program that have IRS agents on site continually to invite the IRS to participate. In each situation where the IRS was invited to participate, the audit relationship improved.

6.2.2 Construction Phase

The technical implementation (construction phase) of the DART application has the following components:

- Extract configuration and testing
- Addition of fields and segments defined in the analysis phase
- Extract testing with additional segments and fields
- View creation

- View testing
- Promotion to production

The construction phase of the project is the most resource-intensive, usually taking six to eight weeks depending on the amount of customization in the system. Let's take a closer look at each one of the steps outlined before.

6.2.3 Extract Configuration

To access the main DART menu, use Transaction FTWO. For version 4.5 and beyond, you can also use the following menu path:

Tools • Administration • Administration • DART

Once in the main DART menu, configuration is done by drilling down under the **Configuration** line item. Appendix C includes a complete list of DART transaction codes for your reference. Transaction codes may change based on the DART version. The list supplied is based on DART version 2.7, which is the version of DART current as of this writing.

Note

DART configuration is not done in the Implementation Guide (IMG), as is other ECC configuration. Therefore, the DART team does not need Transaction SPRO or access to Solution Manager on implementations entering the IMG through Solution Manager. DART configuration is done within the DART application, which is reached either using transaction FTWO or the menu path given earlier in this section.

Note

Appendix C also has a suggested list of security authorizations for the implementation team. The security profile listed allows the DART team to enter the DART application and perform the necessary configuration. It also allows the team to test the application by reviewing system entries and checking the status of extract jobs.

Figure 6.1 shows the initial DART configuration screen with the **Transaction data** tab selected. Boxes checked on this screen determine what displays on the DART extraction screen (Transaction FTWA). Check all the boxes unless you know that a module is not currently installed on the system and will not be installed in the near future.

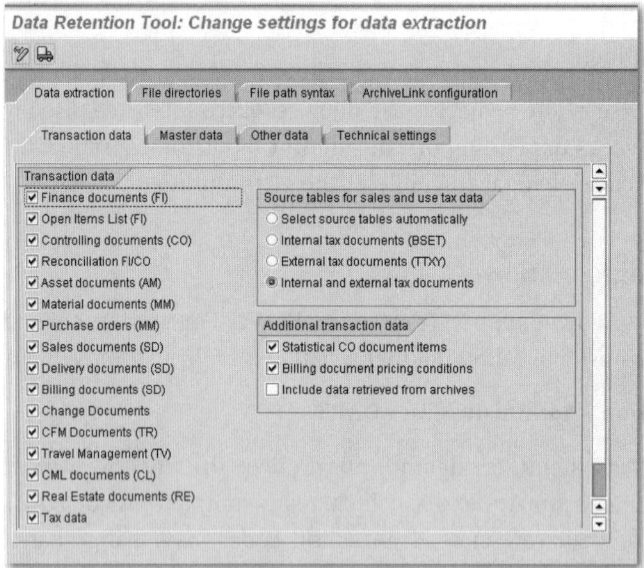

Figure 6.1 Dart Configuration – Transaction Data Tab

Data Check Sums

DART comes with data check sums that give some assurance that the extract is correct. If you will not be performing a more thorough reconciliation, you should indicate that you want check totals by selecting the **Calculate data checksums** box, shown at the bottom of Figure 6.4.

Recommendation

I recommend that a more complete reconciliation be done on each DART extract to more clearly meet the needs of Revenue Procedure 98–25, which in Section 5 states the following:

(2) The taxpayer's machine-sensible records must provide sufficient information to support and verify entries made on the taxpayer's return and to determine the correct tax liability. The taxpayer's machine-sensible records will meet this requirement only if they reconcile with the taxpayer's books and the taxpayer's return. A taxpayer establishes this reconciliation by demonstrating the relationship (i.e., audit trail):

(a) between the total of the amounts in the taxpayer's machine-sensible records by account and the account totals in the taxpayer's books; and

(b) between the total of the amounts in the taxpayer's machine-sensible records by account and the taxpayer's return.

While this seems to imply that an account by account reconciliation is needed to satisfy the procedure, I have not seen a problem raised with DART audits that have used the Check Total functionality.

Compression

A decision also needs to be made concerning data compression. At the bottom of Figure 6.4 (shown later in this chapter) is the data compression indicator. DART compression is usually spoken of as 4–1. There are other tools available that result in a much better compression ratio, but most companies opt for DART compression. The reason is that DART files compressed by a tool other than DART cannot be read until being decompressed. It is often a manual effort for companies to decompress DART files, so most decide to use DART compression or not compress at all. The decision not to compress is often based on performance. The extract will usually run faster if compression is turned off.

The DART Extraction Screen

After you've entered all of the necessary data on Figures 6.1 through 6.4, default information is transferred to the DART extraction screen. This does not complete the configuration stage, however. Figure 6.2 shows the **Master data** tab, where you'll also need to select applicable options. Cost center and profit center hierarchies are used for reporting rollups and may be useful to tax departments. Joint venture accounting is captured in several DART tables, and if used, must be activated. In addition, you can activate master data segment selection here as well.

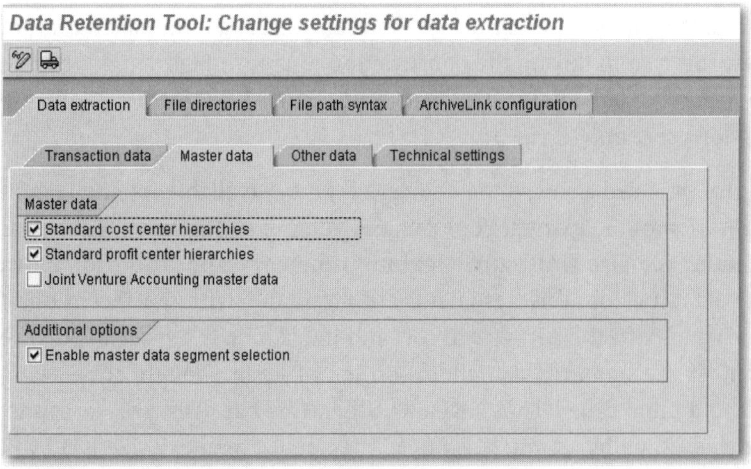

Figure 6.2 DART Configuration — Master Data Tab

Figure 6.3 illustrates the **Other Data** tab on which you specify to **Extract customer-defined data sources**. You must select this checkbox, or you will not get any data added to the standard extract. You must also select the **CO primary posting** and **CO secondary posting** checkboxes, or the extract will not contain CO transactions using these elements.

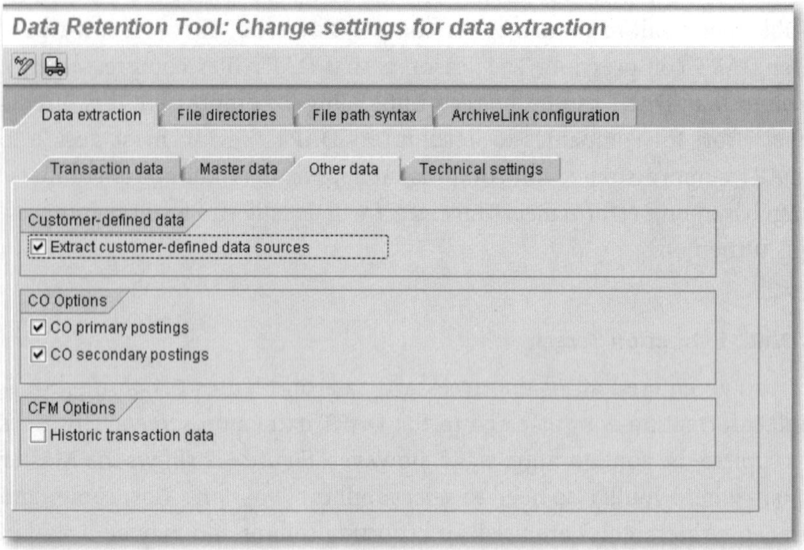

Figure 6.3 DART Configuration — Other Data Tab

Enabling Test Extracts

It is important to enable test extracts so you can extract a minimal amount of data to test the system during the construction phase. In Figure 6.4, you can see this option, called **Enable test run with limited data volume**, in the **Other Options** section.

In this figure, you can also see the choices you have available for the technical configuration of the extract. For example, you can configure items such as the **Maximum file size (MB)** and **Maximum memory allocation for index (MB)**. The default values for these fields are acceptable with the exception of the memory index size. DART has to sort and index data when setting up the extract run. If the memory size allocation is not large enough, the sorting rolls over to a table called TXW_INDEX. When this happens, the sort function is slowed down by as much as 40 %. The default memory size is 50MB; in Figure 6.4, this has been changed to 200MB. Based on the size of the extracts, you might have to raise the value in this field to prevent the rollover.

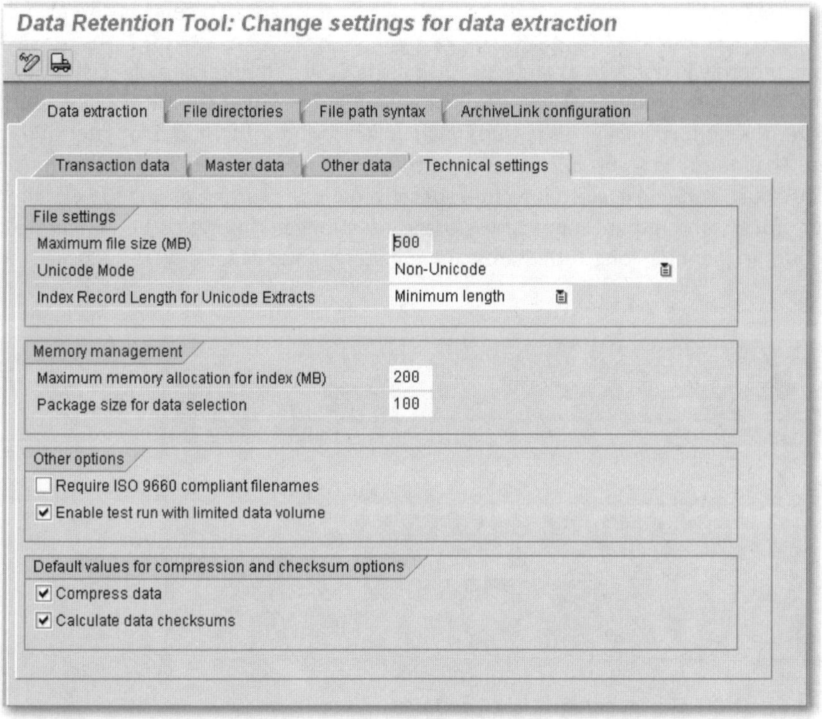

Figure 6.4 DART Configuration — Technical Settings

Specifying the Directory Path

During configuration, you must direct where the DART extract is to be stored. Figures 6.5 and 6.6 demonstrate where the directory path and directory set is actually established. A directory and directory path are required because they define the server location where the DART extracts are to be stored. They also tell the system where to find the extracts again months later when you want to view them again. Figure 6.7 illustrates the syntax used under different storage options.

If a generic set is created without a path such as *DART Tax*, extracts will be saved in the SAP work directory. This may be an option for small test extracts with several hundred documents but not for full extracts because the SAP work directory usually does not have the needed storage space. The DART implementation team will have to get direction from the Basis team as to the proper path for large extracts. During the implementation phase, the DART team should secure at least 5GB of space for DART testing.

Note

Some monthly extracts go as large as 50GB using DART compression. Special problems occur with volumes of this size. For example, the larger the extract size, the slower the performance. This is true for the extraction run itself and for later queries. An extract that runs in 2 hours is much easier to deal with than one that runs in 20 hours. Larger extracts take more space to do index sorting during the extraction process and require more server space for storage. This has to be taken into account in planning long-term hardware and storage needs for the DART project.

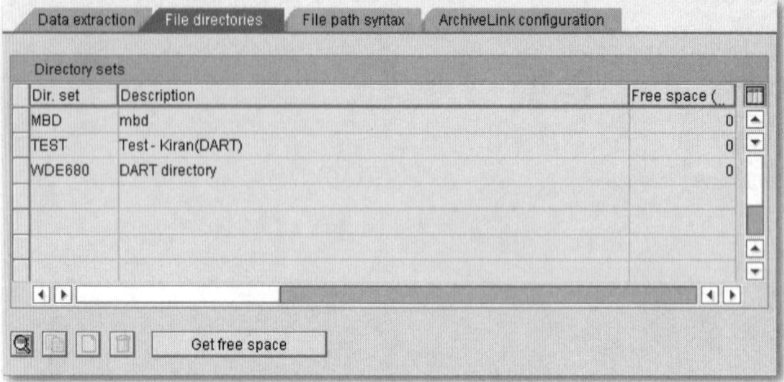

Figure 6.5 DART Configuration — File Directories

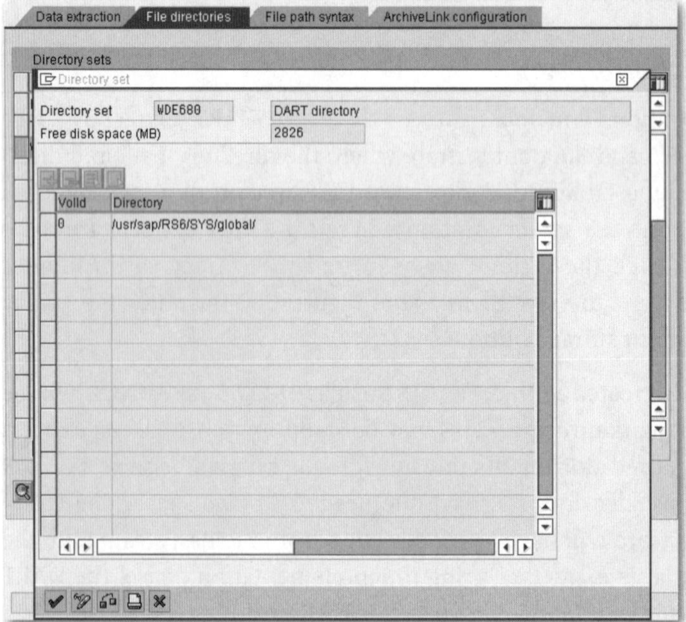

Figure 6.6 DART Configuration — File Directories

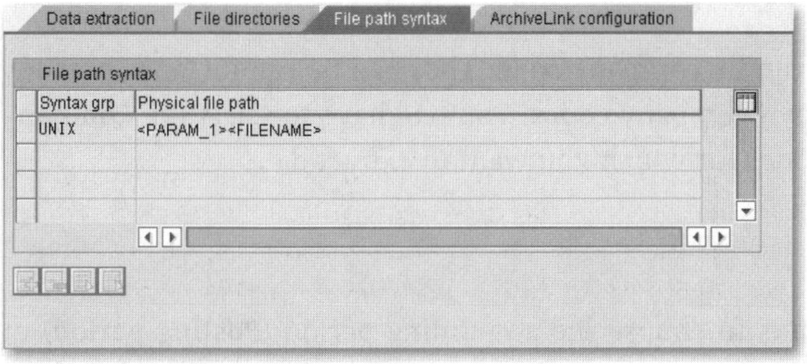

Figure 6.7 Syntax for File Paths

6.2.4 Running a DART Extract

Transaction codes FTWA or FTWA1 are used to start the extract process. Configuration must be done first or the extract will not run. With configuration in place, you are ready to run a DART extract. The transaction codes just mentioned will open up the DART extraction screen shown in Figure 6.8. We'll look at the options on this screen in more detail.

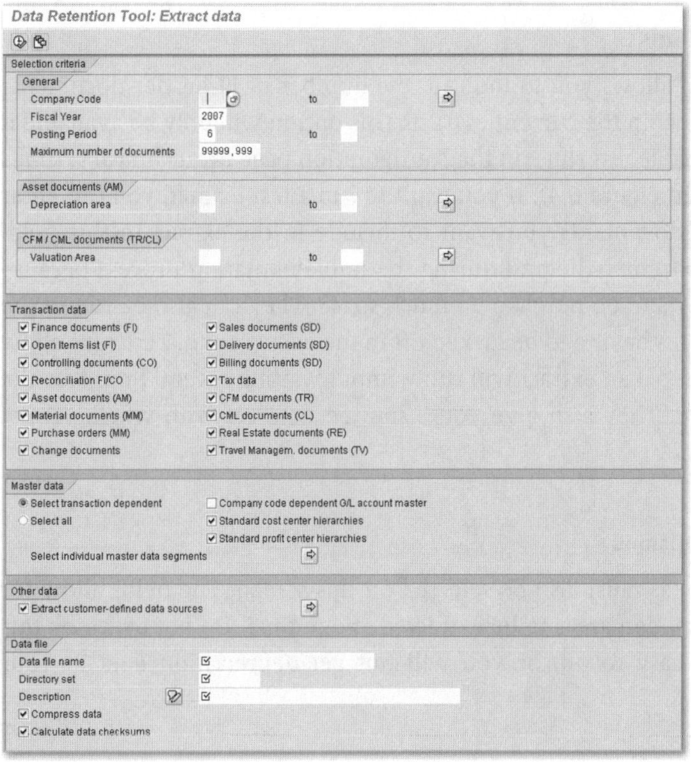

Figure 6.8 The DART Extraction Screen

Company Code

DART extracts are run by company code. They can be run for one company code or for a group of company codes. You will have to select the **Company Code** or range of codes for which you want to extract data.

Posting Period

Your next selection is to choose the accounting period (**Posting period**) or periods for which you want to extract data. DART is able to select data from multiple periods, but in practice, large companies are forced to limit the period selection to a single month because of the size of the extracts.

> **Note**
>
> Nearly 100 % of the companies I have worked with on DART implementations are extracting data on a monthly basis. Although functionality exists to run extracts for multiple months of data, in practice, the extracts become too large and fail to run on a timely basis or simply fail to run at all.

Enabling Test Runs

This screen also allows you to indicate the number of FI header documents you want to select in the current extract. This option will only be available if you chose to enable test runs on the configuration page for technical settings (shown earlier in Figure 6.4). If you want to run a test extract, you can enter the number of documents you want to include in the extract in this field. Test runs are extremely helpful during the implementation process because they run quickly and do not take up much space. They can also be run in the foreground versus having to be kicked off in the background. Test runs allow you to quickly see if an extract will run without waiting several hours for the job to complete. They also give you a limited data set with which to test DART views.

Depreciation Options

Depreciation areas must also be selected on this screen. The fields allow for multiple depreciation areas to be extracted at one time. Do not overlook this step, which is easy to do, or you will not get depreciation data in your extract.

Additional Selection Options

The data extraction screen also shows the default module selections that you selected during configuration. These can be changed at the time of extract kickoff, if desired. The configuration decision concerning Check Sums and Data Compression also defaults into this screen and can be changed at this time if needed.

Naming the Extract

During the extraction kickoff process, you must also assign a name to the extract run in the **Data file name** field. It is best to determine a naming convention before you reach this point. Consistent naming conventions for extracts assist in finding the right extract 4 or 5 years later when the IRS requests this information from you. Remember, you will probably have 12 monthly extracts per year for possibly 10 years, so you need to be able to identify the file you want.

Directory Set

You must also select the **Directory set** at this point. As mentioned earlier, the directory set defines the path to the storage location for the extract. You may have multiple directory sets depending on how you choose to store your extracts.

DART extracts are very large, and anything but small test runs should be executed in the background. After the fields on the screen shown in Figure 6.8 are populated, data extraction can be started. The extract is started in the foreground using the clock icon in the upper-left corner of the screen. Extracts are started in the background by selecting the **Program** item from the left corner of the upper menu bar and then selecting **Background scheduling**.

After the DART extract is complete, you can view the job log that lists the number of documents selected from each DART segment and the total size of the extract. The log also gives the runtime.

6.2.5 DART and the IRS

After an extract is run, it should be stored until needed for a jurisdictional audit. Note that DART extracts cannot be read without an SAP system. Instead, DART has a view (query) tool that lets you select subsets of extract data. If the IRS is part of the implementation, you can build views for them to be supplied at audit time. Views are still large but much more manageable than the extract itself. Views are run and then burned to a CD-ROM or placed on a flash drive and given to the IRS. IRS views are usually dumps of information on a particular DART segment as opposed to queries for specific information. IRS computer audit specialists generally load the view information into a database of their own and do their own data mining. Providing views for auditors allows them to answer many of their own questions and reduces the number of IDRs.

Note

I am often asked whether to give auditors the actual DART extract. The answer is "no" because they cannot read the extract without an SAP system. I have not seen an auditor yet who has access to an SAP system. You also do not want to give auditors access to your SAP system. With DART, there is no reason to do so. The goal is not to hide data from the examine team, but by defining information given to the auditors, you can prevent IDRs that are off target and simply take up time.

6.2.6 DART View Configuration

The DART view tool is rudimentary but does serve the purpose of creating subsets of transactional data from the extract fairly well. In addition, many large companies today leverage information in the DART extract and use it in tax planning and compliance or in other areas of the business by taking DART data out of the SAP environment and placing it in a database that can be used with modern data mining tools.

SAP supplies a number of predefined DART views depending on the DART version you are running. Likely, you'll find it necessary to create additional DART views in specific areas. The view tool allows users to select the DART segments (tables) to be used in the view. Segments can be joined using key fields to select fields from more than one table. Formatting and totaling in DART hardly exists, but the tool was not designed to create great formats. Views can also give you the ability to select all documents with a particular element (cost center) or just the one you want.

DART view configuration is reached through Transaction FTWY (see Figure 6.9). From here, you can **Execute** (run) a view, **Display** view logic, or **Change** view logic. You can use this figure as a reference when running DART views is discussed later in this section.

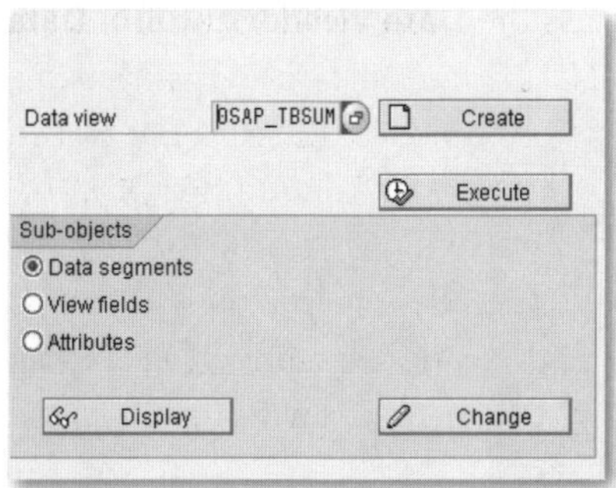

Figure 6.9 DART View Configuration Screen

Creating a DART View

Before beginning view creation, take some time to determine a naming convention for your customer-created views. You might want to start view names with the letter Z or Y, which is customary for custom objects in SAP. The new view name is entered in the view window shown in Figure 6.9. After the name is entered, select the **Create** button also shown in Figure 6.9, and it will take you to the attribute page shown in Figure 6.10.

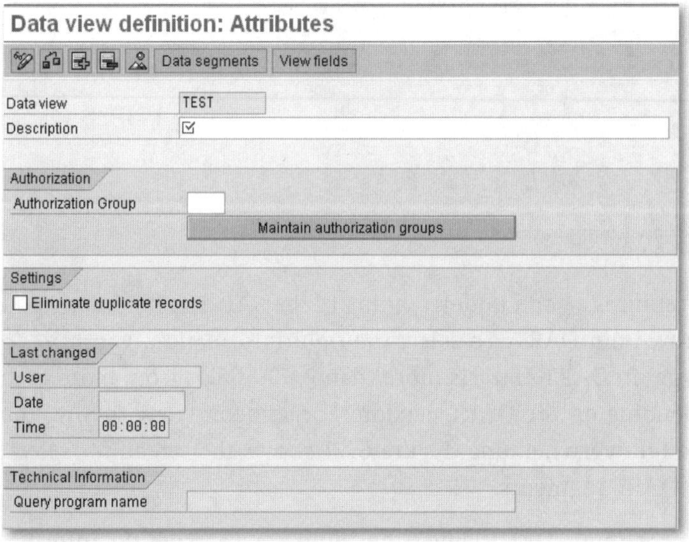

Figure 6.10 DART View Configuration — Attributes

Figure 6.10 displays the DART **Data view definition: Attributes** page. On this screen, you give the view a description, control access to the view, and control duplicates. You continue building the view by clicking the **Data seg-**

ments button at the top of this page to access the **Data view definition: Data segments** page (see Figure 6.11).

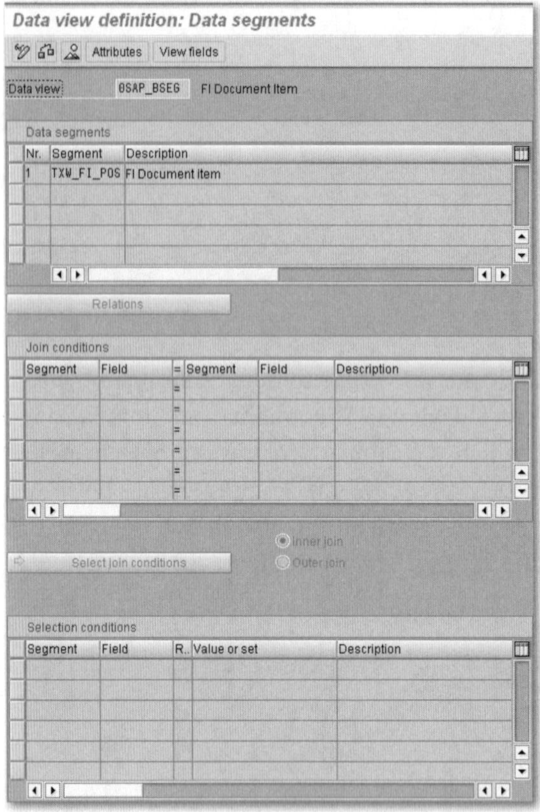

Figure 6.11 DART View Configuration — Data Segments

Building views requires a good understanding of the SAP data dictionary and the file structure within DART. To select the right information, you have to know where to get it. DART extracts more than 2,500 fields from more than 250 tables, depending on the DART version. For someone new to SAP, the information is a bit overwhelming. Figure 6.11 shows the screen for selecting and joining DART segments.

The first step in creating a DART view is deciding where to get the information. DART data is extracted from tables or segments, so you'll need to specify these in the **Data segments** section shown in Figure 6.11. The view segment area is equipped with a dropdown box for selecting the DART segments you desire. If you select more than one segment, you will have to work with the join conditions in the next box down on the screen.

Note

If your view contains only one segment, you will have no join conditions so you can proceed to the bottom of the screen and create **Selection conditions**.

Selection conditions are limited to very few operators but enable the creation of sets that allow for the selection of ranges or groups of data. Most views, however, don't require the use of selection conditions so this area can be bypassed.

Although not required, in many cases, you'll want to link one table to another using a join, so let's now look at how to do this using join conditions.

Join Conditions

Many views require the use of *joins*, which enable users to link one table to another. This is necessary because data is segmented in SAP and remains so in DART. Therefore, if, for example, you need a vendor transaction view that also contains vendor master data, you have to join the vendor transaction table with the vendor master file. To do this, you have to select the proper tables and link them using key fields on each table. DART allows you to use default join conditions, but I have found that this usually results in more join conditions than are needed. Joins can be tricky, and views must be tested to make sure you are getting the right information.

After join conditions have been selected, continue to the **View fields** tab shown in Figure 6.12. The **Select fields** button will bring up the additional box shown in Figure 6.13. On this page, you select the fields from the segments you chose when completing the **Data segments** screen shown in Figure 6.11. If more than one segment has been selected, each will appear when you click the **Select fields** button. Fields are selected by first selecting the proper segment and then selecting the checkbox in front of the field names you want from that segment. The field selection process is shown in Figure 6.13. After the fields are selected, as shown in Figure 6.13, they are populated on the **View fields** tab in Figure 6.12.

You will have to order the fields after selection to get the format you desire. The fields screen also contains columns for sorting, grouping, and totaling. Again, the tool is rudimentary, and totals show up at the end of the report instead of in the body. The **Sel. Field** column allows you to narrow criteria when the view is executed.

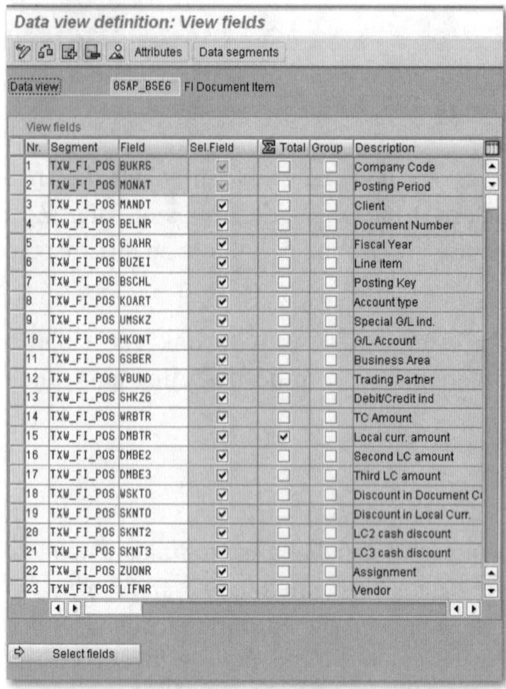

Figure 6.12 DART View Configuration — View Fields Tab

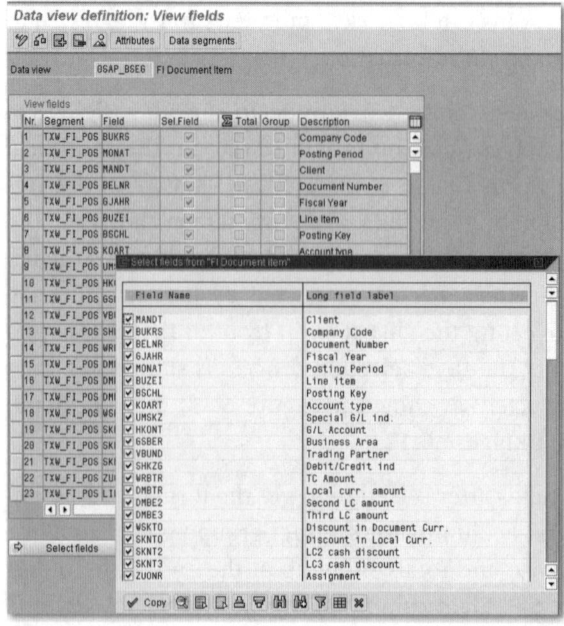

Figure 6.13 DART View Configuration — View Fields Tab — Field Selection

6.2.7 Running DART Views

When a DART view is created, the logic is saved in the system, but the actual view created by execution is not. If you want the actual view saved, it is easily done but requires a few more steps.

Figure 6.8 was mentioned earlier and illustrates the initial screen used to start a DART view. The same screen is used to create or change view logic. You only need to select the view and click on the **Execute** button. You are then taken to a second screen shown in Figure 6.14. This screen allows you to set the parameters for the view run.

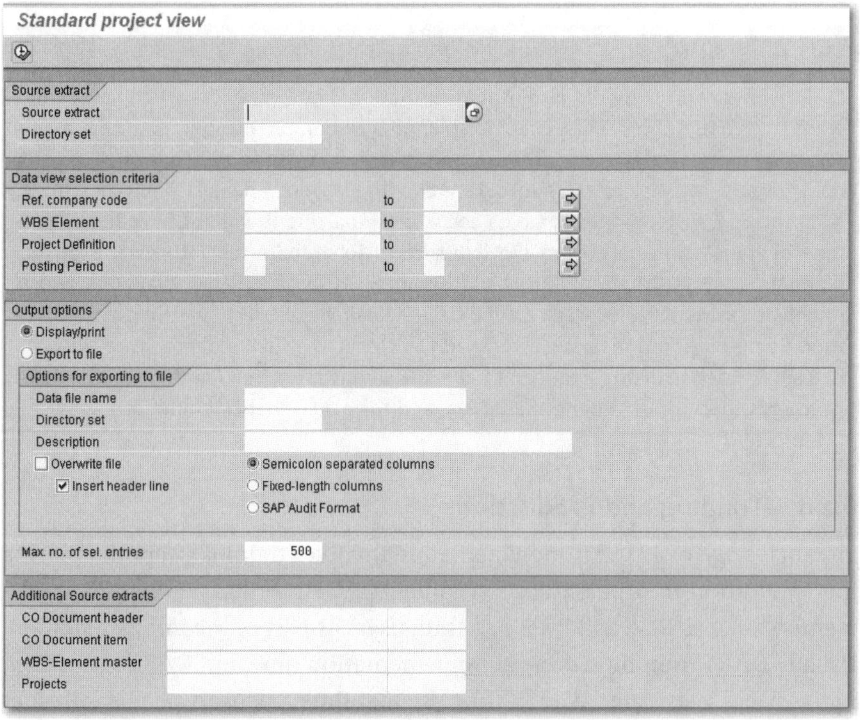

Figure 6.14 DART View Parameter Screen

This screen requires you to select the extract or extracts that you want the view logic applied to. You are also able to indicate selection conditions on this screen. If you checked the boxes by the fields on the field selection screen (refer to Figure 6.12 shown earlier) when building the view, the fields will show up on this screen. For example, if cost center had a check next to it in the selection column, you are able to narrow your cost center selection by indicating what you need on this screen. This is a nice feature that allows the user an easy way to filter the data.

The output mode for the view data is also determined on this screen. A variety of choices exist, but printing views is not a good idea unless you know they are very small. You can elect to save the view results on this screen. If you elect not to save the results, the logic is always saved and can re-create the results unless a new DART extract is run that contains changes. Views can also be downloaded to tools such as Microsoft Excel or Microsoft Access. This is an attractive option if you need to do additional totaling or data mining that cannot be done easily in DART.

Note

DART views can satisfy IRS and other jurisdictional auditors. It is when companies want to leverage the DART extract for planning or compliance purposes that a better data mining tool is useful. Some companies have been forced to leverage DART data because of very aggressive data archiving. Where financial data is archived from the ECC system in less than a year, a tax department will not have the advantage of transaction data from the live system to prepare tax returns and do tax planning. In this situation, the DART extract may be all that is available, and it might be prudent to leverage DART data by using a more powerful data mining tool. Some corporations have leveraged DART data to such a degree that the data is used by departments other than the tax department for identifying duplicate payments, performing financial analysis, and for other financial functions.

6.2.8 Training and Production

The final stage of a DART implementation involves training users and placing the application in production. SAP offers DART training, and DART implementers such as IBM and PwC also train users as part of the implementation. Usually DART training is done at implementation time, but DART is not used until several years later at audit time. By that time, tax users need a refresher course. Training should include documentation of each step in the implementation, as follows:

- DART user manual
- DART configuration
- Fields added to the extract
- Segments added to the extract
- ABAP4 code added to the user exits
- Complete view logic

- Testing procedures and results
- IRS participation and comments (if involved)
- Training slides and narrative
- Promote to production strategy
- Contact numbers for the implementer

DART requires at least two transports to move configuration and views to production. All views can be moved with one transport, whereas the configuration will have to be moved with a second. If the views contain sets as part of the selection criteria, the sets will have to be transported independently as well. They do not move with the views.

Variants can be set up to facilitate running the extract. Some companies start the extract manually each month as a batch job, while others have been able to automate the jobs using a job scheduling tool. After DART is put in production, you will have to catch up with extracts that have not been run. DART extracts are large and compete for hardware resources, so they are best scheduled at a time when the computer is least used. Each company has to decide when that is in their environment. Typical DART user and administrator security roles are included in Appendix E.

6.3 Unstructured Record Retention for Tax

As mentioned earlier, NetWeaver Knowledge Management (KM) is aimed at competing in the content management field. Tax departments create a plethora of unstructured records such as spreadsheets and Microsoft Word documents based on structured reports from SAP systems, thus there is a need to electronically retain these documents and be able to find them at audit time. NetWeaver KM currently offers the functionality listed in Figure 6.15, taken from a 2004 presentation sponsored by the SAP Developer Network and distributed on a CD-ROM titled "SAP NetWeaver Know-How."

> **Note**
>
> The NetWeaver suite of products is shipped with current SAP releases so companies own the right to use the software. This software has excellent potential to solve tax department challenges associated with unstructured data and should therefore be implemented.

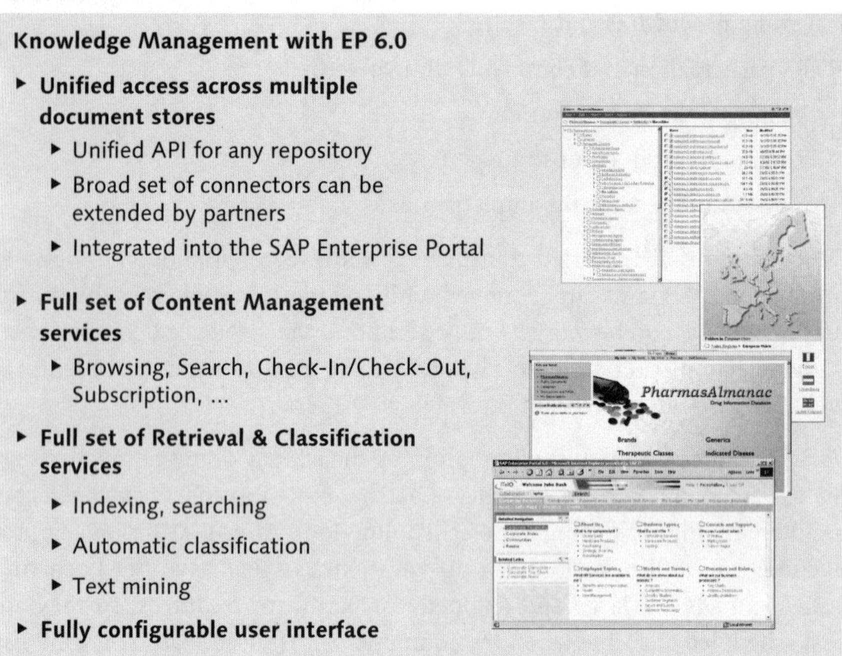

Knowledge Management with EP 6.0
Unified access across multiple document stores
Unified API for any repository
Broad set of connectors can be extended by partners
Integrated into the SAP Enterprise Portal
Full set of Content Management services
Browsing, Search, Check-In/Check-Out, Subscription, ...
Full set of Retrieval & Classification services
Indexing, searching
Automatic classification
Text mining
Fully configurable user interface
PharmasAlmanac

Figure 6.15 NetWeaver Knowledge Management Functionality (Source: SAP AG)

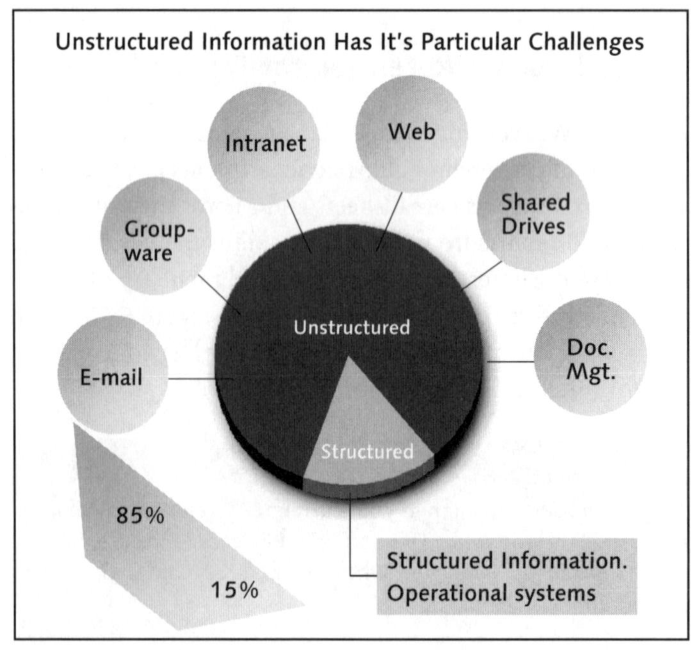

Figure 6.16 The Challenges of Unstructured Data (Source: SAP AG)

Figure 6.16, which is taken from the same source as Figure 6.15, illustrates the ratio of unstructured data as compared to structured data (85 % versus 15 %) found in organizations and lists many of the sources of this type of data.

6.4 Summary

Tax data retention is required by law and is best handled prior to archiving data from SAP. SAP has created DART to facilitate retention of tax data. DART is an extract tool that copies data in preselected fields from preselected SAP tables and stores the data for later use. DART also has a view tool so the extract can be divided into smaller subsets for the IRS. DART implementations require tax analysis to assure that reasonable effort has been made to comply with Revenue Procedure 98–25. DART can be customized to add fields and segments as needed.

Unstructured data also presents retention problems for tax departments. The SAP NetWeaver Knowledge Management tool has promise, and for companies with licenses to the software, it should be used to solve unstructured data retention problems.

In Chapter 7, we will address payroll issues and the important role that payroll expenditures play in tax returns. We will also discuss implementation challenges created by external payroll sytems.

Payroll data often comprises the largest line item on a corporation's tax return and is therefore often an audit target by IRS exam teams. Payroll data is also the basis for many tax calculations and is often interweaved within many tax computations. Regardless of whether SAP HR is part of the implementation, payroll information needs to be addressed as part of tax integration to assure that tax departments will have the information in the format they need.

7 Payroll and Payroll Taxes

Payroll tax compliance is usually not the responsibility of the corporate tax department. Complying with federal, state, and local payroll tax laws is generally handled by HR in most large corporations. That does not mean that tax departments have no concern but that their concern is during the payroll tax audit and not when forms such as W-2, 941, and 940 are filed.

Payroll data plays an important part in many tax calculations and is often the single biggest line on the income statement. Compliance with payroll tax filing laws is the easiest part of the payroll issue. The issue of payroll and payroll taxes is often complicated because of the approach taken to implementing SAP. Many companies choose not to implement the SAP HR module, and many times when they do, it is implemented using a separate SAP instance. Companies not using the SAP HR module and those adopting a separate SAP instance are faced with the challenge of getting payroll data into the main financial instance in some way and at some level.

Many tax calculations can be done using general ledger (G/L) level data, but others, such as state apportionment, must be done at a jurisdictional level. If the SAP HR module is on the same SAP instance, data is available, and it is relatively easy to get the necessary payroll data. Unfortunately, as mentioned before, typically SAP HR is not installed in the same instance as R/3 or ECC. The challenge, simply stated, is how to get the needed payroll data from an unattached system into the SAP system. The solution is an interface of some kind. Designing the interface is actually an easier process than deciding what information needs to be passed and at what level. Appendix E suggests data elements that may need to be brought over from an unattached payroll system to support tax calculations or for tax compliance in R/3 or ECC.

7.1 Payroll Tax Compliance

Although payroll tax compliance is not the responsibility of most tax departments, they are responsible for payroll tax audits. Therefore, they are concerned that compliance is done accurately.

> **Note**
>
> SAP's software did not have elaborate payroll compliance functionality until the updated HR module was released with R/3 4.6. New functionality was released at that time along with the Tax Reporter application (which we'll discuss in more detail later in this section). Therefore, third-party software was often used to compute tax and prepare payroll tax forms.

Looking at tax compliance, large corporations are responsible for complying with the following payroll tax requirements:

- **Form 941**
  Quarterly Payroll Tax Return
- **Form 940**
  Annual Federal Unemployment Tax Return
- **SUTA**
  State Unemployment Tax Returns
- **Form W-2**
  Annual Statement of Employee's Wages
- **Form W-3**
  Annual Summary of Employer's Wages

In addition to filing these forms, corporations are responsible for depositing payroll taxes according to schedules defined by IRS regulations. Failure to deposit timely payments results in penalties. Proper accounting for payroll taxes requires setting up payroll-related G/L accounts and tracking each paycheck, advance, loan, benefit deduction, reimbursement, and so on paid to each employee. If this information is not accounted for in the SAP system, it needs to be brought into the system at a predetermined level.

7.2 Tax Reporter

Tax Reporter is an SAP application that provides payroll tax compliance functionality. The application is designed to create IRS Forms 940, 941, W-2, W-3, and others. Tax Reporter is also capable of tracking and creating 1099R forms.

Payroll tax compliance is complicated by the same jurisdictional requirements as other taxes. That is, jurisidictions want to know where employees live, where they work, and how much money can be attributed to the jurisdiction. Payroll tax compliance is therefore subject to many different rules in many jurisdictions resulting in a multitude of reporting requirements similar to sales and use tax. Let's look at the various jurisdictions and their needs in more detail:

- **The Federal Government**
  The federal government plays a major role in tracking employee income within the United States because W-2's have become the tracking tool for verifying wage information for personal income tax returns. The federal government also works with the states in the unemployment insurance arena, which is the purpose for requesting information on form 940.
- **Individual States**
  States are equally concerned about wage income and especially concerned about where income is earned. To help with this, Tax Reporter, like other payroll compliance systems, tracks payroll by location and can provide the necessary state information. States are also very involved with unemployment insurance and have their own wage reports that gather employment information.
- **Localities**
  Localities also often get involved in where income is earned and want their share of tax for income earned within their city limits.

Tax Reporter Functionality

Tax Reporter configuration is done in the HR module and is very table driven. Tax Reporter is capable of creating all of the tax forms mentioned before and can produce hard copies or electronic formats that meet jurisdictional requirements.

Note

SAP produces a U.S. Tax Reporting Guide that you should read for additional information regarding Tax Reporter functionality and configuration. The guide can be obtained from the SAP website by doing a search on Tax Reporter.

Tax Reporter is also designed to produce all transmittal documents for the forms mentioned previously. Figure 7.1 shows the main screen for Tax Reporter. You will note that test runs are enabled in addition to the production run. All forms and form fields can also be accessed via this screen.

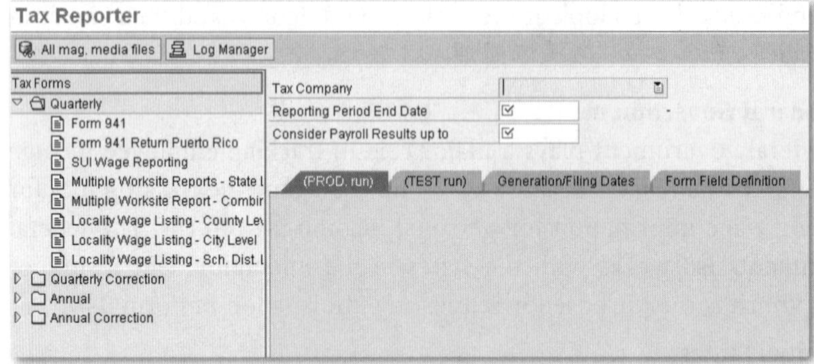

Figure 7.1 Tax Reporter Main Screen

Figure 7.2 shows the county level screen for obtaining wage listings at that level.

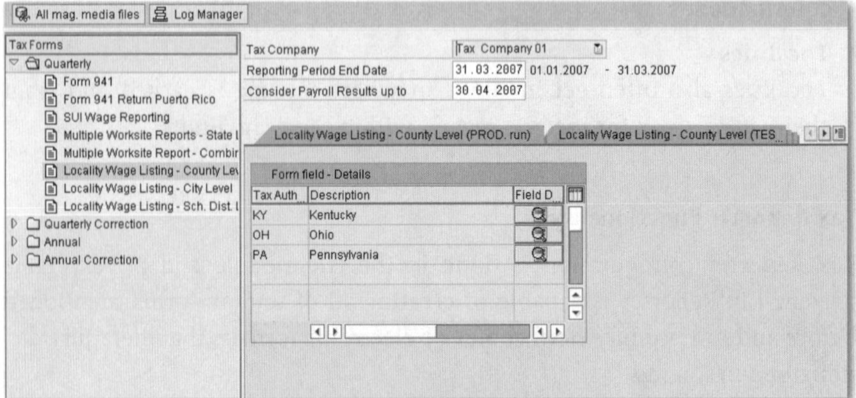

Figure 7.2 County Level Wage Listing Screen

From these screens, you can see that Tax Reporter has the capability to produce reports as well as forms. Manual entries can also be added to data in the HR module. Figure 7.3 is a flow chart from the SAP U.S. Tax Reporting Guide for 2006. It illustrates the functionality in a helpful graphic format.

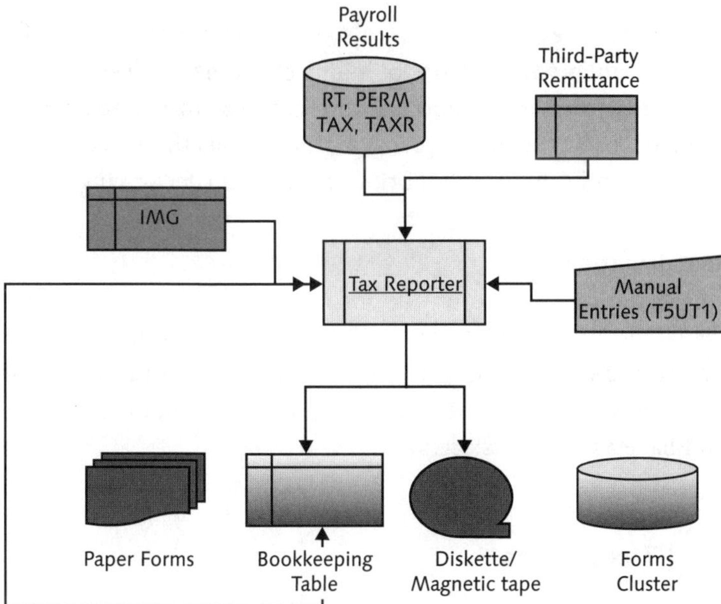

Figure 7.3 Graphic Representation of Tax Reporter (Source: SAP AG)

Figure 7.3 does not show the log within the application that keeps track of run statistics, created by the Tax Reporter Log Manager. The *Tax Reporter Log Manager* keeps track of each report run within the system and is helpful for solving configuration errors and other problems that arise on report execution.

7.3 Tax Uses of Payroll Data

As mentioned earlier, payroll data heavily influences tax calculations. Following is a list of some of the tax calculations affected by payroll information:

- **State Apportionment Calculations**
  One of the ways that corporate income is divided between states for state income taxation is by looking at head count and payroll dollars for a given state versus those for all states.

- **Research and Development Tax Credits**
  The research and development tax credit can be a huge advantage for many corporations and is highly labor driven. Being able to capture the labor costs of those performing research or development activities is vital to calculating and sustaining the credit.
- **Intercompany Labor Fees**
  Most corporations follow the practice of billing out some services to other internal units. Justifying the rate and markup for these intercompany bills requires good payroll accounting. Cross border labor billing is also of interest to the IRS and other tax authorities from a transfer pricing standpoint.
- **Income Tax Calculations**
  Payroll is often the largest line on the income statement and therefore becomes the largest line on IRS Form 1120 and on state and local income tax returns. Because of the variety of uses of payroll data and the size of the numbers, tax departments need to know what the number is comprised of and have a feel for its accuracy.

7.4 Payroll Tax Audits

Payroll data is subject to audit by the IRS and other jurisdictional authorities, not only for the compliance reports filed but also as it relates to other tax calculations. Due to confidentiality, payroll data is seldom captured in DART extracts, but the SAP HR module also faces the same archiving issues that exist in the R/3 or ECC systems. Payroll data is not fragmented as badly as accounts payable (AP) or accounts receivable (AR) data because long lags seldom take place between payment and document closure, but period integrity can be influenced by the timing of payroll runs. Hard copy records usually exist to support payroll-related tax calculations, but attention should be given to retaining payroll data in electronic format as well. SAP archiving will delete electronic payroll information similar to the way it deletes data in other parts of the system, so advance planning should take place to ensure that data is still there when it is needed.

> **Note**
>
> In my experience, IRS examination teams are more interested in payroll as a subset of other tax calculations as opposed to the payroll tax filings (941, 940, etc.) themselves. Although I often see auditors comparing 1099 lists for the year to employee lists to identify individuals that show up on both, the labor component of income tax calculations yields bigger returns. Items such as those mentioned earlier (apportionment, R&D tax credits, and transfer pricing) are often examined on audit, and labor is reviewed as part of that examination. In these cases, it is often helpful to have a contemporaneous time tracking system such as the one provided by SAP or a third-party system to provide support for intercompany labor charges.

7.5 Summary

Accurate payroll data provided at the proper time and in the proper format is essential for tax compliance. Payroll expenses not only need to be reported directly to the IRS but are used in many other tax calculations as well. Tax integration specialists can assist with gathering payroll requirements, which is necessary whether your payroll system is in the SAP HR module, outsourced, or in a third-party system. Tax Reporter can be an efficient compliance tool for those using the SAP HR module. Attention needs to be given to maintaining payroll reports and electronic data for tax audits many years in the future. Payroll data is not captured by the DART tool without modification and is archived similar to other SAP archiving techniques. Unless proactive steps are taken in the payroll area, good audit information may not be available when needed.

Corporations are required to maintain many master data files that serve to provide descriptions and supplemental information concerning their business transactions. Master data in legacy systems must be cleansed and loaded into the new SAP system during implementation. In Chapter 8, we will discuss master data needs for tax and the role of the integration specialists in making sure the tax department's needs are met.

Master data plays a role in every transaction recorded in R/3 or ECC and is essential for accurate tax filings. Incorrect master data can lead to inaccurate tax rates and payments to the wrong tax jurisdictions. In this chapter, we will discuss many of the master files in SAP software and identify fields that are important from a tax standpoint.

8 Master Data

Master data is often overlooked from a tax standpoint when approaching an SAP implementation. That is probably because tax departments have very little master data that they control directly. However, master data is imperative to preparing and supporting tax filings, and bad master data can lead to bad tax decisions. The importance of master data is evident when you consider that DART pulls data from around 27 transaction tables but more than 200 master data tables.

This chapter reemphasizes the need for good jurisdictional and address information that was discussed in Chapter 3 when exploring the importance of jurisdictional information and cost objects. This chapter also discusses other needs for accurate master data. In addition, we will look at data cleansing and loading in this chapter.

Caution

You will be asked to populate certain information on each of the master files we'll discuss next. Much of this information likely will be populated whether requested by the tax department or not, but no harm is done by making sure, especially since address information is sometimes left off storage locations and other lesser known master files.

8.1 The Company Code Master

The company code master is reached from the IMG side of SAP as opposed to the application side. A portion of the company code master data was shown in Chapter 3, Figures 3.1 and 3.2, which showed the basic fields comprising the master file. In addition to the screens shown in Chapter 3, several other screens that contain detailed company code information are shown in this chapter. These screens are also on the IMG side of the software. This means that unless you are authorized to perform configuration in SAP, you will not be able to create, change, or display this master file. You will, however, be able to see what is contained on the master through SAP reports.

The company code is the basic building block in the Financials (FI) module and has nearly every system data element linked to it either directly or indirectly. The name and address information for the company code was shown in Figure 3.2 of Chapter 3. When linked with the **Change View: "Company Code Global Data":Details** screen shown in Figure 8.1, the information is used by the system for vendor payments, 1099 and 1042 forms, and payments to tax jurisdictions.

Tax Requirements — Company Code Master Data

Tax departments need master data describing the company code for a variety of purposes such as supplying address and taxpayer ID information on tax filings and addresses for accounts receivable and payable invoices. The information shown in Table 8.1 should be populated in the ECC table T001 which is the standard SAP company code master data table.

Field	Description
MANDT	Client
BUKRS	Company Code
BUTXT	Name of the Company Code
ORT01	City
LAND1	Country Code
WAERS	Currency Key
SPRAS	Language Key
KTOPL	Chart of Accounts
RCOMP	Company
ADRNR	Address
STCEG	VAT Registration Number
TXJCD	Tax Jurisdiction Number

Table 8.1 Company Code Master (ECC Table T001)

Additional data relevant to the company code, including the company code chart of accounts, the credit control area, field status variants, and the fiscal year variant are all present on the **Change View "Company Code Global Data": Details** screen shown in Figure 8.1. The tax ID number and other regulatory codes are populated in the screen **Maintenance of Additional Data for Company Code xxxx,** as shown in Figure 8.2.

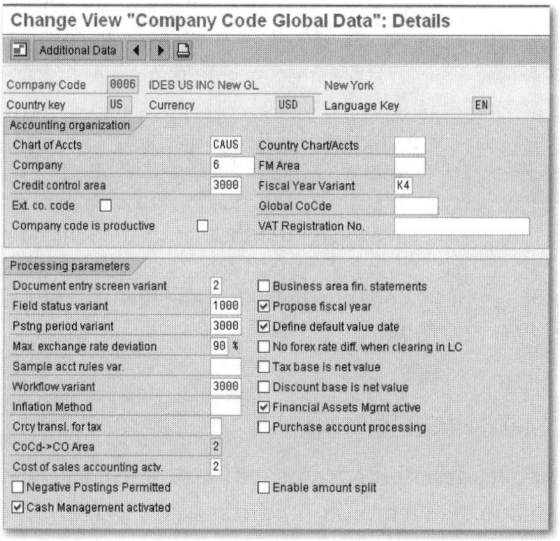

Change View "Company Code Global Data": Details

Additional Data

Company Code	0006 IDES US INC New GL	New York	
Country key	US	Currency USD	Language Key EN

Accounting organization

Chart of Accts	CAUS	Country Chart/Accts	
Company	6	FM Area	
Credit control area	3000	Fiscal Year Variant	K4
Ext. co. code	☐	Global CoCde	
Company code is productive	☐	VAT Registration No.	

Processing parameters

Document entry screen variant	2	☐ Business area fin. statements
Field status variant	1000	☑ Propose fiscal year
Pstng period variant	3000	☑ Define default value date
Max. exchange rate deviation	90 %	☐ No forex rate diff. when clearing in LC
Sample acct rules var.		☐ Tax base is net value
Workflow variant	3000	☐ Discount base is net value
Inflation Method		☑ Financial Assets Mgmt active
Crcy transl. for tax		☐ Purchase account processing
CoCd->CO Area	2	
Cost of sales accounting actv.	2	
☐ Negative Postings Permitted		☐ Enable amount split
☑ Cash Management activated		

Figure 8.1 Company Code Global Parameters

Maintenance of Additional Data for Company Code 0006

Name	Parameter value
Detail Tax Entry with MIRO	
Plants Abroad Not Required	
Tax Without Rounding Tolerance	
LC Tax with Translation Date	
Tax Entry for Ex. Rate Diff.	
ITSR Clerk	
Cash payment order ID number	
INTRASTAT ID number	
INTRASTAT additional number	
EXTRASTAT company number	
EXTRASTAT material number	
Shipper's Auth. Symbol	
Authentification code CUSDEC	
Reprtng prty name (INTRASTAT)	
Reprtng prty city (INTRASTAT)	
ID number EXTRASTAT	
EID number	
Tax number USA (TIN)	SAPTIN
Withholding Tax EDI Referen.No	

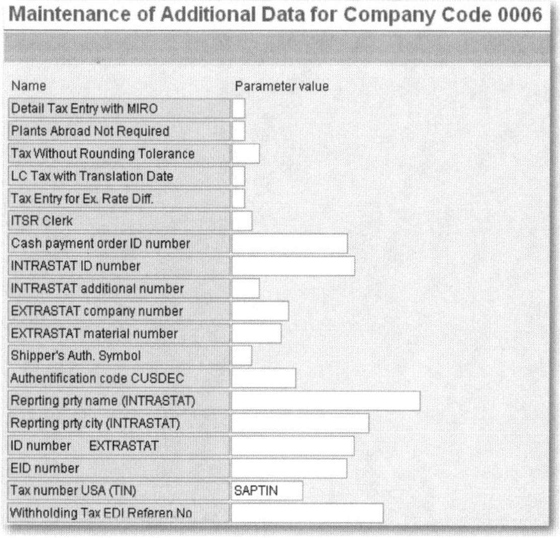

Figure 8.2 Company Code Global Parameters — Additional Data

8.2 The Plant Master

The plant master is also defined from the IMG side of R/3 or ECC and therefore is not available for maintenance by everyone. Plant codes can be used for actual physical plants, office locations, warehouses, distribution centers, and so on. The plant master was shown in Figure 3.10 of Chapter 3. For sales and use tax within the United States, the location of the plant code is often used to derive the *ship to* and *ship from* address.

From My Experience

I worked on a project in my early days working with SAP software where the tax department requested that as much tax data as possible would be defaulted into tax fields, but in the end, only one plant code was used for the entire company. In addition, cost centers were set up on a responsibility basis rather than a jurisdictional basis. This approach meant that manual tax decisions had to be made throughout the system and that very little could be defaulted in without a lot of customization. As a result, the implementation progressed very slowly.

Tax Requirements — Plant Master Data

Tax departments need master data describing plants for purposes such as the domestic manufacturing deduction, inventories, and transaction taxes. The information in Table 8.2 should be populated in the ECC table T001W.

Field	Description
WERKS	Plant Code
NAME1	Plant Name
NAME2	Plant Name 2
STRAS	Street Address
PFACH	P. O. Box
PSTLZ	Postal Code
ORT01	City
LAND1	Country Code
REGIO	Region or State
COUNC	County Code
TXJCD	Jurisdiction Code

Table 8.2 Plant Master (ECC Table T001W)

8.3 The Storage Location Master

The storage location master is a subset of the plant master and can be defined as a building, a warehouse, a distribution center, or any other facility that serves as an appendage to a plant. Like plants, storage locations are set up in the IMG where address information can be maintained. Complete address information should be maintained for each storage location if taxes are going to be computed efficiently.

Tax Requirements — Storage Location Master Data

Tax departments need master data describing storage locations for purposes such as inventories and transaction taxes. The information in Table 8.3 should be populated in ECC table T001L.

Field	Description
WERKS	Plant
LGORT	Storage Location Code
LGOBE	Description of Storage Location

Table 8.3 Storage Location Master (ECC Table T001L)

Address information concerning storage location codes is retained in the address master and needs to be retained along with the jurisdiction code and additional information shown in Table 8.4. This information is maintained in ECC Table ADDR1_DATA.

Field	Description
NAME1	Name of Location
STREET	Street/House Number
POST_CODE1	City Postal Code
COUNTRY	Country
REGION	Region
TAXJURCODE	Jurisdiction
PO_BOX	P. O. Box

Table 8.4 Address Structure (ECC Table: ADDR1_DATA)

Field	Description
POST_CODE2	Postal Code
POST_CODE3	Company Postal Code

Table 8.4 Address Structure (ECC Table: ADDR1_DATA) (cont.)

8.4 The Asset Master

The asset master contains descriptive information on each asset owned by a company, including location and jurisdiction information. It also lists the useful life and depreciation methods under the different depreciation scenarios. Assets and asset depreciation play an integral part in tax calculations and depend on proper master data.

Tax Requirements — Asset Master Data

Tax departments need master data describing assets for a variety of purposes. For example, tax authorities demand descriptive information about assets such as the date placed in service, the cost, the asset description, the useful life, and so on. The information in Table 8.5 should be populated in at least one of the following ECC tables: ANLA, ANLB, ANLC, or ANLZ.

Field	Description
BUKRS	Company Code
ANLN1	Main Asset Number
ANLN2	Asset Sub Number
AIBDT	Original Acquisition Date of AUC/Transferred
AIBN1	Original Asset that was Transferred
AIBN2	Original Asset that was Transferred
AKTIV	Asset Capitalization Date
ANLKL	Asset Class
EIGKZ	Property Indicator
POSNR	WBS Element Investment Project
TXA50	Asset Description
TXT50	Asset Description

Table 8.5 Asset Master (ECC Tables ANLA, ANLB, ANLC, or ANLZ)

Field	Description
URWRT	Original Acquisition Value
AFABE	Real Depreciation Area
AFASL	Depreciation Key
ANLGR	Group Asset
CAUFN	Internal Order
KOSTL	Cost Center
KOSTLV	Cost Center Responsible for Asset
TXJCD	Jurisdiction for Tax Calculation
NDURJ	Original Useful Life in Years
SCHRW	Asset Scrap Date
AFABG	Depreciation Calculation Start Date

Table 8.5 Asset Master (ECC Tables ANLA, ANLB, ANLC, or ANLZ) (cont.)

8.5 The Material Master

The Materials Management (MM) module will be discussed in more detail as part of the sales and use discussion in Chapters 12, 13, and 14. For our purposes here, you need to know that tax logic is limited to a tax indicator, material tax classification codes, and condition records. In earlier versions of SAP software, the indicator could be set to taxable or nontaxable for each material or product. In ECC 6.0, the indicator can be set on a country basis.

Tax Requirements — Material Master Data

Tax departments need master data describing materials to determine the material's ultimate use, the tax jurisdiction where it resides, material descriptions, and other data required for tax accounting. The information in Table 8.6 should be populated in the ECC tables MAKT, MARA, MARC, and MAPE.

Field	Description
MATNR	Material Number
WERKS	Plant
MTART	Material Type

Table 8.6 Material Master (ECC Tables MAKT, MARA, MARC, and MAPE)

Field	Description
MATKL	Material Group
MAKTX	Material Description
NORMT	Industry Standard Description
ATTYP	Material Category
STOFF	Hazardous Material Number
TAXKM	Material MasterTax Classification
TATYP	Material Master Tax Category
TAXIM	Material Master Tax Indicator
KZUMW	Indicator: Environmentally Relevant
TAKLV	Tax Classification of the Material
MTVER	Export/Import Material Group
PRENC	Exemption Certificate: Indicator for Legal Control
PRENO	Number of Exemption Certificate
PREND	Exemption Certificate: Issue Date
PRENE	Indicator: Vendor Declaration Exists
HERBL	State of Manufacture
HERKL	Country of Origin of the Material
HERKR	Region of Origin of the Material

Table 8.6 Material Master (ECC Tables MAKT, MARA, MARC, and MAPE) (cont.)

8.6 The General Ledger Master

The heart of any accounting system is the chart of accounts. The chart of accounts is maintained in the G/L master for SAP systems. This is where new accounts are added and where they are changed or displayed. The G/L master has fields that are relevant to taxes that must be maintained for tax data to flow appropriately in the system.

Tax Requirements — General Ledger Master Data

Table 8.7 lists the minimum accounts needed for tax departments. Several of these fields will be discussed in more detail when sales and use tax is addressed in Chapters 12, 13, and 14. Tax departments need master data describing G/L accounts because the G/L is the backbone of the financial system. Information such as account descriptions, balance sheet indicators, and tax categories are required on tax reports and in tax calculations. The information in Table 8.7 should be populated in ECC tables SKA1, SKAT, and SKB1.

Field	Description
SAKNR	G/L Account Number
TXT20	Short Text
TXT50	G/L Account Long Text
KTOPL	Chart of Accounts
XBILK	Indicator — Account is a Balance Sheet Account
PSTLZ	Postal Code
BUKRS	Company Code
MWSKZ	Tax Category in Account Master Record
XMWNO	Indicator: Tax Code is Not a Required Field

Table 8.7 G/L Master (ECC Tables SKA1, SKAT, and SKB1)

8.7 The Customer Master

The customer master contains information regarding the firm's customers. A separate record must be maintained for each customer address that the firm deals with. A tax jurisdiction code must also be maintained on each customer record. The *sold to* and *ship to* addresses for sales tax are derived from the customer master. The customer master is also used for withholding tax when extended withholding is activated. Master data actually added to the master file is described in Chapter 5.

Tax Requirements — Customer Master Data

Tax departments need master data describing customers to show IRS and state audit teams who sales have been made to and if appropriate sales tax has been collected. Customer location information serves as the basis for apportionment and *ship to* information used in tax calculations. The information in Table 8.8 should be populated in ECC tables KNA1 and KNB1.

Field	Description
MANDT	Client
BUKRS	Company Code
KUNNR	Customer Number
NAME1	Name1
NAME2	Name2
VBUND	Customer ID or Trading Partner
STCD1	Tax Number 1
STCD2	Tax Number 2
STRAS	Street Address
ORT01	City
ORT02	District
PSTL2	Postal Code
PFACH	P. O. Code
REGIO	Region
LAND1	Country Key
TXJCD	Jurisdiction for Tax Calculation
STCEG	VAT Registration Number
AKONT	Reconciliation Account in G/L
BRSCH	Industry Key
TATYP	Customer Tax Category
TAXLD	Customer Tax Classification
FITYP	Tax type

Table 8.8 Customer Master (ECC Tables KNA1 and KNB1)

8.8 The Vendor Master

The vendor master requires full address information as well and must have the jurisdiction code field populated. The vendor master, similar to the customer master, will have a record for each location from which the vendor does business with the firm. The vendor master will determine the *sold from* and *ship from* location for use tax transactions. The vendor master also contains fields that relate to 1099 backup withholding and 1042 NRA withholding. If extended withholding is activated for a company code, the vendor master will also have an extended withholding tab, which is discussed in Chapter 5.

Tax Requirements — Vendor Master Data

Tax departments need master data describing vendors to satisfy use tax requirements for vendor name and jurisdiction information. Vendor information is also requested by the IRS for support of accounts payable transactions. The information in Table 8.9 should be populated in ECC tables LFA1, LFB1, and LFBK.

Field	Description
MANDT	Client
BUKRS	Company Code
LIFNR	Vendor Number
NAME1	Name1
NAME2	Name2
VBUND	Company ID of Trading Partner
STCD1	Tax Number 1
STCD2	Tax Number 2
STCD3	Tax Number 3
STCD4	Tax Number 4
FITYP	Tax Type
STRAS	Street Address
ORT01	City
ORT02	District
PSTL2	Postal Code
PFACH	P. O. Code
REGIO	Region
LAND1	Country Key
TXJCD	Jurisdiction for Tax Calculation

Table 8.9 Vendor Master (ECC Tables LFA1, LFB1, and LFBK)

Field	Description
AKONT	Reconciliation Account in G/L
QSZNR	Certificate Number of Withholding Tax Code
QSZDT	Validity Date for Withholding Tax Exemption Certificate
QSSKZ	Withholding Tax Code
QSREC	Vendor Recipient Type
QSBGR	Authority for Exemption from Withholding
QLAND	Withholding Tax Country Key
MINDK	Minority Indicators
FISKU	Tax Authority
STENR	Tax Code
BANKL	Bank Number
BANKN	Bank Account Number
BANKS	Bank Country Key

Table 8.9 Vendor Master (ECC Tables LFA1, LFB1, and LFBK) (cont.)

8.9 The Cost Center Master

The cost center master, similar to other master files, requires full address information and must have the jurisdiction code field populated. The cost center master location will represent the *ship to* address for use tax when items are shipped to an address other than a plant. The importance of the cost center will be covered in more depth when discussing sales and use tax in Chapters 12, 13, and 14.

Tax Requirements — Cost Center Master Data

Tax departments need master data describing cost centers because the cost center serves as the SAP mainstay in determining the *ship to* address for use tax calculations. Cost center descriptions also assist with determining the purpose of purchases and the ultimate use of products. The information in Table 8.10 should be populated in ECC tables CSKS and CSKT.

Field	Description
BUKRS	Company Code
KOSTL	Cost Center Code
KOKRS	Controlling Area
KTEXT	Cost Center Name
LTEXT	Long Text for Name
KOSAR	Cost Center Category
FUNKT	Cost Center Function
ABTEI	Department
GSBER	Business Area
STRAS	House Number and Street
ORT01	City
ORT02	District
REGIO	Region or State
PSTLZ	Postal Code
LAND1	Country Key
PFACH	P. O. Box
PSTL2	P. O. Box Postal Code
TXJCD	Jurisdiction Code
OBJNR	Object Number
PRCTR	Profit Center
KHINR	Hierarchy Area
ERSDA	Created On

Table 8.10 Cost Center Master (ECC Tables CSKS and CSKT)

8.10 The Internal Order Master

Internal orders are used for project-related work where the length of the project may not warrant using the SAP project system. Internal orders are activated for the majority of implementations. Location information and a jurisdiction code are needed for each internal order in the system if taxes are to be paid to the proper taxing authority.

Tax Requirements — Internal Order Master Data

Tax departments need master data describing internal orders because internal orders are used to capture transactions that have tax impact. Internal orders may capture costs for R&D spending, constructed assets, marketing programs, and other efforts affecting the financial affairs of the enterprise. The information in Table 8.11 should be populated in ECC table AUFK.

Field	Description
BUKRS	Company Code
AUFNR	Order Number
KOKRS	Controlling Area
KTEXT	General Name
AUART	Order Type
ASTKZ	Identifier for Statistical Order
KOSTV	Responsible Cost Center
KOSTL	Cost Center for Basic Settlement
KSTAR	Settlement Cost Element
SAKNR	G/L Account Number for Basic Settlement
ABGSL	Results Analysis Key
AUTYP	Order Category
CCKEY	Cost Collector Key
GSBER	Business Area
KDAUF	Sales Order Number
KDPOS	Item Number in the Sales Order
PRCTR	Profit Center
PSPEL	WBS Element
POSID	WBS Element
SCOPE	Object Class
TXJCD	Jurisdiction Code
WERKS	Plant
ERDAT	Created On Date

Table 8.11 Internal Order Master (ECC Table AUFK)

8.11 The Project/WBS Master

The project code and Work Breakdown Structure (WBS) element are used as alternatives to internal orders. WBS elements allow costs to be broken down into categories that result in more meaningful accounting. WBS elements are actually used with both internal orders and the project system and serve the same purpose in each. One project can therefore have many WBS elements. Projects are basically objects within SAP that comprise a buildup of costs that are captured in WBS elements

Tax Requirements — Project/WBS Master Data

Tax departments need master data describing projects and project/WBS elements for purposes, such as the R&D tax credit. The information in Tables 8.12, 8.13, and 8.14 should be populated in ECC tables PROJ, PRPS, and TCJ1T, respectively.

Field	Description
PSPNR	Project Definition Number
PSPID	Project Definition Description
ERNAM	Name of Person who Created the Project
POST1	Short Description
ERDAT	Date Created
VERNR	Project Manager Number
VERNA	Project Manager Name
PRCTR	Profit Center
KOSTL	Cost Center

Table 8.12 Project Master (ECC Table PROJ)

Field	Description
POSID	WBS Identifier
PSPHI	Current Number of Project
ERNAM	Person who Created the Object
ERDAT	Date Created

Table 8.13 WBS Master (ECC Table PRPS)

Field	Description
VERNR	Project Manager Number
VERNA	Project Manager Name
PRCTR	Profit Center
PRART	Project Type
AKSTL	Requesting Company Code
FKSTL	Responsble Company Code
TPLNR	Location
PWPOS	Currency
KOSTL	Cost Center to which Costs are Posted
TXJCD	Jurisdiction Code
STORT	Location
MATNR	Material Number
ABUKR	Requesting Company Code
KTRG	Cost Object
EQUNR	Equipment Number
WERKS	Plant

Table 8.13 WBS Master (ECC Table PRPS) (cont.)

Field	Description
PRART	Project Type
PRATX	Name of Project Type

Table 8.14 Project Types (ECC Table TCJ1T)

8.12 Master Data Cleansing

Tax departments usually don't have a lot of influence on master data cleansing, but as mentioned earlier, the better the master data, the more accurate the tax filings. Encouraging master data cleansing is an important effort that is discussed in all SAP implementations but often not completed as deadlines grow closer and less money becomes available. However, cleansing address data on each master file prior to loading into SAP software is recommended.

Example

On a recent implementation, several different fields of information were all grouped in the street address field in the legacy system. SAP master data files contained separate fields for different elements of address date. The company was including the following information in the address field:

- Street address
- City
- State
- Building code
- Store code
- ZIP code

As mentioned already, SAP has a place for the different elements of address information. Part of data cleansing should include the parsing of data to reflect information in the proper field. Data cleansing should not only include testing and correcting the integrity of the data but also categorizing data into proper fields where it can be used to its fullest extent.

Note

A good number of companies provide data cleansing services. One such company recently cleansed nearly 150,000 addresses for under $10,000, which, compared to the price of an SAP implementation, is not very much at all. However, be sure to parse address data prior to having it cleansed, or the price tag will end up much higher.

8.13 Loading Master Data

Tax departments do not own any of the master files mentioned in this chapter and therefore are not responsible for the data loads. Instead, SAP implementation teams have data management teams that are responsible for data cleansing and loading. Tax departments may, however, have fields on selected master files where they have to supply master data values to be uploaded. This is true, for example, for the **Withholding Tax** tabs required for the customer and vendor masters if extended withholding functionality is activated. It may also be true for federal ID numbers, jurisdiction codes, and other tax codes. If this data exists in legacy systems, the data may be able to be converted and loaded automatically from the legacy systems. If data does not exist in legacy systems, tax departments may be asked to supply values because they are the ones requesting the functionality.

Extended withholding and additional depreciation areas usually result in values that are not contained in legacy systems and have to be supplied by tax departments. Supplying this kind of data can result in large projects, so it needs to be planned for ahead of time.

Asset loads for tax depreciation areas are typically the biggest items, creating additional work for tax departments. A company with 50,000 assets that only carries 2 or 3 sets of depreciation books faces a big project when it decides to activate 4 or 5 new depreciation areas in SAP. Tax integration specialists need to alert the project team and the tax department of the amount of work required when new depreciation areas are approved. Even with the absence of new depreciation areas, tax departments have a vested interest in the way fixed assets are loaded and should be involved in master data plans throughout the project.

The effort involved in setting up enhanced withholding is largely done in configuration tables with additional values for customers and vendors. This can also amount to considerable effort. Extended withholding functionality is virtually unknown by receivable and payable teams and gets attention only when a new tab suddenly displays on their master files. Coordination with these departments and the data management team needs to be done prior to activating the functionality.

8.14 Summary

Master data affects every transaction in the SAP system and needs to be accurate. Tax professionals working with implementation teams must ensure that needed fields are actually populated in the system and populated accurately. If the tax department is the sole user of the data, tax personnel will likely be called on to supply the field values. Tax departments need to keep this in mind when requesting master data because obtaining proper values and formatting for upload can be a project in itself.

In Chapter 9, we will explore tax reporting and how to work with tax professionals who fear they will lose existing reporting functionality when the new SAP system is turned on. We will also discuss SAP reporting functionality.

Good reporting is essential to timely accurate tax compliance. SAP systems have a variety of reporting tools. Understanding the SAP standard report library will help tax professionals know where much of the information is coming from. An understanding of reporting tools within the SAP system will assist with deciding which custom report writing tool works best in a given circumstance. This helps tax integration specialists identify needs and help with the functional specifications required to make needed custom reports a reality.

9 Tax Reporting

Tax departments use numerous reports to assist in complying with tax laws. When an SAP implementation is about to take place, tax personnel are often concerned that the new system will not deliver the same information as the old one did. Often, they have relied on custom reports from multiple legacy systems to complete tax forms. An understanding of tax compliance and accounting is helpful to understand tax department needs and to determine when standard SAP reports will fit the bill and when customization may be needed. An examination of current reports used for tax compliance, planning, and analysis will result in the information needed to lead to a successful reporting implementation. The earlier a reporting plan is developed, the better. SAP has the following tools available to address reporting needs:

- SAP standard reports
- SAP query
- Report Painter
- Report Writer
- ABAP 4 custom reports
- DART reporting
- Business Warehouse (BW) reporting
- SAP NetWeaver Business Intelligence (BI)

The first five tools in this list retrieve data directly from R/3 or ECC, resulting in real-time reporting. This means that reports using these tools retrieve data directly from the system, getting the very latest data entered.

DART reporting was discussed in Chapter 6 and is used primarily for tax audits but is not limited to the audit period. Many companies leverage the value of the DART extract by using the functionality for compliance as well. DART reporting is not real-time reporting; it is limited to the timing and the time period for which the DART extract is run.

BW and SAP NetWeaver BI reporting is also not real-time reporting but can be very close depending on the frequency that BW is updated from R/3 or ECC. BW and SAP NetWeaver BI are very similar in that SAP NetWeaver BI sits on the BW platform but is capable of stronger data mining functionality than BW alone.

Note

SAP has renamed Business Information Warehouse (BW) to SAP NetWeaver Business Intelligence (BI), so SAP is no longer making any differentiation between the two.

This chapter discusses each of these reporting capabilities so that tax managers and tax integration specialists will understand the strengths and weaknesses of each tool. The decision as to which tool is used to produce tax reports is not made by the tax manager or the tax integration specialist but is left up to the expertise of the reporting team. It is helpful, however, to have an understanding of each of the tools and what each can provide.

9.1 SAP Standard Reports

SAP standard reports are the first option for the reporting team. If a standard report meets the team's requirements, nothing else is needed. R/3 and ECC have an abundance of standard reports available in each system module. Reports that are standard in the Financial Accounting (FI) module will satisfy many tax needs. A corporate income tax return (Form 1120) can be largely prepared using information from a general ledger (G/L) or a trial balance. The aforementioned reports and basic financial statements are part of SAP standard reporting functionality.

The majority of information needed for fixed asset accounting is also available through standard SAP reporting. Figure 9.1 shows the reporting tree in the G/L part of an ECC system. Each part of the system has a similar reporting tree. The majority of SAP standard reports also contains selection conditions that allow the report to be filtered on a single G/L account, cost center, asset, and so on. Figure 9.2 shows the Asset Accounting report tree with some of the reports available in the fixed asset area.

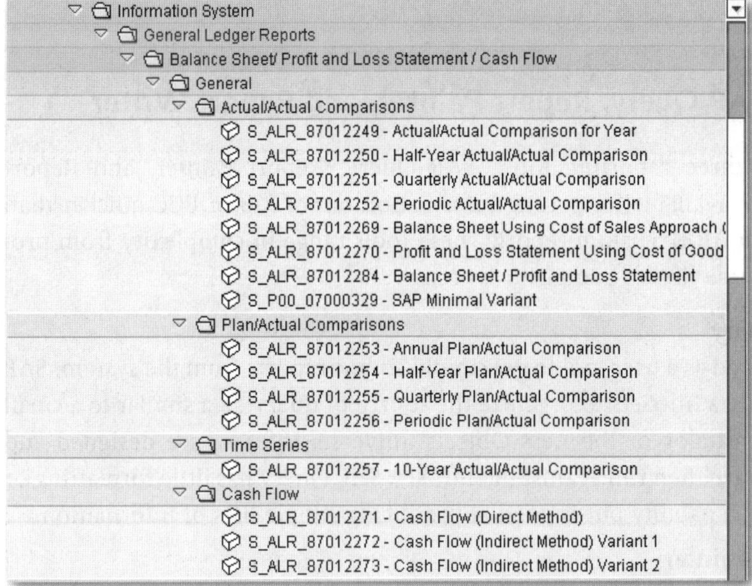

Figure 9.1 The General Ledger Report Tree

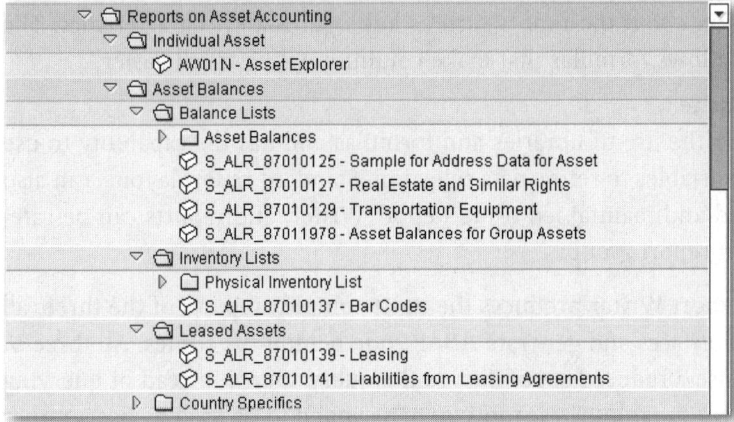

Figure 9.2 The Asset Accounting Report Tree

Although standard reporting can fill many needs, it does not address all tax requirements. Unique requirements such as the domestic manufacturing deduction, the R&D tax credit, and many others require custom reporting and the ability to retrieve data on demand.

Note

You can find in-depth information on SAP standard reports in Thomas Michael's Essentials guide *Reporting for SAP Asset Accounting*, also published by SAP PRESS.

9.2 SAP Query, Report Painter, and Report Writer

The next three reporting tools, SAP Query, Report Painter, and Report Writer, are available for getting information out of R/3 or ECC quicker than creating an ABAP custom report. These tools range in complexity from producing simple lists to complex reports.

- **SAP Query**
  Developed as a user tool to get simple ad hoc reports from the system. SAP Query uses InfoSets to organize the source of query data similar to a small Cognos catalog or Business Objects universe. InfoSets are designed and queries are then run against the InfoSet. SAP Query has little formatting or totaling capability but is good at producing simple lists of information.
- **Report Painter**
  This has more formatting capability then SAP Query and uses the concept of libraries as a source of information. Libraries are linked to summary tables used as the query source and are capable of joins. They also house information about the report such as key figures and characteristics. The tool also allows formulas that make column totaling much easier.
- **Report Writer**
  Allows for the use of libraries and formulas and has the capability to use sets and variables to refine data selection. Standard report layouts can also be created and maintained using Report Writer, and reports can be categorized in report groups.

Although Report Writer produces the most complex reports of the three, all have user interfaces and generate ABAP code behind the scenes. All three of these tools use a reduced set of data as the query source instead of querying against the entire table. These tools were designed to be used by users rather than IT professionals.

Note

These tools caught on quickly in earlier implementations of SAP and can still be valuable if controlled properly. The drawback is that when allowed to be used at will, the amount of queries in the system can dramatically reduce system performance. Current implementations rigorously attempt to control and limit the use of these tools to a few power users.

Accessing SAP Query, Report Painter, and Report Writer

The three reporting applications just reviewed, SAP Query, Report Painter, and Report Writer, are all reached through the following menu path:

SAP Menu • Information Systems • Ad Hoc Reports

Sap Query and Report Painter are both visible under the **Ad Hoc Reports** node on the menu, as shown in Figure 9.3. **Report Writer** is found under the **Report Painter** node, also shown in Figure 9.3. These three tools are intended for ad hoc reporting as opposed to more permanent custom reports usually written in ABAP4.

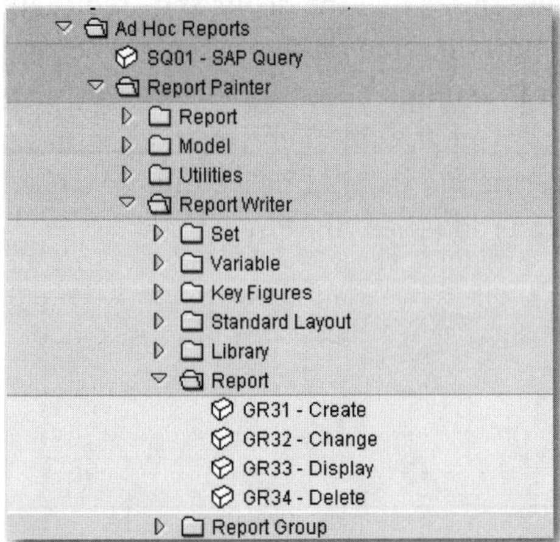

Figure 9.3 SAP Ad Hoc Reports

Figure 9.4 shows a Report Painter report layout. You can see from Figure 9.4 that Report Painter can be used to develop formats with sections and subtotals in an income statement format.

Report 0F-GUV1 IDES Cost of Sales Horizontal page 1 /
Section 0001
Standard layout 0F-CGSA

Format group:	0	0	0	1
Profit and loss statement item	Act. local	Plan local	Var. (abs)	Var. (%)
* Sales deductions	XXX.XXX.XXX	XXX.XXX.XXX	XXX.XXX.XXX	XXXXXXXXX
Total Net Sales	XXX.XXX.XXX	XXX.XXX.XXX	XXX.XXX.XXX	XXXXXXXXX
* Costs of Goods Sold	XXX.XXX.XXX	XXX.XXX.XXX	XXX.XXX.XXX	XXXXXXXXX
* Production variances	XXX.XXX.XXX	XXX.XXX.XXX	XXX.XXX.XXX	XXXXXXXXX
* Production order variance	XXX.XXX.XXX	XXX.XXX.XXX	XXX.XXX.XXX	XXXXXXXXX
Costs of Goods Sold	XXX.XXX.XXX	XXX.XXX.XXX	XXX.XXX.XXX	XXXXXXXXX
Gross Profit	XXX.XXX.XXX	XXX.XXX.XXX	XXX.XXX.XXX	XXXXXXXXX
* Sales costs	XXX.XXX.XXX	XXX.XXX.XXX	XXX.XXX.XXX	XXXXXXXXX
* Administrative costs	XXX.XXX.XXX	XXX.XXX.XXX	XXX.XXX.XXX	XXXXXXXXX
* Research & Development	XXX.XXX.XXX	XXX.XXX.XXX	XXX.XXX.XXX	XXXXXXXXX
Intercompany profits	XXX.XXX.XXX	XXX.XXX.XXX	XXX.XXX.XXX	XXXXXXXXX
* Other Operational Revenue	XXX.XXX.XXX	XXX.XXX.XXX	XXX.XXX.XXX	XXXXXXXXX
* Other Operational Expenses	XXX.XXX.XXX	XXX.XXX.XXX	XXX.XXX.XXX	XXXXXXXXX
* Revenue from Investments	XXX.XXX.XXX	XXX.XXX.XXX	XXX.XXX.XXX	XXXXXXXXX
* Revenue from Other Securities	XXX.XXX.XXX	XXX.XXX.XXX	XXX.XXX.XXX	XXXXXXXXX
* Interest and Other Revenue	XXX.XXX.XXX	XXX.XXX.XXX	XXX.XXX.XXX	XXXXXXXXX
* Depr'n in Fin. Invstmnts, Securities	XXX.XXX.XXX	XXX.XXX.XXX	XXX.XXX.XXX	XXXXXXXXX

Figure 9.4 Report Painter Report

Figure 9.5 shows the layout of a Report Writer report in G/L format that is totaled by balance sheet account. You can see that the debits and credits are included in one total, which is sometimes not the case with some reporting tools. Also, the balance sheet shown in the figure has drill-down capability that is reached by double-clicking each of the line items marked with an asterisk. Report Writer is very powerful and using it needs to be weighed against the time and expense taken to produce an ABAP report.

Avg.balances period version LC YTD

Data selected on 31.05.2007 Page 1 of 1

Account set 0B-GKR.GLT Balance: assests and liabilits

Company code 3000 IDES US INC
Fiscal Year 2006

Account	Period 01	Period 02	Period 03	Period 04
USD American Dollar				
** 1010 Accumulated deprecia				
*** 0FGKR000022.GLT0				
**** 0FGKR000020.GLT0				
USD American Dollar				
** 11000 Plant and Equipment				
*** 0FGKR000024.GLT0				
USD American Dollar				
** 11010 Accumulated deprecia				
*** 0FGKR000025.GLT0				
**** 0FGKR000023.GLT0				
USD American Dollar				
** 21000 Office equipment				
*** 0FGKR000027.GLT0				
USD American Dollar				
** 21010 Accumulated deprecia				
*** 0FGKR000028.GLT0				
**** 0FGKR000026.GLT0				
***** 0FGKR000019.GLT0				
USD American Dollar				
*** 41000 Common Stock - inves				

Figure 9.5 Report Writer Report

9.3 Functional Specifications for Reports

It would be nice to hand over a list of reports to the development team with a copy of a page or two from each report and consider this enough information for developers to produce a group of similar reports in ECC, but it is not that simple. Reports are part of implementation WRICEFs and are treated as development items requiring functional specifications to be completed that explain in detail the report purpose, the source of information, formatting and totaling guidance, field mapping, and other information. WRICEF stands for the following:

- Workflow
- Reports
- Interfaces
- Conversions
- Enhancements
- Forms

Note

The acronym WRICEF is an accepted term on many SAP implementations to refer to development items requiring functional specifications. It is not a tax or SAP term but is commonly used by implementation teams.

Tax integrators will need to assist the tax department with this effort for every custom report identified. Specifications must be accurate and complete so they can be understood by an unrelated third party. This is because many times custom reports will be built by an outside developer who is not part of the project and has no idea how it will be used other than the information in the specification document.

Unfortunately, tax integrators often leave the project before reporting specifications are written and therefore leave this work with someone else on the project or in the tax department. In this case, the best that can be done is to identify the custom reports and as much about them as possible so a file and information is left for the person doing the functional specification to refer to.

9.4 Summary

SAP systems include a variety of tools designed to meet reporting needs. SAP Query, Report Painter, and Report Writer are R/3- or ECC-based ad hoc reporting tools that are capable of producing real-time reports. BW and SAP NetWeaver BI are newer, more powerful, reporting tools that are capable of improved data mining and formatting that produce near real-time reports. DART is also capable of producing large transaction-based reports from R/3 or ECC data extracts but are subject to the extract period and the extract timing as to how current the reports are. Each of these reporting tools have strengths and weaknesses and have to be matched up to the needs of a particular reporting requirement.

Chapter 10 will discuss additional income tax issues, among them being the Domestic Production Activities Deduction. It will also cover meals and entertainment expenses, the R&D tax credit, apportionment, and third-party income tax systems.

In this chapter, you will learn about additional income tax issues that should be addressed during a tax integration project. A job well done in any of these areas can pay for the cost of an integration project many times over. Several of these areas have very high tax impact, and attention needs to be given to assure tax departments get the information required.

10 Other Income Tax Topics

Some calculations required to complete a corporate income tax return are complex and deserve individual attention. In this chapter, we will discuss the following income tax related issues, which can be addressed to some degree when doing a tax integration project:

- Third-party income tax compliance systems
- The domestic production activities deduction
- Travel and entertainment expenses
- Apportionment
- R&D Tax Credits
- FAS 109, FAS 123R, and other Specific Calculations
- M-1 Automation

10.1 Third-Party Income Tax Compliance Systems

Preparation of an IRS form 1120 corporate income tax return is an involved process, so income tax software has been created to assist with data collection, passing information from one form to another, and actually producing the return itself. This income tax software is not linked to the SAP system through the SAP tax interface in the way that sales and use tax software is. In fact, income tax software is generally not linked to R/3 or ECC systems at all, unless a company wants to build an interface between it and the tax software. In the majority of cases, a general ledger (G/L) download is done from the SAP system, and the G/L information is then uploaded into the external income tax software.

> **Note**
>
> The completed return for a large corporation can easily fill several boxes.

Preparing a corporate tax return using external software is G/L intensive in that it is at the G/L level where accounts are consolidated and mapped to line items in the software that comprise line items on the corporate tax return. There is, of course, additional information other than just G/L account balances that need to be fed to the external system, but a G/L trial balance or a list of G/L account balances is the beginning. With an external system, G/L account balances have to get from the SAP system to the tax preparation software either by manual download and upload or through a seamless interface.

Thus, either a manual or electronic interface needs to exist. Federal and state income taxation is more diverse and more complex than other tax areas, so proven tax software is a requirement if companies want to avoid problems with the IRS. Tax integration specialists need to be aware of the income tax preparation software used and determine with the tax department and SAP implementation team the approach to getting data to the tax system. Regardless of whether the method is manual or electronic, functional specifications will be required to define the data that needs to be passed.

10.2 Section 199 — The Domestic Production Activities Deduction

The American Jobs Creations Act passed in 2004 issued guidance under Section 199 of the internal revenue code designed to encourage manufacturing within the United States. The domestic production activities deduction is new and has not been audited to date, but the opportunities for tax savings can result in many millions of dollars for corporations that have manufacturing intensive operations in the United States. To adequately account for and support the deduction, corporate internal accounting needs to be driven to a detail that few companies have achieved. However, newer versions of SAP software can capture the majority of the data needed if the system is designed with the deduction in mind. Fortunately, information needed to support the deduction is also helpful in effectively running the operations end of the business, so you'll likely find operations personnel on SAP implementation teams very helpful when introduced to the requirements needed to support the manufacturing deduction. Let's now take a closer look at the requirements of Section 199.

An Introduction to Section 199

Section 199 explains in detail when the domestic production activities deduction can be taken and when it cannot. However, even with the detail contained in the section, many questions still exist, which will likely only be answered after years of audits and court cases that interpret the intent of the law.

> **Note**
>
> This book provides an overview of the Section 199 law and what needs to be done in R/3 or ECC to best account for expenditures in a way to calculate and support the deduction. For more information on Section 199 and all of the details in the provision, you can go to *www.irs.gov* or do a Web search on Section 199.

When doing tax integration, the approach is usually to identify the data elements or bits of information that need to be captured in the SAP system. This is consistent with the tax data matrix concept discussed in Chapter 1. After the important tax data elements are identified, then a determination is made as to which can be captured by R/3 or ECC and which must be gathered from outside the system. The challenge is how to capture the data elements in the system in a way that is easily reportable.

The domestic production activities deduction has data elements that need to be captured either in the SAP software or outside the system. The more that can be included in the SAP software, the easier the reporting will be. The first step in solving problems created by Section 199 is to identify what needs to be captured and then agressively pursue their capture. The second step is to pull the data out so the tax calculation can be made.

The Calculation

The formula for calculating the domestic manufacturing deduction appears quite simple and is included in this section. In reality, however, the information required to make the calculation is one of the most difficult to obtain because companies have historically not been able to track domestic production costs down to the SKU or even the product level.

The calculation is the following:

The lesser of

Taxable income derived from a qualified production activity

or

Taxable income for the taxable year

multiplied by

applicable percentage rate (2005, 2006 = 3%; 2007 – 2009 = 6%; 2010 and beyond = 9%)

Note

The deduction is limited by the W-2 wages paid out in the taxable year.

The Provisions

The list of qualified production activities is expansive. The following list is taken from a fact sheet published by the Department of Treasury entitled "A Brief Overview of the New Domestic Production Activities Deduction." This and other information about the deduction can be found by going to *www.irs.gov* and doing a search for the "Domestic Production Activities Deduction".

The following information is applicable to taxable years beginning after December 31, 2004:

- The manufacture, production, growth, or extraction in whole or significant part in the United States of tangible personal property (e.g., clothing, goods, and food), software development, or music recordings.
- Film production (with exclusions provided in the statute), provided at least 50% of the total compensation relating to the production of the film is compensation for specified production services performed in the United States.
- Production of electricity, natural gas, or water in the United States.
- Construction or substantial renovation of real property in the United States, including residential and commercial buildings and infrastructure such as roads, power lines, water systems, and communications facilities.
- Engineering and architectural services performed in the United States and relating to construction of real property.

Because the calculation outlined earlier is based on net income produced from tangible personal property, accounting has to be in place that can account for revenue and expenses associated with a specific line of the business. It is uncertain whether taxpayers have to account at an SKU level, a product level, or a product group level. In the past, it has been difficult for corporations to produce accurate division-level financial statements, let alone product-based income statements. The IRS will accept some level of allocation, but specific cost identification is perferred at least through gross income. During an SAP implementation, care should be taken to determine the proper level of reporting and then how net income is going to be calculated after that level is decided. When income statements are needed at the SKU level, the level of reporting is not a problem.

As mentioned earlier, the IRS code states that a substantial part of the manufacturing must be done in the United States. It is therefore a requirement when configuring SAP software to show that the product was manufactured in the United States. If a product is comprised of a combination of materials manufactured in the United States and internationally, the domestic portion must be identifiable and must be the more substantial portion.

An additional requirement is that the manufacturer must bear the benefits and burdens of ownership of the tangible personal property. In other words, the manufacturer must be subject to the risks and rewards of the process. Contract manufacturers that merely provide a service but bear no risks are not eligible for the deduction. When configuring R/3 or ECC, it is therefore essential to separate products resulting from contract manufacturing operations from those that are eligible for the deduction.

Figure 10.1 shows a copy of a portion of IRS form 8903, the form used to report the domestic production activities deduction.

Form **8903** Department of the Treasury Internal Revenue Service	**Domestic Production Activities Deduction** ▶ Attach to your tax return. ▶ See separate instructions.	OMB No. 1545-1984 **2006** Attachment Sequence No. 143
Name(s) as shown on return		Identifying number

1	Domestic production gross receipts (DPGR)			1	
2	Allocable cost of goods sold. If you are using the small business simplified overall method, skip lines 2 and 3	2			
3	If you are using the section 861 method, enter deductions and losses definitely related to DPGR. Estates and trusts, see instructions. All others, skip line 3	3			
4	If you are using the section 861 method, enter your pro rata share of deductions and losses not definitely related to DPGR. All others, see instructions	4			
5	Add lines 2 through 4			5	
6	Subtract line 5 from line 1			6	

Figure 10.1 Domestic Production Activities Deduction

As mentioned, the first line of the return presents the biggest challenge, that is, tracking the gross receipts for all of the products manufactured in the United States, which SAP software does not handle easily. Note that if difficulties exist in this area, allocation is possible.

Figures 10.2 and 10.3 are excerpts from the instructions for form 8903 and offer some guidance. If you are experienced with taxation, you'll usually want to go straight to the internal revenue code or the regulations, but these screenshots from the instructions will give you the IRS view on things.

Gross receipts. Gross receipts include the following amounts from your trade or business activities.
- Total sales (net of returns and allowances).
- Amounts received for services, not including wages received as an employee.
- Income from incidental or outside sources (including sales of business property).

Figure 10.2 IRS Definition of Gross Receipts (Source: Instructions for Form 8903 [2006] www.irs.gov/instructions/i8903/ch02.html)

Allocation of gross receipts. You generally must allocate your gross receipts between DPGR and non-DPGR. Allocate gross receipts using a reasonable method that accurately identifies gross receipts that are DPGR. However, if less than 5% of your gross receipts are non-DPGR, you can treat all of your gross receipts as DPGR. Also, under the final regulations, if less than 5% of your gross receipts are DPGR, you can treat all of your gross receipts as non-DPGR.

Figure 10.3 IRS Instructions for Allocation of Gross Receipts (Source: Instructions for Form 8903 [2006] www.irs.gov/instructions/i8903/ch02.html)

If the cost of goods cannot be specifically identified, allocation is permitted here as well. Figure 10.4 shows instructions for the cost of goods sold area of the form. Cost of goods sold as indicated in Figure 10.4 can also be allocated if specific cost identification cannot be accomplished. Tax departments usually cannot influence production accounting but can jump on board if the operating department decides to report at a product line level or a lower level.

Note

Achieving specific cost identification through gross profit if possible and then allocating general and administrative expenses as needed is the preferable method.

Cost of Goods Sold
For purposes of the DPAD, cost of goods sold includes the:
- Cost of goods sold to customers, and
- Adjusted basis of other property you sold or otherwise disposed of in your trade or business.

Allocation of cost of goods sold. Generally, you must allocate your cost of goods sold between DPGR and non-DPGR using a reasonable method. If you use a method to allocate gross receipts between DPGR and non-DPGR, the use of a different method to allocate cost of goods sold will not be considered reasonable, unless it is more accurate. However, if you qualify to use the small business simplified overall method (discussed on page 4), you can use it to apportion both cost of goods sold and other deductions, expenses, and losses between DPGR and non-DPGR.

Figure 10.4 IRS Instructions for the Allocation of Cost of Goods Sold (Source: Instructions for Form 8903 [2006] www.irs.gov/instructions/i8903/ch02.html)

Reports from the SAP system are useful when preparing form 8903. Let's now look at a sample report that will give you the data needed to complete the return.

Report Format

The report format shown in Figure 10.5 is one possibility of what a report for the domestic production activity deduction could look like, but it is not certain exactly what information will be required after an audit starts. The format shown, however, is a good starting point.

General and Administrative Costs
Very few costs on a project or SKU will be direct costs so allocation is expected in this area.

Earnings before Interest and Taxes
Earnings before Interest and taxes is as low as you have to go. This would equate to Taxable Income Derived from a Qualified Production Activity and would be multiplied by the applicable rate to figure the deduction.

Remember that this is for one SKU or product and similar information must be computed for each domestically manufactured product the company has.

Statement of Profit and Losses		
XXX Corporation US09		
20 oz Beverage		
December 31, 2006		
Domestic Production Gross Receipts (DPGR)		$XXX,XXX,XXX
Less: Returns and Allowances		X,XXX
Net Revenue		$XXX,XXX,XXX
(Gross receipts less returns)		
At this point, it is necessary to subtract expenses directly related to production of product.		
Beginning Inventory	$ XX,XXX	
Direct Labor	X,XXX	
Factory Burden	XX,XXX	
Materials	XXX,XXX	
Freight	XXX	
Other Direct Expenses	XX	
Ending Inventory	XX,XXX	
Cost of Goods Sold**		$ X,XXX,XXX
Net Margin		$ XX,XXX,XXX

Figure 10.5 Domestic Production Activities Report — Part A

Note

The Cost of Goods Sold section is important because it provides support for where and what constitutes the production activities. It provides an audit trail for meeting the substantially all test. Part of the provision provides that the "in significant part" all test is met if at least 20 % of the product costs represent manufacturing labor and overhead costs. The more detailed the accounting is in this area the better the audit support for the deduction.

Form 8903 is actually simpler than the report shown in Figure 10.5, but the additional information will give facts needed to meet the "in significant part" or 20 % tests. It's advisable to start here with your integration requirements and then make concessions as necessary. To prepare a report like the one shown here or have the necessary data to complete form 8903, it is important to look at the data elements needed and ensure that they will be captured in SAP. Data elements and the need for a tax data matrix was discussed in Chapter 1.

Proper use of the product hierarchy and profitability analysis (CO-PA) can produce income and expense information that will get you to an adequate level to support this deduction. As mentioned before, attention to this area can produce large amounts in deductions for your company (possibly millions), so it's clearly worth spending time on this area.

10.3 Travel and Entertainment Expenses

Travel and entertainment expenses impact tax in two ways. The first is separating 50 % deductible expenses from 100 % deductible expenses. This decision determines how the categories are reported on the tax return and directly impact taxable income. The second is the tax professional's ability to defend the expenses on audit. The ability to defend the expenses is determined by the purpose and documentation that is filed with the expense report.

The 50 % Limitation

The IRS took the position around 10 years ago that meals and entertainment expenses inheritantly include a portion of personal gratification or pleasure. They therefore cut the deduction from 100 % to 50 % on the majority of meal and entertainment costs. Since that time, corporations have had difficulty keeping up with what is 100 % deductible and what is 50 % deductible.

To determine what falls into the 50 % bucket, it is easiest to look at what does not. Costs of meals and entertainment eligible for the 100 % deduction are defined as being for the convenience of the employer. They consequently must be taken on the business premises and must be provided for over 50 % of the employees.

Some corporations capture 50 % and 100 % meals and entertainment expenses using G/L accounts. This, however, is often inaccurate because neither the expense report processor nor the individual incurring the expense is usually versed in tax law. At the very least, the individual incurring the expenses needs to provide adequate documentation on the expense report to ensure proper classification. Another approach is using one of the big four CPA firms that do cost studies to help with this issue.

So far, we have addressed meals and entertainment, which are the only items subject to the 50 % limitation. Travel, lodging, and other nonmeal/entertainment expenses are 100 % deductible and are much easier to assign to G/L accounts.

Note

When configuring R/3 or ECC, it is best to automatically code as much as possible without human intervention and leave the exceptions for personal decisions. Automation can provide consistancy for the majority of the charges and leave fewer decisions.

Information about the transaction must be kept in the system or with the expense record in some way. That takes us to the second way tax departments are impacted by expense reporting, which is in the audit area.

Expense Report Audits

When it comes to expense reporting, the best policy is to prepare for the audit at the time the expense report is filed, which means that questions should be asked concerning the business purpose of the expense. An expense reporting system should therefore be able to answer the following questions.

- **Who incurred the expense?**
  - Name of individual submitting report
  - Street address
  - City
  - State
  - Country
  - ZIP + 4
  - Social security number
  - Personnel number
  - Other individuals present
  - Business relationship to other individuals present
- **What was the purpose of the expense?**
  - Description of activity
  - Type of activity (transportation, meal, entertainment, etc.)
  - Business purpose of activity
  - Employer's convenience checkbox for meals
  - De Minimus fringe checkbox
  - Moving related checkbox

- Recreational event checkbox
- Overtime/group meal checkbox
- Nonemployee reimbursement indicator
- Charitable sports event indicator

- **When did the activity take place?**
  - Date activity began
  - Date activity ended
- **Where was the expense incurred?**
  - Location activity took place
  - Street address
  - City
  - State
  - Country
  - ZIP + 4
  - On business site/off site checkbox
  - Location of origination
  - Location of destination
- **How much did the activity cost?**
  - Amount of the transaction
  - Tax amount on the transaction
  - Currency of the transaction
  - Charge code or department to be billed

Travel Management Modules

Many companies running SAP software use a variety of travel management modules and elect to keep their old expense module even though a travel management application comes with the SAP software they are installing. The reluctance to change systems is an indication of the challenges often experienced in this area. Companies feel that if something is working, it is wise not to change it.

However, the SAP travel management application works well and can be configured to consider all of the requirements outlined so far in this chapter. Further, the travel management module can be reached from the FI or the

HR module in R/3 or ECC. From a tax perspective, it includes the bulk of the information needed for tax audits and can be configured or customized to include anything that is missing.

> **Note**
>
> Often the implementation of the travel management module is done by the HR team as opposed to the FI team.

Figure 10.6 displays the **Travel Expense Manager** screen in SAP's travel management module.

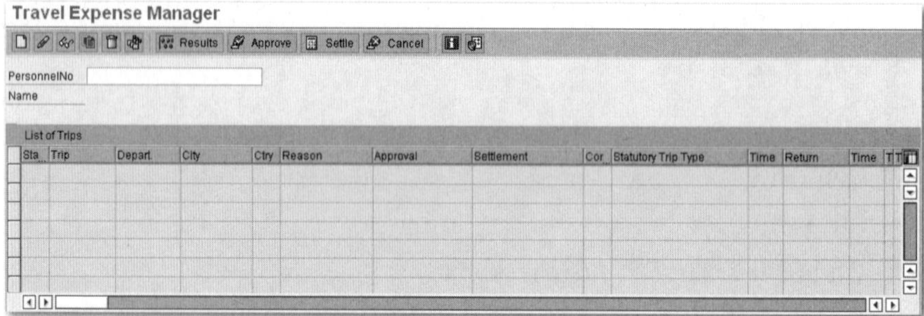

Figure 10.6 Travel Expense Manager

Figure 10.7 shows the entry screen for the expense report.

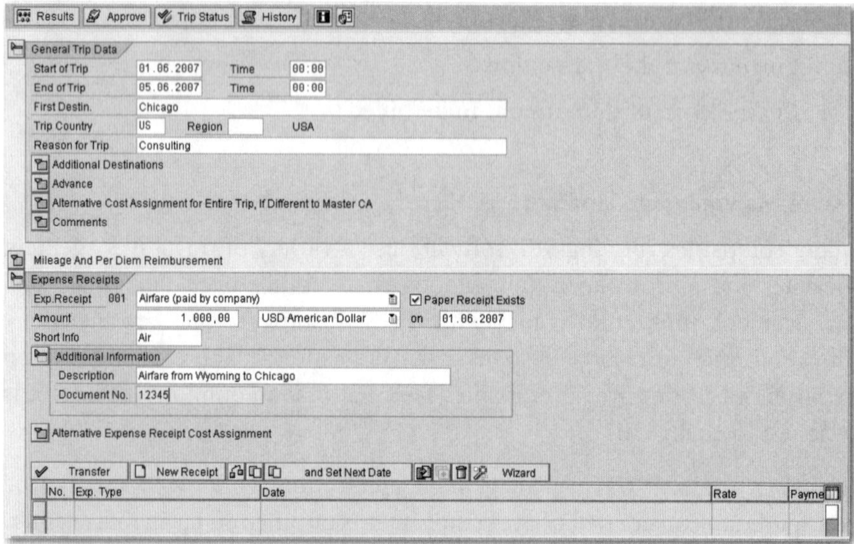

Figure 10.7 Expense Report Entry Screen

10.4 Apportionment

Often, tax department personnel dealing with state income tax have problems getting apportionment information. Let's look at a summary of the basic procedures of apportionment so you can better understand what integration needs to be done in R/3 or ECC.

10.4.1 An Introduction to Apportionment Concepts

Apportionment information is used in most types of taxation but nowhere more than in state income tax. States are looking for additional revenue, and as a result, apportionment calculations are being looked at more and more by state tax audiors.

If you have ever lived and had earnings in two different states in the same year, you have had to do apportionment when filing your personal state income tax return. The personal apportionment formula usually splits taxable earnings based on the number of days lived or worked in each state. Corporate apportionment is aimed at the same thing but has a more complicated formula.

Traditionally, states have required a three-factor formula for corporate apportionment. These three factors are sales, payroll, and property. The factors were applied using a weighting of one-third for each. Over the years, many states, however, have experimented with the factors and the weighting formulas to a degree that the traditional calculations are barely recognizable. Figure 10.8 shows the current corporate formulas for the states, and Figure 10.9 lists the footnotes that accompany Figure 10.8.

Many states have adopted 200 % sales formulas as you can see from Figure 10.8. Some businesses are able to justify apportionment factors based on the nature of their business. Airlines, for example, often use factors different from the traditional ones shown in Figure 10.8.

Some state tax administrators are authorized to have taxpayers use different factors if the state is not collecting what the state tax administrator feels to be their fair share of a corporation's income tax. Provisions adopted by the states such as this are modelled after the Uniform Division of Income for Tax Purposes Act (UDITPA) "equitable apportionment" provision.

STATE APPORTIONMENT OF CORPORATE INCOME

(Formulas for tax year 2007 -- as of January 1, 2007)

State	Formula
ALABAMA *	3 Factor
ALASKA *	3 Factor
ARIZONA * (2)	60% Sales, 20% Property & Payroll
ARKANSAS *	Double wtd. sales
CALIFORNIA *	Double wtd. sales
COLORADO *	3 Factor/Sales & Property
CONNECTICUT	Double wtd. sales/Sales
DELAWARE	3 Factor
FLORIDA	Double wtd. sales
GEORGIA (3)	90% Sales, 5% Property & Payroll
HAWAII *	3 Factor
IDAHO *	Double wtd. sales
ILLINOIS *	Sales
INDIANA (3)	60% Sales, 20% Property & Payroll
IOWA	Sales
KANSAS *	3 Factor
KENTUCKY *	Double wtd. sales
LOUISIANA	Sales
MAINE *	Double wtd. sales
MARYLAND	Double wtd. Sales/Sales
MASSACHUSETTS	Double wtd. sales/Sales
MICHIGAN	92.5% Sales, 3.75% Property & Payroll
MINNESOTA (3)	78% Sales, 11% Property, & Payroll
MISSISSIPPI	Accounting/3 Factor
MISSOURI *	3 Factor/sales
MONTANA *	3 Factor
NEBRASKA	Sales
NEVADA	No State Income Tax
NEW HAMPSHIRE	Double wtd. Sales
NEW JERSEY (1)	Double wtd. Sales
NEW MEXICO *	Double wtd. Sales/3 Factor
NEW YORK (3)	80% Sales, 10% Property & Payroll
NORTH CAROLINA *	Double wtd. sales
NORTH DAKOTA *	3 Factor
OHIO *	60% Sales, 20% Property & Payroll
OKLAHOMA	3 Factor
OREGON *	Sales
PENNSYLVANIA *	60% Sales, 20% Property & Payroll
RHODE ISLAND	Double wtd. Sales
SOUTH CAROLINA (4)	Double wtd. Sales/Sales
SOUTH DAKOTA	No State Income Tax
TENNESSEE *	Double wtd. sales
TEXAS	Sales
UTAH *	3 Factor/Double wtd. Sales
VERMONT	Double wtd. Sales
VIRGINIA	Double wtd. sales
WASHINGTON	No State Income Tax
WEST VIRGINIA *	Double wtd. sales
WISCONSIN * (3)	80% Sales, 10% Property & Payroll
WYOMING	No State Income Tax
DIST. OF COLUMBIA *	3 Factor

Source: Compiled by FTA from various sources.
Note: The formulas listed are for general manufacturing businesses. Some industries have special formula different than those reported. A slash separating two formula's indicate taxpayer option.

** State has adopted substantial portions of the UDITPA.*
(1) A 3-factor formula is used for corporations not subject to the corporation business franchise tax.
(2) For tax years beginning in 2008, formula changes to 70% Sales and 15% Property and Payroll.
(3) State is phasing in a single sales factor. Weightings will change each year until 100% sales factor in 2008 for Georga, New York and Wisconsin, 2001 in Indiana, and 2013 in Minnesota.
(4) Taxpayers are allowed only 20% of the reduced taxes from a single sales factor (40% in 2008).

FEDERATION OF TAX ADMINISTRATORS -- MARCH 2007

Figure 10.8 State Apportionment Formulas (Source: www.taxadmin.org/fta/rate/apport.pdf)

Source: Compiled by FTA from various sources.
Note: The formulas listed are for general manufacturing businesses. Some industries have special formula different than those reported. A slash separating two formula's indicate taxpayer option.

** State has adopted substantial portions of the UDITPA.*
(1) A 3-factor formula is used for corporations not subject to the corporation business franchise tax.
(2) For tax years beginning in 2008, formula changes to 70% Sales and 15% Property and Payroll.
(3) State is phasing in a single sales factor. Weightings will change each year until 100% sales factor in 2008 for Georga, New York and Wisconsin, 2001 in Indiana, and 2013 in Minnesota.
(4) Taxpayers are allowed only 20% of the reduced taxes from a single sales factor (40% in 2008).

Figure 10.9 Footnotes for Information Shown in Figure 10.8

Tax administrators may require the following information regarding all or any part of a taxpayer's business, written as follows under Section 18:

- Separate accounting
- The exclusion of any one or more of the factors

- The inclusion of one or more additional factors, which will fairly represent the taxpayer's business activity in this state
- The employment of any other method to effectuate an equitable allocation and apportionment of the taxpayer's income

10.4.2 Capturing Apportionment Factors

Regardless of what the weighting formula and the factors are, your tax department will know what needs to be captured by the SAP system for apportionment. Capturing the data is the only requirement from R/3 or ECC. The SAP system is not designed or expected to work the formulas.

Capturing apportionment factors appears as easy as setting up G/L accounts, but nothing is ever as simple as it appears. For example, the sales factor is defined differently in different states. Payroll requirements may differ between work location, office location, and home location. Some taxpayers have home location data but have difficulty determining a work location for employees who travel constantly. And property is generally defined in different ways in different states.

Complicating things even more is that payroll data is often in a different system or at least in a different SAP instance and therefore requires a different approach. A different fixed asset system may also be used.

Integrating apportionment into SAP should therefore take the following steps:

1. Understand all of the factors (sales, payroll, and property) used within the corporation for apportionment. This will be more expansive than the three factors mentioned previously due to the different state definitions of the main three factors.
2. Devise a way to capture the apportionment factors by location. A location level below the state level may be needed in some cases.
3. Develop reports that retrieve the necessary data from the SAP system in a format useful to the tax department.

10.4.3 Apportionment Reports

Apportionment reports usually require selection criteria and formats that do not lend themselves to standard SAP reporting. They therefore become custom reports requiring report specification documents and are added to the project development requirements. Specification documents have deadlines that need to be met and approvals that need to be obtained. Tax department personnel have a role in assisting with specification documents and should be notified ahead of time that they will need to play a role in preparing needed documentation. Specification documents are tracked in project management software such as Solution Manager, so tax integrators must also be profficient with that tool.

You can use DART reports to get the necessary data, but usually not in the nice clean format previously existing custom reports offered. You should remember that DART is used after the live data for the accounting period has been purged from the system. At that time, the DART extracts contain the only information available. Custom SAP reports can no longer be run for the same accounting period. Also, limitations in the DART view tool may require several reports to obtain the data. Adding a stronger data mining tool to the extract environment as mentioned in Chapter 6 makes it much easier.

10.5 R&D Tax Credits

The R&D tax credit for some companies exceeds $50 million per year. This is a lot of money for the corporation and a lot of money for the tax department. The tax credit is calculated using a base year formula compared to current R&D expenditures. The base years are usually not a factor or a problem for SAP software. The main emphasis then is on capturing the current R&D expenditures. Generally speaking, three elements of cost need to be captured to calculate the credit, as follows:

Note

Again, this chapter only focuses on what needs to be done in R/3 or ECC to get the credit and file the tax form. For more information about R&D tax credits, see *www.irs.gov* and do a search on "Research and Development Tax Credit."

- Payroll data
- Supplies
- Contract labor

This seems easy enough, but again, nothing is ever that simple. All of the elements have to be tied to a given R&D project. The project therefore must be defined in SAP as a cost object of some kind. The IRS prefers that project accounting be used to neatly capture all of the costs for R&D projects, but using project accounting usually results in a lower credit because much of the R&D work that goes on in a corporation is captured by cost centers or internal orders. Tax departments therefore do not feel bound to use cost centers or projects to calculate the credit but may use a mixture of the two.

10.5.1 Labor Cost

Labor costs have to be linked to the projects the employees worked on. On the surface, it would seem that finding out who worked on a project and then totaling the W-2 income for each would get you the correct labor cost per project. However, there are several things wrong with this perception:

- Engineers tend to work on multiple projects during the year.
- Supervisory wages above the first line are not allowed in whole for the credit unless it can be shown that the individual worked exclusively on the project and had some impact.
- W-2 wages cannot be linked to projects unless a contemporanious time tracking system is used by the corporation. The IRS loves contemporanious time tracking systems. Even with a time tracking system, the tie to W-2 wages involves an allocation based on hours on the project versus total hours for the year. Attempting to take each individual and track the W-2 wages and the total hours worked to arrive at an hourly rate for each project is a daunting task if you have 400 or 500 projects and hundreds of employees. Many corporations will use a blended rate per hour for this reason.
- Wage detail may not be in the same SAP instance or even in an SAP system. In these situations, wage data must be brought into the SAP system, but it is often at a summarized level that may not be low enough for the R&D calculation.
- Labor costs allocated to projects often contain a markup that has to be removed from the total before doing the calculation. This is only a factor if labor costs are captured from the cost object and not linked to the employee W-2 and allocated on an hourly basis. Capturing total labor at the cost object is a frequently followed practice but lacks the link to the W-2 that the IRS prefers. Capturing labor at the cost object still requires a time tracking system to show the employees that make up the labor dollars. In the absence of a time tracking system, a survey must be done of employees that gives an estimate of time worked on the project. In this case, you will probably only recover a percentage of the expenses on audit.

It seems clear then that the best way to handle payroll issues regarding the R&D tax credit is to maintain a contemporanious time tracking system. If this is not done within the SAP system, there is little more that tax integrators can do but maintain G/L accounts for salary data and divide out supervisory labor for special attention. If project labor is allocated to projects or other cost objects using an hourly rate based on anything other than actual direct labor hours, tax integrators can assist with removing the markup, but audit adjustments should be anticipated.

10.5.2 Supplies

If supplies can be captured in a G/L account and linked to the R&D project, then you are done with capturing supply-related data. There are some nuances regarding computer equipment dedicated to the project, but the tax department will handle this aspect.

10.5.3 Contract Labor

Contract labor and consulting costs can also be captured in G/L accounts but still need to be linked to the project. Tax integrators need to make sure the G/L accounts are set up and that cost objects will be used to capture R&D costs. Related consulting charges then need to be charged to the cost object and adequate descriptive information maintained.

10.5.4 R&D Reporting

Typically, you don't have to develop specialized R&D reports as part of an SAP implementation. Tax departments can take data from standardized R/3 or ECC reports and arrange the figures using Microsoft Excel or Access. A great deal of work coming up with qualified research expenditures is gathering information concerning the development process and the process of experimentation. Much of the determination does not lend itself to inclusion in an SAP system, and therefore general financial data is usually taken from the system and specific reports completed in other tools.

10.6 FAS 109, FAS 123R, and Other Accounting Issues

Accounting standards boards have been coming up with accounting methods that have challenged electronic accounting systems for years. Over the years, SAP has continually improved its software in response to some of these pronouncements. This is especially true in the leasing area. All of these accounting issues are considered by the IRS and often adopted for tax accounting.

FAS 109 specifically relates to tax accounting and deferred tax issues related to the income tax provision. When doing tax integration, there is little that can be done concerning these issues within the SAP system. Most companies either purchase external software or perform the calculation manually. In either case, however, plans for downloading information or creating necessary reports must be made to enable the calculation to be completed. Additional plans must also be made if interfaces back to SAP are to be built or manual information needs to be uploaded.

123R, dealing with employee equity instruments, is also difficult to track even with the SAP Treasury module. If a third-party treasury system is maintained, there isn't much need to load data at a detail level into SAP. Summary input can be done using standard SAP functionality.

M-1 Automation

Many companies have hundreds of Ms that require adjustments at year end. If you have not dealt with corporate income tax, M-1s and M-2s refer to schedules on the fourth page of IRS Form 1120 where adjustments between taxable income and book income are entered. Corporations may have hundreds of adjustments of this sort that are collectively referred to as "Ms."

Example

One project for one large company had more than 300 legal entities and was doing Ms at three different levels within the organization. In situations like this, tax departments sometimes build a database or tax warehouse to keep track of tax information and manually perform some of the calculations that are difficult to keep up with.

If done correctly, a tax warehouse can be useful for tax data retention and can also automate some of the workload and recurring adjustments such as M-1s. Some of the calculations, such as those discussed concerning accounting pronouncements, may also be added there. Further, some accounting and consulting firms have created packaged products in these areas that may also be helpful.

Note

If you embark on a course of putting SAP system data into a tax warehouse to automate some of these calculations, be advised that it is a big project that takes a huge commitment. It might be a good idea to find resource people who are experienced with these kinds of projects.

10.7 Summary

SAP systems were not originally built to handle U.S. taxes. However, since the early versions of SAP software, SAP has added functionality that has improved the software from a tax standpoint. This is clearly evident, for example, when you look at travel expense and lease accounting. At the same time, tax professionals faced with SAP implementations have to ensure that they get the information they need regarding new tax legislation and accounting pronouncements. In this chapter, we discussed the importance of the domestic production activity deduction and the R&D tax credit. Both of these tax breaks can result in savings for corporations. Ideas and information concerning how to improve the data from the SAP system were discussed.

Chapter 11 will lead us away from income tax and into a discussion of property tax and what can be done in ECC to integrate this very jurisdictional-based tax into the SAP system.

Although no certified property tax products work seamlessly with SAP software, integration can be accomplished nonetheless to improve the quality of data used in the property tax calculation. Attention to the cost buildup of assets is a key within SAP software that can save corporations money and contribute to the business case for the project.

11 Property Tax

Property tax is heavily jurisdictionally based, similar to most other U.S. taxes. Most of us are familiar with the property tax calculation because we have to pay property tax on the homes we own. If understanding mil rates and assessment percentages challenges you concerning your home, imagine having to deal with 50,000 assets and 10,000 or 20,000 tax jurisdictions. That's the challenge a corporate property tax manager must face.

However, the property tax calculation is relatively simple when you understand the concept of a mil rate and how assessments are done in various jurisdictions. Further, the challenge in R/3 or ECC is not making the calculation — because the system will not do that for you — but keeping track of property acquisitions, values, dispositions, abandonments, and depreciation. We already discussed many of these processes when discussing asset management in Chapter 4. In this chapter, we will discuss many of the concepts in more detail, especially as they relate to property tax. Let's start by discussing the asset cost buildup for property tax purposes.

11.1 Asset Cost Buildup

Many assets have a variety of cost layers that add up to the total cost of the asset. Tax jurisdictions differ in the way these layers are treated for property tax purposes. Some of the costs that comprise total asset cost include the following:

- Sales tax
- Freight and delivery fees

- Installation fees
- Embedded software
- Labor
- The actual acquisition cost of the asset

11.1.1 Challenges to Asset Cost Buildup

The challenge with breaking cost layers out is that they are often not broken out neatly on a vendor invoice for purchased assets. Constructed assets have so many invoices that it is difficult to break the cost out. Thus, the tendency is to book everything to one line in the asset account. Although this is the easiest approach, a great deal of money is at stake, so it's worth putting the effort into breaking out costs. But first let's look at some of the problems confronting detailed asset buildup:

- Costs have to be broken down at the time they are charged to the project. Many times, the different characteristics of cost are not known at the time a purchase order is processed.
- If costs are detailed when charged to the project, it is difficult to retain the detail when settling to the asset account.
- Detail on incoming invoices is often ignored, and the whole amount is charged to a single asset account. Change management and training is required to make sure the detail is not ignored.
- Electronic invoices that include detail may require customization to enable processing in R/3 or ECC.

11.1.2 What Is Needed in R/3 or ECC

To accomplish detailed cost buildup in R/3 or ECC, a number of things need to happen:

- Procedures or processes must be implemented to enable cost layers to be identified and split out when the costs are charged to the project.
- Cost layers must be retained when settling to the asset account.
- Assets must first be assigned to an ECC asset class. As mentioned before, asset classes within SAP systems determine the useful life and depreciation method for that category of asset. Segregating assets by asset class allows tax departments to depreciate the asset appropriately.

- Cost layers within a given asset class must be identifiable when looking at the final asset. This can be done by segregating the layers using different cost elements on settlement.
- The system must have the capability to automatically record incoming electronic invoices from turn-key contractors. Some companies have the capability to automatically enter vendor turn-key invoices via electronic spreadsheets. SAP R/3 or ECC must be configured or customized to handle these types of invoices.

Segregating asset costs takes two forms, and both are beneficial for property tax. The first is illustrated in "Example One" that follows this paragraph, which deals with breaking cost down into the proper depreciable classes. The second we have talked about earlier in this chapter and involves breaking out cost layers that are nontaxable in some property tax juridictions. This is illustrated in "Example Two."

Example One

Acme Corporation executes a turn-key contract with Scottland Construction to construct a mineral extraction plant in Wyoming for a cost of 500 million dollars. Two scenarios exist for depreciation purposes:

- The invoice is booked as one asset for $500 million and depreciated over 39 years.
- The invoice is broken down into component assets as shown in Table 11.1.

Asset	Cost	# Years for Depreciation
Building	$350 million	39 years
Machinery and equipment	$100 million	7 years
Computer equipment	$50 million	5 years

Table 11.1 Breaking Invoice Components Out by Asset, Cost, and the Number of Years Components Will Depreciate

Under the first scenario, depreciation during the first year using straight-line would result in $12.821 million of depreciation. The second scenario would result in straight line depreciation during the first year of $33.260 million; a tax savings of $20.439 million. Actual tax savings would be much higher due to bonus depreciation and accelerated depreciation methods.

This example illustrates the tax savings in income tax by segregating assets by asset class. Savings would also result from property tax due to the cost segregation. It is also possible to save on property tax by segregating parts of an asset even though the asset class does not change. Charges to an asset must be detailed to identify the characteristics discussed earlier concerning asset cost buildup. Many property tax jurisdictions allow the cost elements discussed here to be subtracted from the total cost of the asset before applying the property tax rate.

Example Two

Using the scenario outlined in "Example One," machinery and equipment totaled $100 million. If a mill levy of .80 were applied to an appraised value of $100 million, the tax would amount to $80,000. Acme segregates its nontaxable asset components as shown in Table 11.2.

Asset component	Amount
Sales and Use Tax	$ 1.0 million
Freight	$ 2.5 million
Labor	$20.0 million
Installation	$ 5.0 million
Software	$12.5 million
Total	$41.0 million

Table 11.2 Acme's Nontaxable Asset Components

By breaking out the nontaxable components of $41.0 million, Acme will save $32,800 per year.

11.1.3 Configuring the System to Make It Happen

When discussing fixed assets in Chapter 4, we talked about the advantages of running all assets through a project code and the Asset under Construction (AuC) account. The AuC account in an SAP system is an asset class that represents a holding account until settlement to the final resting place can be made. The AuC account is generally combined with the project system within R/3 or ECC. When using project accounting, all of the costs related to a constructed project are assigned to a project code. Purchased assets are not normally run through a project code, but doing so can result in several benefits:

- Constructed assets appropriately fall under this scenario.
- The acquisition volumes created by central purchasing departments can lead to problems determining the location of the asset for accounting treatment for a month or two following purchase. Charging to an AuC account creates a holding area for the asset until accurate accounting decisions can be made.
- Accounting treatment for bulk asset acquisitions and drop shipments can be determined accurately while the asset sits in the AuC account.
- Through the use of cost elements, the various aspects of an asset acquisition can be divided out in the asset account. For example, sales tax, freight, embedded software, and installation costs can be recorded separately from the basic asset value. These items receive different treatment in many property tax jurisdictions and can lead to huge savings for asset-intensive organizations.

The trick then is to activate the project system and to train the organization to make all asset purchases through a project using the AuC asset class. Asset settlement then must be done in a way that retains the detail. Retaining the detail can be done through the proper use of G/L accounts or WBS elements within the project. The downside to this approach involves primarily the rigor needed to stay on top of the AuC account.

11.2 External Property Tax Software

The R/3 or ECC jurisdiction code can be constructed to work at a variety of levels, but generally it is identified using the five-digit ZIP code. While this can work effectively for sales and use tax, often property tax managers want to go to a street address level. Some property tax systems, although not connected to the SAP system, have been designed to use the SAP jurisdiction code, which in some cases cannot be totally relied upon for accurate property tax jurisdictional information. The challenge is to figure out what information needs to be sent to an external property tax system. Let's look at how to do this.

Project Approach

Dealing with external property tax systems requires the following steps:

1. Performing an analysis of what data needs to be sent to the external system.
2. Deciding whether to use a download and upload approach or to develop an electronic interface.
3. Deciding how to bring information back from the external system so tax jurisdictions can be paid and liability accounts relieved.

1. Analytical Phase

As a result of multiple jurisdiction codes ocurring for some five-digit ZIP codes, another code is often needed to pinpoint the location for property tax accounting. As it is, SAP software does a good job with location information. In addition to the jurisdiction code, the software has a location code, building codes, and address information. If property tax requires any of this information, however, plans must be made ahead of time to populate these fields in a way that is useful to the external system. Regardless of the location or site code sent to the external system, complete address information is generally sent as well.

After an accurate way has been devised to identify the proper tax jurisdiction, care needs to be given to identify the property. The majority of property will be in the SAP asset management application, which needs to be examined to determine the fields sent to the external system. Some assets subject to property tax, however, are not capitalized and tracked in the fixed asset system. Corporations have hundreds of low-value assets that have been expensed for financial purposes and are not tracked in fixed assets. Information concerning these property items must be transferred to the external property tax system for accurate compliance.

Identifying the asset base to send to the external system is a major step. The next step is to identify the proper information about the assets and the level of information to send to the external property tax system If assets can be grouped into consistent asset types permissable to a jurisdiction, it is acceptable to send over summarized information. In many cases, detailed information may need to be sent across the interface.

The identification of field information concerning property items should have been done when the detailed tax matrix discussed in Chapter 1 was prepared. The data elements identified at that time then need to be compared to the fields required by the external property tax system. Making this comparison should provide assurance that nothing has been missed. Table 11.3 lists 40 data elements or fields that are examples of what might be passed to external property tax systems.

Item #	Data Element	Item #	Data Element
1	Company Code	21	Leased/Owned
2	Location Code	22	Serial #
3	Asset Class	23	G/L Account
4	Asset_Number	24	Model
5	Description	25	License #
6	Date Placed in Service	26	GVW
7	Date Purchased	27	Style
8	Retirement Date	28	Unit Value
9	Historical Cost	29	Sq. Feet
10	Sales Tax Amount	30	#units
11	Freight	31	#units
12	Installation Fees	32	Project Name
13	Embedded Software Amount	33	Parent Asset
14	Labor	34	Parent Asset Number
15	Net book Value	35	Address 1
16	Salvage Value	36	Address 2
17	Depreciation Expense	37	County Name
18	Accumulated Depreciation	38	City
19	Depreciation Method	39	State
20	Useful Life	40	ZIP Code

Table 11.3 Property Tax Data Elements

The data elements related to depreciation shown in Table 11.3 may not need to be passed if the external property tax system is going to calculate and maintain the values for property tax depreciation. In some cases, property tax depreciation is tracked in the SAP system, but in many more cases, an external property tax system takes care of depreciation. Property tax systems are usually built to handle the differing useful lives across the multiple jurisdictions and accessed values.

It is also helpful to pass additional information concerning asset additions, retirements, and transfers to the external system. This can be done using the asset transaction type field in R/3 or ECC.

2. Deciding on an Approach to the Interface

Most companies elect to get a download from the SAP system and then upload the data into the external property tax system. This is initally less expensive and less time-consuming than an electronic interface but needs to be weighed against the cost of making the manual effort over the life of the system.

Regardless of the approach, functional specifications and mapping have to take place. If a manual interface is chosen, the information going to the external system must be defined in the analysis phase so downloads can be developed. The design will be more complicated with an electronic interface, but both deal with removing data from one system and passing it to another.

3. Returning Data to the SAP System

After the external property tax system has made its calculations, data needs to be brought back to the SAP system. The amount of data depends on the functionality of the external system. Some property tax systems are capable of not only creating compliance reports but also of cutting checks to the tax jurisdictions.

Caution

Only R/3 or ECC should be used for cutting checks to jurisdictional vendors because SAP systems are designed to handle things like that. Having the liabilties brought back into the SAP software and having the checks cut as they would be for any other vendor is preferable. If checks are cut from the external system, accounting is still required in R/3 or ECC so that financial statements will be accurate.

When returning information to the SAP software, enough information must be brought back from the property tax system to identify the jurisdictional vendor and the amount of payment, and to remove tax liabilities set up in the SAP system. Returning data to SAP will ensure proper financial accounting.

11.3 Summary

SAP software has no provisions for calculating property tax or preparing property tax returns, and no certified bolt-on software exists. Large corporations usually use external software programs that are interfaced to SAP either through a manual download and upload procedure or through an electronic interface. SAP does provide differing levels of location information, and the level of location data needed for property tax must be considered during the implementation. Not all property is captured in the SAP asset management module, so attention needs to be given to low-value assets and how they are tracked within the SAP software. Interfaces to external property tax systems require a plan that includes an analysis phase, a decision concerning the type of interface, and decisions regarding the movement of data back into the SAP system to facilitate necessary accounting treatment.

In Chapter 12, we start our discussion of sales and use tax and concentrate on the tools within R/3 or ECC that aid with the tax calculation either inside or outside of the SAP system. We will also discuss tax procedures TAXUS and TAXUSJ for calculating tax inside the SAP system.

Sales and use tax gets more attention than any other area of tax during an SAP implementation. In this chapter, you will become familiar with the basic tools in R/3 and ECC to configure and calculate sales and use tax within the SAP system.

12 Calculating Sales and Use Tax Within the SAP System

Nearly every corporation regardless of its size and business is required to either collect *sales* tax on its sales or pay *use* tax on its purchases. Sales and use tax is referred to as an indirect tax because it is not paid directly to a taxing jurisdiction. Sales tax is collected from the buyer by the seller of goods and later remitted to a tax jurisdiction. Use tax is either paid to the vendor at the time of purchase or accrued by the purchasing corporation and remitted to the taxing authority. Corporations are continously buying and selling goods as part of their business and are therefore subject to sales and use tax laws. They are required to collect sales tax on sales and pay use tax on purchases.

In simple terms, sales and use tax statutes are legislated or created at multiple levels, and the tax is generally a combination of taxes levied by city, county, and state taxing juridictions. Governments have also granted additional organizations the power to tax, such as metropolitan transit authorities.

12.1 The Sales and Use Tax Calculation

Most jurisdictions base the calculation of sales and use tax on three factors:

- **The jurisdiction in which the buyer takes possession (Ship to Jurisdiction)**
  We have talked about the importance of jurisdictional information in Chapters 3, 4, and 8, and only need to emphasize here that appropriate sales and use tax compliance absolutly requires good *ship from* and *ship to* jurisdictional information. We also discussed that assigning jurisdiction codes to master file records facilitates jurisdictional reporting in SAP. In

the remainder of this chapter, you will learn how to put jurisdictional data together with other data elements to obtain proper tax rates and amounts.

- **The ultimate use of the material, product, or service**
  Juridictions have developed tax legislation and tax rates based on the type of material, product, or service changing hands during a transaction. Jurisdictions have varying rules concerning what materials or services are taxable in their locality. A material, product, or service that is exempt from tax in one jurisdiction is probably taxable in another. This chapter will discuss ways SAP software and third-party tax packages receive ultimate use information and how they act upon it.
- **The tax status of the legal entity that is purchasing the product**
  Many legal entities do not pay tax in certain localities for different reasons. Some entities are tax exempt because of their legal entity status, such as churches and charitable orgainizations. Other entities are not taxed because they have resale certificates that prevent them from paying tax on purchases because they collect tax from the consumer when they sell the goods. Still other companies have obtained direct pay permits giving them the authority to remit their tax liability directly to the jurisdiction instead of paying it to the seller and having him remit it. Regardless of the situation, knowing the legal entity is a must for accurate tax compliance. If your SAP system is configured properly, legal entity information is easily obtained.

12.2 Tax Procedures and the Condition Technique

Current SAP software contains tax procedures for many countries. Tax procedures are activated on a countrywide basis. A company code in Spain cannot, for example, have a different tax procedure than any other company code in the same country. Tax procedures are built similar to pricing procedures in the SAP system. They use the *condition technique*, which allows flexibility to change the procedure as necessary, although it is usually not necessary to change the standard SAP tax procedures. If change is necessary, it is best to copy the standard tax procedure under a new name and make the changes to the newly created procedure.

Tax Procedure TAXUSJ is shown in Figure 12.1. In this case, you can see four levels of condition types. You will also note that the condition types are arranged in groups depending on the type of tax (sales or use) and whether tax is paid to the vendor or self assessed. Account keys are shown on the right that assist with account determination.

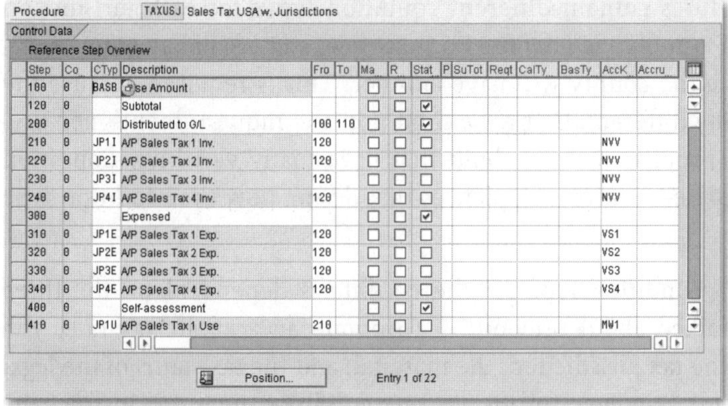

Procedure: TAXUSJ Sales Tax USA w. Jurisdictions

Control Data

Reference Step Overview

Step	Co	CTyp	Description	Fro	To	Ma	R	Stat	P	SuTot	Reqt	CalTy	BasTy	AccK	Accru
100	0	BASB	[illegible]se Amount			☐	☐	☐							
120	0		Subtotal			☐	☐	☑							
200	0		Distributed to G/L	100	110	☐	☐	☑							
210	0	JP1I	A/P Sales Tax 1 Inv.	120		☐	☐	☐						NVV	
220	0	JP2I	A/P Sales Tax 2 Inv.	120		☐	☐	☐						NVV	
230	0	JP3I	A/P Sales Tax 3 Inv.	120		☐	☐	☐						NVV	
240	0	JP4I	A/P Sales Tax 4 Inv.	120		☐	☐	☐						NVV	
300	0		Expensed			☐	☐	☑							
310	0	JP1E	A/P Sales Tax 1 Exp.	120		☐	☐	☐						VS1	
320	0	JP2E	A/P Sales Tax 2 Exp.	120		☐	☐	☐						VS2	
330	0	JP3E	A/P Sales Tax 3 Exp.	120		☐	☐	☐						VS3	
340	0	JP4E	A/P Sales Tax 4 Exp.	120		☐	☐	☐						VS4	
400	0		Self-assessment			☐	☐	☑							
410	0	JP1U	A/P Sales Tax 1 Use	210		☐	☐	☐						MW1	

Position... Entry 1 of 22

Figure 12.1 Tax Procedure TAXUSJ

A detailed analysis of how complicated tax procedures function is beyond the scope of this book, but the following paragraphs contain a summary of some of the basic elements and principles.

Tax procedures are comprised of different condition types that define the variables that make up the tax calculation. General examples of tax condition types are shown in Figure 12.2.

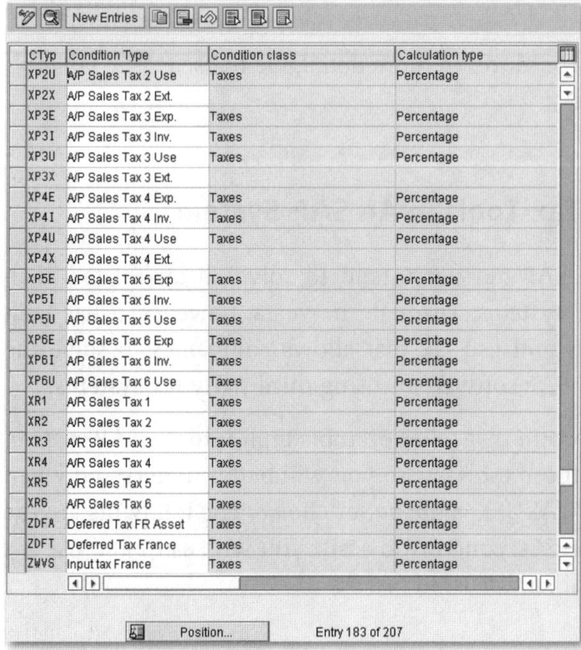

New Entries

CTyp	Condition Type	Condition class	Calculation type
XP2U	A/P Sales Tax 2 Use	Taxes	Percentage
XP2X	A/P Sales Tax 2 Ext.		
XP3E	A/P Sales Tax 3 Exp.	Taxes	Percentage
XP3I	A/P Sales Tax 3 Inv.	Taxes	Percentage
XP3U	A/P Sales Tax 3 Use	Taxes	Percentage
XP3X	A/P Sales Tax 3 Ext.		
XP4E	A/P Sales Tax 4 Exp.	Taxes	Percentage
XP4I	A/P Sales Tax 4 Inv.	Taxes	Percentage
XP4U	A/P Sales Tax 4 Use	Taxes	Percentage
XP4X	A/P Sales Tax 4 Ext.		
XP5E	A/P Sales Tax 5 Exp	Taxes	Percentage
XP5I	A/P Sales Tax 5 Inv.	Taxes	Percentage
XP5U	A/P Sales Tax 5 Use	Taxes	Percentage
XP6E	A/P Sales Tax 6 Exp	Taxes	Percentage
XP6I	A/P Sales Tax 6 Inv.	Taxes	Percentage
XP6U	A/P Sales Tax 6 Use	Taxes	Percentage
XR1	A/R Sales Tax 1	Taxes	Percentage
XR2	A/R Sales Tax 2	Taxes	Percentage
XR3	A/R Sales Tax 3	Taxes	Percentage
XR4	A/R Sales Tax 4	Taxes	Percentage
XR5	A/R Sales Tax 5	Taxes	Percentage
XR6	A/R Sales Tax 6	Taxes	Percentage
ZDFA	Defered Tax FR Asset	Taxes	Percentage
ZDFT	Deferred Tax France	Taxes	Percentage
ZWVS	Input tax France	Taxes	Percentage

Position... Entry 183 of 207

Figure 12.2 Some SAP Condition Types

U.S. tax procedures contain different condition types for each jurisdiction comprising the cumulative tax rate. For example, a city will have one condition type, while the county will have another. This is required because the tax rate is usually different. Using the condition technique as mentioned previously allows procedures to be built that have many variables. Condition types are comprised of access sequences that define how the condition type is arrived at.

For example, a condition type for the tax rate is dependent on the three types of data talked about previously. To obtain an accurate tax rate, you need to know the tax jurisdiction, the material, and the tax status of the legal entity. The access sequence for the tax rate condition type will instruct the system to look for condition records that match the jurisdiction code, the material, and the legal entity. When a matching entry is found, the condition record is chosen, and the proper tax rate is selected.

The tax procedure also contains account keys that determine the general ledger (G/L) account determination for each condition type. The following are the three U.S. tax procedures shipped with SAP software:

- TAXUS
- TAXUSJ
- TAXUSX

Before we look at these procedures in more detail, we'll discuss the tax tools you have available to you.

12.3 Overview of Tax Tools in An SAP System

As discussed previously, SAP did not intend to solve all tax-related challenges within R/3 or ECC systems. Through the years, however, it has built an approach to U.S. sales and use tax that allows companies to solve the issues either internally in SAP software or using third-party tax systems.

TAXUSJ is an internal solution that relies on tools built into the SAP system. We'll now explore what those tools are so you will better understand when to use TAXUSJ and when TAXUSX is the better choice. The following are the codes or tools that R/3 or ECC contains to assist you with sales and use tax calculations. Each one will be discussed briefly:

- Company code
- Tax jurisdiction code

- Tax code
- Tax category code on the G/L master
- Tax indicator on the G/L master
- Tax classification on the material master
- Tax indicator on the material master
- Materials Management (MM) condition records
- Sales and distribution (SD) condition records
- Customer tax classification code

12.3.1 Company Code

The importance of the company code was discussed in Chapters 1, 2, 3, and 8. Modern multinational corporations are rarely comprised of only one legal entity. Many are comprised of hundreds. Sales and use tax returns are filed on a legal entity basis, which means that an SAP company code is generally set up to capture transactions between that legal entity and external parties.

12.3.2 Tax Jurisdiction Code

By now, you should understand that SAP approaches *ship from* and *ship to* information by providing fields for tax jurisdiction codes on nearly every master file in the system. When jurisdiction codes are populated in the master files, a trail is provided from the manufacture of goods to their sale and from the purchase of goods to their consumption. Jurisdictional tracking is at the heart of SAP's attempt to handle U.S. tax requirements.

12.3.3 Tax Code

SAP approaches sales and use taxation within the system by using tax codes. Tax codes are configurable and are designed to fulfill a variety of functions in the system. The following functions are all leveraged when using procedure TAXUSJ. The tax code plays a lesser role when used with procedure TAXUSX.

When using TAXUSJ, jurisdiction codes are assigned to the tax codes, and the tax rate is maintained in the condition records for the code. A TAXUSJ tax code can be used with multiple jurisdictions because multiple condition records exist, but when the jurisdiction code from the transaction and the transaction tax code are combined, the proper condition record is selected to yield the proper rate. TAXUSX tax codes are not assigned jurisdiction codes or tax rates. They are maintained in the external system.

Several tax codes are shipped with standard SAP software and have names that are not conducive to U.S. taxation. SAP was developed in Germany and is used internationally where many companies follow tax methodologies similar to VAT instead of U.S. sales and use tax. The names of the standard codes can be changed, however, or new codes set up to to satisfy U.S. norms. Let's explore the functions next.

Choosing Between Sales and Use Tax

Different tax codes are used for sales tax than for use tax. Tax codes are different depending on account determination. Since different G/L accounts are used when tax is paid versus when it is accrued or collected, a different tax code is necessary. The tax codes shipped with SAP software are shown in Figure 12.3.

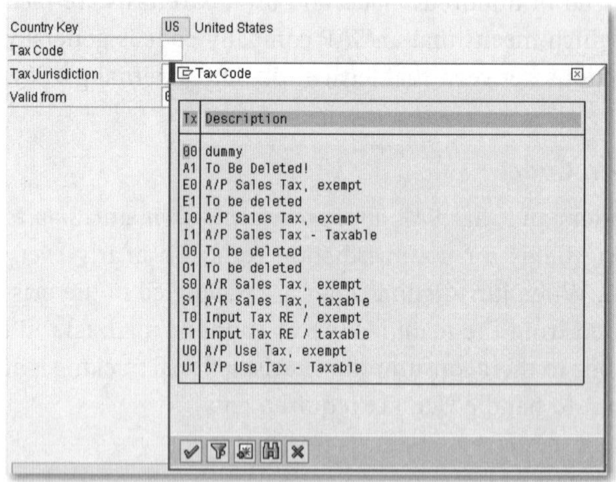

Figure 12.3 Tax Codes Shipped with SAP

Discerning Whether Tax on a Transaction Is Determined Within R/3 and ECC or by an External System

When tax codes are set up as part of a configuration using TAXUSX, the properties for the code contains a field that indicates whether tax is calculated in SAP or by an external system. This is not the case using TAXUSJ because it is entirely an internal R/3 or ECC calculation.

Figure 12.4 shows the properties for a TAXUSJ tax code. The most important property, the **Tax type** box, allows you to indicate whether the tax code is used for input tax, output tax, or both.

Note

The other properties are rarely used in the United States, but they are used extensively for VAT internationally.

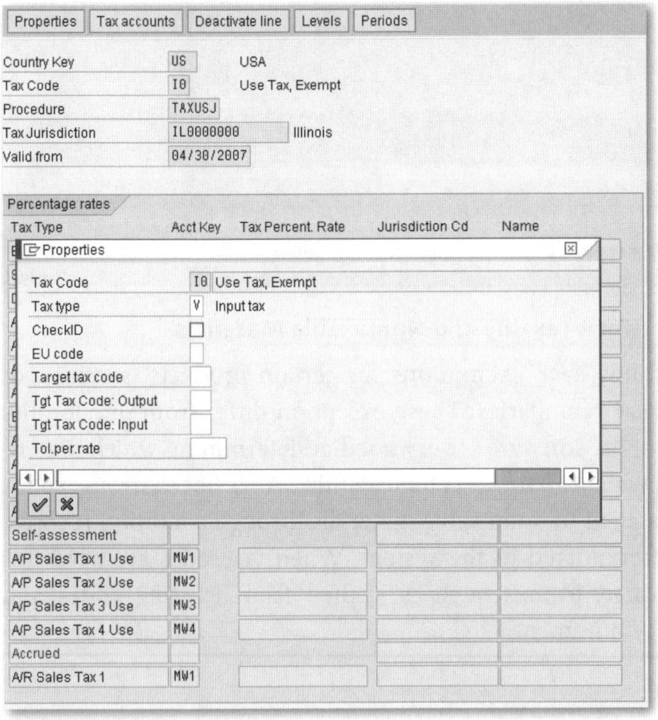

Figure 12.4 Tax Code Properties

Controlling the Account Determination for the Tax Amount Portion of the Transaction

Account codes are mapped to G/L accounts to determine consistancy in the entry of the tax amount. Account determination is set up during configuration of the tax code. Figure 12.5 illustrates this step in the configuration process.

Account determination for a tax code is based on the account or **Transaction** key that can be seen in Figure 12.5. Transaction keys are defined in the system and cannot be changed by the user. Each condition type in the tax code has a transaction or account key. This means that for procedure TAXUSJ the different parts of the tax rate (state, county, city, MTA) can be posted to four different G/L accounts. In practice, only one G/L account is generally used.

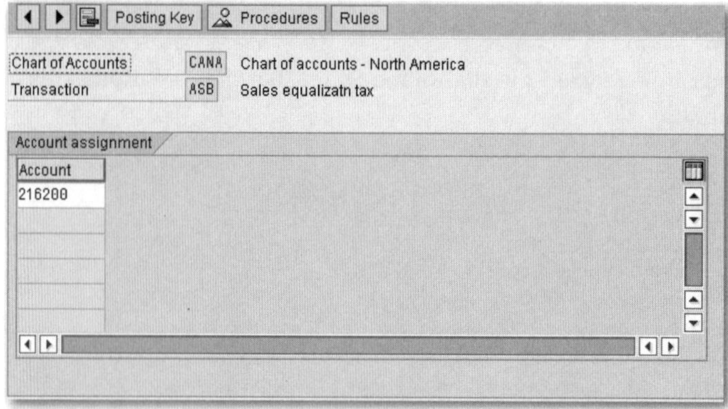

Figure 12.5 Setting Up Account Determination for a Tax Code

Differentiating Between Taxable and Nontaxable Materials

Many tax jurisdictions have exemptions for certain products, services, or materials within their boundaries. These exception differ from one locality to another. External tax software is very good at determining which materials are taxable and which are not. Tax logic within SAP is not as strong, so tax codes are often assigned to nontaxable materials through condition records, so they can be differentiated in the system. When tax codes are used this way, they are created from scratch or copied from existing codes and changed to fit the requirement.

Additional Tax Code Configuration

We have discussed tax code properties and the configuration needed for account assignment, however, additional steps exist. Figure 12.6 illustrates additional configurations for tax codes, which will be discussed in more detail in this section.

As mentioned previously, tax procedures contain condition types for each layer of tax, for example, state, county, city, Metropolitan Transit Authority (MTA), and so on. TAXUSJ will hold up to four layers of tax. Condition types also determine the base amount to apply the tax rate percentage. When tax is calculated by R/3 or ECC, the condition records need values to react appropriately. Each tax code is configured to supply the tax procedure with the correct information. Tax codes are also set up using condition records. The condition records within the tax code correspond to the condition types within the tax procedure and tell the tax procedure how to handle tax when that tax code is used as part of a transaction.

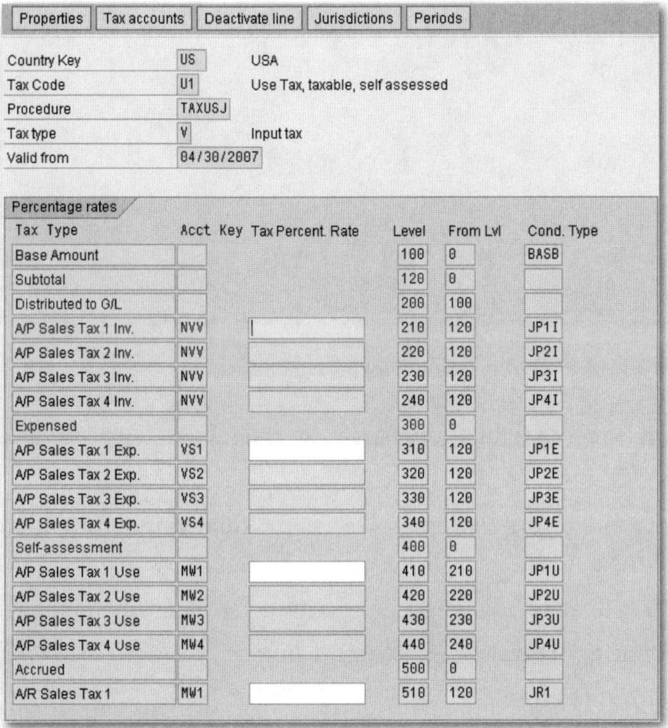

Tax Type	Acct Key	Tax Percent. Rate	Level	From Lvl	Cond. Type
Base Amount			100	0	BASB
Subtotal			120	0	
Distributed to G/L			200	100	
A/P Sales Tax 1 Inv.	NVV		210	120	JP1I
A/P Sales Tax 2 Inv.	NVV		220	120	JP2I
A/P Sales Tax 3 Inv.	NVV		230	120	JP3I
A/P Sales Tax 4 Inv.	NVV		240	120	JP4I
Expensed			300	0	
A/P Sales Tax 1 Exp.	VS1		310	120	JP1E
A/P Sales Tax 2 Exp.	VS2		320	120	JP2E
A/P Sales Tax 3 Exp.	VS3		330	120	JP3E
A/P Sales Tax 4 Exp.	VS4		340	120	JP4E
Self-assessment			400	0	
A/P Sales Tax 1 Use	MW1		410	210	JP1U
A/P Sales Tax 2 Use	MW2		420	220	JP2U
A/P Sales Tax 3 Use	MW3		430	230	JP3U
A/P Sales Tax 4 Use	MW4		440	240	JP4U
Accrued			500	0	
A/R Sales Tax 1	MW1		510	120	JR1

Figure 12.6 Configuration of a Tax Code

Let's look at an example in Table 12.1, which illustrates the similarity between the tax code linked to a transaction and tax procedure TAXUSJ.

Tax Type	TAXUSJ	Tax Code I1		
Distributed to G/L				
A/P Sales Tax 1 Inv.	NVV	JPI1	NVV	JP1I
A/P Sales Tax 2 Inv.	NVV	JPI2	NVV	JP2I
A/P Sales Tax 3 Inv.	NVV	JPI3	NVV	JP3I
A/P Sales Tax 4 Inv.	NVV	JPI4	NVV	JP4I
Expensed				
A/P Sales Tax 1 Exp.	VS1	JP1E	VS1	JP1E
A/P Sales Tax 2 Exp.	VS2	JP2E	VS2	JP2E
A/P Sales Tax 3 Exp.	VS3	JP3E	VS3	JP3E

Table 12.1 Comparing a Tax Code to the Tax Procedure

Tax Type	TAXUSJ	Tax Code I1		
A/P Sales Tax 4 Exp.	VS4	JP4E	VS4	JP4E
Self Assessment				
A/P Sales Tax 1 Use	MW1	JP1U	VS1	JP1E
A/P Sales Tax 2 Use	MW2	JP2U	VS2	JP2E
A/P Sales Tax 3 Use	MW3	JP3U	VS3	JP3E
A/P Sales Tax 4 Use	MW4	JP4U	VS4	JP4E

Table 12.1 Comparing a Tax Code to the Tax Procedure (cont.)

When a transaction is recorded in a company code assigned to tax procedure TAXUSJ, the following events occur:

- The tax code attached to the transaction relays the following information to the tax procedure:
  - The account key that points to the G/L account for recording tax
  - The G/L accounting treatment (Expense or Accrue)
  - The character or tax type
- The jurisdictional tax rate maintained as part of the tax code is supplied to the transaction. (Not shown in the preceding table.)
- The tax rate is multiplied by the transaction base amount, and a tax amount is computed.

Some transactions are not relevant for sales and use tax, but jurisdiction and tax codes are required by the tax procedure. In these cases, a dummy jurisdiction code can be set up and the tax code defaulted in through configuration. Figure 12.7 shows the configuration screen where the default code is maintained.

12.3.4 Tax Category Code on the G/L Master

As we have already discussed, SAP has designed its system with tax codes. Each G/L account contains an indicator in the master file that governs which type of tax code it will accept. Accounts payable and purchase-related accounts are classified with codes designed for use tax. Accounts receivable and sales-related accounts are designed for sales tax. It is impossible to create an FI transaction using a G/L account if the appropriate tax code is not populated as part of the transaction.

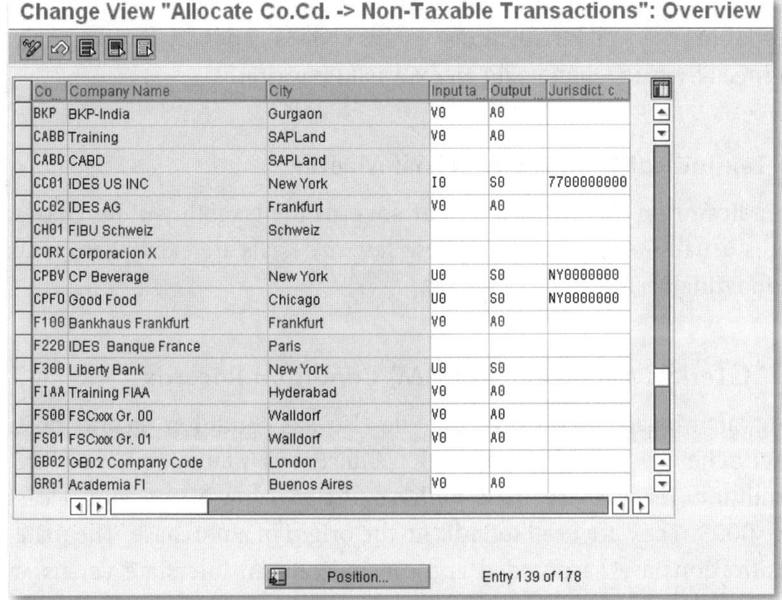

Change View "Allocate Co.Cd. -> Non-Taxable Transactions": Overview

Co	Company Name	City	Input ta	Output	Jurisdict. c
BKP	BKP-India	Gurgaon	V0	A0	
CABB	Training	SAPLand	V0	A0	
CABD	CABD	SAPLand			
CC01	IDES US INC	New York	I0	S0	7700000000
CC02	IDES AG	Frankfurt	V0	A0	
CH01	FIBU Schweiz	Schweiz			
CORX	Corporacion X				
CPBV	CP Beverage	New York	U0	S0	NY0000000
CPFO	Good Food	Chicago	U0	S0	NY0000000
F100	Bankhaus Frankfurt	Frankfurt	V0	A0	
F220	IDES Banque France	Paris			
F300	Liberty Bank	New York	U0	S0	
FIAA	Training FIAA	Hyderabad	V0	A0	
FS00	FSCxxx Gr. 00	Walldorf	V0	A0	
FS01	FSCxxx Gr. 01	Walldorf	V0	A0	
GB02	GB02 Company Code	London			
GR01	Academia FI	Buenos Aires	V0	A0	

Position... Entry 139 of 178

Figure 12.7 Default for Nontaxable Transactions

> **Note**
>
> Some accounts are set up to accept any tax code and others are set up to accept none. If a G/L account is set up as tax relevant, it must have a code in the tax category field.

12.3.5 Tax Indicator on the G/L Master

The G/L master also contains an indicator that can be used to determine tax relevancy. Tax can also be totally turned off for a G/L account if desired. For example, a nontaxable material could be represented by a G/L account and have tax totally turned off. Although this can be done, it requires the material to be nontaxable for the entire country. The same effect can be achieved through the material master, which will be discussed next. Some accounts should never be tax relevant, and good control dictates that the indicator should be used for these.

12.3.6 Tax Classification on the Material Master (SD)

The tax classification code in the sales area of the material master record indicates whether the material is taxable or nontaxable. If taxable is noted on the material master, it can still be overridden at the time of sale. Few materials are nontaxable across all jurisdictions, so this code is generally set to taxable. This is especially true when using an external tax system.

12.3.7 Tax Indicator on the Material Master

The tax indicator on the material master governs the taxability of purchases. Again, it is usually set to taxable because few materials are exempt from tax on a nationwide basis.

12.3.8 Materials Management (MM) Condition Records

The Materials Management (MM) module also has condition records of its own that can be maintained to help with tax decisions internal to R/3 or ECC. MM condition records are used with condition type NAVS and access sequence 0003. They are used to indicate the origin of a purchase. The material classifications are hard coded and can indicate an interstate versus an intrastate purchase and a domestic purchase versus an import. MM condition records are optional but will allow for automatic determination of the tax code when used. Figures 12.8 and 12.9 illustrate the NAVS condition type and a condition record for the condition type. The condition type governs the format and contains Metadata about the condition record.

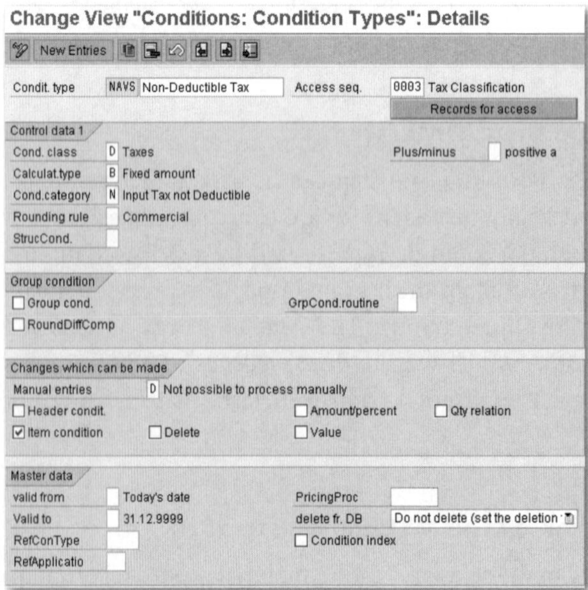

Figure 12.8 Details of the NAVS Condition Type

The MM module also takes advantage of condition records contained in the FI tax codes. Accounts payable and accounts receivable transactions make use of condition records maintained in FI tax codes.

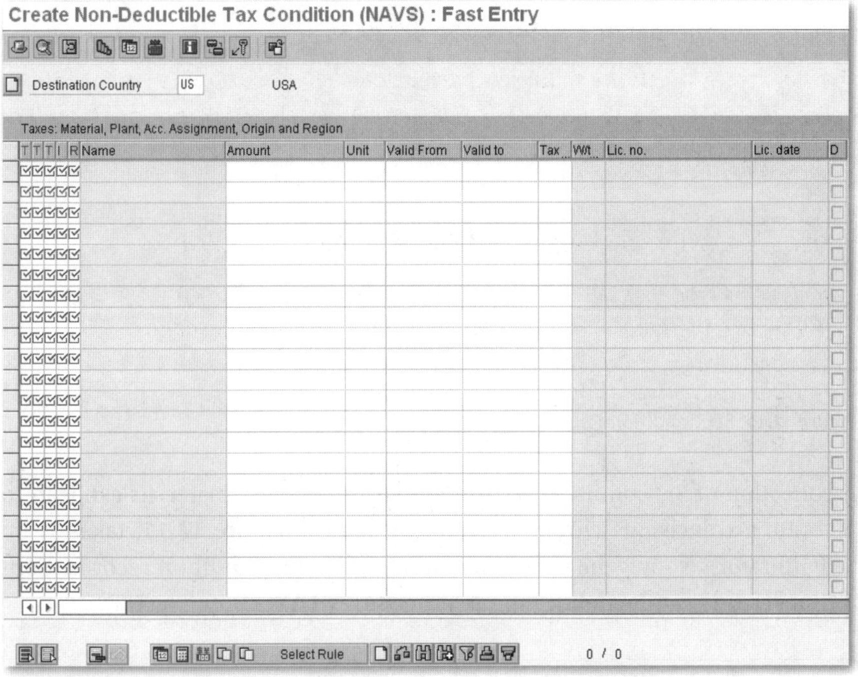

Create Non-Deductible Tax Condition (NAVS) : Fast Entry

Destination Country US USA

Taxes: Material, Plant, Acc. Assignment, Origin and Region

T	T	T	I	R	Name	Amount	Unit	Valid From	Valid to	Tax	W/t	Lic. no.	Lic. date	D

Select Rule 0 / 0

Figure 12.9 A NAVS Condition Record

When filled out, the MM condition record can hold information about the tax status of a material. For example, if the destination country is the United States, the tax indicator can be used to indicate whether the material is non-taxable, partially taxable, or wholly taxable. It can also contain data indicating that the material is nontaxable in Texas and that the material was imported or came from a neighboring state. When hundreds of these records are compiled, they can determine a material's taxability in every state under a variety of circumstances. Material condition records can point directly to a tax code.

12.3.9 Sales and Distribution (SD) Condition Records

Taxation in the SD module is done within the pricing procedure and not done using TAXUSJ. We will discuss this in more detail when discussing TAXUSX. Pricing procedures also use the condition technique and rely on condition records. The SD module houses its own condition records, which are tied to tax codes. Tax codes used in SD are equivalent to tax codes maintained in FI. Condition records in the SD pricing procedure are linked to TAXUSJ through the tax code. Figure 12.10 shows an SD condition record.

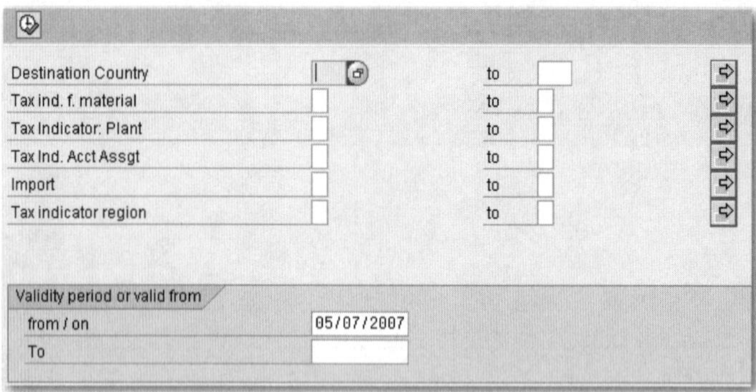

Figure 12.10 SD Condition Record Search Screen

A collection of SD condition records for customers and materials can lead to accurate tax decisions within a given jurisdiction. Figure 12.11, taken from SAP literature, shows the different combinations for condition records. Condition records can be helpful in tax procedures TAXUSJ or TAXUSX.

Menu Path: ***Logistics>Sales and distribution>Master data>Conditions> Prices>Taxes>Create/Change***

Transaction: **VK11** create / **VK12** change

To maintain U.S. condition records, select the condition type **UTXJ** or to maintain Canadian condition records, select **CTXJ**.

Example:

Delivery Country	Customer tax classification	Material tax classification	Rate	Tax Code
US	1 (taxable)	1 (taxable)	100%	01
US	1 (taxable)	0 (non-taxable)	100%	00
US	0 (exempt)	1 (taxable)	100%	00
US	0 (exempt)	0 (non-taxable)	100%	00

Figure 12.11 Example of Condition Records from SAP's 4.6 Configuration Guide (Source: SAP AG)

12.3.10 Customer Tax Classification Code

The customer master also contains a tax classification code that indicates the taxability or exempt status of the customer. Customers that are exempt in all or given jurisdictions can be exempted on the customer master without having to use condition records or other tools. Figure 12.12 shows the **Billing Documents** tab of the customer master and the tax classification code. The customer tax classification is linked to the tax code on the SD condition record and can therefore be used to default in the desired tax code.

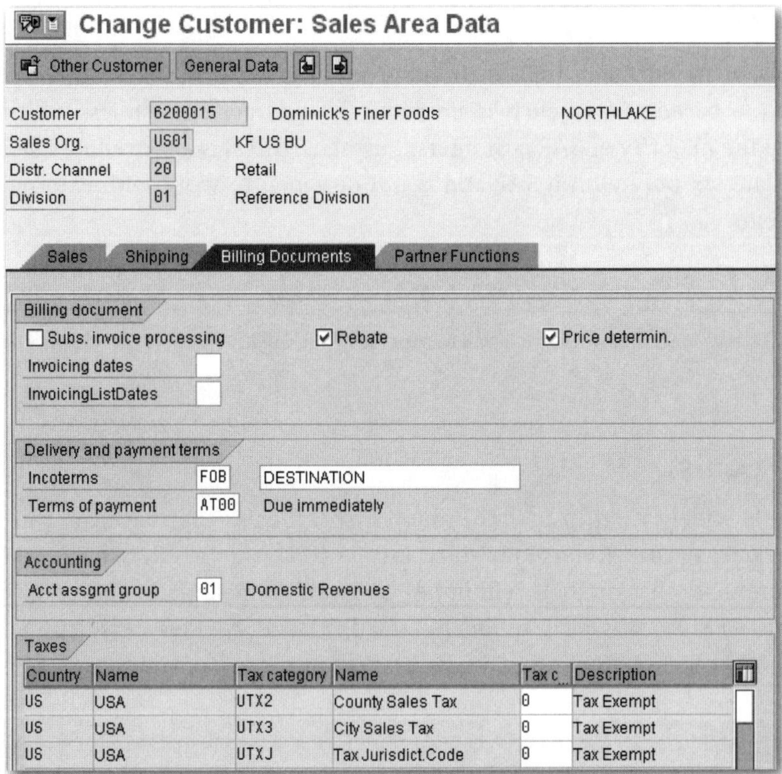

Figure 12.12 Tax Classification Code

12.4 U.S. Tax Procedures

The three tax procedures that come standard with SAP software, TAXUS, TAXUSJ, and TAXUSX, usually do not need to be changed. They do, however, produce very different results, and integrators must be familiar with each of them because only one can be chosen for U.S. taxation. TAXUS and TAXUSJ are tax procedures defined to calculate and account for tax within the SAP software. TAXUSX is designed to be used with an external tax system and will be discussed in Chapter 13.

Note

Although the U.S. tax procedures were developed for handling sales and use tax, the procedure chosen can have a direct effect on the ability to accurately comply with income tax and property tax requirements.

12.4.1 TAXUS

We will not spend much time with tax procedure TAXUS because it is not jurisdiction based and as such is impractical for larger companies, which make up the majority of SAP customers. Further, TAXUS is a procedure used to calculate tax only within SAP and is not designed to work with external tax systems.

Note

TAXUS is only recommended for small companies that sell and receive in one jurisdiction.

12.4.2 TAXUSJ

TAXUSJ is widely used in practice today by companies that have not purchased external sales and use tax software. TAXUSJ is a jurisdictional-based procedure that relies on logic within SAP software to make sales and use tax decisions. Because it is jurisdictionally based, it also provides jurisdictional data for other jurisdictional-based taxes such as property tax and income tax.

Note

There is no standard approach or procedure for implementing sales and use tax using TAXUSJ. Companies using TAXUSJ generally have nexus in fewer tax jurisdictions than those using TAXUSX and build processes that work for those jurisdictions. Although no standard implementation procedure exists, the tools discussed earlier in this chapter are all available to assist with tax processes. The key to configuring TAXUSJ is knowing these tools and then approaching the tax implementation one jurisdiction at a time.

TAXUSJ has the following strengths:

- The procedure is jurisdictionally based and requires a jurisdiction code when activated.
- The procedure is capable of returning proper tax rates for simple sales and use tax calculations.

- Juridictional information required by the procedure can be useful for other tax calculations.
- The procedure is entirely internal to R/3 or ECC and does not require the purchase of external sales and use tax software.

TAXUSJ has the following weaknesses:

- Use of TAXUSJ requires you to maintain jurisdiction codes and tax rates within SAP. Tax rates change continually, and companies using external tax software are provided updates of jurisdiction and rate changes on a constant basis. Maintaining this information by yourself is a burdensome task.
- The procedure cannot make accurate decisions in complex tax situations. TAXUSJ is dependent on logic within R/3 or ECC to make tax decisions and that logic is not as deep as logic within external tax software.
- TAXUSJ requires more maintenance of condition records in the Sales and Distribution (SD) module, tax classification codes in the Materials Management (MM) module, and tax codes in the Financial Accounting (FI) module than external tax software. External software requires maintenance of a few tax codes, but maintenance of SD condition records and MM tax classification codes in the material master is very minor.

12.4.3 Implementing TAXUSJ

The tools discussed earlier can result in effective tax compliance when put together properly. The trick is figuring out how to do that. One step is to realize that TAXUSJ is truly a jurisdictional-based procedure. It not only requires jurisdiction codes on R/3 or ECC master files, but the approach to implementation is one jurisdiction at a time, not the entire nation all at once, which means that each state has to be approached separatly when using TAXUSJ. We'll illustrate this using a sample company, Titus Corporation, that does business in Dallas, Texas.

Titus Corporation

Titus Corporation manufactures and sells batting helmets to sports teams in Texas. They also market batting gloves, replacement chin straps, and decorative helmet covers within Texas. The company buys plastic, leather, and miscellaneous parts solely from Dallas suppliers. Office supplies and equipment are also purchased in the Dallas area. All of the products are manufactured by

Titus, except for the helmet covers which are bought locally and then resold. The helmet covers are tax exempt in Texas because they have a picture of Nolan Ryan on the front.

Table 12.2 shows the tax treatment of the Titus purchases in Texas.

Material	Tax Treatment
Plastic	Nontaxable
Leather	Nontaxable
Miscellaneous	Nontaxable
Office Supplies	Taxable
Equipment	Taxable
Helmet Covers	Exempt

Table 12.2 Titus' Materials and Assets

The taxablity of Titus products held for sale is listed in Table 12.3.

Product	Tax Treatment
Batting Helmets	Taxable
Batting Gloves	Taxable
Chin Straps	Taxable
Helmet Covers	Tax Exempt

Table 12.3 Titus' Products

In addition to the information listed in Tables 12.2 and 12.3, Titus' customers have the tax status outlined in Table 12.4.

Customer	Tax Treatment	Jurisdiction
Texas Rangers	Taxable	Arlington, TX
Baptist Church	Tax Exempt	Dallas, TX
Houston Astros	Taxable	Houston, TX

Table 12.4 Titus' Customers

Based on the information presented in Tables 12.2, 12.3, and 12.4, three jurisdiction codes are needed: one for Dallas, one for Arlington, and one for Houston. The address of the Titus plant in Dallas is used as the ship from address for Titus sales, and the customer address is the ship to. For Titus purchases, the plant in Dallas is the ship to address, and the vendor address is used as the ship from. Using TAXUSJ means that jurisdiction codes and tax rates are assigned to tax codes, so the tax codes in Table 12.5 are necessary.

Tax Code	Tax Code Description
I0	Use Tax — Tax Exempt
I1	Use Tax — Taxable
S0	Sales Tax — Tax Exempt
S1	Sales Tax — Taxable

Table 12.5 Titus' Tax Codes

Condition records for the tax codes are shown in Table 12.6.

Tax Code	Jurisdiction	Tax Rate
I0	Dallas, TX	0.00 %
I1	Dallas, TX	8.25 %
S0	Dallas, TX	0.00 %
S1	Arlington, TX	8.25 %
S1	Houston, TX	7.50 %

Table 12.6 Tax Code Condition Records

The nontaxable material purchases are easily marked nontaxable through codes on the material master. Although if Titus buys helmet covers in the future from jurisdictions outside of Texas, they will not be exempt, and a better means of tax determination will be necessary. A separate tax code would work best in this case.

The Baptist Church, one of Titus' customers, can quickly be exempted through the customer tax classification code on the customer master. The customer tax classification code is a good solution here because any products sold to the church will always be nontaxable.

Titus has a tax liability for the office supplies and equipment. Assigning tax code I1 to the transaction and using the proper jurisdiction code will allow the tax procedure to return the proper rate of 8.25 %. The tax code will also point to the G/L account.

On the sales tax side, the helmet covers can be exempted using the SD condition records linked to code S0. Titus will collect tax on the remaining products barring a customer resale certificate or a direct pay permit from the customer. Tax code S1 will be used on both the Dallas and Houston sales, but the jurisdiction codes on the transaction will result in different tax rates for the two sales.

When we look at the criteria discussed earlier for arriving at the proper tax rate (the ship to location or jurisdication; the material, product, or service; and the tax status of the legal entity making the purchase), TAXUSJ does a reasonable job of defining each area. One problem is that TAXUSJ does not have a way to recognize a tax-exempt material, product, or service except through condition records that point to tax codes. That means for every exempt product in every jurisdiction, a separate condition record needs to be set up. The number of records and rates needing maintainence therefore grows quickly.

TAXUSJ is not designed that differently from a matrix in an external system except that the tax rate and the jurisdiction have been combined in the tax codes that are linked to condition records. Therefore, tax codes have to be set up for each jurisdiction, and new condition records need to be set up to point to the tax codes. The system will work well in most circumstances, but the design requires that condition records be repeated in each tax jurisdiction.

An external system contains records similar to condition records, but they are not necessarily tied to a rate and jurisdiction and can be reused across the system. For example, if a product is tax exempt in both Texas and New Mexico, the product exemption can be used again by logic in the software. In TAXUSJ, two separate condition records are required for the two states. Multiple this by 50 states and hundreds of materials, and it results in a huge maintenance effort.

Thus, companies doing business in multiple jurisdictions soon run into a very difficult situation in terms of maintenance. This partially explains why larger companies usually opt out of TAXUSJ and choose TAXUSX, which, as mentioned earlier, we'll discuss in detail in Chapter 13. Another reason is that max tax rules legislated by some states are impossible to do in TAXUSJ without customization.

12.5 Sales and Use Tax Analysis

Any SAP system implementation should include an analysis or blueprint phase prior to undertaking the project. To determine the direction needed, research must be done about the company and its current tax structure and processes. The following information should be solicited as a starting point:

- How many states require you to file sales/use tax returns?
- How many legal reporting entities do you have?
- Do you currently hold direct pay permits?
  - If so, for which states?
- Do you have manufacturing operations?
  - If so, in which states?
- In which states do you have distribution centers?
- How much sales tax do you collect monthly?
- How much use tax do you pay monthly?
- Approximately how many different products do you sell?
- How many customers do you have?
- Approximately how many customers have tax exempt status?
- Are your resale certificates from customers in good shape?
- How many customers hold direct pay permits?
- How many states do you do business in that have max tax rules?
- Do you currently calculate tax net of discount?
- Is freight currently identified as a separate item on the invoice?
- Are your vendor and customer addresses complete and parsed out to different address fields?
- Do your vendor addresses currently represent the shipping point for your sales?
- Are your cost objects currently set up on a geographical or a responsibility basis?
- How much manual intervention do you want in the tax decision process?
- Do you currently have sales and use tax compliance automated (using a tool that automatically prepares sales and use tax tax forms)?

Answers to these questions give tax integrators an understanding of how the company is handling taxes. The purpose of the analysis phase is to gain enough information so different solutions can be discussed with tax management. Integrators are charged with working with the client until the optimal solution is reached given the existing constraints. The list of questions presented here offers a starting point for discussions about various solutions and will also allow the client to consider approaches available with SAP software. After integrators and clients are familiar with how SAP software addresses sales and use tax challenges, it is time to discuss the U.S. tax procedures in more detail.

12.6 Summary

Three U.S. tax procedures are shipped with standard SAP software, TAXUS, TAXUSJ, and TAXUSX. The former two are designed to calculate and account for tax within the SAP system. TAXUS is not jurisdictionally defined and is only relevant for the very smallest of companies doing business in a single jurisdiction. TAXUSJ is jurisdictionally defined, but for a company in multiple jurisdictions, it may require maintenance of thousands of conditions records with tax rates and jurisdiction codes to properly calculate and account for tax. All of the tools contained in SAP software that were discussed in this chapter can be used with any of the tax procedures. Analysis should be done prior to starting a sales and use tax implementation to determine the effort involved and the tax procedure best fitted to the company.

In Chapter 13, we will continue our discussion of sales and use tax but this time concentrate on tax procedure TAXUSX. TAXUSX is the procedure used with an external tax program.

In Chapter 12, we discussed the calculation and accounting for tax within the SAP system. In this chapter, we'll address using an external system to do the tax calculation so that the results can be recorded in R/3 or ECC. The tax procedure used for this is TAXUSX.

13 Calculating Sales and Use Tax Using External Tax Software

TAXUSX is the third U.S. tax procedure. It is capable of communicating with an external tax system and bringing back tax data into R/3 or ECC. In this chapter, you will learn how the communication link works when using TAXUSX.

TAXUSX is widely used by the nation's largest corporations. It requires the use of an external tax system, which can be SAP-certified bolt-on software or a company's custom built system. TAXUSX uses many of the tools discussed in Chapter 12, including taking advantage of tax codes. The procedure communicates with an external tax program through the SAP tax interface system. Using the interface system, TAXUSX calls out to the external system where it obtains a tax rate and then returns the rate to the SAP system on a real-time basis so tax can be entered in a transaction. Let's look at the strengths and weaknesses of this procedure.

13.1 Strengths And Weaknesses of TAXUSX

The TAXUSX tax procedure is jurisdictionally based and has the following strengths:

- External systems remove the administrative burden of maintaining jurisdiction tables, tax rate tables, and multiple condition records because tax rates and jurisdiction code changes are maintained by the software company. Updates are sent on a periodic basis or can be downloaded from the company website. SAP users that want to retain their own tax software must find a source for jurisdiction codes and tax rates and follow a procedure of maintaining them.

- External systems are generally capable of more accurate and more complex tax decisions because they contain a tax matrix that can be customized to the company's requirements.
- External systems minimize the configuration effort as compared to that needed with TAXUSJ.
- External systems have a method to identify material, product, or service exemptions without proliferating the use of SAP tax codes.
- External tax systems are usually capable of transaction storage for audit response and are created with reporting capability.

TAXUSX also has a couple of weaknesses:

- External tax systems are generally more costly than using TAXUSJ.
- External tax systems may lower system performance as opposed to doing calculations within R/3 or ECC.

Implementing TAXUSX

All of the tax tools discussed in Chapter 12 are to some degree used when implementing TAXUSX. However, TAXUSX makes less use of condition records and tax codes because the tax logic is contained in the external system. TAXUSX therefore requires a communication link to the outside system.

SAP created a standard sales and use tax interface system to communicate with third-party tax packages. It can also be used for client custom tax systems. The tax interface is designed to carry data out of R/3 or ECC via a user exit and make it available to an application programming interface (API) created by the client or the third-party software vendor. The information is then compared to a matrix in the external software to reach tax decisions.

Let's now discuss tax configuration using an external tax system, including contrasting common tax software with that of a client-developed tax package where possible. Although much of the following discussion is very technical in nature but will be explained in a way that everyone can understand, without needing IT training.

Note

The use of an external tax system together with procedure TAXUSX offers a preferred solution to those possible using TAXUS or TAXUSJ. All of the SAP-certified software vendors offer capable products that can be designed to meet any company's needs when implemented properly. At the same time, several companies I have worked with have developed in-house tax systems that they have used with SAP software and these have worked as well.

13.2 Configuring the Communication Link Between R/3 or ECC and External Tax Software

To use an external software program, R/3 and ECC require a communication link. As mentioned earlier, SAP has developed an interface that makes this possible. The interface was designed to make Remote Function Calls (RFCs) to the external tax program. For the RFC to be successful, a path must be entered during configuration because the RFC must know the destination it is calling.

Figure 13.1 shows the **Configuration of RFC Connections** screen for entering the physical destination. The transactions used to reach the IMG configuration screens are not provided in this chapter, but they are given in Chapter 14. You simply have to define the RFC protocol as a TCP/IP connection and use **T** for the **Type**. The name of the system you are connecting to is placed in the **Comment** field.

Configuration of RFC Connections

RFC Connections	Type	Comment
R/2 Connections	2	
ABAP Connections	3	
HTTP Connections to External Server	G	
HTTP Connections to ABAP System	H	
Internal Connections	I	
Logical Connections	L	
TCP/IP connections	T	
1A_PRODUCTION	T	
ALEMANU	T	Test ALE communication with Manugistics
AL_RFC2.1	T	Archive RFC2.1
AL_RFC3.0	T	ArchiveLink
AMADEUS_JRES_TRAINING	T	AMADEUS_JRES_TRAINING
AMADEUS_SYNC	T	AMADEUS
AMA_JRES_TRAINING_US	T	AMA_JRES_TRAINING_US

Figure 13.1 Configuring the Physical Destination

After the configuration type is created, you can enter the path to the external system. Figure 13.2 shows the **Technical Settings** tab of the **RFC Destination EXTERNAL TAX PROGRAM** window, where, in the **Start on Application Server** section, you enter the path in the **Program** text field.

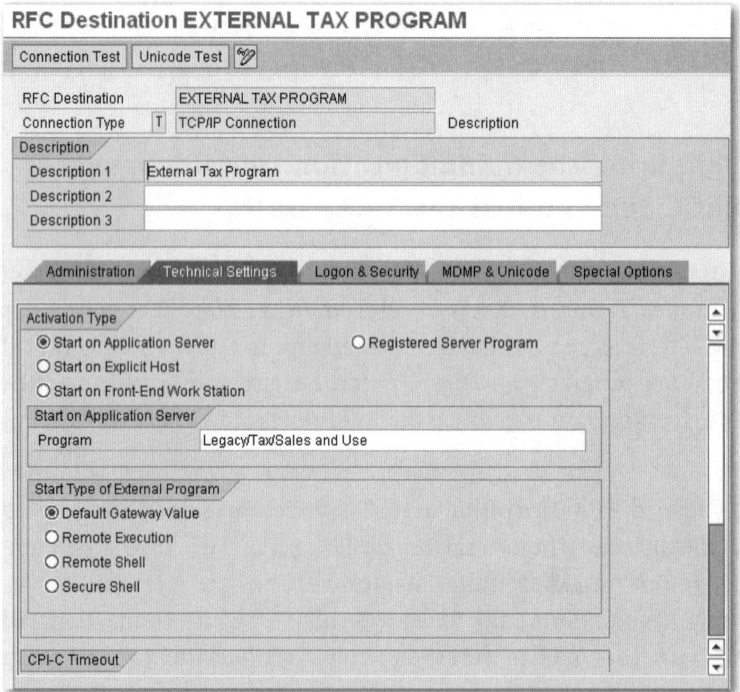

Figure 13.2 Configuring the External Path

Figure 13.3 is an illustration of the screen where the logical destination is established. A function module in SAP is designed to make the type of call needed. Each **Function Module** requires an **RFC Destination** name, which is user defined.

As shown in Figure 13.3, there are several RFC function modules. This is because the external tax system is called more than once during tax processing. You may also note that AVP and Vertex are defined as RFC destinations. It could also be Taxware, Sabrix, or a name given to software created inhouse. More importantly, because more than one function call is made from R/3 or ECC to the external software, it is necessary to explore the purpose of each call.

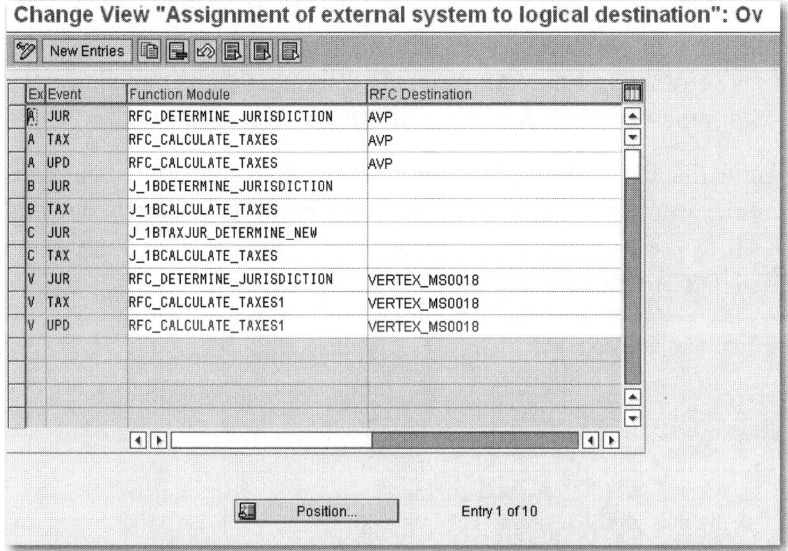

Change View "Assignment of external system to logical destination": Ov

New Entries

Ex	Event	Function Module	RFC Destination
A	JUR	RFC_DETERMINE_JURISDICTION	AVP
A	TAX	RFC_CALCULATE_TAXES	AVP
A	UPD	RFC_CALCULATE_TAXES	AVP
B	JUR	J_1BDETERMINE_JURISDICTION	
B	TAX	J_1BCALCULATE_TAXES	
C	JUR	J_1BTAXJUR_DETERMINE_NEW	
C	TAX	J_1BCALCULATE_TAXES	
V	JUR	RFC_DETERMINE_JURISDICTION	VERTEX_MS0018
V	TAX	RFC_CALCULATE_TAXES1	VERTEX_MS0018
V	UPD	RFC_CALCULATE_TAXES1	VERTEX_MS0018

Position... Entry 1 of 10

Figure 13.3 Configuring the Logical Destination

13.2.1 SAP Function Modules

The first two function modules are shown in the following list in the order in which they are made. The third and forth function modules are an either/or situation, depending on the validity of the tax data and whether the external tax software has a document register or database. All of these function modules can be used to test the standard SAP tax interface during implementation to ensure it is working properly.

- RFC_DETERMINE_JURISDICTION
- RFC_CALCULATE_TAXES_DOC
- RFC_UPDATE_TAXES_DOC
- RFC_FORCE_TAXES_DOC

Let's look at each module in more detail.

RFC_DETERMINE_JURISDICTION

Generally, the first call made to the external system will be the call made to populate the jurisdiction code field on a master file. For example, when a vendor master record is created and the address fields are populated, an RFC call to the external system will be made in an attempt to populate the jurisdiction code field. If R/3 or ECC is not communicating properly with the external system, the call will fail and result in an error message. The master record can therefore not be created until the communication between the external tax software and the SAP system is working. Figure 13.4 shows the coding within the RFC_DETERMINE_JURISDICTION module.

You will note that the coding in this function module is commented out. This is because the structure LOCATION_DATA is filled by another program and then passed to the external system. A portion of the program loading the LOCATION_DATA structure is shown in Figure 13.4.

```
FUNCTION RFC_DETERMINE_JURISDICTION.
*"----------------------------------------------------------------------
*"*"Lokale Schnittstelle:
*"       IMPORTING
*"             VALUE(LOCATION_DATA) LIKE  COM_JUR STRUCTURE  COM_JUR
*"       EXPORTING
*"             VALUE(LOCATION_ERR) LIKE  COM_ERR STRUCTURE  COM_ERR
*"       TABLES
*"              LOCATION_RESULTS STRUCTURE  COM_JUR
*"----------------------------------------------------------------------



ENDFUNCTION.
```

Figure 13.4 Function Module RFC_DETERMINE_JURISDICTION

This program runs when address information is entered in most SAP master files. At that point, the program attempts to make a call to the external system. If the link is configured, a jurisdiction code is returned. If the link is not configured, an error message results, and the master data record cannot be completed. Figure 13.5 is the result of running the debugger and tracing an error through to the program creating it. You can see from the right side of the screen that the system attempted to pass address information to the external system. In this case, it failed because the link was not completed.

For the RFC call to return the correct jurisdiction code, information has to reach the external tax software and match up with a table within the system. The RFC_DETERMINE_JURISDICTION functional module contains a structure or temporary table that temporarily houses information from the master record and sends it to the external tax software in search of a match. The structure is named LOCATION_DATA and has the following fields:

- Country
- State
- County
- City

- ZIP Code
- TXJCD_L1
- TXJCD_L2
- TXJCD_L3
- TXJCD_L4

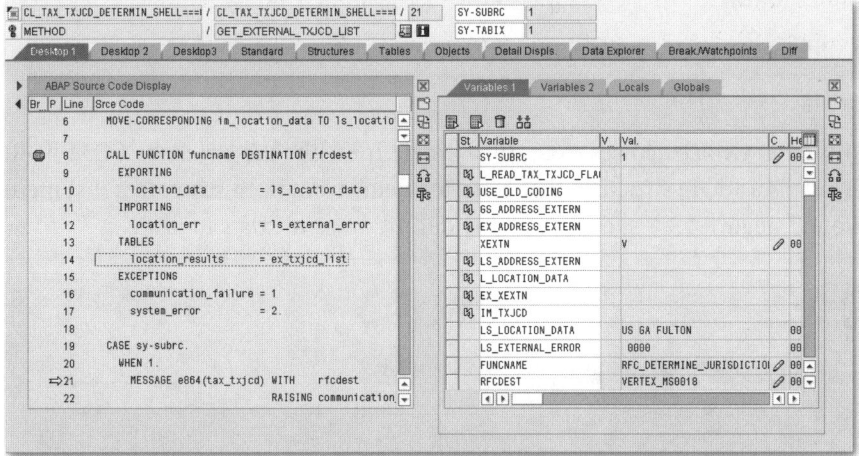

Figure 13.5 Method: get_external_txjcd_list

Not all of the values need to be passed to return a jurisdiction code; state and ZIP code are sufficient. However, in many instances, ZIP codes cross jurisdictional boundries and a pop-up window will display offering a choice of jurisdiction codes. When this happens, the person creating or changing the record is forced to choose a jurisdiction code from the list. Unfortunately, this can result in errors, so it is best to send as much information as possible.

The address information shown is self-explanatory, but the last four fields are not. SAP software clients using an external system are required to define the format of the jurisdiction code as part of tax configuration. Vertex, Taxware, and Sabrix all have naming conventions for the jurisdiction codes used in their system. Vertex, for example, has a 2,3,4,1 naming standard. That means that the Vertex jurisdiction code is broken down so that the first two digits equal the state, the second three the county, the next four the city, and the last digit is an in-city or out-of-city indicator.

The four fields starting with TXJCD communicate to the external system the jurisdiction code format that the SAP software is expecting to have returned. We will talk about the value of this when we discuss the function module dealing with the tax calculation. There is not, however, a requirement that the jurisdiction code be broken down into the tax jurisdictions that compose it. If a company wants to return a 10-digit string, it would only use the first field and not the remainder.

Information is returned by the function module through the use of a second structure call LOCATION_RESULTS. The parameters for this temporary table are as follows:

- Jurisdiction Code (TXJCD)
- OUT_OF_CITY

Although two structures exist, they are defined like the structure COM_JUR, which is a single structure that contains fields from both structures just mentioned. Figure 13.6 shows the table definition as it exists in SAP.

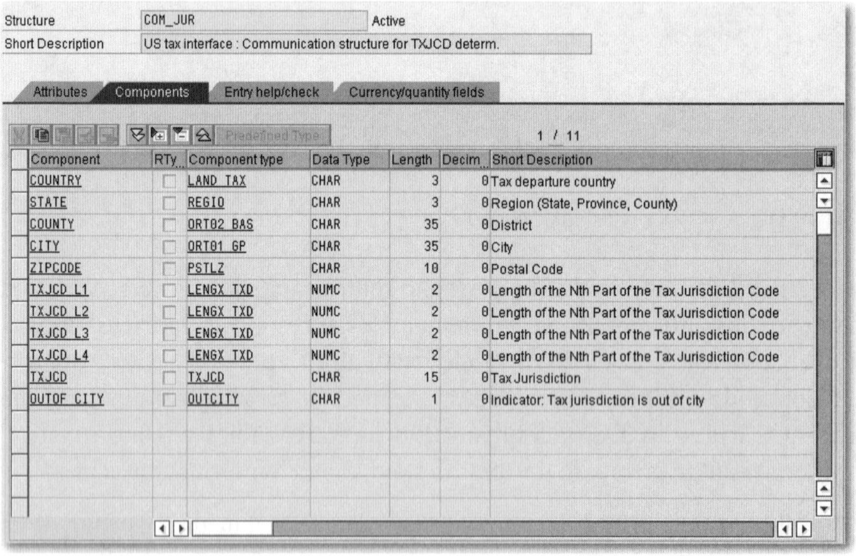

Structure: COM_JUR — Active
Short Description: US tax interface : Communication structure for TXJCD determ.

Attributes | Components | Entry help/check | Currency/quantity fields

1 / 11

Component	RTy	Component type	Data Type	Length	Decim	Short Description
COUNTRY		LAND_TAX	CHAR	3	0	Tax departure country
STATE		REGIO	CHAR	3	0	Region (State, Province, County)
COUNTY		ORT02_BAS	CHAR	35	0	District
CITY		ORT01_GP	CHAR	35	0	City
ZIPCODE		PSTLZ	CHAR	10	0	Postal Code
TXJCD_L1		LENGX_TXD	NUMC	2	0	Length of the Nth Part of the Tax Jurisdiction Code
TXJCD_L2		LENGX_TXD	NUMC	2	0	Length of the Nth Part of the Tax Jurisdiction Code
TXJCD_L3		LENGX_TXD	NUMC	2	0	Length of the Nth Part of the Tax Jurisdiction Code
TXJCD_L4		LENGX_TXD	NUMC	2	0	Length of the Nth Part of the Tax Jurisdiction Code
TXJCD		TXJCD	CHAR	15	0	Tax Jurisdiction
OUTOF_CITY		OUTCITY	CHAR	1	0	Indicator: Tax jurisdiction is out of city

Figure 13.6 The COM_JUR StructureDefinition

The jurisdiction code is returned and an in-city and out-of-city flag may be returned as well. When the communication link is working and jurisdictions codes are being returned, they just need to be verified to make sure they are correct. Once tested, the system continues to work properly unless interrupted.

Case Study

I recently worked with a company that wanted to retain a custom-built tax system because they felt the logic developed for its business lines was superior to that available from external vendors. We wrestled with what to use for a jurisdiction code. The firm was getting a ZIP code feed with tax rates from a vendor, but I was not completely comfortable using a five- or nine-digit ZIP code for a jurisdiction code in SAP because the ZIP code was not designed for tax use and could not be parsed out to equate to the different jurisdictions that build up to the total tax rate. We later found that a GEO code was also contained on the vendor feed and elected to use that.

The structure of the jurisdiction code can also make a difference. If you have elected to use a program from a certified third-party vendor, you don't need to worry about comparing the structure of one code to that of another, but if you are customizing your own system, take some time to consider the structure of the code and how you are going to maintain it.

RFC_CALCULATE_TAXES_DOC

With jurisdiction code information included in the master files and other configuration complete, you are in good shape to start booking transactions and determining the proper tax. At the time of invoice entry, R/3 or ECC will make an RFC call to the external tax system to determine the correct tax rate. The RFC call carries data with it as if in an envelope to the external system, and the external tax system then employs the data by comparing it to records contained in its tables. When a match is found, a tax rate is returned to ECC. The RFC_CALCULATE_TAXES_DOC function module is more complex than RFC_DETERMINE_JURISDICTION but again involves structures or tables that temporarily house data during the processing of a given invoice. Figure 13.7 illustrates the code in the RFC_CALCULATE_TAXES_DOC function module.

You will note that a number of structures or tables are used to ship information back and forth between R/3 or ECC and the external tax system. The SAP system has to send some information just to introduce itself to the external system and establish communication; this is a type of handshake between the two systems.

Information contained in the structures under the **IMPORTING** command is mostly handshake information. The external system in return has to send information back to R/3 or ECC to again communicate in the other direction. Information in the structures under the **EXPORTING** command is handshake information going in the other direction.

```
FUNCTION RFC_CALCULATE_TAXES_DOC.
*"----------------------------------------------------------------------
*"*"Lokale Schnittstelle:
*"  IMPORTING
*"     VALUE(I_SAP_CONTROL_DATA) LIKE  SAP_CONTROL_DATA
*"       STRUCTURE  SAP_CONTROL_DATA
*"     VALUE(I_TAX_CAL_HEAD_IN) LIKE  TAX_CAL_HEAD_IN00
*"       STRUCTURE  TAX_CAL_HEAD_IN00
*"  EXPORTING
*"     VALUE(O_EXT_CONTROL_DATA) LIKE  EXT_CONTROL_DATA
*"       STRUCTURE  EXT_CONTROL_DATA
*"     VALUE(O_COM_ERR_DOC) LIKE  COM_ERR_DOC
*"       STRUCTURE  COM_ERR_DOC
*"  TABLES
*"      I_TAX_CAL_ITEM_IN STRUCTURE  TAX_CAL_ITEM_IN00
*"      O_TAX_CAL_ITEM_OUT STRUCTURE  TAX_CAL_ITEM_OUT00
*"      O_TAX_CAL_JUR_LEVEL_OUT STRUCTURE  TAX_CAL_JUR_LEVEL_OUT00
*"----------------------------------------------------------------------

ENDFUNCTION.
```

Figure 13.7 Function RFC_CALCULATE_TAXES_DOC

As was the case with the RFC_DETERMINE_JURISDICTION function module, you will note that the code in the function module RFC_CALCULATE_TAXES_DOC shown in Figure 13.7 is commented out. Again, the structures in the module are filled by other programs.

From a tax standpoint, the really interesting part is what is passed in the remaining tables. You will note in Figures 13.8 and 13.9 that many different fields can be passed to the external system using the RFC. Although so far, all we have discussed are items such as company code, jurisdiction code, and material code or group, it's possible to have a lot more complexity.

Structure: TAX_CAL_ITEM_IN00 — Active

Short Description: Tax Interface: document item input (version TAXDOC00)

Attributes | Components | Entry help/check | Currency/quantity fields

Predefined Type — 1 / 29

Component	RTy	Component type	Data Type	Length	Decim	Short Description	Group
ITEM_NO		TAX_ITEM_NO	NUMC	6	0	Tax interface communication item number.	
POS_NO		TAX_POSNR	NUMC	6	0	Tax document item number	
GROUP_ID		TAX_GROUP_ID	CHAR	18	0	Grouping code for components that are part of the same set	
COUNTRY		LANDTX	CHAR	3	0	Tax departure country	
DIVISION		DIVISION	CHAR	4	0	Business area/division code	
MATNR		TAX_MATNR	CHAR	18	0	Material number for taxes	
PROD_CODE		PROCD_TTXP	CHAR	10	0	SAP internal product code (external interface)	
GROUP_PROD_CODE		GRP_PROCD	CHAR	10	0	Group product code	
QUANTITY		QUANT_13	CHAR	13	0	Quantity	
UNIT		UNIT_3	CHAR	3	0	Unit	
APAR_IND		APAR_IND	CHAR	1	0	Indicator for A/P or A/R	
TAX_TYPE		TAXTYPEXT	CHAR	1	0	Indicator: Sales/use/rental/service/tax	
EXEMP_IND		EXTEXMTFLG	CHAR	1	0	Indicator: Transaction is tax exempt/taxable	
TAX_DATE		DATE	CHAR	8	0	Date in CHAR format	
TXJCD_ST		TXJCD_ST	CHAR	15	0	Jurisdiction code "Ship-to"	
TXJCD_SF		TXJCD_SF	CHAR	15	0	Jurisdiction code "Ship-from"	
TXJCD_POA		TXJCD_POA	CHAR	15	0	Jurisdiction code "Point of order acceptance"	
TXJCD_POO		TXJCD_POO	CHAR	15	0	Jurisdiction code "Point of order origin"	
AMOUNT		BASAMOUNT	CHAR	15	0	Tax base amount	

Figure 13.8 TAX_CALC_ITEM_IN00 — Upper Portion

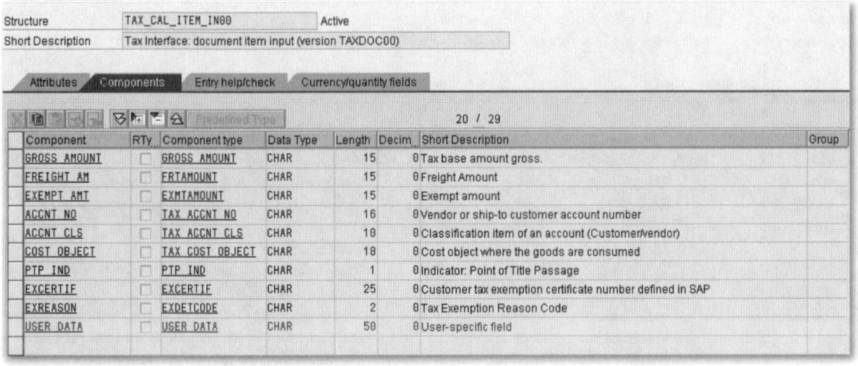

Structure: TAX_CAL_ITEM_IN00 Active
Short Description: Tax Interface: document item input (version TAXDOC00)

Attributes | Components | Entry help/check | Currency/quantity fields

20 / 29

Component	RTy	Component type	Data Type	Length	Decim	Short Description	Group
GROSS_AMOUNT		GROSS_AMOUNT	CHAR	15	0	Tax base amount gross.	
FREIGHT_AM		FRTAMOUNT	CHAR	15	0	Freight Amount	
EXEMPT_AMT		EXMTAMOUNT	CHAR	15	0	Exempt amount	
ACCNT_NO		TAX_ACCNT_NO	CHAR	16	0	Vendor or ship-to customer account number	
ACCNT_CLS		TAX_ACCNT_CLS	CHAR	10	0	Classification item of an account (Customer/vendor)	
COST_OBJECT		TAX_COST_OBJECT	CHAR	18	0	Cost object where the goods are consumed	
PTP_IND		PTP_IND	CHAR	1	0	Indicator: Point of Title Passage	
EXCERTIF		EXCERTIF	CHAR	25	0	Customer tax exemption certificate number defined in SAP	
EXREASON		EXDETCODE	CHAR	2	0	Tax Exemption Reason Code	
USER_DATA		USER_DATA	CHAR	50	0	User-specific field	

Figure 13.9 TAX_CALC_ITEM_IN00 — Lower Portion

The screen shown in Figure 13.9 allows you to pass detailed information between R/3 or ECC and the external system. If more detail is needed, a user exit is provided, which will be discussed in section 13.2.2. There are many instances where some of these additional fields are needed, and they can make the difference to end up with a successful tax implementation.

You have now seen what can be sent to the external system, so let's next take a look at what can be brought back. The remaining two tables in the RFC_CALCULATE_TAXES_DOC function module deal with the information brought back into the SAP software.

Figure 13.10 shows table TAX_CALC_ITEM_OUT00. You might be surprised to see that more than just the tax rate and amount can be brought back to the SAP system. For example, if the customer exemption certificate is stored by the external tax system, it can be brought back into the SAP system and be used to populate the exemption certificate field on the customer master. You will note that the reason code can also be brought back, as well as codes for the material or customer tax exemptions. This information can be very useful when dealing with audits several years after the transactions are recorded.

Figure 13.11 shows the second table entitled TAX_CALC_JUR_OUT00. We discussed earlier the ability to maintain tax amounts for each jurisdiction within R/3 and ECC. The table shown in Figure 13.10 communicates the number of jurisdiction levels being passed back to the SAP system from the external tax system. The table shown in Figure 13.11 passes tax rates and amounts for each of the jurisdiction levels (state, county, city, MTA, etc.) back to R/3 or ECC. A separate record is created for each level of the jurisdiction code indicated in the NR_JUR_LEVELS field in the TAX_CALC_ITEM_OUT00 table shown in Figure 13.10.

Structure: TAX_CAL_ITEM_OUT00 — Active
Short Description: Tax Interface: document item input (version TAXDOC00)

Attributes | Components | Entry help/check | Currency/quantity fields

1 / 9

Component	RTy	Component type	Data Type	Length	Decim	Short Description
ITEM_NO		TAX_ITEM_NO	NUMC	6	0	Tax interface communication item number.
TXJCD_IND		TXJCDIND	CHAR	1	0	Indicator: Jurisdiction code used for tax calculation
TAXPCOV		TAXPERCNTG	CHAR	15	0	Total tax rate
TAXAMOV		TAXAMOUNTG	CHAR	15	0	Total tax amount
EXMATFLAG		EXMATCODE	CHAR	2	0	Code for material tax exemption
EXCUSFLG		EXCUSCODE	CHAR	2	0	Code for customer tax exemption
EXT_EXCERTIF		EXT_EXCERTIF	CHAR	25	0	Customer exempt certificate as returned by tax system
EXT_EXREASON		EXT_DETCODE	CHAR	2	0	Tax Exemption Reason Code as returned by tax system
NR_JUR_LEVELS		TAX_NR_LEVELS	NUMC	2	0	Number of levels per item for communication control

Figure 13.10 TAX_CALC_ITEM_OUT00

Structure: TAX_CAL_JUR_LEVEL_OUT00 — Active
Short Description: Results of tax calculation for one jurisdiction level

Attributes | Components | Entry help/check | Currency/quantity fields

1 / 7

Component	RTy	Component type	Data Type	Length	Decim	Short Description
ITEM_NO		TAX_ITEM_NO	NUMC	6	0	Tax interface communication item number.
TXJLV		TXJCD_LEVEL	CHAR	1	0	Tax jurisdiction code level
TAXPCT		TAXPERCNT	CHAR	15	0	Level n tax rate
TAXAMT		TAXAMOUNT	CHAR	15	0	Level n tax amount
TAXBAS		TAXBASE	CHAR	15	0	Tax base amount level n
EXAMT		TAXAMOUNT	CHAR	15	0	Level n tax amount
EXCODE		EXDETCODE	CHAR	2	0	Tax Exemption Reason Code

Figure 13.11 TAX_CALC_JUR_LEVEL_OUT00

Figure 13.11 reinforces the importance of a well structured jurisdiction code. A single 10-digit string would not give you the ability to break down a combined tax rate into its jurisdictional components. The value of doing this is that you can retrieve this information from R/3 or ECC for audit purposes using DART. You can also customize reports that will assist in sales and use tax compliance. We'll look at this in more detail later in this chapter when disucssing user exits. For now, we'll continue with the discussion of the remaining function modules.

RFC_UPDATE_TAXES_DOC

Third-party tax software systems provide a means for reporting and storing transaction documents in what is referred to as a *register*. RFC_UPDATE_TAXES_DOC is used to pass the completed transaction or document back to the external tax system through the tax interface so that it can be stored for audit or reporting purposes.

From My Experience

One advantage that third-party software has over a client's custom solution is that the client system usually does not have a storage area that is updated by the SAP system for retention of sales and use documents. I am not, however, convinced that having external storage and reporting is that much of a benefit.

An external storage system and audit file is valuable if every sales and use tax decision is made by the external tax system. This requires that every transaction created in R/3 or ECC be sent to the external system for processing. In practice, I have simply not seen this to be the case. In every implementation I have seen, some tax decisions are made using logic within the SAP system. Because of this, it is important to go to R/3 or ECC to defend against audits. If the reason for tax exemption exists in the SAP software, it is best to use that software to get audit detail.

The fact that not all documents are updated to the external register creates another problem on audit. If an invoice has no tax associated with it, the document may not be updated to the audit file. Invoices without tax are often looked at by auditors to ascertain why tax was not charged.

The audit tool of choice within R/3 or ECC is DART. DART, discussed in Chapter 6, is used for sales and use tax audits at many companies. Tax integration specialists with a good understanding of DART can get the information from the SAP system needed for audit defense. DART includes 99% of the fields needed for a sales and use tax audit without customization.

RFC_FORCE_TAXES_DOC

In some situations, an inconsistency may exist when the tax document is recalculated in R/3 or ECC. The calculation occurs after tax has been brought back from the external system. Jurisdiction codes are verified, and the amount of tax is checked. If the jurisdiction code cannot be validated, the transaction is stopped at that point. If a difference occurs between the amount to be posted to the external audit file and what is to be posted in the general ledger (G/L), the document then must be forced to the external system. RFC_FORCE_TAXES_DOC is the function module used to force the document to the external audit file when inconsistencies are found during the final calculation procedure.

External audit files can be very helpful and offer an additional means of reporting and additional reporting tools, but you have to be aware of limitations that may be created based on the way your SAP system is configured.

13.2.2 Enhancement FYTX0002 — The Tax User Exit

SAP has created an enhancement to the standard tax interface that provides a user exit to be used within the interface programming logic. The enhancement does not need to be used in all cases. The existing function modules discussed earlier in this chapter provide solutions for most tax situations. Coding for user exit EXIT_SAPLFYTX_USER_001 is shown in Figure 13.12.

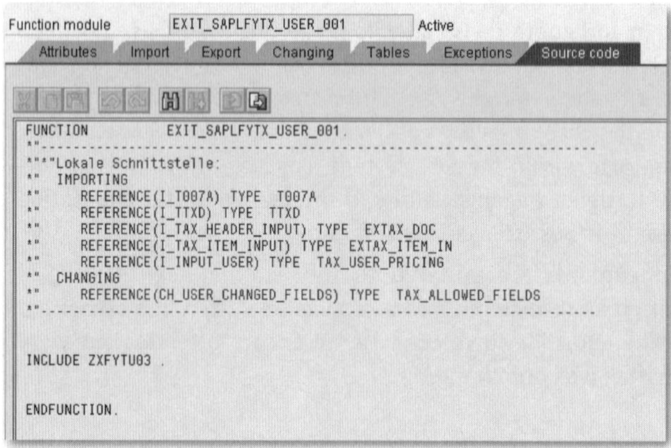

Figure 13.12 EXIT_SAPLFYTX_001

You will note that structures exist similar to those in the function modules perviously discussed for carrying and returning information between R/3 or ECC and the external tax system. Table T007A is also available from the user exit, which allows you to specifically reference tax codes or tax code properties. In addition, structures exist that allow users to either add or change field values. Notice input parameter I_INPUT_USER and the structure TAX_ALLOWED_FIELDS. You need to understand the purpose of these two items to better understand the user exit, so let's take a detailed look at them.

I_INPUT_USER

I_INPUT_USER is defined as the type TAX_USER_PRICING, which means that it uses the structure TAX_USER_PRICING for temporary storage of information. The table and field definition for TAX_USER_PRICING is shown in Figure 13.13.

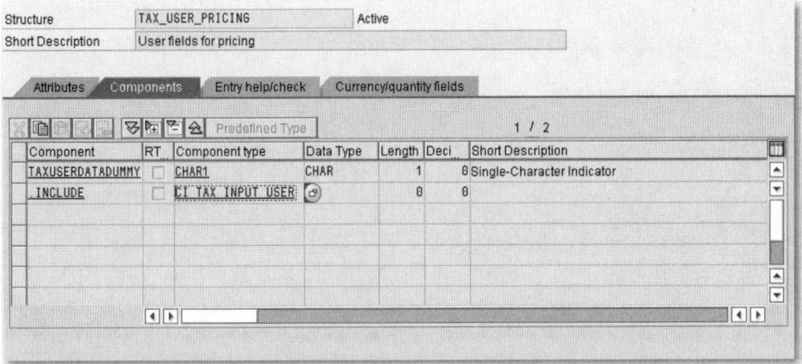

Figure 13.13 TAX_USER_PRICING

You can see that the definition is very short. The important item to notice is the include file CI_TAX_INPUT_USER. An include file is basically a structure that allows you to add or append additional files to a table. In this case, user-defined fields can be added to structure TAX_USER_PRICING.

As mentioned in Chapter 12, tax computations in SD rely on the pricing procedure and not the tax procedure. A structure in the user exit is therefore necessary to work with the pricing procedure and allow additional fields to be added from the SD application. CI_TAX_INPUT_USER is the tool that allows this to happen. Structures in the user exit are filled from the SD module using pricing structures KOMP, KOMK, and XKOMV. If additional fields are needed from SD, these are the tables they are taken from, and CI_TAX_INPUT_USER is the means to get them to the external tax system.

TAX_ALLOWED_FIELDS

TAX_ALLOWED_FIELDS is the structure that houses the fields that can be changed. Figures 13.14 and 13.15 show the upper and lower portions of the table definition for TAX_ALLOWED_FIELDS.

The primary input parameters for carrying information to the external tax system are listed in Figure 13.12, shown previously. They consist of a header structure and a line item structure and are TAX_HEADER_INPUT and TAX_ITEM_INPUT. As mentioned before, they are similar to the function modules contained in the standard tax interface. The structure TAX_ALLOWED_FIELDS allows users to change some of the fields in these input parameters. Some of the fields in TAX_ALLOWED_FIELDS come with default data in them prior to calling the user exit, but many of them can be filled in the user exit, which allows the user to direct values into these fields.

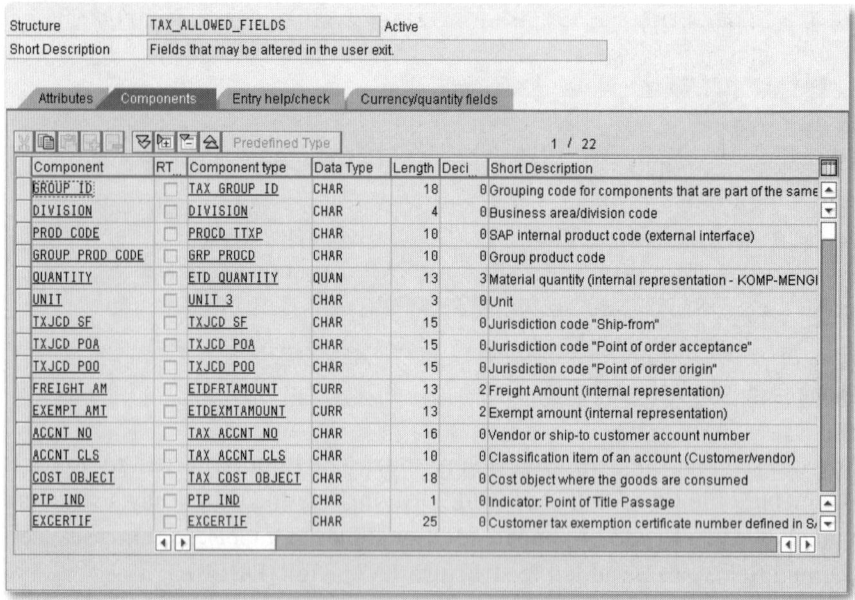

Structure: TAX_ALLOWED_FIELDS Active
Short Description: Fields that may be altered in the user exit.

Attributes / Components / Entry help/check / Currency/quantity fields

Predefined Type 1 / 22

Component	RT...	Component type	Data Type	Length	Deci...	Short Description
GROUP_ID		TAX_GROUP_ID	CHAR	18	0	Grouping code for components that are part of the same
DIVISION		DIVISION	CHAR	4	0	Business area/division code
PROD_CODE		PROCD_TTXP	CHAR	10	0	SAP internal product code (external interface)
GROUP_PROD_CODE		GRP_PROCD	CHAR	10	0	Group product code
QUANTITY		ETD_QUANTITY	QUAN	13	3	Material quantity (internal representation - KOMP-MENGI
UNIT		UNIT_3	CHAR	3	0	Unit
TXJCD_SF		TXJCD_SF	CHAR	15	0	Jurisdiction code "Ship-from"
TXJCD_POA		TXJCD_POA	CHAR	15	0	Jurisdiction code "Point of order acceptance"
TXJCD_POO		TXJCD_POO	CHAR	15	0	Jurisdiction code "Point of order origin"
FREIGHT_AM		ETDFRTAMOUNT	CURR	13	2	Freight Amount (internal representation)
EXEMPT_AMT		ETDEXMTAMOUNT	CURR	13	2	Exempt amount (internal representation)
ACCNT_NO		TAX_ACCNT_NO	CHAR	16	0	Vendor or ship-to customer account number
ACCNT_CLS		TAX_ACCNT_CLS	CHAR	10	0	Classification item of an account (Customer/vendor)
COST_OBJECT		TAX_COST_OBJECT	CHAR	18	0	Cost object where the goods are consumed
PTP_IND		PTP_IND	CHAR	1	0	Indicator: Point of Title Passage
EXCERTIF		EXCERTIF	CHAR	25	0	Customer tax exemption certificate number defined in S/

Figure 13.14 TAX_ALLOWED_FIELDS — Upper Portion of Table

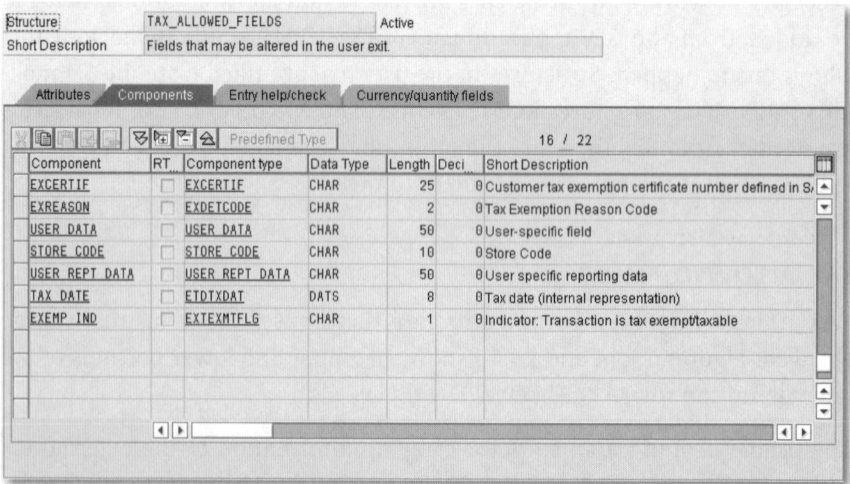

Structure: TAX_ALLOWED_FIELDS Active
Short Description: Fields that may be altered in the user exit.

Attributes / Components / Entry help/check / Currency/quantity fields

Predefined Type 16 / 22

Component	RT...	Component type	Data Type	Length	Deci...	Short Description
EXCERTIF		EXCERTIF	CHAR	25	0	Customer tax exemption certificate number defined in S/
EXREASON		EXDETCODE	CHAR	2	0	Tax Exemption Reason Code
USER_DATA		USER_DATA	CHAR	50	0	User-specific field
STORE_CODE		STORE_CODE	CHAR	10	0	Store Code
USER_REPT_DATA		USER_REPT_DATA	CHAR	50	0	User specific reporting data
TAX_DATE		ETDTXDAT	DATS	8	0	Tax date (internal representation)
EXEMP_IND		EXTEXMTFLG	CHAR	1	0	Indicator: Transaction is tax exempt/taxable

Figure 13.15 TAX_ALLOWED_FIELDS — Lower Portion of Table

13.3 Building the Logic Matrix Within the External Software System

Rarely do external tax systems come with the logic needed to correctly calculate taxes. Thus, you have to build the tax matrix required in the external system. Building the tax matrix is a major project that is rarely part of the SAP implementation budget, and the logic matrices will also always need work, whether you have been using the same external tax software and are adapting it for the SAP system or you are starting from scratch.

Large U.S. corporations usually operate in every state. Setting up a tax logic matrix for every state can be a daunting task, and tax professionals should find out if their company has set aside funding for this project when an SAP implementation is planned in the future. If not, they need to start requesting it. If tax logic has already been built for each state, the challenge is to replace the codes in your existing system so they match the codes passed to it from the SAP system. If the codes are not the same, the systems cannot talk to each other. Several options exist:

- **Build mapping tables that convert the codes coming from the SAP system to those used in your external tax software.**
  This option requires permanent mapping for existing codes in the system. When new logic is set up, you have to decide whether to continue to use the old naming convention or adopt the SAP naming convention. Mapping tables add overhead to the solution, which diminishes performance.
- **Convert the codes in your existing tax software to SAP numbering conventions and upload them to your tax system.**
  This solution is great if your system has an easy way to upload data into it and if your data is in good shape. It is certainly preferable to making manual entries into the system. If your data is in poor shape, cleansing may need to take place prior to the loading process.
- **Build or rebuild your matrix manually.**
  You should consider this option only if you are building your matrix for the first time or your external tax software does not have a way to upload your logic.

Note

Tax departments usually do not take on the task of researching and building tax decision logic in the external software without getting help from the implementor or another outside consultant.

13.4 Summary

Using an external tax system requires a communication link to the SAP software. SAP has provided a tax interface system to carry information to and from external sales and use tax software. A tax user exit is also provided for more complex tax calculations. The SAP system must be configured for use with any of the three U.S. tax procedures. The external system requires a tax decision matrix that matches the data passed to it from R/3/ECC to make proper tax decisions. Tax professionals need to anticipate and plan ahead for this project.

Chapter 14 addresses configuration for all three U.S. tax procedures and gives transaction codes where available so that configuration screens can be reached. It also discusses the master data settings needed on the application side of the SAP system.

Chapters 12 and 13 have discussed tools that are available in the SAP system and the communication link required for an external tax system. In this chapter, we will discuss the configuration needed on both the application side and in the IMG to make everything work together.

14 Tax Configuration in the SAP System

In Chapter 12, we discussed many of the tax tools available in SAP systems that can be used to assist with tax computations. Chapter 13 discussed the communication link and tax interface system. However, we still need to discuss tax configuration in detail, which we'll do in this chapter.

All three of the U.S. tax procedures require some configuration. In this section, we'll look at the configuration needed and identify for which tax procedure each is necessary. Several configuration steps are unique to an external tax system, but the majority of the steps are required regardless of the tax procedure.

Configuring the SAP system is important under each of the tax procedures, but those internal to R/3 and ECC have heavier configuration requirements than TAXUSX. As was mentioned earlier, when using TAXUSX, tax codes are not used as intensively as in the other two procedures. Tax codes used with TAXUSX are best maintained for account determination and not for tax decisions, which means that very few tax codes are needed when using TAXUSX.

Note

Implementations using an external tax system can still have 40 or 50 tax codes. Implementing tax within R/3 and ECC is an art and not a science, so I do not choose to structure implementations using external software by making heavy use of tax codes, but some implementors may prefer that method.

When using an external tax system, a judgement is usually made to default all transactions within R/3 or ECC to either a taxable or nontaxable state. After this is done, records are set up in the external tax software to handle the exceptions. Typically, internal SAP system configuration is set up so that the majority of transactions are taxable and then sent to the external tax software for the real tax decision. The external system contains table information similar to the condition records in the SAP system. The external tax system will usually have, at a minimum, the following data:

- A list of all jurisdiction codes and tax rates
- A list of tax exempt customers
- A list of tax exempt products by jurisdiction

Transactions will pass through the SAP tax interface and be compared to the information in the external table. The customer number, material group, and jurisdiction code will leave the SAP system and will then be compared to the data in the external system. If records are found that match all three conditions, the transaction may be exempted, and a zero tax rate and zero amount are returned to R/3 or ECC. If no exception records are found, the transaction will remain taxable, and a tax rate and amount will be returned to the SAP system through the tax interface.

14.1 Assigning a Tax Procedure to a Country

The first step in the configuration process is assigning a tax procedure to a country. As mentioned before, a country can only have one tax procedure. You therefore must choose from TAXUS, TAXUSJ, and TAXUSX. Table 14.1 shows the transaction code used to access the IMG screen where you assign the tax procedure, as well as the tax procedures to which this action applies.

Note

All of the tables in this chapter list the action required for a configuration step, the appropriate transaction code(s), the tax procedure(s) to which the action applies, and additional comments (if appropriate).

Action	T-Code	TAXUS	TAXUSJ	TAXUSX	Comments
Assign a tax procedure.	OBBG	X	X	X	One per country

Table 14.1 Transaction Code Used to Assign a Tax Procedure

Figure 14.1 shows the IMG screen where the assignment is made.

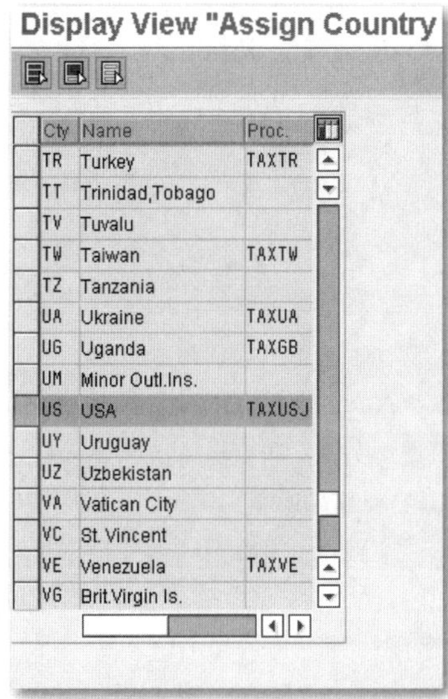
Display View "Assign Country

Cty	Name	Proc.
TR	Turkey	TAXTR
TT	Trinidad,Tobago	
TV	Tuvalu	
TW	Taiwan	TAXTW
TZ	Tanzania	
UA	Ukraine	TAXUA
UG	Uganda	TAXGB
UM	Minor Outl.Ins.	
US	USA	TAXUSJ
UY	Uruguay	
UZ	Uzbekistan	
VA	Vatican City	
VC	St. Vincent	
VE	Venezuela	TAXVE
VG	Brit.Virgin Is.	

Figure 14.1 Assigning a Country to a Tax Procedure

14.2 Configuration Steps Unique to TAXUSX

If you're using an external tax system, you must perform several configuration steps not required when you're using the two internal tax procedures. In Chapter 13, we already discussed the first two, defining the physical and logical destinations, and related screenshots were shown in that chapter. You then have to activate the external tax calculation, as shown in Figure 14.2. The last two steps include defining number ranges for the external tax document (audit file or register) using Transaction OBETX, as shown in Figure 14.3, and setting the **Activ** flag, which ensures that the external audit file will be updated, as shown in Figure 14.4.

Display View "TTXD: View of External System": Overview

TTXD: View of External System

Sche...	Ext...	tax interface vers.	RFC Destination	Update RFC destination	TC
TAXCAJ					☐
TAXUSJ					☐
TAXUSX	V				☐

Figure 14.2 Activating the External Tax Calculation

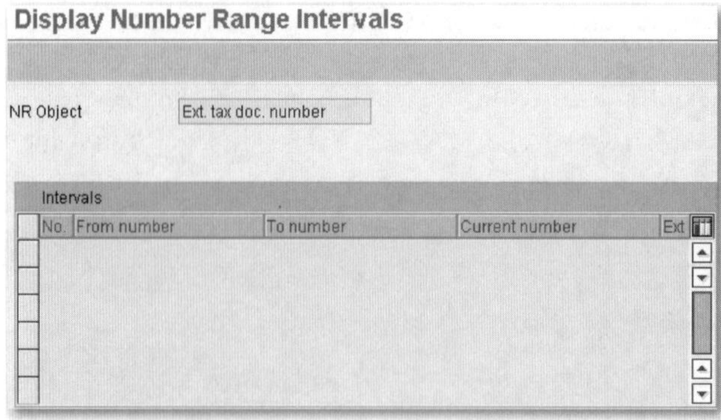

Figure 14.3 Defining Number Ranges for the External Tax Document

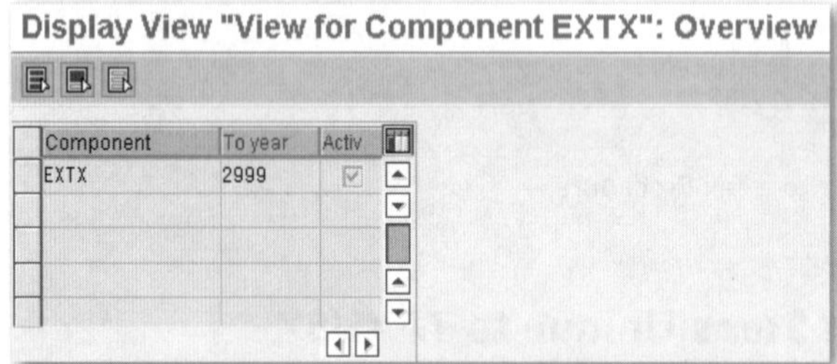

Figure 14.4 Activating the External Tax Document

Table 14.2 summarizes these actions for easy reference.

Action	T-Code	TAXUS	TAXUSJ	TAXUSX	Comments
Define the physical destination.				X	Shown in Chapter 13, Section 1.2.
Define the logical destination.				X	Shown in Chapter 13, Section 1.2.
Activate the external tax calculation.				X	
Define number ranges for the external tax document.	OBETX			X	
Activate the external tax document.				X	If you don't set the flag, the external audit file will not be updated.

Table 14.2 Configuration Specific to an External Tax System

14.3 Defining the Structure of the Tax Jurisdiction Code

Next, you need to define the tax jurisdiction code structure, the importance of which we've discussed already in Chapter 12. You'll find the transaction code for this action and the tax procedures to which it applies in Table 14.3.

Action	T-Code	TAXUS	TAXUSJ	TAXUSX	Comments
Define the tax jurisdiction code structure.	OBCO		X	X	

Table 14.3 Defining the Jurisdiction Code Structure

Figure 14.5 shows the IMG screen where the structure is maintained.

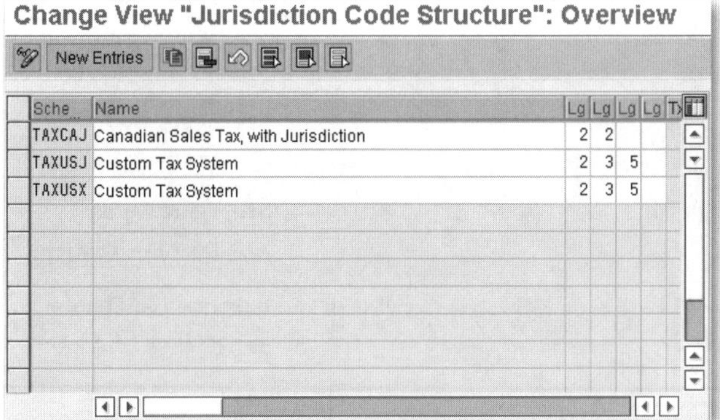

Figure 14.5 Defining the Tax Jurisdiction Code Structure

14.4 Master Data Configuration and Master Data in SD

The next steps in configuration deal with defining tax classification values for master data fields in the SD module. The values are limited based on the country code of the plant or the company code. Also, the customer and material master may display a different tax category code based on the sales organization of the plant and company code.

Let's now look at defining the range of tax classification values for each of the tax categories. The tax classification values are used by R/3 or ECC to determine taxability within the SAP system and make it possible to make exempt decisions in the SAP system. This is absolutly necessary using tax procedures TAXUS or TAXUSJ and elective using TAXUSX.

Most configuration done using TAXUSX does not pass every transaction to the external system for a tax decision. If every transaction were passed to the extenal system, the tax classification code would simply be a taxable code. It is often easier, and it takes the load off the external system, to make some tax decisions in the SAP environment. Generally, the assigned codes are equal to 0 for tax exempt and 1 for taxable. They can, however, be anything you want to use for the assignment.

The first four actions, including their transaction codes and applicable tax procedures, are shown in Table 14.4. The following transactions are done in the IMG and establish the values available for selection during master data creation or maintenance on the application side of the SAP system.

Action	T-Code	TAXUS	TAXUSJ	TAXUSX	Comments
Define tax category by departure country.	OVK1	X	X	X	See Figure 14.6.
Configure customer master.	OVK3	X	X	X	See Figure 14.7.
Configure material master (SD).	OVK4	X	X	X	See Figure 14.8. A/R Tax Classification.
Maintain SD condition records.	VK11 VK12	X	X	X	Illustrated in Chapter 12, Section 12.3.9.

Table 14.4 Master Data Settings in SD

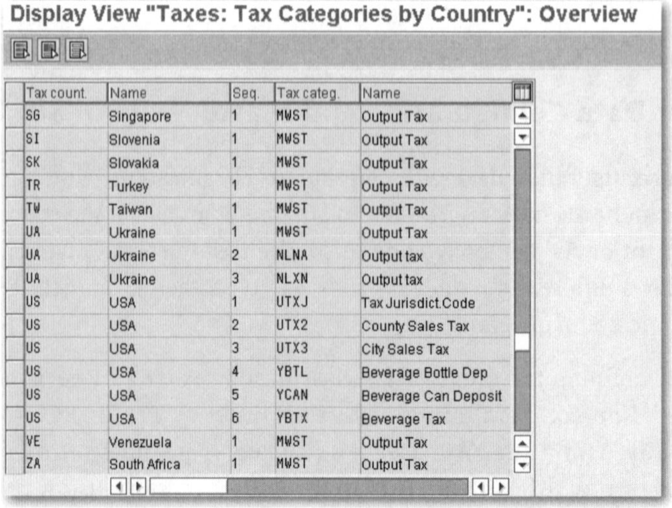

Display View "Taxes: Tax Categories by Country": Overview

Tax count.	Name	Seq.	Tax categ.	Name
SG	Singapore	1	MWST	Output Tax
SI	Slovenia	1	MWST	Output Tax
SK	Slovakia	1	MWST	Output Tax
TR	Turkey	1	MWST	Output Tax
TW	Taiwan	1	MWST	Output Tax
UA	Ukraine	1	MWST	Output Tax
UA	Ukraine	2	NLNA	Output tax
UA	Ukraine	3	NLXN	Output tax
US	USA	1	UTXJ	Tax Jurisdict.Code
US	USA	2	UTX2	County Sales Tax
US	USA	3	UTX3	City Sales Tax
US	USA	4	YBTL	Beverage Bottle Dep
US	USA	5	YCAN	Beverage Can Deposit
US	USA	6	YBTX	Beverage Tax
VE	Venezuela	1	MWST	Output Tax
ZA	South Africa	1	MWST	Output Tax

Figure 14.6 Defining Tax Category by Departure Country

Display View "Customer Taxes": Overview

Tax categ.	Name	Tax class.	Description
NLNA	Output tax	1	Full tax
NLNA	Output tax	2	Half tax
NLXN	Output tax	0	Tax Exempt
NLXN	Output tax	1	Tax Exempt
UTX2	County Sales Tax	0	Exempt
UTX2	County Sales Tax	1	Taxable
UTX3	City Sales Tax	0	Exempt
UTX3	City Sales Tax	1	Taxable
UTXJ	Tax Jurisdict.Code	0	Exempt
UTXJ	Tax Jurisdict.Code	1	Taxable
WUST	Sales Tax	0	Tax Exempt
WUST	Sales Tax	1	Liable for Taxes
YBTL	Beverage Bottle Dep	0	Exempt
YBTL	Beverage Bottle Dep	1	Taxable
YBTL	Beverage Bottle Dep	Z	Customer Pays State
YBTX	Beverage Tax	0	Exempt

Figure 14.7 Defining Customer Tax Classification Indicators

Display View "Material Taxes": Overview

Tax categ.	Name	Tax class.	Description
MWST	Output Tax	5	N/A
MWST	Output Tax	6	N/A
MWST	Output Tax	7	DE-WTRD
MWST	Output Tax	8	SE-WTRD
NLNA	Output tax	0	Exempt
NLNA	Output tax	1	Full tax
NLXN	Output tax	1	Full tax
UTX2	County Sales Tax	0	Exempt
UTX2	County Sales Tax	1	Taxable
UTX3	City Sales Tax	0	Exempt
UTX3	City Sales Tax	1	Taxable
UTXJ	Tax Jurisdict.Code	0	Exempt
UTXJ	Tax Jurisdict.Code	1	Taxable
WUST	Sales Tax	0	No tax
WUST	Sales Tax	1	Full tax
WUST	Sales Tax	2	Half tax

Figure 14.8 A/R Material Tax Classification Indicator

The material master in R/3 or ECC acts as both a repository for master data concerning products (SD) and as a repository concerning materials (MM). That means that a tax indicator exists on the SD side used during accounts receivable entry (A/R) and one on the MM side for accounts payable (A/P) transactions.

The final step involving SD master data is defining values for the A/R tax classification indicators on the material master. This step is especially useful because it allows a tax code to be defaulted into a transaction when dealing with the two internal tax procedures that are both tax code intensive. It can also be used with an external tax system. As in the preceding step, the A/R material tax classification indicator is part of the SD condition record and helps determine which tax code to use.

14.4.1 Tax Procedures and Condition Records

When using the two internal tax procedures, condition records are the key to making tax decisions concerning product or service taxability. You will remember that the tax code also determines the tax rate. If, for example, your company offers both products and services in a jurisdiction, it is possible that the products may be taxed at a different rate than the services. It is therefore necessary to have a condition record that points to a specific tax code for the product and a different tax code for the services. If your company had nontaxable products or services, a third condition record and tax code would be needed to handle that situation.

When the external tax procedure is used, condition records are still often used to point to either a taxable or nontaxable tax code. Because the product or service is a variable in the taxability decision, at least two values are needed to satisfy this requirement. It is, however, possible to use SD condition records to point to tax codes that represent materials or products with corresponding codes in the external tax system.

14.4.2 SD Master Data Settings

The next four steps, outlined in Table 14.5, do not deal with IMG configuration but with master data settings on the application side of the SAP software. We have talked a great deal about the importance of good jurisdiction information, and screenshots of the jurisdiction code field on the majority of the master files were included in Chapter 3. The customer tax classification code was displayed in Chapter 12. Now, we'll take a look at the values that need to be entered in selected master data fields to determine how the tax procedure and tax codes process different combinations of jurisdiction, customer, and material code information

When using procedure TAXUSJ, the jurisdiction code field will be selected from the internal jurisdiction code table based on address information. This is true for both the customer and plant jurisdiction codes referred to in Table 14.5. TAXUSX automatically populates the field on both the customer and plant masters based on the address data. TAXUS is not jurisdictionally based and will not require jurisdiction codes. The other two fields, the customer tax classification code and the material master tax classification code, require population. The available values for these two fields was determined in the configuration activities described in Table 14.4.

Tax classification indicators can be used within the SAP system to determine taxability using the two internal U.S. tax procedures. When using TAXUSX, the indicators are usually set to *taxable*, and the external system makes the final tax decision.

Action	T-Code	TAXUS	TAXUSJ	TAXUSX	Comments
Maintain customer tax jurisdiction code (SD).	V-03 V-09 VD02 XD02		X	X	
Maintain customer tax classification (SD).	V-03 V-09 VD02 XD02	X	X	X	Billing screen shown in Chapter 12, Section 1.3.10.
Maintain material master tax classification (SD).	MM01 MM02	X	X	X	Sales Org 1 Tab from the material master.
Maintain plant master jurisdiction code (SD).	MM01 MM02		X	X	Shown in Chapter 3, Section 1.2.6.

Table 14.5 Settings for Maintaining SD Master Data

Figure 14.9 shows the screen where the material tax classification indicator is set.

14.4.3 The Pricing Procedure in SD

As mentioned before, the pricing procedure in the SD module is used in combination with the tax procedure when using an external tax system. As of release 4.6A, SAP created an additional pricing procedure named RVAXUD to handle more complex tax situations and now recommends using that pricing procedure in place of RVAXUS.

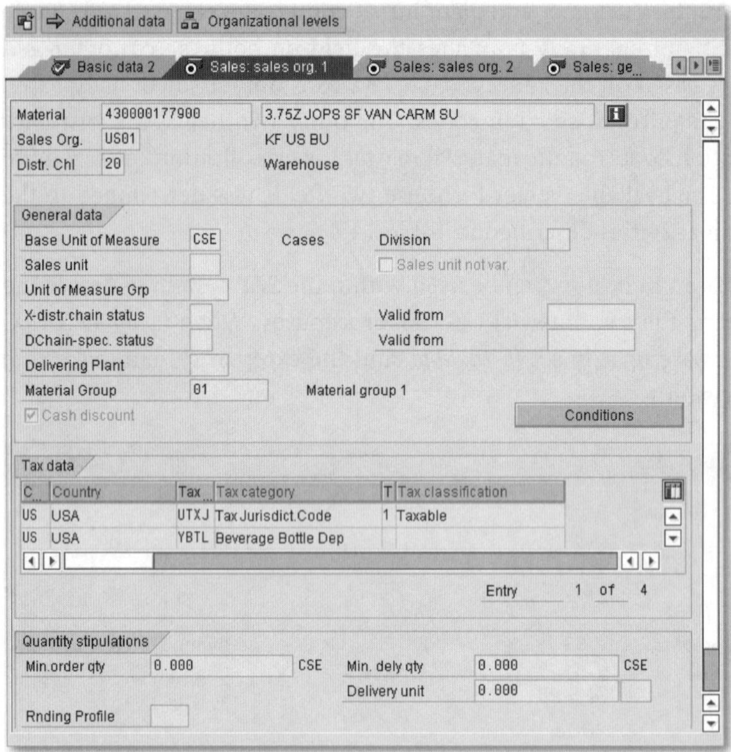

Figure 14.9 The Material Tax Classification Code

Both pricing procedures work with FI tax codes, and the tax code is the link between the pricing procedure and the tax procedure. TAXUSX is only used on the SD side for account determination purposes for booking the tax liability. From a configuration standpoint, the use of the pricing procedure instead of the tax procedure is fairly transparent and does not create major differences between the way SD is configured versus MM. Luckily, most of the work is handled by the SAP tax interface system behind the scenes.

14.5 Master Data Configuration and Master Data in MM

The A/P material tax classification indicator is used in the same way as the A/R indicator to indicate material taxability. The material tax classification indicator is a part of the MM condition record and points to a tax code. The A/P record is used for materials, whereas the A/R indicator is used for products or services. The A/P indicator can default in the tax code and is used to a larger extent with the internal tax procedures, but it serves a purpose with

TAXUSX as well. MM condition type and condition record maintenance will be discussed in Section 1.5.1. Table 14.6 shows the transaction code for setting the A/P tax classification indicator.

Action	T-Code	TAXUS	TAXUSJ	TAXUSX	Comments
Configure material master (MM).	OMKK	X	X	X	

Table 14.6 The Transaction for the A/P Tax Classification Indicator

Figure 14.10 illustrates the configuration screen for creating the A/P material tax classification indicators.

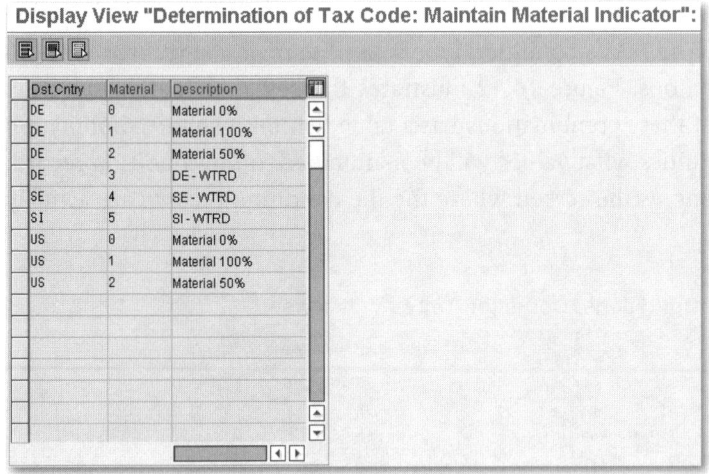

Figure 14.10 A/P Material Tax Classification Indicator

14.5.1 MM Condition Type and Condition Record Maintenance

MM condition records need to be maintained when using an internal tax procedure just as those in SD. You will remember that when using an external tax system for SD, the pricing procedure is actually used for the tax calculation in harmony with the tax procedure. This is not the case on the MM side, making the use of MM condition records more of an elective process when using an external tax procedure. Table 14.7 shows the transactions for maintaining MM condition types and condition records.

The condition type NAVS is used in the MM module. If configuration in this area is completed, the tax code can be defaulted automatically. Automatic selection of the tax code requires maintenance of MM condition records.

Note

When creating either SD or MM condition records, you are required to select the key combination desired.

Action	T-Code	TAXUS	TAXUSJ	TAXUSX	Comments
Maintain MM condition type.	M/06	X	X	X	Condition type NAVS.
Maintain MM condition.	MEK1 MEK2	X	X	X	

Table 14.7 MM Condition Type Maintenance

Figure 14.11 illustrates the NAVS condition type that comes preconfigured in the system. The NAVS condition type is used to maintain records for non-taxable transactions. Figure 14.12 illustrates the key combination selection screen. Each of these combinations has a table behind it so the combination selected determines what values will be maintained in the condition record. Figure 14.13 shows the screen where the the condition records are actually maintained.

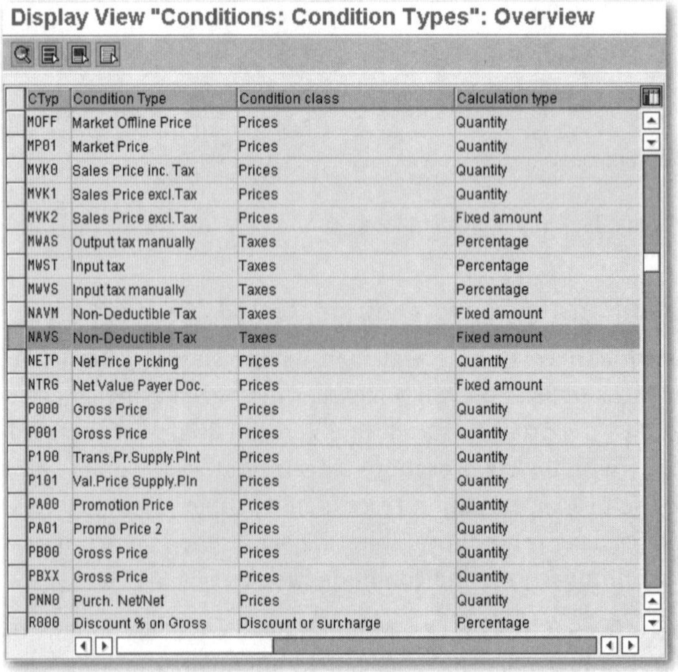

Display View "Conditions: Condition Types": Overview

CTyp	Condition Type	Condition class	Calculation type
MOFF	Market Offline Price	Prices	Quantity
MP01	Market Price	Prices	Quantity
MVK0	Sales Price inc. Tax	Prices	Quantity
MVK1	Sales Price excl.Tax	Prices	Quantity
MVK2	Sales Price excl.Tax	Prices	Fixed amount
MWAS	Output tax manually	Taxes	Percentage
MWST	Input tax	Taxes	Percentage
MWVS	Input tax manually	Taxes	Percentage
NAVM	Non-Deductible Tax	Taxes	Fixed amount
NAVS	Non-Deductible Tax	Taxes	Fixed amount
NETP	Net Price Picking	Prices	Quantity
NTRG	Net Value Payer Doc.	Prices	Fixed amount
P000	Gross Price	Prices	Quantity
P001	Gross Price	Prices	Quantity
P100	Trans.Pr.Supply.Plnt	Prices	Quantity
P101	Val.Price Supply.Pln	Prices	Quantity
PA00	Promotion Price	Prices	Quantity
PA01	Promo Price 2	Prices	Quantity
PB00	Gross Price	Prices	Quantity
PBXX	Gross Price	Prices	Quantity
PNN0	Purch. Net/Net	Prices	Quantity
R000	Discount % on Gross	Discount or surcharge	Percentage

Figure 14.11 The NAVS Condition Type

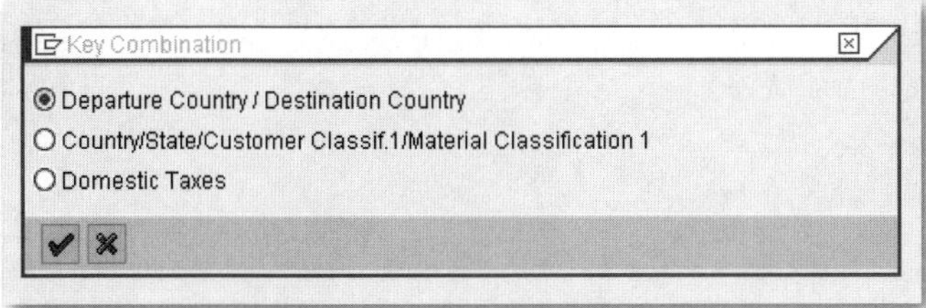

Figure 14.12 Key Combinations for Condition Records

Create Non-Deductible Tax Condition (NAVS) : Fast Entry

Purch. Organization

Vendor

Vendor	Description	Amount	Unit	Valid From	Valid to	Tax	Wt...	Lic. no.	Lic. date	D

Figure 14.13 An MM Condition Record

14.5.2 MM Configuration for Plants

It is possible to specify a default tax code by assigning tax classification indicators to the plant. In the first step, you define the indicators, and in the second step, you assign them to your plants using the transaction codes outlined in Table 14.8. Note that these two steps are not mandatory.

Note

A U.S. plant that purchases only nontaxable goods is rare if not nonexistent, therefore, the realistic usefulness of this configuration is suspect. Essentially, the plant will have to be assigned a taxable code of 1, and the final taxability decision will be left up to condition records or the external system.

Action	T-Code	TAXUS	TAXUSJ	TAXUSX	Comments
Define tax classification indicators for plant.	OMKM	X	X	X	
Assign tax classification indicators for plant.	OMKN	X	X	X	

Table 14.8 Plant Tax Classification Indicators

Figures 14.14 and 14.15 show the screens used to perform the plant configurations steps.

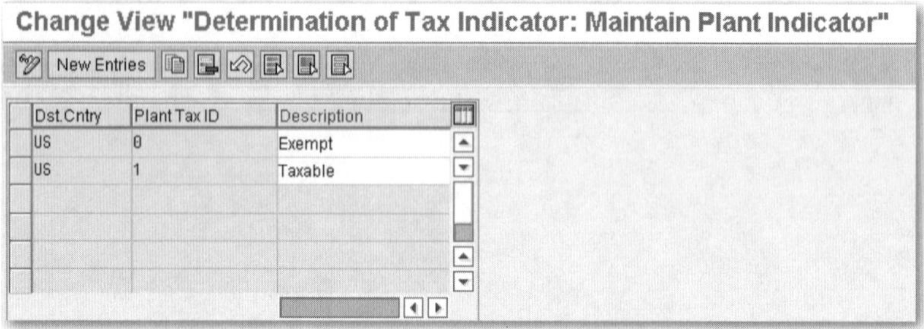

Figure 14.14 Define Tax Classification Indicators for Plants

Change View "Assignment of Tax Indicator to Plant": Overview

Plnt	Name 1	Plant Tax ID	Descriptio
0001	SAP Standard Plant	1	

Figure 14.15 Assign Tax Indicators to Plants

14.5.3 Determine MM Account Assignment

Tax classification indicators can also be set up for account assignment. When using an external tax system, these indicators are generally set to *taxable*, and the external system looks for exceptions. Similar to the plant tax classification indicators, these are also elective. Using these classification codes, it is possible to make a group of transactions nontaxable within the SAP system. For example, using Transaction OMKO, you can turn off tax on a complete account assignment category if desired; however, this is unlikely, and in reality, everything is set to taxable using the internal tax procedures as well. Table 14.9 shows the configuration transactions where the assignment indicators are defined and set.

Action	T-Code	TAXUS	TAXUSJ	TAXUSX	Comments
Define tax classification indicators for account assignment.	OMKL	X	X	X	
Assign tax classification indicators for account assignment.	OMKO	X	X	X	

Table 14.9 Account Assignment Indicators (MM)

Figures 14.16 and 14.17 illustrate the screens for the MM account assignment tax classification indicators.

Display View "Determine Tax Code: Maintain Account Assignment Indicato

Dst.Cntry	Tax Ind. AccAss.	Description
US	0	Exempt
US	1	Taxable

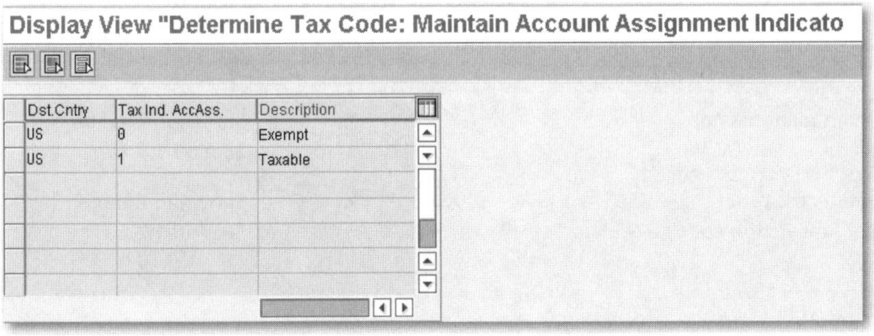

Figure 14.16 Determine MM Account Assignment Tax Classification Indicators

Display View "Assignment of Tax Indicator to Account Assignment Catego

AAC	Dst.Cntry	Description	Name	Tax Ind. AccAss.
A	US	Asset	USA	1
F	US	Order	USA	1
K	US	Cost center	USA	1
P	US	Project	USA	1

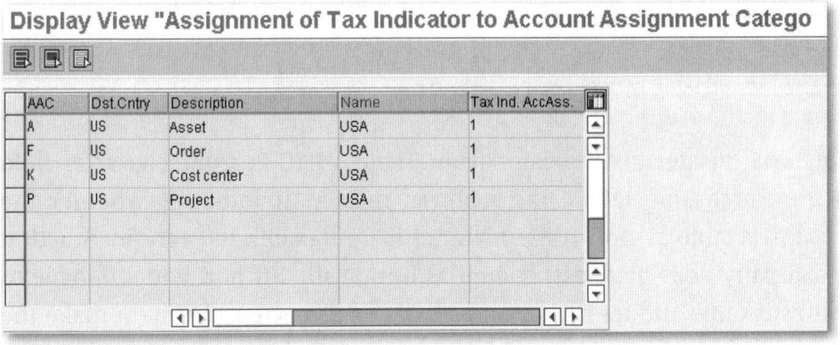

Figure 14.17 Assign Tax Classification Indicators for Account Assignment

14.5.4 MM Master Data Settings

There are more master files that affect A/P than impact the SD module. Three of these master files are mentioned in Table 14.10. The plant master, the cost center master, and the vendor master are included in Table 14.10, but as stated in Chapter 3 and Chapter 8, jurisdiction code information is needed on all revenue and cost object master files.

Note

The reasons for good jurisdiction code information were also discussed in Chapter 3. In addition, Chapter 3 includes a list of the remaining master files requiring jurisdictional information. Refer to Chapter 3 as a guide for master files requiring jurisdiction codes.

When using an external tax system, the jurisdiction code on all of these files will be populated when completing or changing the address information on the record. With TAXUSJ, you will be prompted for a jurisdiction code. Jurisdiction codes should be required on all of these master files.

Action	T-Code	TAXUS	TAXUSJ	TAXUSX	Comments
Maintain plant master jurisdiction code (MM).		X	X	X	Shown in Chapter 3, Section 1.2.6.
Maintain cost center master jurisdiction code (MM).	KS01 KS02	X	X	X	Shown in Chapter 3, Section 1.2.1.
Maintain vendor master jurisdiction code (MM).	MK01 MK02	X	X	X	
Maintain material master tax indicator.	MM01 MM02	X	X	X	Purchasing tab.

Table 14.10 Maintaining MM Related Master Data

The material master tax indicator from Table 14.10 is a one-character field from the Purchasing tab of the material master. It indicates whether the material is taxable or not. If the material is nontaxable in every jurisdiction your company does business, code it as nontaxable. If not, you will have to code it as taxable and let condition records or the external system make the final taxability decision. Figure 14.18 shows the screen where the material master tax indicator is set.

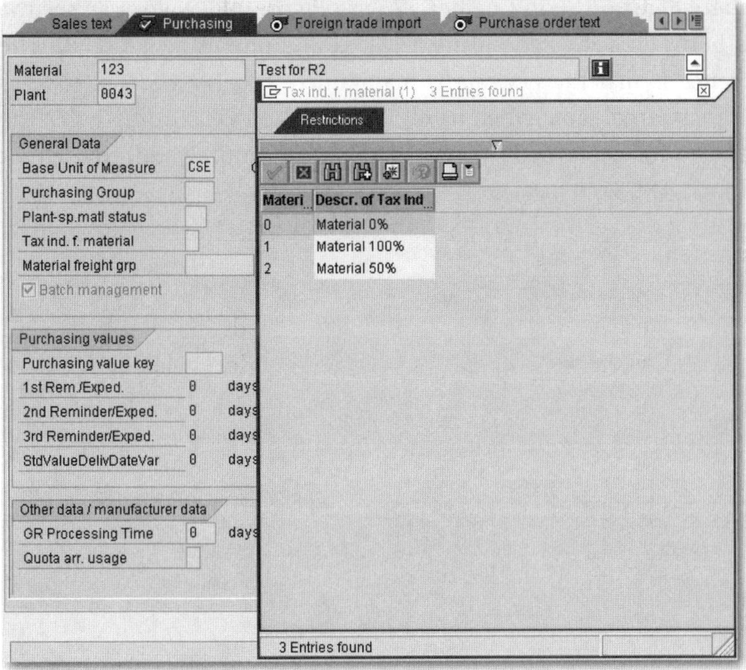

Figure 14.18 Material Master Tax Indicator

14.6 Maintaining Tax Codes

A great deal was said about tax codes in Chapter 12 when we discussed tax procedure TAXUSJ. In the introduction to this chapter, we also dicussed using tax codes with the external tax procedure, TAXUSX. Although tax codes are used with both procedures, a significant difference exists. When using procedure TAXUSJ, the tax code actually houses the tax rate for the jurisdiction. This is not the case when using TAXUSX. With this tax procedure, the tax code will still house a rate, but the rate will be 100 % (or –100 % in the case of self-assessed tax).

When using TAXUSX, the external system supplies the tax rate so the tax code simply multiplies the rate coming from the external system by one and comes up with the same result. An additional difference between tax codes under the two procedures is that while TAXUSJ tax codes can be used for multiple jurisdictions, they are in a sense tied to each juridiction because the jurisdictional rate is contained within the tax code. TAXUSX tax codes can be used with any jurisdiction code regardless of rate because the rate is contained in the external system.

If you compare Figure 12.6 in Chapter 12 with Figure 14.19, you can see the differences between a tax code using TAXUSJ and one using TAXUSX. The main difference is that the tax rate is maintained in a TAXUSJ tax code as opposed to an external table when using TAXUSX. You will also note that the condition types for a tax code using TAXUSX are entirely different from those used for TAXUSJ.

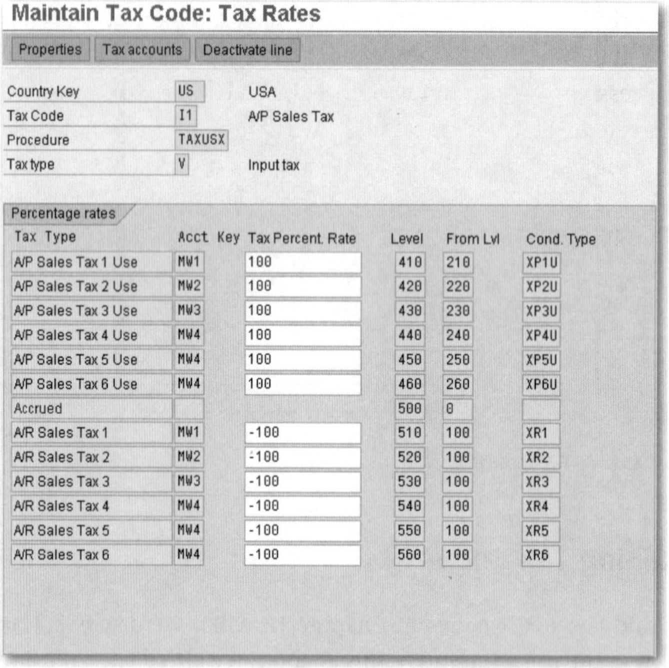

Maintain Tax Code: Tax Rates

Properties | Tax accounts | Deactivate line

Country Key	US	USA
Tax Code	I1	A/P Sales Tax
Procedure	TAXUSX	
Tax type	V	Input tax

Percentage rates

Tax Type	Acct Key	Tax Percent. Rate	Level	From Lvl	Cond. Type
A/P Sales Tax 1 Use	MW1	100	410	210	XP1U
A/P Sales Tax 2 Use	MW2	100	420	220	XP2U
A/P Sales Tax 3 Use	MW3	100	430	230	XP3U
A/P Sales Tax 4 Use	MW4	100	440	240	XP4U
A/P Sales Tax 5 Use	MW4	100	450	250	XP5U
A/P Sales Tax 6 Use	MW4	100	460	260	XP6U
Accrued			500	0	
A/R Sales Tax 1	MW1	-100	510	100	XR1
A/R Sales Tax 2	MW2	-100	520	100	XR2
A/R Sales Tax 3	MW3	-100	530	100	XR3
A/R Sales Tax 4	MW4	-100	540	100	XR4
A/R Sales Tax 5	MW4	-100	550	100	XR5
A/R Sales Tax 6	MW4	-100	560	100	XR6

Figure 14.19 A TAXUSX Tax Code

The account determination for the tax liability was also shown in Chapter 12, and the approach used is the same regardless of tax procedure. We did not, however, discuss how the system decides whether to record a liability, so let's look at this now.

SAP software uses three objects in combination to decide how tax is recorded:

- An accounting key
- A process key
- A transaction key

The Accounting Key

Each condition type in the tax procedure has an accounting key assigned to it. The accounting key can also be seen by looking at the tax code. The accounting key is always equal to a process key.

The Process Key

The process key carries a posting indicator in its master data that indicates how tax amounts will be handled. For example, Figure 14.20 shows the master data for the process key MW1. You will note that each process key is tied to a tax type and has a posting indicator field. A posting indicator of 2 specifies a separate line item. A posting indicator of 3 indicates that the tax amount will be recorded to relevant expense or revenue accounts. The posting indicator should be assigned based on condition types in the tax code.

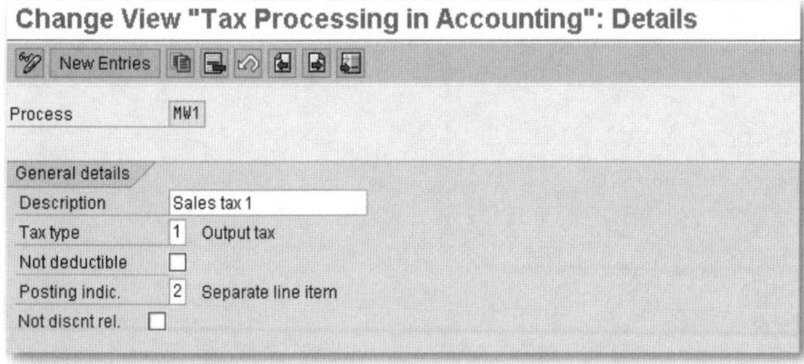

Figure 14.20 Process Key MW1

The Transaction Key

Process keys with posting indicators other than 3 have related transaction keys that specify the account for posting. Those with posting indicators of 3 do not need additional account assignment because the tax amounts are distributed to the related expense or revenue items. The transaction key is where you will make the account assignment for process keys with a liability account. In configuring the process key, you will first have to select the chart of accounts and then the proper account from that chart. Table 14.11 shows the transaction necessary for the system to properly determine the account for a tax code.

Figures 14.21 and 14.22 illustrate the screens where the process keys and transaction keys are maintained in the IMG, respectively.

Action	T-Code	TAXUS	TAXUSJ	TAXUSX	Comments
Maintain tax code.	FTXP	X	X	X	Also shown in Chapter 12, Section 1.3.3.
Determine account for tax codes.	OBCN OB40	X	X	X	Process keys.
Determine account for tax codes.	OB40	X	X	X	Transaction keys.

Table 14.11 Account Determination for a Tax Code

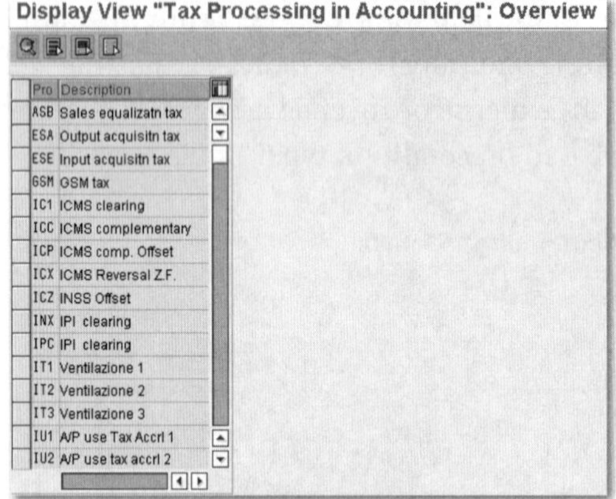

Figure 14.21 Process Keys

Display FI Configuration: Automatic Posting - Procedures

Group %TX Taxes on sales/purchases

Procedures

Description	Transaction	Account determ.
Special fuel tax	J3A	☑
Additional tax	LUX	☑
Sales tax 1	MW1	☑
Sales tax 2	MW2	☑
Sales tax 3	MW3	☑
Sales tax 4	MW4	☑
Output tax GST	MW5	☑
Output tax	MWS	☑
Non-deduct.input tax	NAV	☑
Entertainment tax	NZ1	☑
Reduction	NZ2	☑
Sales tax 1	VS1	☑
Sales tax 2	VS2	☑
Sales tax 3	VS3	☑
Sales tax 4	VS4	☑
Input Tax PST Gross	VS5	☑
Input Tax HST s/a	VS6	☑
Input tax GST s/a	VS7	☑
Input tax QST	VSC	☑

Figure 14.22 Transaction Keys

14.7 Nontaxable Transactions

Transactions not relevant to tax were discussed briefly in Chapter 12 and are covered here in more detail. Transactions such as goods receipts and goods issues are not relevant for sales and use tax, but because a jurisdiction code and tax code are required by the tax procedure, it is necessary to default in a nontaxable tax code and set up a dummy jurisdiction code to assign to these transactions. The transaction code for this is shown in Table 14.12. An illustration of this was included in Chapter 12 and another is included here in Figure 14.23.

Action	T-Code	TAXUS	TAXUSJ	TAXUSX	Comments
Set codes for nontaxable transactions.	OBCL	X	X	X	Set tax code and jurisdiction code.

Table 14.12 Configuration for Nontaxable Transactions

The nontaxable jurisdiction code is generally set to XX00000000, as shown in Figure 14.23.

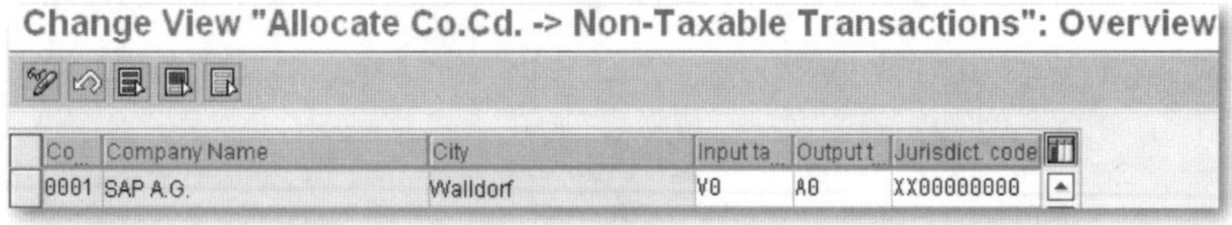

Change View "Allocate Co.Cd. -> Non-Taxable Transactions": Overview

Co...	Company Name	City	Input ta...	Output t...	Jurisdict. code
0001	SAP A.G.	Walldorf	V0	A0	XX00000000

Figure 14.23 Configuration for Nontax Relevant Transactions

14.8 G/L Account Maintenance

Each G/L account carries a one-character **Tax category** field indicating whether the account can be posted to without tax. If the indicator is left blank, it means the account is tax-relevant and requires a tax category code. If the field is checked, a tax category field need not be entered for the G/L account.

The **Tax category** field on the **Control Data** tab of the G/L account master needs to be maintained for each tax-relevant G/L account. The **Tax category** value can be an individual tax code or can be customized to the requirements of the company. Table 14.13 shows several standard tax category values.

Value	Description
*	All tax types allowed
+	Only output tax allowed
-	Only input tax allowed
>	Output tax
<	Input tax

Table 14.13 Standard Tax Category Values

If a G/L account cannot be posted to without tax and the **Tax category** field is blank, transactions using the G/L account cannot be processed. The system looks for tax amounts where tax-relevant G/L accounts are used and will not proceed if tax line items are not found in the transaction. Table 14.14 lists the G/L master file settings that need to be reviewed for each account.

Action	T-Code	TAXUS	TAXUSJ	TAXUSX	Comments
Use the posting without tax allowed indicator.	FS01 FS02 FS03	X	X	X	
Maintain G/L tax account.	FS01 FS02 FS03	X	X	X	Tax category on the G/L master.

Table 14.14 Maintaining Tax Fields on a G/L Account

Figure 14.24 displays the G/L **Tax category** field and the **Posting without tax allowed** indicator.

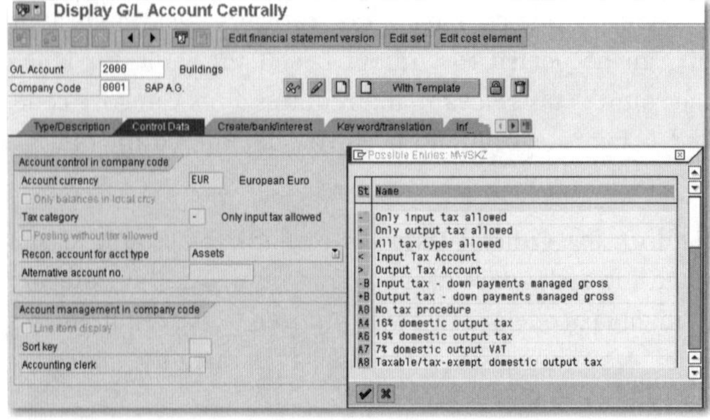

Figure 14.24 The G/L Tax Category Code and Posting Without Tax Allowed Indicator

14.9 A Final Word About Sales and Use Tax Configuration

This chapter and Chapters 12 and 13 have given you a great deal of information about configuration for sales and use taxes. This configuration usually coincides with other configuration on the project, so when testing starts, if tax-related issues crop up, you'll have knowledge to fall back on for troubleshooting.

However, while the information contained in these chapters will help you a great deal, it is not a replacement for experience. Thus, if you are in charge of sales and use tax, it is still helpful to have experienced assistance from an individual with a good understanding of the tax processes involved, so be sure to seek assistance from experienced tax integration specialists.

Further, many nuances in this area often require special solutions that have not been addressed in these chapters. Experienced assistance is especially helpful when these nuances arise. Each company faces unique situations when installing SAP software, and skilled consultting in this area will usually result in a more efficient tax solution in a shorter period of time.

14.10 Summary

Configuration for sales and use tax requires maintaining data on both the IMG and the application side of the SAP system. This chapter has discussed the settings necessary in the SD, MM, and FI modules and provided transaction codes where available. Screenshots illustrating the majority of the settings have also been included. In addition, this chapter discussed the role of pricing procedures in SD and identified the configuration steps for the different U.S. tax procedures. However, tax configuration is complicated, and challenges may arise that are not discussed in this book. Thus, although this chapter has imparted a great deal of knowledge, only through hands-on experience can you fully understand the processes required to create an efficient sales and use tax solution. You should work with skilled tax integration specialists in addition to using this chapter as a reference.

In Chapter 15, we will depart from our discussion of sales and use tax and look at integration techniques for so-called "green" taxes. In particular, we will look at beverage taxes, bottle and can deposits, and waste taxes.

A number of additional taxes exist that often cause difficulty for corporate tax departments and SAP implementation teams. In this chapter, we'll discuss these taxes and what can be done in your SAP software to assist with compliance.

15 Miscellaneous Taxes

Corporate tax departments are usually organized around and geared toward handling the major taxes we have discussed already, including the following:

- Federal income taxes
- State and local income taxes
- Sales and use taxes
- Property taxes

In addition, larger corporate tax departments typically have a group dedicated to audits, planning, and legal issues. International taxation is also a consideration, but we are focused on U.S. tax and have discussed the federal aspect of international taxation that does get attention by tax departments. Beyond this, however, there are also smaller taxes like those in the following list:

- Franchise taxes
- Beverage taxes and bottle and can deposits
- Waste taxes and environmental fees

These taxes are typically handled by other groups or are added to the responsibilities of a tax manager who already has a full plate handling bigger dollar issues. In addition, there is often no tax package that produces the necessary returns, so someone is assigned to do this manually. Tax departments want and attempt to comply with these issues, and any assistance is welcome during an SAP implementation. To help with these tax issues, we'll look at each of these smaller taxes in detail. Let's take a look at franchise taxes first.

15.1 Franchise Taxes

Franchise tax is generally a tax on income or capital levied at the state level. Of the taxes mentioned earlier, franchise taxes tend to get the most attention because they are easily computed from a company's financial records, and the state jurisdictions can cause a corporation real problems. Further, tax directors don't want the corporate charter suspended in a given state, so this tax is generally taken care of. Thankfully, very little in the SAP system needs to be done to obtain data needed to calculate the tax other than maintaining a complete chart of accounts and good financial records.

As an example, Figures 15.1 and 15.2 illustrate the two ways the state of Texas calculates franchise tax. Both illustrations are portions of the actual Texas franchise tax return and are taken from the website for the Texas State Comptroller of Public Accounts (*http://window.state.tx.us/taxinfo/taxforms/05-forms.html*).

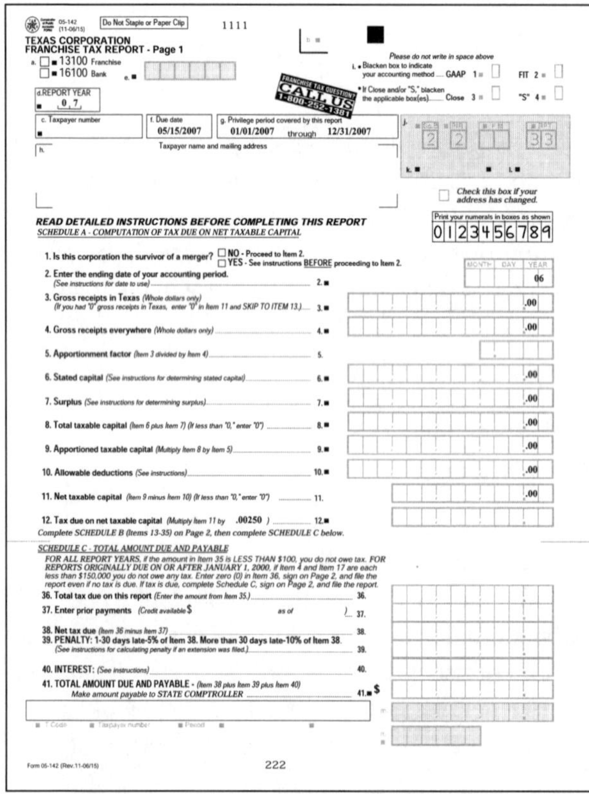

05-142 (11-06/15) Do Not Staple or Paper Clip 1111

TEXAS CORPORATION
FRANCHISE TAX REPORT - Page 1

a. ☐ 13100 Franchise
☐ 16100 Bank
e.

d. REPORT YEAR 0 7

Please do not write in space above

i. • Blacken box to indicate your accounting method ... GAAP 1 ☐ FIT 2 ☐
• If Close and/or "S," blacken the applicable box(es) ... Close 3 ☐ "S" 4 ☐

FRANCHISE TAX QUESTION? CALL US 1-800-252-1381

c. Taxpayer number	f. Due date	g. Privilege period covered by this report
	05/15/2007	01/01/2007 through 12/31/2007

h. Taxpayer name and mailing address

j. 2 2 3 3

k. l.

☐ Check this box if your address has changed.

Print your numerals in boxes as shown: 0 1 2 3 4 5 6 7 8 9

READ DETAILED INSTRUCTIONS BEFORE COMPLETING THIS REPORT

SCHEDULE A - COMPUTATION OF TAX DUE ON NET TAXABLE CAPITAL

1. Is this corporation the survivor of a merger? ☐ NO - Proceed to Item 2. ☐ YES - See instructions BEFORE proceeding to Item 2.
2. Enter the ending date of your accounting period. (See instructions for date to use) ... 2. MONTH DAY YEAR 06
3. Gross receipts in Texas (Whole dollars only) (If you had "0" gross receipts in Texas, enter "0" in Item 11 and SKIP TO ITEM 13.) ... 3. .00
4. Gross receipts everywhere (Whole dollars only) ... 4. .00
5. Apportionment factor (Item 3 divided by Item 4) ... 5.
6. Stated capital (See instructions for determining stated capital) ... 6. .00
7. Surplus (See instructions for determining surplus) ... 7. .00
8. Total taxable capital (Item 6 plus Item 7) (If less than "0," enter "0") ... 8. .00
9. Apportioned taxable capital (Multiply Item 8 by Item 5) ... 9. .00
10. Allowable deductions (See instructions) ... 10. .00
11. Net taxable capital (Item 9 minus Item 10) (If less than "0," enter "0") ... 11. .00
12. Tax due on net taxable capital (Multiply Item 11 by .00250) ... 12.

Complete SCHEDULE B (Items 13-35) on Page 2, then complete SCHEDULE C below.

SCHEDULE C - TOTAL AMOUNT DUE AND PAYABLE

FOR ALL REPORT YEARS, if the amount in Item 35 is LESS THAN $100, you do not owe tax. FOR REPORTS ORIGINALLY DUE ON OR AFTER JANUARY 1, 2000, if Item 4 and Item 17 are each less than $150,000 you do not owe any tax. Enter zero (0) in Item 36, sign on Page 2, and file the report even if no tax is due. If tax is due, complete Schedule C, sign on Page 2, and file the report.

36. Total tax due on this report (Enter the amount from Item 35.) ... 36.
37. Enter prior payments (Credit available $ as of) ... 37.
38. Net tax due (Item 36 minus Item 37) ... 38.
39. PENALTY: 1-30 days late-5% of Item 38. More than 30 days late-10% of Item 38. (See instructions for calculating penalty if an extension was filed.) ... 39.
40. INTEREST: (See instructions) ... 40.
41. TOTAL AMOUNT DUE AND PAYABLE - (Item 38 plus Item 39 plus Item 40) Make amount payable to STATE COMPTROLLER ... 41. $

T Code Taxpayer number Period

Form 05-142 (Rev.11-06/15) 222

Figure 15.1 Franchise Tax Based on Corporate Capital
(Source: http://window.state.tx.us/taxinfo/taxforms/2007rep.pdf)

Note

Tax jurisdictions differ in the calculations for franchise tax returns. Delaware, for example, uses two methods that both deal with outstanding stock. The first is called the *Authorized Shares Method*, and the second is called the *Assumed Par Value Actual Method*. You will note that while Texas taxes capital or earned surplus, Delaware does not.

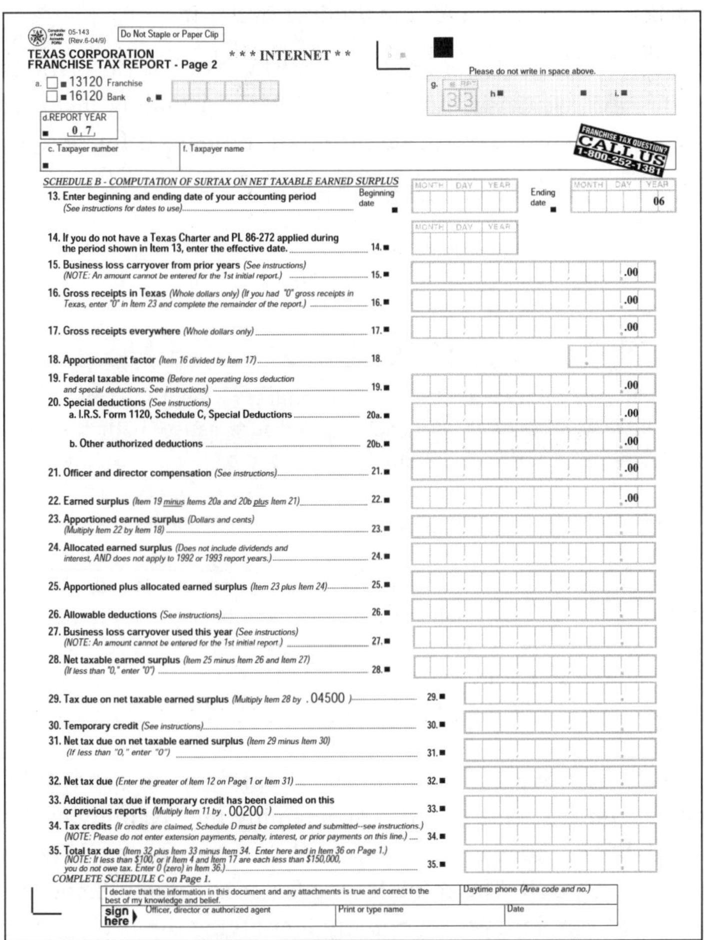

05-143 (Rev.6-04/9)

Do Not Staple or Paper Clip

TEXAS CORPORATION
FRANCHISE TAX REPORT - Page 2

* * * INTERNET * *

Please do not write in space above.

a. ☐ ■ 13120 Franchise
☐ ■ 16120 Bank

e. ■

g. 33 h■ ■ i.■

d.REPORT YEAR ■ 0 7

c. Taxpayer number ■ | f. Taxpayer name

FRANCHISE TAX QUESTION? CALL US 1-800-252-1381

SCHEDULE B - COMPUTATION OF SURTAX ON NET TAXABLE EARNED SURPLUS

13. Enter beginning and ending date of your accounting period *(See instructions for dates to use)* — Beginning date ■ MONTH DAY YEAR — Ending date ■ MONTH DAY YEAR 06
14. If you do not have a Texas Charter and PL 86-272 applied during the period shown in Item 13, enter the effective date. 14.■ MONTH DAY YEAR
15. Business loss carryover from prior years *(See instructions)* *(NOTE: An amount cannot be entered for the 1st initial report.)* 15.■ .00
16. Gross receipts in Texas *(Whole dollars only) (If you had "0" gross receipts in Texas, enter "0" in Item 23 and complete the remainder of the report.)* 16.■ .00
17. Gross receipts everywhere *(Whole dollars only)* 17.■ .00
18. Apportionment factor *(Item 16 divided by Item 17)* 18.
19. Federal taxable income *(Before net operating loss deduction and special deductions. See instructions)* 19.■ .00
20. Special deductions *(See instructions)*
    a. I.R.S. Form 1120, Schedule C, Special Deductions 20a.■ .00
    b. Other authorized deductions 20b.■ .00
21. Officer and director compensation *(See instructions)* 21.■ .00
22. Earned surplus *(Item 19 minus Items 20a and 20b plus Item 21)* 22.■ .00
23. Apportioned earned surplus *(Dollars and cents)* *(Multiply Item 22 by Item 18)* 23.■
24. Allocated earned surplus *(Does not include dividends and interest, AND does not apply to 1992 or 1993 report years.)* 24.■
25. Apportioned plus allocated earned surplus *(Item 23 plus Item 24)* 25.■
26. Allowable deductions *(See instructions)* 26.■
27. Business loss carryover used this year *(See instructions)* *(NOTE: An amount cannot be entered for the 1st initial report.)* 27.■
28. Net taxable earned surplus *(Item 25 minus Item 26 and Item 27)* *(If less than "0," enter "0")* 28.■
29. Tax due on net taxable earned surplus *(Multiply Item 28 by .04500)* 29.■
30. Temporary credit *(See instructions)* 30.■
31. Net tax due on net taxable earned surplus *(Item 29 minus Item 30)* *(If less than "0," enter "0")* 31.■
32. Net tax due *(Enter the greater of Item 12 on Page 1 or Item 31)* 32.■
33. Additional tax due if temporary credit has been claimed on this or previous reports *(Multiply Item 11 by .00200)* 33.■
34. Tax credits *(If credits are claimed, Schedule D must be completed and submitted--see instructions.)* *(NOTE: Please do not enter extension payments, penalty, interest, or prior payments on this line.)* 34.■
35. Total tax due *(Item 32 plus Item 33 minus Item 34. Enter here and in Item 36 on Page 1.)* *(NOTE: If less than $100, or if Item 4 and Item 17 are each less than $150,000, you do not owe tax. Enter 0 (zero) in Item 36.)* 35.■

COMPLETE SCHEDULE C on Page 1.

I declare that the information in this document and any attachments is true and correct to the best of my knowledge and belief.		Daytime phone *(Area code and no.)*
sign here ▸ Officer, director or authorized agent	Print or type name	Date

Figure 15.2 Franchise Tax Based on Corporate Income
(Source: http://window.state.tx.us/taxinfo/taxforms/2007rep.pdf)

As mentioned earlier, SAP software will meet franchise tax needs fairly easily, but requirements for given states need to be looked at for anything that might be peculiar. Tax integration specialists can assist in this area if brought on board early in the implementation.

15.2 Beverage Taxes and Bottle and Can Deposits

Beverage taxes take many forms and are levied by many jurisdictions. Alcoholic beverage taxes are the most common and are generally calculated based on apportioned sales in the locality, times a tax rate. Nonalcholic soft drinks may be taxed on the finished product, on the syrup used to make the finished product, the powder used to make it, or the base. Rates differ based on the form and quantity of the container the product comes in.

Bolt-on software that works with R/3 or ECC to assist with these calculations isn't available. The SAP system is, however, capable of handling many of these types of taxes. We'll discuss two ways this can be done, as follows:

- Using condition types and records within the pricing procedures
- Using an internal tax procedure (TAXUSJ or TAXUSX) or the SAP tax interface to call an internal or external table maintained by the tax department

Note

In Chapters 13 and 14, we discussed SAP's tax procedures at length. From those discussions, you will remember that the pricing procedure assists with the tax calculation in the SD module and that the link between the pricing procedure and the tax procedure is the tax code. The tax code is also necessary for account determination or deciding the general ledger (G/L) account status for the amount of tax collected from the customer. You may also remember that only one tax procedure can be used for a given country. This means that the tax procedure used will be decided by the team who configures sales and use tax, and because beverage tax and deposit issues are not going to take priority over sales and use tax issues, you will need to work with the procedure given. This might be TAXUSJ or TAXUSX, so we'll look at both.

When using either of the two approaches, similar information needed for sales and use tax is required. This includes maintaining the taxability of the customer, the taxability of the material, the jurisdiction code of the delivery location, and the tax rate itself. The complicating factor in computing beverage tax and bottle and can deposits is properly identifying the tax per unit and associating the tax with the appropriate container size. Beverages are sold in a variety of container sizes, which are packed and shipped in various ways. For a given transaction, the tax may be a penny an ounce, but there may be 20 cases shipped to the customer. Calculating the number of ounces in a case is hard enough but can be complicated more if 100 pallets are shipped with each pallet containing 50 cases. It may be necessary to do some customization to assist with the conversions.

15.2.1 Using the Pricing Procedure Without a Tax Procedure

Beverage tax conditions and rates can be calculated using the pricing procedure, however, it does require maintaining a large number of records in the system. To help with this, because tax rates change per package size, you should break the package size down to its lowest common denominator, such as an ounce, or a can, and then break the tax rate down the same way. The tax per product size can be calculated by multiplying the rate times the units of measure; thus, by adding this functionality to the solution, the number of rates maintained in the system will be much fewer.

When using the pricing procedure, you also need to set up condition types and records for the additional charge to the customer. The tax rate and material can be maintained in the condition records for the condition type, and the delivery location can be taken from the jurisdiction code on the customer master. The process will work well but is very record-intensive.

Note

The number of states adopting beverage and container deposit laws is growing quickly. Oregon is the most recent state to pass legislation adopting these types of rules.

15.2.2 Using the Pricing Procedure with TAXUSJ

Let's look at what is required if you are given tax procedure TAXUSJ to work with. SD condition records are maintained under SD condition type UTXJ and pricing procedure RVAJUS. Condition records under condition type UTXJ point to a tax code that will contain a tax rate for a given jurisdiction. UTXJ condition records contain both the tax classification of the customer and the material. They also can contain a region code (state), depending on the key combination used for the record. Figure 15.3 shows a condition record for condition type tax UTXJ.

The tax code under TAXUSJ can be tied to many jurisdictions. As long as the tax rate is the same, the code can be used a number of times. It is still generally necessary, however, to maintain a high number of codes for taxable situations. Nontaxable situations can all use the same zero-rate tax code and have it tied to multiple jurisdictions.

Using one condition type, UTXJ, with separate tax codes for beverage tax, bottle deposits, and can deposits will lead to a high number of tax codes. An alternate solution is to set up additional condition types, one for each type of tax, which should reduce the number of tax codes in the system. This may be the only solution if you have vendors that have more than one type of tax on the same invoice.

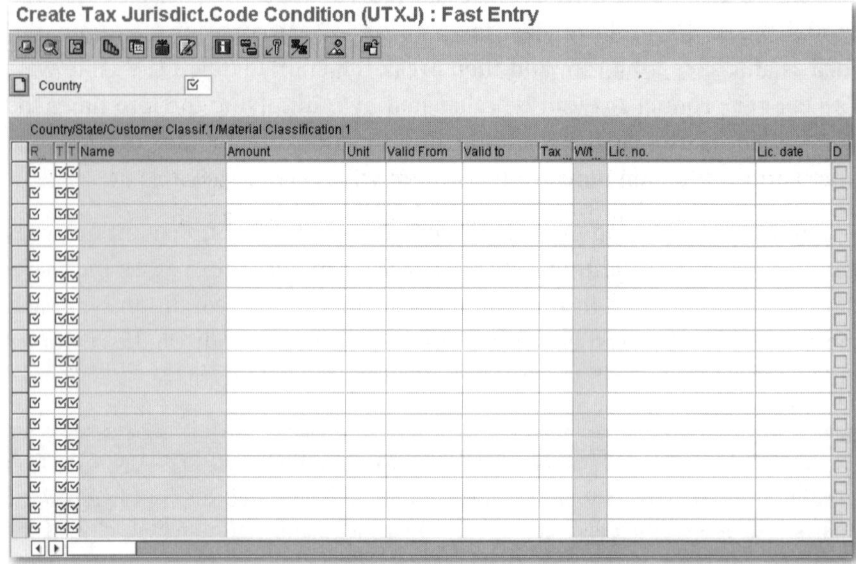

Figure 15.3 An SD Condition Record Under UTXJ

> **Note**
>
> Using the pricing procedure and TAXUSJ works very well, but note that it still has the drawback of having to maintain a large number of records.

15.2.3 Using the Pricing Procedure with TAXUSX

If your company has chosen TAXUSX for sales and use tax, you will have to work within its confines for beverage tax, and bottle and can deposits. As mentioned in Chapters 12 and 13, two pricing procedures come with SAP software for use with TAXUSX, as follows:

- RVAXUS
- RVAXUD

Depending on the pricing procedure selected by the team doing the sales and use tax integration, the approach for beverage tax will be slightly different. Pricing procedure RVAXUS has been around for years and is still in place for many implementations. Pricing procedure RVAXUD is a newer pricing procedure introduced with SAP R/3 release 4.6B. The newer pricing procedure was introduced because some jurisdictions started using creative taxing schemes such as max tax rules, step tax, tiered rates, and other progressive tax methods.

SAP recommends using pricing procedure RVAXUD because it handles the tax methods mentioned earlier much easier. The difference in the two procedures is that with RVAXUD, the external tax software is able to look at an entire document instead of individual line items. This does not mean that it ignores the individual line items, however. On the contrary, it takes all of the items in the document into account before making the tax rate decision.

Note

Ultimately, the only difference the pricing procedure makes is what SD condition type is used when preparing the condition records. RVAXUS uses UTXJ, whereas RVAXUD uses UTXD. We looked at a condition record for UTXJ earlier. Records for UTXD are identical to UTXJ. New condition types can be created for each type of tax under pricing procedure RVAXUD, as I mentioned as an option when discussing the process using TAXUSJ. The RFC call will fire for each condition type and bring back separate amounts that can be detailed on the customer invoice.

When either of the two pricing procedures are used with an external system, there is no need for condition records to be tied to jurisdictions and tax codes. Tax rates, product information, and jurisdictional data can be maintained either in an internal SAP table or in an external table.

Clarification and Caution

Let me clarify a statement made earlier about no bolt-on software being available for SAP for calculating beverage taxes and bottle and can deposits. That is true, so we are talking about either creating a custom table to hold the information needed or working with a third-party vendor to buy the data. However, very few vendors exist that have this type of data.

It is also a bit of a risk to say that an internal SAP table can be used to hold the data, as I have not actually seen this done before. However, a client I am working with is implementing this approach, which means that the function modules in the SAP tax interface system need to be pointed to an internal SAP table and that the internal table has to have a communication link built that can receive and give back data.

Regardless of where the table is located, the functionality is the same as was covered in Chapter 13. Beverage tax and bottle and can deposits are levied at the transaction level similar to sales and use tax, and the functionality of the tax user interface can be leveraged here as well.

15.3 Waste Taxes and Environmental Fees

The arena of environmental tax provisions is one of the fastest growing areas of tax. For example, the bottle and can deposits just discussed, although often not considered a tax, certainly fall into the bucket of enviromental provisions. In general, so-called "green" taxes seem to be catching on all over the United States and are taking many forms. Thus, in the remainder of this chapter, we will explore the different types of green taxes, the different ways they are levied, and whether anything can be done in R/3 or ECC to assist companies with compliance.

In 1998, the Center for a Sustainable Economy published its survey of state initiatives titled "Harnessing the Tax Code for Environmental Protection: A Survey of State Initiatives." The study stated that in 1998 only five states had fewer than 5 environmental tax provisions and that as of 1996, 462 provisions were in place nationwide. That was nearly 10 years ago, and the number has only grown since then.

Fortunately, R/3 or ECC can usually easily deal with these types of tax payments.

Many of the issues require self-assessment of the tax and remittance to tax authorities. Others offer incentives that many companies are missing out on because they require corporations to track and prove efforts taken to improve the environment. Environmental provisions, or *waste taxes,* as they are often called, sometimes take the following forms:

- Resource severance charges
- Direct fees related to disposal
- Self-assessed fees
- Tax incentives

Let's look at each of these in more detail.

15.3.1 Resource Severance Charges

Resource severance charges require measurement of the amount of oil and gas or other mineral extracted. Oil and gas is more easily measured than a mineral such as ore. All can be measured, however. This type of tax requires tracking and remitting to tax authorities on a periodic basis.

15.3.2 Direct Fees Related to Disposal

Direct fees related to disposal are handled most easily because they require a payment through the AP system based on a predetermined rate per unit. The remaining charges are based on some type of self assessment, which is more difficult.

15.3.3 Self-Assessed Fees

Many self-assessed fees are not as easily measured, such as those involving air and water pollution. Because many self-assessed taxes are specific to industries, they can be planned for and captured in G/L accounts or cost centers.

15.3.4 Tax Incentives

Tax incentives present the biggest challenges because corporations are eager to comply to receive the rebates, but the incentives can span all areas of a corporation. A corporation may be required to track expenditures for pollution control equipment, savings on utilities, expenditures for alternative fuel automobiles, and a host of other initiatives. Tracking these types of costs not only involve G/L accounts but possibly the use of internal orders and projects. They also often involve operations personnel at the plant level having knowledge of state statutes so efforts can be effectively reported. Tax departments often have difficulty gathering information for these types of activities.

Tax integrations specialists may be able to assist with specific high-impact taxes if addressed during the implementation process and should at least give the area a look. This is an area where new taxes are being created every year, and tweaking in R/3 or ECC may create some relief.

15.4 Summary

Environmental taxes have expanded rapidly since the 1970s. SAP software can handle some of these taxes, depending on how they are calculated, and if they are considered during the implementation process. Taxes that require self-assessment and data from across an organization are much more difficult to deal with than those specific to a particular business process. Tax integration specialists should review these taxes during the implementation process to determine what assistance can be obtained from the SAP software.

Chapter 16 discusses transfer pricing issues in more detail and measures that can be taken within the SAP software to help tax professionals comply with this important issue.

Transfer pricing requires a great deal of attention from tax departments of multinational corporations. In this chapter, we will discuss transfer pricing projects, best practices, and what can be done within SAP software to lighten the transfer pricing load for tax professionals.

16 Transfer Pricing

From a tax standpoint, *transfer pricing* refers to the IRS requiring a fair market or arm's length price on goods or services transferred between two legal entities of the same company when the transaction crosses a U.S. border. However, transfer pricing in the minds of many is much more encompassing than the tax definition of the term. In Releases ECC 5.0 and ECC 6.0, SAP addressed the issue by integrating transfer pricing functionality into its software. This has made it possible for corporations to look at each of their operating divisions or business segments on a standalone basis from a profitability standpoint. Corporations have attempted to do this for years, but previously did not have the tools available they now do with the new transfer pricing functionality in the ECC releases mentioned, and with the new general ledger (G/L). With this new functionality, it is possible for one division to charge another at a fair market value and for both to produce an accurate internal income statement and balance sheet.

Note

Prior to this functionality being available, transfer pricing was done using pricing procedures and the cost objects available at the time. The problem that quickly became apparent was that it was difficult to look at transfer prices between two legal entities of a company and two operating divisions of a company at the same time. Tax departments are required by law to report on transfer pricing between two company codes or legal entities of an enterprise and not on an operational basis. Upper management wants to see profitability by identifing and controlling prices between the operating divisions. Management's need to accurately track division net income and hold operations leadership responsible has led to improvements in the transfer pricing area.

16.1 The SAP Solution to Transfer Pricing Issues

With ECC releases 5.0 and 6.0, transfer pricing took a step forward, especially in the area of divisional profitability. SAP leveraged two current applications, material ledger and document splitting, and developed two new applications, the new G/L and profit center transfer pricing, to improve financial accounting, managerial accounting, and transfer pricing.

The new transfer pricing functionality was placed in the Contolling module and can be found in the IMG under **Controlling** and **Profit Center Accounting.** Figure 16.1 shows the IMG screen where the configuration is done.

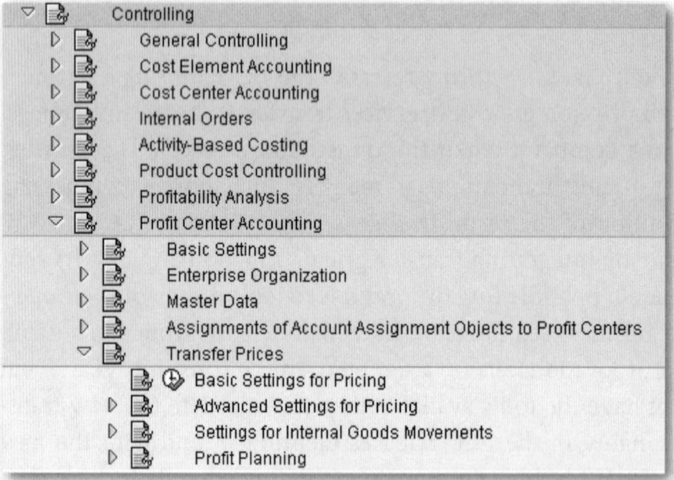

Figure 16.1 The IMG Node Where Transfer Pricing Is Found

The new process still uses the pricing procedure for controlling the arm's length markup but offers SAP-supplied functionality for options such as fixed rate versus percentage markups. When coupled with the material ledger and the new G/L, three valuation approaches are available:

- Legal valuation
- Group valuation
- Profit center valuation

In addition, multiple currencies are now available.

Note

The addition of the new valuation areas does not assist tax departments as much as it does internal operations management. The legal valuation area has always been available. But it is possible now to use one valuation approach for legal entity accounting and a different one for profit center accounting. When coupled with document splitting, a complete set of balanced financial statements can now be obtained on a profit center, segment, or cost center basis.

From a tax standpoint, the arm's length markup is still maintained in the pricing procedure, but additional pricing procedures have been supplied as part of the enhancement. Figure 16.2 shows the screen where condition types and pricing procedures are maintained.

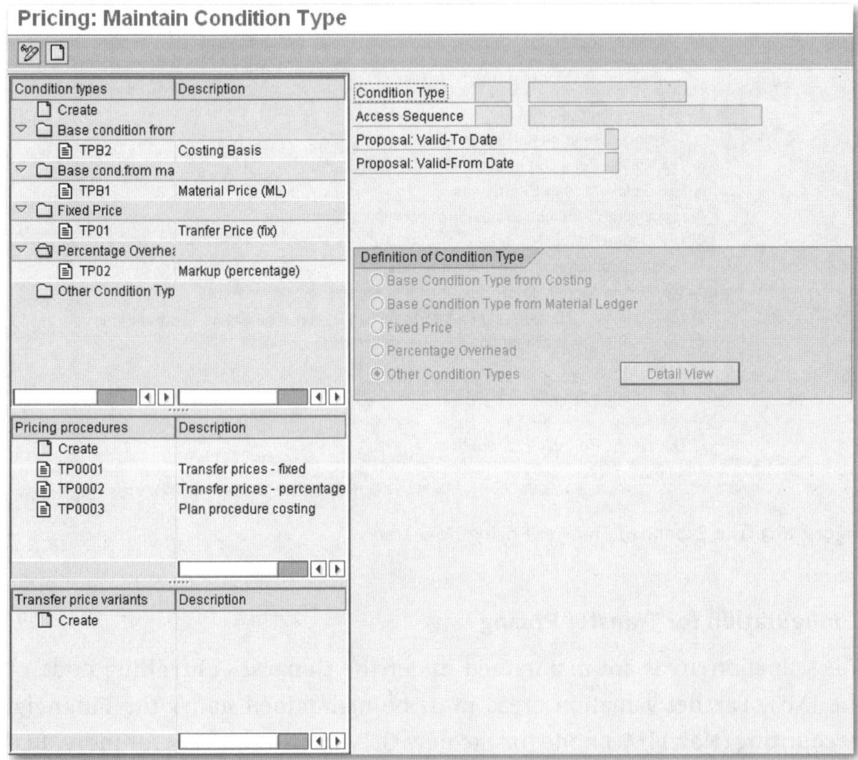

Figure 16.2 Maintaining Condition Types and Pricing Procedures

If the condition types and pricing procedures supplied are not adequate, new pricing procedures can also be created. Figure 16.3 shows the expanded IMG tree where advanced settings for pricing is maintained. Report creation is also available.

In addition, account determination is available within profit center accounting that allows for internal revenue to be recognized on intercompany transactions. These are based off the Financials (FI) postings but do not impact the financial records in FI. The third activity shown in Figure 16.3 is the planning functionality built into profit center accounting. Additional nodes exist in the IMG for other transfer pricing activities.

> **Note**
>
> The account determination and planning functionalities both again benefit operations management in more ways than they do tax departments.

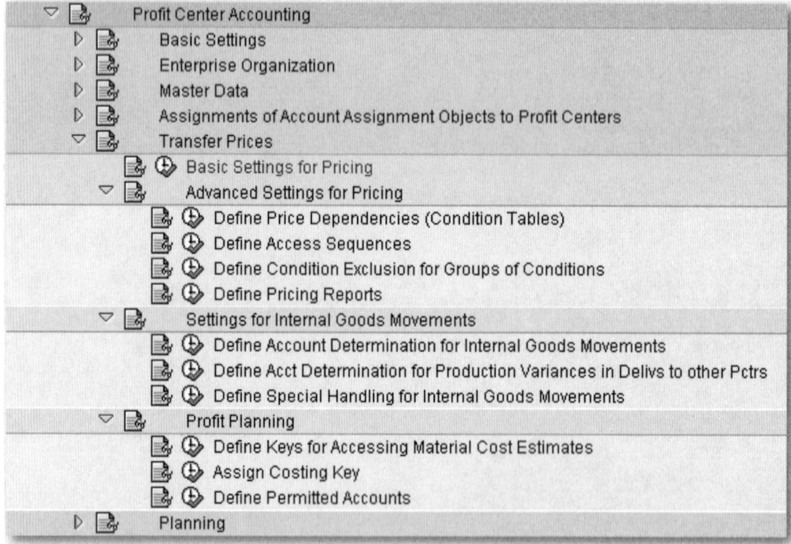

Figure 16.3 The Expanded Transfer Pricing IMG Tree

Configuration for Transfer Pricing

The valuation areas are maintained under the **General Controlling** node of the IMG. Parallel valuation areas must be maintained under the **Financial Accounting (New)** IMG node for the new G/L. Transfer pricing for individual projects can also be maintained in the project system under the **Project System** node of the IMG as long as the controlling area is set up for multiple valuation. All the configuration in the material ledger, the new G/L, document splitting, and profit center transfer pricing is new and complex and must be done in unison for everything to work properly.

Caution

Be sure to find experienced help configuring the new functionality before going forward.

The application side of the SAP system is also impacted by the new functionality. Figure 16.4 shows the **Profit Center Accounting** menu and the **Transfer Pricing** node on the menu. Transfer pricing condition records are created, changed, or displayed in this menu area.

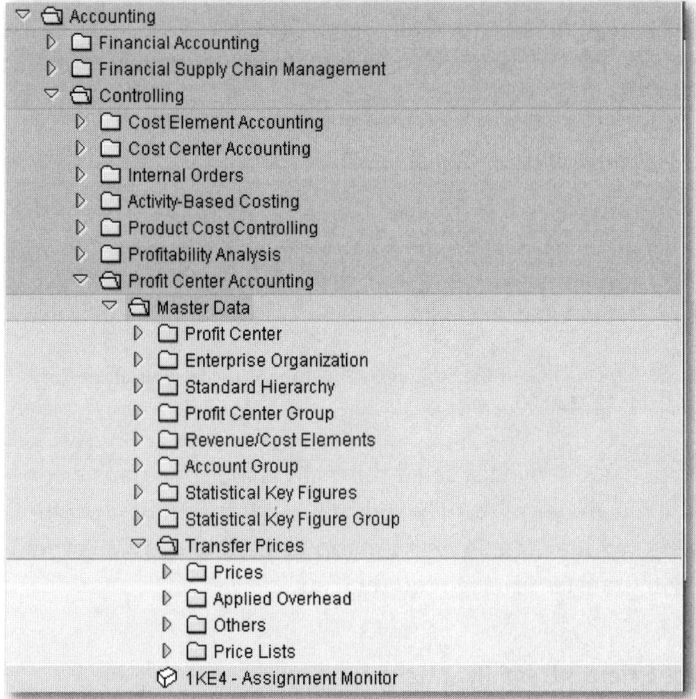

Figure 16.4 Transfer Pricing Condition Record Maintenance

In summary, new ECC functionality has radically improved the ability to track internal operational profits between a company's divisions with tools like the new G/L, material ledger, transfer pricing, and document splitting. The improvements in a tax department's ability to account for transfer pricing on a legal entity basis has not been as dramatic but has provided standard pricing procedures. With the improved functionality in mind, let's turn our attention to tax requirements and other items obtainable from the SAP system.

16.2 Transfer Pricing for Tax

Section 482 of the internal revenue code addresses transfer pricing requirements for U.S. commonly controlled taxpayers. Figure 16.5 shows an IRS statement concerning intercompany transactions and transfer pricing. It says that the IRS has the right to adjust pricing between controlled entities if it is not done at a fair market price. You can conclude from this that these adjustments will result in an increase in a corporation's tax liability.

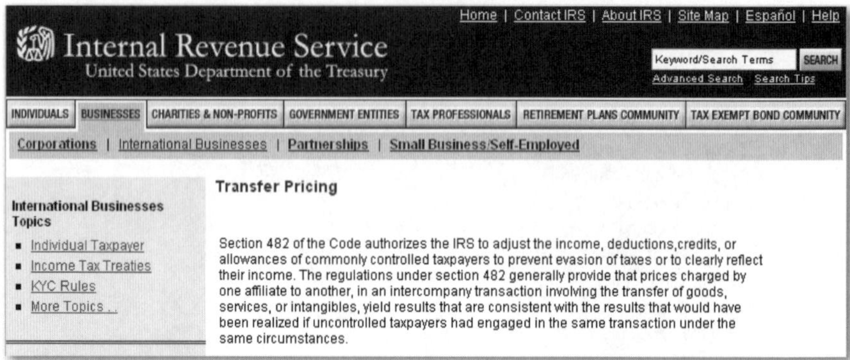

Figure 16.5 IRS Transfer Pricing Statement (Source: IRS website www.irs.gov/businesses/international/article/0,,id=120220,00.html)

In Chapter 4, Section 4.3.1, we discussed the main phases of a transfer pricing project. In the remainder of this chapter, we will focus on best practices for transfer pricing and how the SAP system can be used to assist a corporation to comply with transfer pricing requirements.

16.2.1 Transfer Pricing Best Practices

PricewaterhouseCooper (PwC) maintains a Global Best Practices group that collects information concerning best practices on a variety of tax and accounting issues. PwC also has a number of transfer pricing experts in its tax practice. The information in Table 16.1 is a partial list of items included on a Process Appraisal Tool prepared by the PwC Global Best Practices group.

Note

The actual appraisal tool is much longer but I have included those items that can be influenced by tax integration in an SAP system.

PricewaterhouseCoopers	Global Best Practices	Process Appraisal Tool
Section	**Practice**	**Response**
10.2.6 Part B 1	Transfer pricing analysts use historical operating and profit data to determine the impact of current pricing methods on individual units.	Yes
10.2.6 Part B 3	The company conducts a functional analysis when selecting a new transfer pricing method.	Yes
10.2.6 Part D 3	The company calculates transfer prices as needed for each intercompany transaction.	No
10.2.6 Part D 5	An automated accounting system generates ordering and billing documents for intercompany transactions.	Yes

Table 16.1 A Sample from the PwC Transfer Pricing Best Practices Appraisal Tool (Source: www.globalbestpractices.com/Home/)

Note

PwC's Global Best Practices website can be accessed at *www.globalbestpractices.com/Home/*. Global Best Practices are available through subscription obtainable on the website.

Appendix G at the end of this book contains reports needed to support prices used in cross border transfers of goods and services. Item 10.2.6 Part B 1 from Table 16.1 calls for the use of historical operating and profit data in determining pricing methods. IRS auditors often request information supporting the premise that the price used in an intercompany transaction is truly a fair market price. SAP software is capable of capturing the data required to produce both of the report formats given in Appendix G.

Tax integration specialists need to assure that reports such as those included in Appendix G are developed as part of the implementation. These reports calculate a gross margin that can be used to support the markup used for intercompany transactions. Arm's length prices often differ around the world so reports run for Mexican operations may support a different markup than those for Germany. One of the IRS's intentions is to ensure that U.S. corporations are not shifting income from the United States to another country with more favorable tax treatment. One of the ways to demonstrate this is by providing legal entity reports in foreign countries showing that the internal pricing margin used between the United States and the foreign entity is the same as that used for external vendors/customers in that country.

Item 10.2.6 Part B 3 recommends a functional analysis that looks at the organization structure of the company and the relevant business units in determining a transfer pricing policy and transfer prices. This should be done each year. ECC functionality incorporating transfer pricing capabilities at the legal entity, group, and profit center levels supports this type of analysis, as does the material ledger, document splitting, and the new G/L.

Item 10.2.6 Part D 3 desires a negative response meaning that transfer prices are best established by agreement between controlled entities trading between countries on an annual basis and not every time a transaction takes place. Pricing conditions for cross border intercompany transactions should be updated with adjusted markups once a year based on supporting data and agreements between the countries. SAP software provides pricing conditions that are easily updated and the tools needed to create necessary reports. Tax specialists need to introduce the SAP team to these requirements and ensure that something is done.

Item 10.2.6 Part D 5 deals with the intercompany documents that should be produced by the system to support the arm's length premise and document the transaction. Cross border intercompany transactions within SAP should have documentation and be based on the proper transfer price. Purchase orders and sales orders similar to those produced between external parties is the ideal situation with the markup dispalyed on the invoice. SAP software tracks and documents every transaction in the system, but invoicing does not accompany all intercompany transactions. Tax professionals should work with the goal of having invoicing on all cross border intercompany transactions.

16.2.2 Pricing Procedures for Transfer Pricing

Pricing procedures for transfer pricing uses the condition technique referred to in Section 1.2 of Chapter 12. Transfer pricing audits not only require support for the transfer price but proof that the agreed price is actually used in the transaction. To this end, auditors will sample cross border intercompany transactions to see if the transfer pricing markup is indeed used. The easiest way to convince an auditor that the proper markup is being used is to have the markup displayed on the intercompany invoice. If that is not possible, an explanation of pricing procedures, condition types, access sequences, and condition records may be required. Some IRS auditors may be familiar with SAP pricing concepts, but most will not and most tax professionals coordinating the audit will require explanations as well. Printing the markup on the intercompany invoice is possible in R/3 or ECC and will save audit questions down the road.

16.3 Summary

Transfer pricing requires charging a fair market price for transactions of goods, services, and intangibles between related entities of the same company. SAP applications such as the new G/L, document splitting, material ledger, and profit center transfer pricing in ECC releases improve transfer pricing capabilities for operating management and for taxes.

Although most improvement is in the operations management area, tax departments benefit from additional pricing procedures and pricing methods. SAP software is able to assist with transfer pricing efforts and capable of bringing tax departments to a best practice level in system-related areas.

16.4 Book Summary

Tax integration involves assisting tax departments and SAP implementation teams solve tax-related challenges in ways that benefit both parties. In this book, we have discussed the management of SAP projects and the role of the tax integration specialist. We also discussed the importance of the way companies are organized when the system structure is defined and the importance of legal entity accounting and defining cost objects on a jurisdictional basis. Chapter 4 introduced you to income tax concepts and discussed integration techniques involving the chart of accounts, fixed assets, and intercompany accounting. That was followed by federal and state withholding tax issues and a discussion of classic withholding and extended withholding. Chapter 6 reviewed requirements for tax data retention and discussed the DART tool. Unstructured data and NetWeaver KM was also discussed. The importance of payroll data in tax returns and the issues related to payroll data in SAP was next reviewed in Chapter 7, and master data was covered in Chapter 8.

Chapter 9 addressed tax reporting and the need for tax departments to be equipped with equal or improved reporting tools after the implementation as they had prior to it. In that regard, SAP standard reports, SAP Query, Report Painter, and Report Writer were all reviewed. Chapter 10 addressed other federal tax issues such as the domestic production activities deduction, third-party income tax software, meals and entertainment expenses, apportionment, and the R&D tax credit. We next went into property tax and integration techniques available to break down property into components that are nontaxable in some jurisdictions. Chapters 12, 13, and 14 discussed sales and use tax and processing taxes internally in SAP versus using an external tax system. Configuration of sales and use tax under each of the three U.S. tax procedures was also reviewed. Chapter 15 discussed state franchise taxes and then went into "green" taxes such as beverage tax and bottle and can deposits. We concluded the chapter with a discussion of waste taxes. Chapter 16 concluded the book with a review of transfer pricing methodology in SAP and its links to the material ledger, new G/L, and document splitting. We discussed how SAP functionality can assist corporations to develop best practices in the transfer pricing area.

I hope you have enjoyed this book and were able to learn much from it. If I have missed subjects that you feel need to be covered or better explanations are needed in specific areas, please let me know. You can reach me by email at *scottem@us.ibm.com*.

Appendix

A Suggested Tax Accounts

Table A.1 contains accounts that have been added at a number of SAP implementations for tax purposes. All of them will not be needed in all cases but the list should serve as a reminder of the various accounts that may be needed for tax purposes.

Account Title
Lobbying Expense Payable
Lobbying Expense
Personal Property Tax Payable
Personal Property Tax Expense
Real Property Tax Payable
Real Property Tax Expense
Provincial Sales Tax Payable (PST — Canada)
Provincial Sales Tax Expense (PST — Canada)
General Sales Tax Payable (GST — Canada)
General Sales Tax Expense (GST — Canada)
State Income Tax Payable
State Income Tax Expense
Local Income Tax Payable
Local Income Tax Expense
Charitable Contributions — Noncash
Late Fees and Penalties
Political Contributions
Group Insurance
Worker's Compensation
Capital Leases — Rents
Legal Expense
R&D Expenses
Amortization — Goodwill
Federal Backup Withholding — 1099
Foreign Taxes Paid or Withheld — Receipted
Foreign Taxes Paid or Withheld — Unreceipted
International — International Sales — Third Parties
International — Intercompany Sales
International — Intercompany Service Income
International — Service Income — Third Parties
International — Intercompany Service Expense

Table A.1 Suggested Tax Accounts

International – Service Expense – Third Parties
International – Intercompany Royalty Income
International – Royalty Income – Third Parties
International – Intercompany Royalty Expense
International – Royalty Expense – Third Parties
International – Intercompany Rental Income
International – Rental Income – Third Parties
International – Intercompany Rental Expense
International – Rental Expense – Third Parties
International – Intercompany Lease Income
International – Lease Income – Third Parties
International – Intercompany Lease Expense
International – Lease Expense – Third Parties
International – Intercompany Interest Income
International – Interest Income – Third Parties
International – Intercompany Interest Expense
International – Interest Expense – Third Parties
International – Intercompany Management Fee Income
International – Management Fee Income – Third Parties
International – Intercompany Management Fee Expense
International – Management Fee Expense – Third Parties
International – Realized Foreign Exchange Gain
International – Realized Foreign Exchange Loss
International – Unrealized Foreign Exchange Gain
International – Unrealized Foreign Exchange Loss
International: Amortization Expense – Foreign
International – Withholding – Royalty Income
International – Withholding – Interest Income
International – Withholding – Rental Income
International – Withholding – Lease Income
International – Withholding – Service Income
International – Withholding – Dividend Income
International – Withholding – Other Income
International – Dividends Paid or Received – Related Parties **(Note: This is an account that rolls into Retained Earnings.)**
Cumulative Translation Adjustment (CTA) **(Note: This is an account that rolls into Retained Earnings.)**
Other Comprehensive Income (OCI) **(Note: This is an account that rolls into Retained Earnings.)**

Table A.1 Suggested Tax Accounts (cont.)

International: FAS 109 Accounts
▶ Deferred tax asset (Current)
▶ Deferred tax asset (Noncurrent)
▶ Deferred tax liability (Current)
▶ Deferred tax liability (Noncurrent)
▶ Income Tax payable
▶ Income Tax Expense — Current — U.S.
▶ Income Tax Expense — Current — Foreign
▶ Income Tax Expense — Deferred — U.S.
▶ Income Tax Expense — Deferred — Foreign

Table A.1 Suggested Tax Accounts (cont.)

B Asset Classes and Depreciation Areas

Table B.1 shows an asset class matrix used to supply information to configuration specialists for fixed assets. In this case, the depreciation areas are listed across the top and the asset classes down the left side. Asset classes can be used across depreciation areas and houses information concerning the depreciation method, the useful life, and the G/L account for that asset class in a given depreciation area. This matrix contains 5 depreciation areas, but some corporations may have twice that number. A matrix with 10 depreciation areas and 200 asset classes can be a chore to prepare; especially if depreciation areas are not currently maintained in the legacy system. Asset classes are used to group similar assets but also should represent a unique set of depreciation methods and lives. If an asset class has the same method and life as another asset class, there is no reason to establish two classes unless a descriptive grouping is required.

	Asset Class	Asset Class Short Description	Asset Class Long Description	Fin MTD	Fin Life	FED Tax MTD	FED Tax Life	ACE MTD	ACE Life	AMT MTD	AMT Life	State w/o Bonus MTD	State w/o Bonus Life	G/L Account
Construction in Progress	2000	Asset Under Construction (AuC)	Asset Under Construction	None		None								
Buildings	3000	Buildings — 50yr	Buildings Structures	STL	50	STL	39	STL	40	STL	40	STL	39	1234567
		Buildings — 20yr STL	Buildings-Pollution Control Roofs	STL	20	STL	39		20		20		20	1234567
		Buildings — 15yr STL	Buildings-Portable	STL	15	STL			15		15		15	
		Buildings — 10yr STL	Buildings-roofs	STL	10	STL	39		10		10		10	
Building Equipment	4000	Bldg Eqp — 25yr STL	Elevators, Escalators	STL	25	STL	39		40		40		39	
		Bldg Eqp — 20yr STL	HVAC, Pollution, Alarm, Electrical, Central Utility Systems	STL	20	STL	39							

Table B.1 Asset Classes and Depreciation Areas

	Asset Class	Asset Class Short Description	Asset Class Long Description	Fin MTD	Fin Life	FED Tax MTD	FED Tax Life	ACE MTD	ACE Life	AMT MTD	AMT Life	State w/o Bonus MTD	State w/o Bonus Life	G/L Account
		Bldg Eqp — 15yr STL	Receiving and Shipping Apparatus (Overhead Doors, Dock Levelers, etc.)	STL	15	STL	39							
		Bldg Eqp — 10yr STL	Lighting Fixtures, Meters and Instruments, Pumps, Compressors, Blowers, Conveyors	STL	10	STL	39							
Interest	5000	Capitalized Interest	Capitalized Interest Book and Tax	NA	NA	STL	Life of Major Asset							
Computer Hardware	6000	Mainframe Computers and Peripheral Equipment	Large Computers, 5 yr Servers, etc.	STL	5	DDB	5							
		PC Computers and Peripheral Equipment	PC's, 3yr Servers, Routers, etc.	STL	3	DDB	5							

Table B.1 Asset Classes and Depreciation Areas (cont.)

C DART Team Application Process

DART implementation teams require authorization to carry out their responsibilities. Team members are tasked with data mapping, extract and view configuration, and understanding the differences between SAP tables and DART segments and how they exist in the SAP data dictionary. The authorization listed in Table C.1 will get the DART team off to a great start. Please note that the DART team security authorization is more expansive than the Administrator or the User authorization shown in Appendix E.

Module or Area	Create	Change	Display	Authorization Object	T-Code	Environment
FI	X	X	X			Development or Sandbox
SD	X	X	X			Development or Sandbox
MM	X	X	X			Development or Sandbox
Data Dictionary			X		SE84 and SE16	Development or Sandbox and Production or Production Copy
DART						
Extract configuration	X	X	X	F_TXW_TFCF		Development or Sandbox
Data extract	X	X	X	F_TXW_TF		Development or Sandbox
View configuration	X	X	X	F_TXW_TVCF		Development or Sandbox
Data views	X	X	X	F_TXW_TV		Development or Sandbox
Data Retention Tool	X	X	X		FTWO	Development or Sandbox

Table C.1 DART Team Application Authorization

Module or Area	Create	Change	Display	Authorization Object	T-Code	Environment
Information about DART installation	X	X	X		FTW9	Development or Sandbox
Extract data	X	X	X		FTWA	Development or Sandbox
Retrieve archived data	X	X	X		FTWB	Development or Sandbox
Merge data files	X	X	X		FTWA	Development or Sandbox
Verify data file checksums	X	X	X		FTWD	Development or Sandbox
Verify control totals (FI documents)	X	X	X		FTWE	Development or Sandbox
Data extract browser	X	X	X		FTWF	Development or Sandbox
Data view queries	X	X	X		FTWH	Development or Sandbox
Create background job	X	X	X		FTWI	Development or Sandbox
Clear data retrieved from archives	X	X	X		FTWJ	Development or Sandbox
Delete data files	X	X	X		FTWK	Development or Sandbox
Display extract log	X	X	X		FTWL	Development or Sandbox
Rebuild data file	X	X	X		FTWM	Development or Sandbox
Display view query log	X	X	X		FTWN	Development or Sandbox
Settings for data file extraction	X	X	X		FTWP	Development or Sandbox
Configure data file data segments	X	X	X		FTWQ	Development or Sandbox

Table C.1 DART Team Application Authorization (cont.)

Module or Area	Create	Change	Display	Authorization Object	T-Code	Environment
File size work-sheet	X	X	X		FTWR	Development or Sandbox
Transport config-uration and logs	X	X	X		FTWS	Development or Sandbox
List segment information	X	X	X		FTWW	Development or Sandbox
Data file view authority groups	X	X	X		FTWX	Development or Sandbox
Maintain data file view	X	X	X		FTWY	Development or Sandbox

Table C.1 DART Team Application Authorization (cont.)

D DART Transaction Codes for DART Release 2.4

Table D.1 lists transaction codes available in the DART application.

DART Action	Transaction Code
Access Data Retention Tool	FTW0
Extract data	FTW1A
Retrieve archived data	FTWB
Merge data files	FTWC
Field catalog	FTWCF
Segment catalog	FTWCS
Verify data file checksums	FTWD
Verify control totals (FI documents)	FTWE
Verify all control totals (FI documents)	FTWE1
Data extract browser	FTWF
Data view queries	FTWH
Create background job	FTWI
Clear data retrieved from archives	FTWJ
Delete data files	FTWK
Display extract log	FTWL
Rebuild data file	FTWM
Display view query log	FTWN
Settings for data file extraction	FTWP
Configure data segments	FTWQ
File size worksheet	FTWR
Transport configuration and logs	FTWS
List segment information	FTWW

Table D.1 DART Transaction Codes for DART Release 2.4

DART Action	Transaction Code
Data file view authority groups	FTWX
Define data extract views	FTWY
Display extract splitter log	S_P6D_40000025
Associated data detector	S_P6D_40000026
Data Extract Splitter	S_P6D_40000027

Table D.1 DART Transaction Codes for DART Release 2.4 (cont.)

E DART Administrator Role

A suggested security role and configuration for the DART administrator and another for a DART user are given in Tables E.1 and E.2, respectively. These roles might need to be changed depending on which party will run views but should serve as a starting point for building DART security roles.

Module or Area	Create	Change	Display	T-Code
Data Retention Tool	X	X	X	FTW0
Verify data file checksums	X	X	X	FTWD
Verify control totals (FI documents)	X	X	X	FTWE
Verify control totals (Entire Extract)	X	X	X	FTWE1
Data extract browser	X	X	X	FTWF
Data view queries	X	X	X	FTWH
List segment information	X	X	X	FTWW
File size worksheet	X	X	X	FTWR
Transport configuration and logs	X	X	X	FTWS
Data file view authority groups	X	X	X	FTWX
Maintain data file view	X	X	X	FTWY
Extract data	X	X	X	FTWA
Extract data	X	X	X	FTWA1
Retrieve archived data	X	X	X	FTWB
Create background job	X	X	X	FTWI
Clear data retrieved from archives	X	X	X	FTWJ
Delete extracts	X	X	X	FTWK
Rebuild data extract	X	X	X	FTWM
Display view query log	X	X	X	FTWN
Settings for data extraction	X	X	X	FTWP

Table E.1 DART Administrator Role

Module or Area	Create	Change	Display	T-Code
Configure data file data segments	X	X	X	FTWQ
Segment catalog	X	X	X	FTWCS
Field catalog	X	X	X	FTWCF
Overview of job selection	X	X	X	SM37
R/3 Repository Information System	X	X	X	SE84

Table E.1 DART Administrator Role (cont.)

Module or Area	Create	Change	Display	T-Code
FI			X	
SD			X	
CO			X	
MM			X	
Report S_ALR_87012301: Totals and Balances***			X	
Report S_ALR_87012277: G/L Account Balances***			X	
Data Retention Tool			X	FTW0
Verify data file checksums			X	FTWD
Verify control totals (FI documents)			X	FTWE
Verify control totals (entire extract)			X	FTWE1
Data extract browser			X	FTWF
Data view queries			X	FTWH
List segment information			X	FTWW
*** Tax departments need the ability to run this report and print it to reconcile the extract to the books of record.				

Table E.2 DART User Role

F Suggested Payroll Data Elements

Table F.1 lists suggested payroll data elements. This list is particularly helpful if you are implementing a system where the SAP HR module is on a different instance of SAP or your company is using an HR system other than an SAP system. When payroll is in a different instance or in a non-SAP system, decisions have to made concerning which data elements are needed in the SAP system. Again, the list is long and probably has more data elements than may be needed in your system but will provide a good checklist.

Payroll Field Descriptions
G/L Account
G/L Account Description
Legal Entity
FICA Limit
Wages Subject to FICA
FICA Rate
Medicare Limit
Wages Subject to Medicare
Medicare Rate
FUTA Limit
Wages Subject to FUTA
SUTA Limit by State
SUTA Wages by State
Compensation Country
Compensation State
Compensation City
Compensation Locality
Compensation ZIP Code

Table F.1 Suggested Payroll Data Elements

Payroll Field Descriptions
Compensation Charge Code
Compensation Entity Code
Compensation Paid Amount
Compensation Accrued Amount
Compensation Posting Date
Other Compensation or Compensatory Benefits
Personnel Type Code
Employee Visa Code
Employment Date
Employee Illness Code
Employee Benefits Code
Employee Locality Description
Employee Termination Date
Employee Rehire Date
Employee Position Code
Employee Birth Date
Employee Gender
Employee Exempt/Nonexempt Status
Employee SSN
Employee Class Group
Employee Practice Function Code
Employee Discipline Code
Employee Cost Code
Employee Citizenship
Employee State Exemptions
Employee Federal Exemptions
Employee Marital Status
Employee Locality
Employee First Name

Table F.1 Suggested Payroll Data Elements (cont.)

Payroll Field Descriptions
Employee Middle Name
Employee Last Name
Employee Number
Employee Status
Employee Street Address
Employee City
Employee State or Region
Employee ZIP or Postal Code
Employee Country
Employee Withholding Amounts: ▶ FICA ▶ Medicare ▶ Retirement Plans, 401K, etc. ▶ Stock Ownership Plans ▶ Loans and Advances ▶ Employer-Sponsored Day Care ▶ Flexible Spending Withheld ▶ Health Insurance ▶ Life Insurance ▶ Accident Insurance ▶ Dental Insurance ▶ Vision Insurance ▶ Savings ▶ Other
Employer Contributions: ▶ FICA ▶ Medicare ▶ Retirement Plans, 401K, etc. ▶ Stock Ownership Plans ▶ Loans and Advances ▶ Employer-Sponsored Day Care ▶ Flexible Spending Withheld ▶ Health Insurance ▶ Life Insurance

Table F.1 Suggested Payroll Data Elements (cont.)

Payroll Field Descriptions
Employer Contributions: ▶ Accident Insurance ▶ Dental Insurance ▶ Vision Insurance ▶ Savings ▶ Other
Withholding Type
Tax Jurisdiction
Date Withheld
Withholding Amount Paid to Taxing Jurisdiction
Withholding Paid Date
Withholding Amount Paid to Plan Administrators, etc.
Sick Time
Sick Pay Amount
Vacation Time Accrued
Vacation Time Taken
Vacation Pay
Other Paid Leave
Payroll Credits
Posting Date
Transaction Date
Check Number
Transaction Number

Table F.1 Suggested Payroll Data Elements (cont.)

G Data Requirements for Intercompany Transaction Analysis

Section 482 of the internal revenue code and related treasury regulations require the analysis of related party (intercompany) transactions to ensure compliance with an arm's length standard. To complete the analysis of a company's intercompany transactions, legal entity based financial statements are required. The following data requirements are generally used to analyze a company's intercompany transactions with regard to transfer pricing regulations.

G.1 Legal Entity Profit and Loss Reports in U.S. GAAP

- Gross revenue
- Contra-revenue items
- Net revenues
- Net revenues by brand
  - For related party sales
  - For third-party sales
- Net revenues by customer
- Cost of sales/cost of goods sold
- COGS by brand
  - For related party sales
  - For third-party sales
- COGS by customer
- Gross profit

The following expenses should be broken down out by legal entity, project, and brand (where possible):

- Administrative expense
- Marketing expense

- R&D expense
- Royalty expense
  - Paid to related parties
  - Paid to third parties
- Royalty income
  - Received from related parties
  - Received from third parties
- Service fee income
  - Received from related parties
  - Received from third parties
- Service fee expense
- Freight expenses
  - On sales to related parties
  - On sales to third parties
- Depreciation
- Other operating expenses
- Operating profit
- Transfer pricing adjustments

G.2 Legal Entity Balance Sheet Reports in U.S. GAAP Cash

- Accounts receivable
  - From related parties
  - From third parties
- Notes receivable
  - From related parties
  - From third parties
- Investments in affiliates
- Broken out by affiliate
- Other investments
- Total assets

- Accounts payable
  - To related parties
  - To third parties
- Notes payable
  - To related parties
  - To third parties
- Other liabilities
- Total liabilities
- Shareholders' equity

The following data is required on a division basis and broken out by project and brand:

- Profit and loss summary reports
- Net revenue
- Gross profit
- Operating profit
- R&D spending
- Administrative expense
- Marketing expense

H IRS Tax Forms

Appendix H shows IRS and other jurisdictional tax forms that are mentioned in this book, organized by chapter. Many SAP team members not directly involved in tax work may not have seen some of these forms. The following forms give an idea of some of the types of data that need to be maintained in the SAP system. Many of these forms have more than one page so all the pages have been included. This book discusses just a sample of tax forms filed by corporate tax departments. Hundreds of forms such as these are filed each year.

All of the federal income and payroll tax forms were taken from the Internal Revenue website at: *www.irs.gov/Formspubs/lists/0,,id=97817,00.html.* Other sources are mentioned in figure captions as appropriate.

H.1 Tax Forms for Chapter 1

Figures H.1 through H.4 show Form 1120 — U.S. Corporation Income Tax Return (4 pages).

Form **1120** — Department of the Treasury, Internal Revenue Service

U.S. Corporation Income Tax Return

For calendar year 2006 or tax year beginning .... , 2006, ending .... , 20 ....
▶ See separate instructions.

OMB No. 1545-0123 — **2006**

A Check if:
1 Consolidated return (attach Form 851) ☐
2 Personal holding co. (attach Sch. PH) ☐
3 Personal service corp. (see instructions) ☐
4 Schedule M-3 required (attach Sch. M-3) ☐

Use IRS label. Otherwise, print or type.
Name
Number, street, and room or suite no. If a P.O. box, see instructions.
City or town, state, and ZIP code

B Employer identification number
C Date incorporated
D Total assets (see instructions) $

E Check if: (1) ☐ Initial return (2) ☐ Final return (3) ☐ Name change (4) ☐ Address change

Income

1a	Gross receipts or sales ______ b Less returns and allowances ______ c Bal ▶	1c	
2	Cost of goods sold (Schedule A, line 8)	2	
3	Gross profit. Subtract line 2 from line 1c	3	
4	Dividends (Schedule C, line 19)	4	
5	Interest	5	
6	Gross rents	6	
7	Gross royalties	7	
8	Capital gain net income (attach Schedule D (Form 1120))	8	
9	Net gain or (loss) from Form 4797, Part II, line 17 (attach Form 4797)	9	
10	Other income (see instructions—attach schedule)	10	
11	**Total income.** Add lines 3 through 10 ▶	11	

Deductions (See instructions for limitations on deductions.)

12	Compensation of officers (Schedule E, line 4)	12	
13	Salaries and wages (less employment credits)	13	
14	Repairs and maintenance	14	
15	Bad debts	15	
16	Rents	16	
17	Taxes and licenses	17	
18	Interest	18	
19	Charitable contributions	19	
20	Depreciation from Form 4562 not claimed on Schedule A or elsewhere on return (attach Form 4562)	20	
21	Depletion	21	
22	Advertising	22	
23	Pension, profit-sharing, etc., plans	23	
24	Employee benefit programs	24	
25	Domestic production activities deduction (attach Form 8903)	25	
26	Other deductions (attach schedule)	26	
27	**Total deductions.** Add lines 12 through 26 ▶	27	
28	Taxable income before net operating loss deduction and special deductions. Subtract line 27 from line 11	28	
29	**Less:** a Net operating loss deduction (see instructions) — 29a		
	b Special deductions (Schedule C, line 20) — 29b	29c	

Tax and Payments

30	**Taxable income.** Subtract line 29c from line 28 (see instructions)	30	
31	**Total tax** (Schedule J, line 10)	31	
32a	2005 overpayment credited to 2006 — 32a		
b	2006 estimated tax payments — 32b		
c	2006 refund applied for on Form 4466 — 32c ( ) d Bal ▶ 32d		
e	Tax deposited with Form 7004 — 32e		
f	Credits: (1) Form 2439______ (2) Form 4136______ — 32f		
g	Credit for federal telephone excise tax paid (attach Form 8913) — 32g	32h	
33	Estimated tax penalty (see instructions). Check if Form 2220 is attached ▶ ☐	33	
34	**Amount owed.** If line 32h is smaller than the total of lines 31 and 33, enter amount owed	34	
35	**Overpayment.** If line 32h is larger than the total of lines 31 and 33, enter amount overpaid	35	
36	Enter amount from line 35 you want: **Credited to 2007 estimated tax** ▶ ______ **Refunded** ▶	36	

Sign Here

Under penalties of perjury, I declare that I have examined this return, including accompanying schedules and statements, and to the best of my knowledge and belief, it is true, correct, and complete. Declaration of preparer (other than taxpayer) is based on all information of which preparer has any knowledge.

Signature of officer — Date — Title

May the IRS discuss this return with the preparer shown below (see instructions)? ☐ Yes ☐ No

Paid Preparer's Use Only

Preparer's signature — Date — Check if self-employed ☐ — Preparer's SSN or PTIN
Firm's name (or yours if self-employed), address, and ZIP code — EIN — Phone no. ( )

For Privacy Act and Paperwork Reduction Act Notice, see separate instructions. Cat. No. 11450Q Form **1120** (2006)

Figure H.1 Form 1120 — U.S. Corporation Income Tax Return, Page 1

Form 1120 (2006) Page 2

Schedule A Cost of Goods Sold (see instructions)

1	Inventory at beginning of year	1	
2	Purchases	2	
3	Cost of labor	3	
4	Additional section 263A costs (attach schedule)	4	
5	Other costs (attach schedule)	5	
6	**Total.** Add lines 1 through 5	6	
7	Inventory at end of year	7	
8	**Cost of goods sold.** Subtract line 7 from line 6. Enter here and on page 1, line 2	8	

9a Check all methods used for valuing closing inventory:

(i) ☐ Cost

(ii) ☐ Lower of cost or market

(iii) ☐ Other (Specify method used and attach explanation.) ▶

b Check if there was a writedown of subnormal goods ▶ ☐

c Check if the LIFO inventory method was adopted this tax year for any goods (if checked, attach Form 970) ▶ ☐

d If the LIFO inventory method was used for this tax year, enter percentage (or amounts) of closing inventory computed under LIFO | 9d |

e If property is produced or acquired for resale, do the rules of section 263A apply to the corporation? ☐ Yes ☐ No

f Was there any change in determining quantities, cost, or valuations between opening and closing inventory? If "Yes," attach explanation ☐ Yes ☐ No

Schedule C Dividends and Special Deductions (see instructions)

		(a) Dividends received	(b) %	(c) Special deductions (a) × (b)
1	Dividends from less-than-20%-owned domestic corporations (other than debt-financed stock)		70	
2	Dividends from 20%-or-more-owned domestic corporations (other than debt-financed stock)		80	
3	Dividends on debt-financed stock of domestic and foreign corporations		see instructions	
4	Dividends on certain preferred stock of less-than-20%-owned public utilities		42	
5	Dividends on certain preferred stock of 20%-or-more-owned public utilities		48	
6	Dividends from less-than-20%-owned foreign corporations and certain FSCs		70	
7	Dividends from 20%-or-more-owned foreign corporations and certain FSCs		80	
8	Dividends from wholly owned foreign subsidiaries		100	
9	**Total.** Add lines 1 through 8. See instructions for limitation			
10	Dividends from domestic corporations received by a small business investment company operating under the Small Business Investment Act of 1958		100	
11	Dividends from affiliated group members		100	
12	Dividends from certain FSCs		100	
13	Dividends from foreign corporations not included on lines 3, 6, 7, 8, 11, or 12			
14	Income from controlled foreign corporations under subpart F (attach Form(s) 5471)			
15	Foreign dividend gross-up			
16	IC-DISC and former DISC dividends not included on lines 1, 2, or 3			
17	Other dividends			
18	Deduction for dividends paid on certain preferred stock of public utilities			
19	**Total dividends.** Add lines 1 through 17. Enter here and on page 1, line 4 ▶			
20	**Total special deductions.** Add lines 9, 10, 11, 12, and 18. Enter here and on page 1, line 29b ▶			

Schedule E Compensation of Officers (see instructions for page 1, line 12)

Note: *Complete Schedule E only if total receipts (line 1a plus lines 4 through 10 on page 1) are $500,000 or more.*

	(a) Name of officer	(b) Social security number	(c) Percent of time devoted to business	Percent of corporation stock owned: (d) Common	(e) Preferred	(f) Amount of compensation
1			%	%	%	
			%	%	%	
			%	%	%	
			%	%	%	
			%	%	%	

2	Total compensation of officers	
3	Compensation of officers claimed on Schedule A and elsewhere on return	
4	Subtract line 3 from line 2. Enter the result here and on page 1, line 12	

Form **1120** (2006)

Figure H.2 Form 1120 — U.S. Corporation Income Tax Return, Page 2

Form 1120 (2006) Page **3**

Schedule J **Tax Computation** (see instructions)

1	Check if the corporation is a member of a controlled group (attach Schedule O (Form 1120)) ▶ ☐		
2	Income tax. Check if a qualified personal service corporation (see instructions) ▶ ☐	2	
3	Alternative minimum tax (attach Form 4626)	3	
4	Add lines 2 and 3	4	
5a	Foreign tax credit (attach Form 1118) — 5a		
b	Qualified electric vehicle credit (attach Form 8834) — 5b		
c	General business credit. Check applicable box(es): ☐ Form 3800 ☐ Form 6478 ☐ Form 8835, Section B ☐ Form 8844 — 5c		
d	Credit for prior year minimum tax (attach Form 8827) — 5d		
e	Bond credits from: ☐ Form 8860 ☐ Form 8912 — 5e		
6	**Total credits.** Add lines 5a through 5e	6	
7	Subtract line 6 from line 4	7	
8	Personal holding company tax (attach Schedule PH (Form 1120))	8	
9	Other taxes. Check if from: ☐ Form 4255 ☐ Form 8611 ☐ Form 8697 ☐ Form 8866 ☐ Form 8902 ☐ Other (attach schedule)	9	
10	**Total tax.** Add lines 7 through 9. Enter here and on page 1, line 31	10	

Schedule K **Other Information** (see instructions)

		Yes	No
1	Check accounting method: a ☐ Cash b ☐ Accrual c ☐ Other (specify) ▶		
2	See the instructions and enter the:		
a	Business activity code no. ▶		
b	Business activity ▶		
c	Product or service ▶		
3	At the end of the tax year, did the corporation own, directly or indirectly, 50% or more of the voting stock of a domestic corporation? (For rules of attribution, see section 267(c).)		
	If "Yes," attach a schedule showing: **(a)** name and employer identification number (EIN), **(b)** percentage owned, and **(c)** taxable income or (loss) before NOL and special deductions of such corporation for the tax year ending with or within your tax year.		
4	Is the corporation a subsidiary in an affiliated group or a parent-subsidiary controlled group?		
	If "Yes," enter name and EIN of the parent corporation ▶		
5	At the end of the tax year, did any individual, partnership, corporation, estate, or trust own, directly or indirectly, 50% or more of the corporation's voting stock? (For rules of attribution, see section 267(c).)		
	If "Yes," attach a schedule showing name and identifying number. (Do not include any information already entered in **4** above.) Enter percentage owned ▶		
6	During this tax year, did the corporation pay dividends (other than stock dividends and distributions in exchange for stock) in excess of the corporation's current and accumulated earnings and profits? (See sections 301 and 316.)		
	If "Yes," file **Form 5452,** Corporate Report of Nondividend Distributions.		
	If this is a consolidated return, answer here for the parent corporation and on **Form 851,** Affiliations Schedule, for each subsidiary.		
7	At any time during the tax year, did one foreign person own, directly or indirectly, at least 25% of **(a)** the total voting power of all classes of stock of the corporation entitled to vote or **(b)** the total value of all classes of stock of the corporation?		
	If "Yes," enter: **(a)** Percentage owned ▶ and **(b)** Owner's country ▶		
c	The corporation may have to file **Form 5472,** Information Return of a 25% Foreign-Owned U.S. Corporation or a Foreign Corporation Engaged in a U.S. Trade or Business. Enter number of Forms 5472 attached ▶		
8	Check this box if the corporation issued publicly offered debt instruments with original issue discount ▶ ☐		
	If checked, the corporation may have to file **Form 8281,** Information Return for Publicly Offered Original Issue Discount Instruments.		
9	Enter the amount of tax-exempt interest received or accrued during the tax year ▶ $		
10	Enter the number of shareholders at the end of the tax year (if 100 or fewer) ▶		
11	If the corporation has an NOL for the tax year and is electing to forego the carryback period, check here ▶ ☐		
	If the corporation is filing a consolidated return, the statement required by Temporary Regulations section 1.1502-21T(b)(3) must be attached or the election will not be valid.		
12	Enter the available NOL carryover from prior tax years (Do not reduce it by any deduction on line 29a.) ▶ $		
13	Are the corporation's total receipts (line 1a plus lines 4 through 10 on page 1) for the tax year **and** its total assets at the end of the tax year less than $250,000?		
	If "Yes," the corporation is not required to complete Schedules L, M-1, and M-2 on page 4. Instead, enter the total amount of cash distributions and the book value of property distributions (other than cash) made during the tax year. ▶ $		

Note: If the corporation, at any time during the tax year, had assets or operated a business in a foreign country or U.S. possession, it may be required to attach **Schedule N (Form 1120),** *Foreign Operations of U.S. Corporations, to this return. See Schedule N for details.*

Form **1120** (2006)

Figure H.3 Form 1120 — U.S. Corporation Income Tax Return, Page 3

Form 1120 (2006) Page 4

Schedule L Balance Sheets per Books

Assets	Beginning of tax year (a)	(b)	End of tax year (c)	(d)
1 Cash				
2a Trade notes and accounts receivable				
b Less allowance for bad debts	( )		( )	
3 Inventories				
4 U.S. government obligations				
5 Tax-exempt securities (see instructions)				
6 Other current assets (attach schedule)				
7 Loans to shareholders				
8 Mortgage and real estate loans				
9 Other investments (attach schedule)				
10a Buildings and other depreciable assets				
b Less accumulated depreciation	( )		( )	
11a Depletable assets				
b Less accumulated depletion	( )		( )	
12 Land (net of any amortization)				
13a Intangible assets (amortizable only)				
b Less accumulated amortization	( )		( )	
14 Other assets (attach schedule)				
15 Total assets				
Liabilities and Shareholders' Equity				
16 Accounts payable				
17 Mortgages, notes, bonds payable in less than 1 year				
18 Other current liabilities (attach schedule)				
19 Loans from shareholders				
20 Mortgages, notes, bonds payable in 1 year or more				
21 Other liabilities (attach schedule)				
22 Capital stock: a Preferred stock				
b Common stock				
23 Additional paid-in capital				
24 Retained earnings—Appropriated (attach schedule)				
25 Retained earnings—Unappropriated				
26 Adjustments to shareholders' equity (attach schedule)				
27 Less cost of treasury stock		( )		( )
28 Total liabilities and shareholders' equity				

Schedule M-1 Reconciliation of Income (Loss) per Books With Income per Return

Note: Schedule M-3 required instead of Schedule M-1 if total assets are $10 million or more—see instructions

1 Net income (loss) per books		7 Income recorded on books this year not included on this return (itemize): Tax-exempt interest $	
2 Federal income tax per books			
3 Excess of capital losses over capital gains			
4 Income subject to tax not recorded on books this year (itemize):		8 Deductions on this return not charged against book income this year (itemize):	
5 Expenses recorded on books this year not deducted on this return (itemize):		a Depreciation . . . . $	
a Depreciation . . . . $		b Charitable contributions $	
b Charitable contributions $			
c Travel and entertainment $		9 Add lines 7 and 8	
6 Add lines 1 through 5		10 Income (page 1, line 28)—line 6 less line 9	

Schedule M-2 Analysis of Unappropriated Retained Earnings per Books (Line 25, Schedule L)

1 Balance at beginning of year		5 Distributions: a Cash	
2 Net income (loss) per books		b Stock	
3 Other increases (itemize):		c Property	
		6 Other decreases (itemize):	
		7 Add lines 5 and 6	
4 Add lines 1, 2, and 3		8 Balance at end of year (line 4 less line 7)	

Form **1120** (2006)

Figure H.4 Form 1120 — U.S. Corporation Income Tax Return, Page 4

H.2 Tax Forms for Chapter 4

Figure H.5 and H.6 show Form 4562 – Depreciation and Amortization (2 pages).

Form **4562** — Department of the Treasury, Internal Revenue Service

Depreciation and Amortization
(Including Information on Listed Property)
▶ See separate instructions. ▶ Attach to your tax return.

OMB No. 1545-0172 — **2006** — Attachment Sequence No. **67**

Name(s) shown on return	Business or activity to which this form relates	Identifying number

Part I Election To Expense Certain Property Under Section 179
Note: *If you have any listed property, complete Part V before you complete Part I.*

1	Maximum amount. See the instructions for a higher limit for certain businesses	1	$108,000
2	Total cost of section 179 property placed in service (see instructions)	2	
3	Threshold cost of section 179 property before reduction in limitation	3	$430,000
4	Reduction in limitation. Subtract line 3 from line 2. If zero or less, enter -0-	4	
5	Dollar limitation for tax year. Subtract line 4 from line 1. If zero or less, enter -0-. If married filing separately, see instructions	5	

	(a) Description of property	(b) Cost (business use only)	(c) Elected cost
6			

7	Listed property. Enter the amount from line 29	7	
8	Total elected cost of section 179 property. Add amounts in column (c), lines 6 and 7	8	
9	Tentative deduction. Enter the **smaller** of line 5 or line 8	9	
10	Carryover of disallowed deduction from line 13 of your 2005 Form 4562	10	
11	Business income limitation. Enter the smaller of business income (not less than zero) or line 5 (see instructions)	11	
12	Section 179 expense deduction. Add lines 9 and 10, but do not enter more than line 11	12	
13	Carryover of disallowed deduction to 2007. Add lines 9 and 10, less line 12 ▶	13	

Note: *Do not use Part II or Part III below for listed property. Instead, use Part V.*

Part II Special Depreciation Allowance and Other Depreciation (Do not include listed property.) (See instructions.)

14	Special allowance for qualified New York Liberty or Gulf Opportunity Zone property (other than listed property) placed in service during the tax year (see instructions)	14	
15	Property subject to section 168(f)(1) election	15	
16	Other depreciation (including ACRS)	16	

Part III MACRS Depreciation (Do not include listed property.) (See instructions.)

Section A

17	MACRS deductions for assets placed in service in tax years beginning before 2006	17	
18	If you are electing to group any assets placed in service during the tax year into one or more general asset accounts, check here ▶ ☐		

Section B—Assets Placed in Service During 2006 Tax Year Using the General Depreciation System

(a) Classification of property	(b) Month and year placed in service	(c) Basis for depreciation (business/investment use only—see instructions)	(d) Recovery period	(e) Convention	(f) Method	(g) Depreciation deduction
19a 3-year property						
b 5-year property						
c 7-year property						
d 10-year property						
e 15-year property						
f 20-year property						
g 25-year property			25 yrs.		S/L	
h Residential rental property			27.5 yrs.	MM	S/L	
			27.5 yrs.	MM	S/L	
i Nonresidential real property			39 yrs.	MM	S/L	
				MM	S/L	

Section C—Assets Placed in Service During 2006 Tax Year Using the Alternative Depreciation System

(a) Classification of property	(b) Month and year placed in service	(c) Basis for depreciation	(d) Recovery period	(e) Convention	(f) Method	(g) Depreciation deduction
20a Class life					S/L	
b 12-year			12 yrs.		S/L	
c 40-year			40 yrs.	MM	S/L	

Part IV Summary (see instructions)

21	Listed property. Enter amount from line 28	21	
22	**Total.** Add amounts from line 12, lines 14 through 17, lines 19 and 20 in column (g), and line 21. Enter here and on the appropriate lines of your return. Partnerships and S corporations—see instr.	22	
23	For assets shown above and placed in service during the current year, enter the portion of the basis attributable to section 263A costs	23	

For Paperwork Reduction Act Notice, see separate instructions. Cat. No. 12906N Form **4562** (2006)

Figure H.5 Form 4562 – Depreciation and Amortization, Page 1

Form 4562 (2006) Page 2

Part V **Listed Property** (Include automobiles, certain other vehicles, cellular telephones, certain computers, and property used for entertainment, recreation, or amusement.)

Note: *For any vehicle for which you are using the standard mileage rate or deducting lease expense, complete* ***only*** *24a, 24b, columns (a) through (c) of Section A, all of Section B, and Section C if applicable.*

Section A—Depreciation and Other Information (Caution: *See the instructions for limits for passenger automobiles.***)**

24a Do you have evidence to support the business/investment use claimed? ☐ **Yes** ☐ **No** **24b** If "Yes," is the evidence written? ☐ **Yes** ☐ **No**

(a) Type of property (list vehicles first)	(b) Date placed in service	(c) Business/ investment use percentage	(d) Cost or other basis	(e) Basis for depreciation (business/investment use only)	(f) Recovery period	(g) Method/ Convention	(h) Depreciation deduction	(i) Elected section 179 cost
25 Special allowance for qualified New York Liberty or Gulf Opportunity Zone property placed in service during the tax year and used more than 50% in a qualified business use (see instructions) 25								
26 Property used more than 50% in a qualified business use:								
		%						
		%						
		%						
27 Property used 50% or less in a qualified business use:								
		%				S/L –		
		%				S/L –		
		%				S/L –		
28 Add amounts in column (h), lines 25 through 27. Enter here and on line 21, page 1. . 28								
29 Add amounts in column (i), line 26. Enter here and on line 7, page 1. 29								

Section B—Information on Use of Vehicles

Complete this section for vehicles used by a sole proprietor, partner, or other"more than 5% owner," or related person.
If you provided vehicles to your employees, first answer the questions in Section C to see if you meet an exception to completing this section for those vehicles.

	(a) Vehicle 1		(b) Vehicle 2		(c) Vehicle 3		(d) Vehicle 4		(e) Vehicle 5		(f) Vehicle 6	
30 Total business/investment miles driven during the year (**do not** include commuting miles)												
31 Total commuting miles driven during the year												
32 Total other personal (noncommuting) miles driven												
33 Total miles driven during the year. Add lines 30 through 32												
	Yes	**No**	**Yes**	**No**	**Yes**	**No**	**Yes**	**No**	**Yes**	**No**	**Yes**	**No**
34 Was the vehicle available for personal use during off-duty hours?												
35 Was the vehicle used primarily by a more than 5% owner or related person?												
36 Is another vehicle available for personal use?												

Section C—Questions for Employers Who Provide Vehicles for Use by Their Employees

Answer these questions to determine if you meet an exception to completing Section B for vehicles used by employees who **are not** more than 5% owners or related persons (see instructions).

	Yes	No
37 Do you maintain a written policy statement that prohibits all personal use of vehicles, including commuting, by your employees?		
38 Do you maintain a written policy statement that prohibits personal use of vehicles, except commuting, by your employees? See the instructions for vehicles used by corporate officers, directors, or 1% or more owners		
39 Do you treat all use of vehicles by employees as personal use?		
40 Do you provide more than five vehicles to your employees, obtain information from your employees about the use of the vehicles, and retain the information received?		
41 Do you meet the requirements concerning qualified automobile demonstration use? (See instructions.)		

Note: *If your answer to 37, 38, 39, 40, or 41 is "Yes," do not complete Section B for the covered vehicles.*

Part VI **Amortization**

(a) Description of costs	(b) Date amortization begins	(c) Amortizable amount	(d) Code section	(e) Amortization period or percentage	(f) Amortization for this year
42 Amortization of costs that begins during your 2006 tax year (see instructions):					
43 Amortization of costs that began before your 2006 tax year.				43	
44 **Total.** Add amounts in column (f). See the instructions for where to report.				44	

Form **4562** (2006)

Figure H.6 Form 4562 — Depreciation and Amortization, Page 2

Figures H.7 through H.14 show Form 1118 — Foreign Tax Credit — Corporations (8 pages).

Form **1118**
(Rev. December 2004)
Department of the Treasury
Internal Revenue Service

Foreign Tax Credit—Corporations
▶ **Attach to the corporation's tax return.**
▶ **See separate instructions.**

OMB No. 1545-0122

For calendar year 20 , or other tax year beginning , 20 , and ending , 20

Name of corporation | **Employer identification number**

Use a **separate** Form 1118 for each applicable category of income listed below. See **Categories of Income** on page 1 of instructions. Also, see **Specific Instructions** on page 5. Check only one box on each form.

☐ Passive Income
☐ High Withholding Tax Interest
☐ Financial Services Income
☐ Shipping Income
☐ Dividends From a DISC or Former DISC
☐ Taxable Income Attributable To Foreign Trade Income
☐ Certain Distributions From a FSC or Former FSC
☐ Section 901(j) Income: Name of Sanctioned Country ▶ ________
☐ Income Re-sourced by Treaty: Name of Country ▶ ________
☐ General Limitation Income

Schedule A **Income or (Loss) Before Adjustments** *(Report all amounts in U.S. dollars. See page 5 of instructions.)*

	1. Foreign Country or U.S. Possession (Enter two-letter code from list beginning on page 11 of instructions. Use a separate line for each.)*	**Gross Income or (Loss) From Sources Outside the United States (*INCLUDE* Foreign Branch Gross Income here *and* on Schedule F)**								
		2. Deemed Dividends (see instructions)		3. Other Dividends		4. Interest	5. Gross Rents, Royalties, and License Fees	6. Gross Income From Performance of Services	7. Other (attach schedule)	8. Total (add columns 2(a) through 7)
		(a) Exclude gross-up	(b) Gross-up (sec. 78)	(a) Exclude gross-up	(b) Gross-up (sec. 78)					
A										
B										
C										
D										
E										
F										
Totals (add lines A through F)										

* For section 863(b) income, use a single line and enter "863(b)."

Deductions (*INCLUDE* Foreign Branch Deductions here *and* on Schedule F)

	9. Definitely Allocable Deductions					10. Apportioned Share of Deductions Not Definitely Allocable (enter amount from applicable line of Schedule H, Part II, column (d))	11. Total Deductions (add columns 9(e) and 10)	12. Total Income or (Loss) Before Adjustments (subtract column 11 from column 8)
	Rental, Royalty, and Licensing Expenses							
	(a) Depreciation, Depletion, and Amortization	(b) Other Expenses	(c) Expenses Related to Gross Income From Performance of Services	(d) Other Definitely Allocable Deductions	(e) Total Definitely Allocable Deductions (add columns 9(a) through 9(d))			
A								
B								
C								
D								
E								
F								
Totals								

For Paperwork Reduction Act Notice, see separate instructions. Cat. No. 10900F Form **1118** (Rev. 12-2004)

Figure H.7 Form 1118 — Foreign Tax Credit — Corporations, Page 1

Form 1118 (Rev. 12-2004) Page **2**

Schedule B **Foreign Tax Credit** *(Report all foreign tax amounts in U.S. dollars.)*

Part I—Foreign Taxes Paid, Accrued, and Deemed Paid *(see page 5 of instructions)*

	1. Credit is Claimed for Taxes: ☐ Paid ☐ Accrued		2. Foreign Taxes Paid or Accrued (attach schedule showing amounts in foreign currency and conversion rate(s) used)								3. Tax Deemed Paid (from Schedule C—Part I, column 10, Part II, column 8(b), and Part III, column 8)
			Tax Withheld at Source on:			Other Foreign Taxes Paid or Accrued on:					
	Date Paid	Date Accrued	(a) Dividends	(b) Interest	(c) Rents, Royalties, and License Fees	(d) Section 863(b) Income	(e) Foreign Branch Income	(f) Services Income	(g) Other	(h) Total Foreign Taxes Paid or Accrued (add columns 2(a) through 2(g))	
A											
B											
C											
D											
E											
F											
Totals (add lines A through F)											

Part II—Separate Foreign Tax Credit *(Complete a **separate** Part II for **each** applicable category of income.)*

1 Total foreign taxes paid or accrued (total from Part I, column 2(h))
2 Total taxes deemed paid (total from Part I, column 3)
3 Reductions of taxes paid, accrued, or deemed paid (enter total from Schedule G) ( )
4 Total carryover of foreign taxes (attach schedule showing computation in detail—see page 6 of the instructions)
5 Total foreign taxes (combine lines 1 through 4)
6 Enter the amount from the applicable column of Schedule J, Part I, line 11 (see page 6 of instructions). If Schedule J is **not** required to be completed, enter the result from the "Totals" line of column 12 of the applicable Schedule A
7a Total taxable income from all sources (enter taxable income from the corporation's tax return)
b Adjustments to line 7a (see page 6 of instructions)
c Subtract line 7b from line 7a
8 Divide line 6 by line 7c. Enter the resulting fraction as a decimal (see instructions). If line 6 is greater than line 7c, enter 1
9 Total U.S. income tax against which credit is allowed (regular tax liability (see section 26(b)) minus possessions tax credit determined under section 936 or 30A)
10 Credit limitation (multiply line 8 by line 9) (see page 6 of instructions)
11 **Separate foreign tax credit** (enter the smaller of line 5 or line 10 here and on the appropriate line of Part III)

Part III—Summary of Separate Credits (Enter amounts from Part II, line 11 for **each** applicable category of income. **Do not** include taxes on taxable income attributable to foreign trade income or taxes paid to sanctioned countries.)

1 Credit for taxes on passive income
2 Credit for taxes on high withholding tax interest
3 Credit for taxes on financial services income
4 Credit for taxes on shipping income
5 Credit for taxes on dividends from a DISC or former DISC
6 Credit for taxes on certain distributions from a FSC or former FSC
7 Credit for taxes on general limitation income
8 Credit for taxes on income re-sourced by treaty (combine all such credits on this line)
9 Total (add lines 1 through 8)
10 Reduction in credit for international boycott operations (see page 6 of instructions)
11 **Total foreign tax credit** (subtract line 10 from line 9). Enter here and on the appropriate line of the corporation's tax return

Figure H.8 Form 1118 — Foreign Tax Credit — Corporations, Page 2

Form 1118 (Rev. 12-2004) Page **3**

Schedule C **Tax Deemed Paid by Domestic Corporation Filing Return**

Use this schedule to figure the tax deemed paid by the corporation with respect to dividends from a first-tier foreign corporation under section 902(a), and deemed inclusions of earnings from a first- or lower-tier foreign corporation under section 960(a). ***Report all amounts in U.S. dollars unless otherwise specified.***

Part I—Dividends and Deemed Inclusions From Post-1986 Undistributed Earnings

1. Name of Foreign Corporation (identify DISCs and former DISCs)	2. Tax Year End (Yr-Mo) (see instructions)	3. Country of Incorporation (enter country code from instructions)	4. Post-1986 Undistributed Earnings (in functional currency—attach schedule)	5. Opening Balance in Post-1986 Foreign Income Taxes	6. Foreign Taxes Paid and Deemed Paid for Tax Year Indicated		7. Post-1986 Foreign Income Taxes (add columns 5, 6(a), and 6(b))	8. Dividends and Deemed Inclusions		9. Divide Column 8(a) by Column 4	10. Tax Deemed Paid (multiply column 7 by column 9)
					(a) Taxes Paid	(b) Taxes Deemed Paid (from Schedule D, Part I—see instructions)		(a) Functional Currency	(b) U.S. Dollars		

Total (Add amounts in column 10. Enter the result here and include on "Totals" line of Schedule B, Part I, column 3) . . . . ▶

Part II—Dividends Paid Out of Pre-1987 Accumulated Profits

1. Name of Foreign Corporation (identify DISCs and former DISCs)	2. Tax Year End (Yr-Mo) (see instructions)	3. Country of Incorporation (enter country code from instructions)	4. Accumulated Profits for Tax Year Indicated (in functional currency computed under section 902) (attach schedule)	5. Foreign Taxes Paid and Deemed Paid on Earnings and Profits (E&P) for Tax Year Indicated (in functional currency) (see instructions)	6. Dividends Paid		7. Divide Column 6(a) by Column 4	8. Tax Deemed Paid (see instructions)	
					(a) Functional Currency	(b) U.S. Dollars		(a) Functional Currency	(b) U.S. Dollars

Total (Add amounts in column 8b. Enter the result here and include on "Totals" line of Schedule B, Part I, column 3) . . . . ▶

Part III—Deemed Inclusions From Pre-1987 Earnings and Profits

1. Name of Foreign Corporation (identify DISCs and former DISCs)	2. Tax Year End (Yr-Mo) (see instructions)	3. Country of Incorporation (enter country code from instructions)	4. E&P for Tax Year Indicated (in functional currency translated from U.S. dollars, computed under section 964) (attach schedule)	5. Foreign Taxes Paid and Deemed Paid for Tax Year Indicated (see instructions)	6. Deemed Inclusions		7. Divide Column 6(a) by Column 4	8. Tax Deemed Paid (multiply column 5 by column 7)
					(a) Functional Currency	(b) U.S. Dollars		

Total (Add amounts in column 8. Enter the result here and include on "Totals" line of Schedule B, Part I, column 3) . . . . ▶

Figure H.9 Form 1118 — Foreign Tax Credit — Corporations, Page 3

Form 1118 (Rev. 12-2004) Page **4**

Schedule D Tax Deemed Paid by First- and Second-Tier Foreign Corporations under Section 902(b)

Use Part I to compute the tax deemed paid by a first-tier foreign corporation with respect to dividends from a second-tier foreign corporation. Use Part II to compute the tax deemed paid by a second-tier foreign corporation with respect to dividends from a third-tier foreign corporation. ***Report all amounts in U.S. dollars unless otherwise specified.***

Part I—Tax Deemed Paid by First-Tier Foreign Corporations

Section A—Dividends Paid Out of Post-1986 Undistributed Earnings (Include the column 10 results in Schedule C, Part I, column 6(b).)

1. Name of Second-Tier Foreign Corporation and Its Related First-Tier Foreign Corporation	2. Tax Year End (Yr-Mo) (see instructions)	3. Country of Incorporation (enter country code from instructions)	4. Post-1986 Undistributed Earnings (in functional currency—attach schedule)	5. Opening Balance in Post-1986 Foreign Income Taxes	6. Foreign Taxes Paid and Deemed Paid for Tax Year Indicated		7. Post-1986 Foreign Income Taxes (add columns 5, 6(a), and 6(b))	8. Dividends Paid (in functional currency)		9. Divide Column 8(a) by Column 4	10. Tax Deemed Paid (multiply column 7 by column 9)
					(a) Taxes Paid	(b) Taxes Deemed Paid (see instructions)		(a) of Second-tier Corporation	(b) of First-tier Corporation		

Section B—Dividends Paid Out of Pre-1987 Accumulated Profits (Include the column 8(b) results in Schedule C, Part I, column 6(b).)

1. Name of Second-Tier Foreign Corporation and Its Related First-Tier Foreign Corporation	2. Tax Year End (Yr-Mo) (see instructions)	3. Country of Incorporation (enter country code from instructions)	4. Accumulated Profits for Tax Year Indicated (in functional currency—attach schedule)	5. Foreign Taxes Paid and Deemed Paid for Tax Year Indicated (in functional currency—see instructions)	6. Dividends Paid (in functional currency)		7. Divide Column 6(a) by Column 4	8. Tax Deemed Paid (see instructions)	
					(a) of Second-tier Corporation	(b) of First-tier Corporation		(a) Functional Currency of Second-tier Corporation	(b) U.S. Dollars

Part II—Tax Deemed Paid by Second-Tier Foreign Corporations

Section A—Dividends Paid Out of Post-1986 Undistributed Earnings (Include the column 10 results in Section A, column 6(b), of Part I above.)

1. Name of Third-Tier Foreign Corporation and Its Related Second-Tier Foreign Corporation	2. Tax Year End (Yr-Mo) (see instructions)	3. Country of Incorporation (enter country code from instructions)	4. Post-1986 Undistributed Earnings (in functional currency—attach schedule)	5. Opening Balance in Post-1986 Foreign Income Taxes	6. Foreign Taxes Paid and Deemed Paid for Tax Year Indicated		7. Post-1986 Foreign Income Taxes (add columns 5, 6(a), and 6(b))	8. Dividends Paid (in functional currency)		9. Divide Column 8(a) by Column 4	10. Tax Deemed Paid (multiply column 7 by column 9)
					(a) Taxes Paid	(b) Taxes Deemed Paid (from Schedule E, Part I, column 10)		(a) of Third-tier Corporation	(b) of Second-tier Corporation		

Section B—Dividends Paid Out of Pre-1987 Accumulated Profits (Include the column 8(b) results in Section A, column 6(b), of Part I above.)

1. Name of Third-Tier Foreign Corporation and Its Related Second-Tier Foreign Corporation	2. Tax Year End (Yr-Mo) (see instructions)	3. Country of Incorporation (enter country code from instructions)	4. Accumulated Profits for Tax Year Indicated (in functional currency—attach schedule)	5. Foreign Taxes Paid and Deemed Paid for Tax Year Indicated (in functional currency—see instructions)	6. Dividends Paid (in functional currency)		7. Divide Column 6(a) by Column 4	8. Tax Deemed Paid (see instructions)	
					(a) of Third-tier Corporation	(b) of Second-tier Corporation		(a) In Functional Currency of Third-tier Corporation	(b) U.S. Dollars

Figure H.10 Form 1118 — Foreign Tax Credit — Corporations, Page 4

Form 1118 (Rev. 12-2004) Page **5**

Schedule E **Tax Deemed Paid by Certain Third-, Fourth-, and Fifth-Tier Foreign Corporations Under Section 902(b)**

Use this schedule to report taxes deemed paid with respect to dividends from eligible post-1986 undistributed earnings of fourth-, fifth- and sixth-tier controlled foreign corporations. ***Report all amounts in U.S. dollars unless otherwise specified.***

Part I—Tax Deemed Paid by Third-Tier Foreign Corporations (Include the column 10 results in Schedule D, Part II, Section A, column 6(b).)

1. Name of Fourth-Tier Foreign Corporation and Its Related Third-Tier Foreign Corporation	**2.** Tax Year End (Yr-Mo) (see instructions)	**3.** Country of Incorporation (enter country code from instructions)	**4.** Post-1986 Undistributed Earnings (in functional currency—attach schedule)	**5.** Opening Balance in Post-1986 Foreign Income Taxes	**6.** Foreign Taxes Paid and Deemed Paid for Tax Year Indicated		**7.** Post-1986 Foreign Income Taxes (add columns 5, 6(a), and 6(b))	**8.** Dividends Paid (in functional currency)		**9.** Divide Column 8(a) by Column 4	**10.** Tax Deemed Paid (multiply column 7 by column 9)
					(a) Taxes Paid	**(b)** Taxes Deemed Paid (from Part II, column 10)		**(a)** Of Fourth-tier CFC	**(b)** Of Third-tier CFC		

Part II—Tax Deemed Paid by Fourth-Tier Foreign Corporations (Include the column 10 results in column 6(b) of Part I above.)

1. Name of Fifth-Tier Foreign Corporation and Its Related Fourth-Tier Foreign Corporation	**2.** Tax Year End (Yr-Mo) (see instructions)	**3.** Country of Incorporation (enter country code from instructions)	**4.** Post-1986 Undistributed Earnings (in functional currency—attach schedule)	**5.** Opening Balance in Post-1986 Foreign Income Taxes	**6.** Foreign Taxes Paid and Deemed Paid for Tax Year Indicated		**7.** Post-1986 Foreign Income Taxes (add columns 5, 6(a), and 6(b))	**8.** Dividends Paid (in functional currency)		**9.** Divide Column 8(a) by Column 4	**10.** Tax Deemed Paid (multiply column 7 by column 9)
					(a) Taxes Paid	**(b)** Taxes Deemed Paid (from Part III, column 10)		**(a)** Of Fifth-tier CFC	**(b)** Of Fourth-tier CFC		

Part III—Tax Deemed Paid by Fifth-Tier Foreign Corporations (Include the column 10 results in column 6(b) of Part II above.)

1. Name of Sixth-Tier Foreign Corporation and Its Related Fifth-Tier Foreign Corporation	**2.** Tax Year End (Yr-Mo) (see instructions)	**3.** Country of Incorporation (enter country code from instructions)	**4.** Post-1986 Undistributed Earnings (in functional currency—attach schedule)	**5.** Opening Balance in Post-1986 Foreign Income Taxes	**6.** Foreign Taxes Paid For Tax Year Indicated	**7.** Post-1986 Foreign Income Taxes (add columns 5 and 6)	**8.** Dividends Paid (in functional currency)		**9.** Divide Column 8(a) by Column 4	**10.** Tax Deemed Paid (multiply column 7 by column 9)
							(a) Of Sixth-tier CFC	**(b)** Of Fifth-tier CFC		

Figure H.11 Form 1118 — Foreign Tax Credit — Corporations, Page 5

Form 1118 (Rev. 12-2004) Page **6**

Schedule F **Gross Income and Definitely Allocable Deductions for Foreign Branches**

	1. Name of Foreign Country or U.S. Possession (Use a separate line for each.)	2. Gross Income	3. Definitely Allocable Deductions
A			
B			
C			
D			
E			
F			
Totals (add lines A through F)* ▶			

* **Note:** *The Schedule F totals are not carried over to any other Form 1118 Schedule. (These totals were already included in Schedule A.) However, the IRS requires the corporation to complete Schedule F under the authority of section 905(b).*

Schedule G **Reductions of Taxes Paid, Accrued, or Deemed Paid**

A	Reduction of Taxes Under Section 901(e)—Attach separate schedule	
B	Reduction of Oil and Gas Extraction Taxes—Enter amount from Schedule I, Part II, line 6	
C	Reduction of Taxes Due to International Boycott Provisions—Enter appropriate portion of Schedule C (Form 5713), line 2b. **Important:** Enter only "specifically attributable taxes" here.	
D	Reduction of Taxes for Section 6038(c) Penalty—Attach separate schedule	
E	Other Reductions of Taxes—Attach schedule(s)	
	Total (add lines A through E). Enter here and on Schedule B, Part II, line 3 . . . . ▶	

Figure H.12 Form 1118 — Foreign Tax Credit — Corporations, Page 6

Form 1118 (Rev. 12-2004) Page 7

Schedule H **Apportionment of Deductions Not Definitely Allocable** *(complete only once)*

Part I—Research and Development Deductions

	(a) Sales Method					**(b)** Gross Income Method—Check method used: ☐ Option 1 ☐ Option 2 (See page 9 of instructions.)		**(c)** Total R&D Deductions Not Definitely Allocable (enter all amounts from column (a)(v) or all amounts from column (b)(vii))
	Product line #1 (SIC Code:)*		Product line #2 (SIC Code:)*		**(v)** Total R&D Deductions Under Sales Method (add columns (ii) and (iv))			
	(i) Gross Sales	**(ii)** R&D Deductions	**(iii)** Gross Sales	**(iv)** R&D Deductions		**(vi)** Gross Income	**(vii)** Total R&D Deductions Under Gross Income Method	
1 Totals (see pages 8 and 9 of instructions)								
2 Total to be apportioned								
3 Apportionment among statutory groupings:								
a General limitation income								
b Passive income								
c High withholding tax interest								
d Financial services income								
e Shipping income								
f Taxable income attributable to foreign trade income								
g Section 901(j) income*								
h Income re-sourced by treaty*								
4 Total foreign (add lines 3a through 3h)								

*Important: *See* ***Computer-Generated Schedule H*** *in instructions.*

Figure H.13 Form 1118 — Foreign Tax Credit — Corporations, Page 7

Form 1118 (Rev. 12-2004) Page 8

Schedule H **Apportionment of Deductions Not Definitely Allocable** *(continued)*

Part II—Interest Deductions, All Other Deductions, and Total Deductions

	(a) Average Value of Assets—Check method used: ☐ Fair market value ☐ Tax book value ☐ Alternative tax book value		**(b)** Interest Deductions		**(c)** All Other Deductions Not Definitely Allocable	**(d)** Totals (add the corresponding amounts from column (c), Part I; columns (b)(iii) and (b)(iv), Part II; and column (c), Part II). Enter each amount from lines 3a through 3j below in column 10 of the corresponding Schedule A.
	(i) Nonfinancial Corporations	**(ii)** Financial Corporations	**(iii)** Nonfinancial Corporations	**(iv)** Financial Corporations		
1a Totals (see pages 9 and 10 of instructions)						
b Amounts specifically allocable under Temp. Regs. 1.861-10T(e)						
c Other specific allocations under Temp. Regs. 1.861-10T						
d Assets excluded from apportionment formula						
2 Total to be apportioned (subtract the sum of lines 1b, 1c, and 1d from line 1a)						
3 Apportionment among statutory groupings:						
a General limitation income						
b Passive income						
c High withholding tax interest						
d Financial services income						
e Shipping income						
f Taxable income attributable to foreign trade income						
g Certain distributions from a FSC or former FSC						
h Dividends from a DISC or former DISC						
i Section 901(j) income*						
j Income re-sourced by treaty*						
4 Total foreign (add lines 3a through 3j)						

* **Important:** *See* ***Computer-Generated Schedule H*** *in instructions.*

Printed on recycled paper

Figure H.14 Form 1118 — Foreign Tax Credit — Corporations, Page 8

Figures H.15 through H.18 show Form 5471 — Information Return of U.S. Persons With Respect to Certain Foreign Corporations (4 pages).

Form **5471** (Rev. December 2005) Department of the Treasury Internal Revenue Service

Information Return of U.S. Persons With Respect To Certain Foreign Corporations

▶ **See separate instructions.**

Information furnished for the foreign corporation's annual accounting period (tax year required by section 898) (see instructions) beginning , 20 , and ending , 20

OMB No. 1545-0704
Attachment Sequence No. **121**

File In Duplicate (see **When and Where To File** in the instructions)

Name of person filing this return	**A Identifying number**
Number, street, and room or suite no. (or P.O. box number if mail is not delivered to street address)	**B** Category of filer (See instructions. Check applicable box(es)): 1 (repealed) 2 ☐ 3 ☐ 4 ☐ 5 ☐
City or town, state, and ZIP code	**C** Enter the total percentage of the foreign corporation's voting stock you owned at the end of its annual accounting period .... %

Filer's tax year beginning , 20 , and ending , 20

D Person(s) on whose behalf this information return is filed:

(1) Name	**(2)** Address	**(3)** Identifying number	**(4)** Check applicable box(es)		
			Shareholder	Officer	Director

Important: *Fill in all applicable lines and schedules. All information* ***must*** *be in English. All amounts* ***must*** *be stated in U.S. dollars unless otherwise indicated.*

1a Name and address of foreign corporation	**b** Employer identification number, if any
	c Country under whose laws incorporated

d Date of incorporation	**e** Principal place of business	**f** Principal business activity code number	**g** Principal business activity	**h** Functional currency

2 Provide the following information for the foreign corporation's accounting period stated above.

a Name, address, and identifying number of branch office or agent (if any) in the United States	**b** If a U.S. income tax return was filed, enter:	
	(i) Taxable income or (loss)	*(ii)* U.S. income tax paid (after all credits)

c Name and address of foreign corporation's statutory or resident agent in country of incorporation	**d** Name and address (including corporate department, if applicable) of person (or persons) with custody of the books and records of the foreign corporation, and the location of such books and records, if different

Schedule A **Stock of the Foreign Corporation**

(a) Description of each class of stock	**(b)** Number of shares issued and outstanding	
	(i) Beginning of annual accounting period	*(ii)* End of annual accounting period

For Paperwork Reduction Act Notice, see instructions. Cat. No. 49958V Form **5471** (Rev. 12-2005)

Figure H.15 Form 5471 — Information Return of U.S. Persons With Respect to Certain Foreign Corporations, Page 1

Form 5471 (Rev. 12-2005) Page 2

Schedule B **U.S. Shareholders of Foreign Corporation** (see instructions)

(a) Name, address, and identifying number of shareholder	(b) Description of each class of stock held by shareholder. **Note:** *This description should match the corresponding description entered in Schedule A, column (a).*	(c) Number of shares held at beginning of annual accounting period	(d) Number of shares held at end of annual accounting period	(e) Pro rata share of subpart F income (enter as a percentage)

Schedule C **Income Statement** (see instructions)

Important: *Report all information in functional currency in accordance with U.S. GAAP. Also, report each amount in U.S. dollars translated from functional currency (using GAAP translation rules). However, if the functional currency is the U.S. dollar, complete only the U.S. Dollars column. See instructions for special rules for DASTM corporations.*

			Functional Currency	U.S. Dollars
Income	1a Gross receipts or sales	1a		
	b Returns and allowances	1b		
	c Subtract line 1b from line 1a	1c		
	2 Cost of goods sold	2		
	3 Gross profit (subtract line 2 from line 1c)	3		
	4 Dividends	4		
	5 Interest	5		
	6 Gross rents, royalties, and license fees	6		
	7 Net gain or (loss) on sale of capital assets	7		
	8 Other income (attach schedule)	8		
	9 Total income (add lines 3 through 8)	9		
Deductions	10 Compensation not deducted elsewhere	10		
	11 Rents, royalties, and license fees	11		
	12 Interest	12		
	13 Depreciation not deducted elsewhere	13		
	14 Depletion	14		
	15 Taxes (exclude provision for income, war profits, and excess profits taxes)	15		
	16 Other deductions (attach schedule—exclude provision for income, war profits, and excess profits taxes)	16		
	17 Total deductions (add lines 10 through 16)	17		
Net Income	18 Net income or (loss) before extraordinary items, prior period adjustments, and the provision for income, war profits, and excess profits taxes (subtract line 17 from line 9)	18		
	19 Extraordinary items and prior period adjustments (see instructions)	19		
	20 Provision for income, war profits, and excess profits taxes (see instructions)	20		
	21 Current year net income or (loss) per books (combine lines 18 through 20)	21		

Form **5471** (Rev. 12-2005)

Figure H.16 Form 5471 — Information Return of U.S. Persons With Respect to Certain Foreign Corporations, Page 2

Form 5471 (Rev. 12-2005) Page 3

Schedule E **Income, War Profits, and Excess Profits Taxes Paid or Accrued** (see instructions)

	(a) Name of country or U.S. possession	Amount of tax (b) In foreign currency	(c) Conversion rate	(d) In U.S. dollars
1	U.S.			
2				
3				
4				
5				
6				
7				
8	Total . . . ▶			

Schedule F **Balance Sheet**

Important: *Report all amounts in U.S. dollars prepared and translated in accordance with U.S. GAAP. See instructions for an exception for DASTM corporations.*

	Assets		(a) Beginning of annual accounting period	(b) End of annual accounting period
1	Cash	1		
2a	Trade notes and accounts receivable	2a		
b	Less allowance for bad debts	2b	( )	( )
3	Inventories	3		
4	Other current assets (attach schedule)	4		
5	Loans to shareholders and other related persons	5		
6	Investment in subsidiaries (attach schedule)	6		
7	Other investments (attach schedule)	7		
8a	Buildings and other depreciable assets	8a		
b	Less accumulated depreciation	8b	( )	( )
9a	Depletable assets	9a		
b	Less accumulated depletion	9b	( )	( )
10	Land (net of any amortization)	10		
11	Intangible assets:			
a	Goodwill	11a		
b	Organization costs	11b		
c	Patents, trademarks, and other intangible assets	11c		
d	Less accumulated amortization for lines 11a, b, and c	11d	( )	( )
12	Other assets (attach schedule)	12		
13	Total assets	13		
	Liabilities and Shareholders' Equity			
14	Accounts payable	14		
15	Other current liabilities (attach schedule)	15		
16	Loans from shareholders and other related persons	16		
17	Other liabilities (attach schedule)	17		
18	Capital stock:			
a	Preferred stock	18a		
b	Common stock	18b		
19	Paid-in or capital surplus (attach reconciliation)	19		
20	Retained earnings	20		
21	Less cost of treasury stock	21	( )	( )
22	Total liabilities and shareholders' equity	22		

Form **5471** (Rev. 12-2005)

Figure H.17 Form 5471 — Information Return of U.S. Persons With Respect to Certain Foreign Corporations, Page 3

Form 5471 (Rev. 12-2005) Page **4**

Schedule G **Other Information**

		Yes	No
1	During the tax year, did the foreign corporation own at least a 10% interest, directly or indirectly, in any foreign partnership? If "Yes," see the instructions for required attachment.	☐	☐
2	During the tax year, did the foreign corporation own an interest in any trust?	☐	☐
3	During the tax year, did the foreign corporation own any foreign entities that were disregarded as entities separate from their owners under Regulations sections 301.7701-2 and 301.7701-3 (see instructions)? If "Yes," you are generally required to attach Form 8858 for each entity (see instructions).	☐	☐

Schedule H **Current Earnings and Profits** (see instructions)

Important: *Enter the amounts on lines 1 through 5c in **functional** currency.*

		Net Additions	Net Subtractions		
1	Current year net income or (loss) per foreign books of account			1	
2	Net adjustments made to line 1 to determine current earnings and profits according to U.S. financial and tax accounting standards (see instructions):				
a	Capital gains or losses				
b	Depreciation and amortization				
c	Depletion				
d	Investment or incentive allowance				
e	Charges to statutory reserves				
f	Inventory adjustments				
g	Taxes				
h	Other (attach schedule)				
3	Total net additions				
4	Total net subtractions				
5a	Current earnings and profits (line 1 plus line 3 minus line 4)			5a	
b	DASTM gain or (loss) for foreign corporations that use DASTM (see instructions)			5b	
c	Combine lines 5a and 5b			5c	
d	Current earnings and profits in U.S. dollars (line 5c translated at the appropriate exchange rate as defined in section 989(b) and the related regulations (see instructions))			5d	

Enter exchange rate used for line 5d ▶

Schedule I **Summary of Shareholder's Income From Foreign Corporation** (see instructions)

1	Subpart F income (line 38b, Worksheet A in the instructions)	1	
2	Earnings invested in U.S. property (line 17, Worksheet B in the instructions)	2	
3	Previously excluded subpart F income withdrawn from qualified investments (line 6b, Worksheet C in the instructions)	3	
4	Previously excluded export trade income withdrawn from investment in export trade assets (line 7b, Worksheet D in the instructions)	4	
5	Factoring income	5	
6	Total of lines 1 through 5. Enter here and on your income tax return. See instructions.	6	
7	Dividends received (translated at spot rate on payment date under section 989(b)(1))	7	
8	Exchange gain or (loss) on a distribution of previously taxed income	8	

	Yes	No
• Was any income of the foreign corporation blocked?	☐	☐
• Did any such income become unblocked during the tax year (see section 964(b))?	☐	☐

If the answer to either question is "Yes," attach an explanation.

Form **5471** (Rev. 12-2005)

Figure H.18 Form 5471 — Information Return of U.S. Persons With Respect to Certain Foreign Corporations, Page 4

Figures H.19 through H.25 show Form 8865 — Return of a U.S. Person With Respect to Certain Foreign Partnerships (7 pages).

Form **8865**

Department of the Treasury
Internal Revenue Service

Return of U.S. Persons With Respect to Certain Foreign Partnerships

▶ **Attach to your tax return. See separate instructions.**

Information furnished for the foreign partnership's tax year beginning , 2006, and ending , 20

OMB No. 1545-1668

2006

Attachment Sequence No. **118**

Name of person filing this return | **Filer's identifying number**

Filer's address (if you are not filing this form with your tax return)

A Category of filer (see **Categories of Filers** in the instructions and check applicable box(es)): 1 ☐ 2 ☐ 3 ☐ 4 ☐

B Filer's tax year beginning ...., 20 ..... , and ending ...., 20 .....

C Filer's share of liabilities: Nonrecourse $ Qualified nonrecourse financing $ Other $

D If filer is a member of a consolidated group but not the parent, enter the following information about the parent:

Name | EIN

Address

E Information about certain other partners (see instructions)

(1) Name	(2) Address	(3) Identifying number	(4) Check applicable box(es)		
			Category 1	Category 2	Constructive owner

F1 Name and address of foreign partnership

2 EIN (if any)

3 Country under whose laws organized

4 Date of organization	5 Principal place of business	6 Principal business activity code number	7 Principal business activity	8a Functional currency	8b Exchange rate (see instr.)

G Provide the following information for the foreign partnership's tax year:

1 Name, address, and identifying number of agent (if any) in the United States

2 Check if the foreign partnership must file:
☐ Form 1042 ☐ Form 8804 ☐ Form 1065 or 1065-B
Service Center where Form 1065 or 1065-B is filed:

3 Name and address of foreign partnership's agent in country of organization, if any

4 Name and address of person(s) with custody of the books and records of the foreign partnership, and the location of such books and records, if different

5 Were any special allocations made by the foreign partnership? . . . ▶ ☐ **Yes** ☐ **No**

6 Enter the number of Forms 8858, Information Return of U.S. Persons With Respect To Foreign Disregarded Entities, attached to this return (see instructions). . . . ▶ ....

7 How is this partnership classified under the law of the country in which it is organized? . . ▶ ....

8 Did the partnership own any separate units within the meaning of Regulations section 1.1503-2(c)(3) or (4)? . . ▶ ☐ **Yes** ☐ **No**

9 Does this partnership meet **both** of the following requirements?
- The partnership's total receipts for the tax year were less than $250,000 and
- The value of the partnership's total assets at the end of the tax year was less than $600,000. } . . . . ▶ ☐ **Yes** ☐ **No**

If "Yes," **do not** complete Schedules L, M-1, and M-2.

Sign Here Only If You Are Filing This Form Separately and Not With Your Tax Return

Under penalties of perjury, I declare that I have examined this return, including accompanying schedules and statements, and to the best of my knowledge and belief, it is true, correct, and complete. Declaration of preparer (other than general partner or limited liability company member) is based on all information of which preparer has any knowledge.

▶ Signature of general partner or limited liability company member ▶ Date

Paid Preparer Sign and Complete Only If Form is Filed Separately.

Preparer's signature ▶	Date	Check if self-employed ▶ ☐	Preparer's SSN or PTIN
Firm's name (or yours if self-employed), address, and ZIP code ▶		EIN ▶	
		Phone no. ( )	

For Privacy Act and Paperwork Reduction Act Notice, see the separate instructions. Cat. No. 25852A Form **8865** (2006)

Figure H.19 Form 8865 — Return of a U.S. Person With Respect to Certain Foreign Partnerships, Page 1

Form 8865 (2006) Page **2**

Schedule A **Constructive Ownership of Partnership Interest.** Check the boxes that apply to the filer. If you check box **b,** enter the name, address, and U.S. taxpayer identifying number (if any) of the person(s) whose interest you constructively own. See instructions.

a ☐ Owns a direct interest **b** ☐ Owns a constructive interest

Name	Address	Identifying number (if any)	Check if foreign person	Check if direct partner

Schedule A-1 **Certain Partners of Foreign Partnership** (see instructions)

Name	Address	Identifying number (if any)	Check if foreign person

Does the partnership have any other foreign person as a direct partner? . . . . ☐ **Yes** ☐ **No**

Schedule A-2 **Affiliation Schedule.** List all partnerships (foreign or domestic) in which the foreign partnership owns a direct interest or indirectly owns a 10% interest.

Name	Address	EIN (if any)	Total ordinary income or loss	Check if foreign partnership

Schedule B **Income Statement—Trade or Business Income**

Caution. *Include **only** trade or business income and expenses on lines 1a through 22 below. See the instructions for more information.*

Income	**1a**	Gross receipts or sales	**1a**			
	b	Less returns and allowances	**1b**		**1c**	
	2	Cost of goods sold			**2**	
	3	Gross profit. Subtract line 2 from line 1c			**3**	
	4	Ordinary income (loss) from other partnerships, estates, and trusts *(attach statement)*			**4**	
	5	Net farm profit (loss) *(attach Schedule F (Form 1040))*			**5**	
	6	Net gain (loss) from Form 4797, Part II, line 17 (attach Form 4797)			**6**	
	7	Other income (loss) *(attach statement)*			**7**	
	8	**Total income (loss).** Combine lines 3 through 7			**8**	
Deductions (see instructions for limitations)	9	Salaries and wages (other than to partners) (less employment credits)			**9**	
	10	Guaranteed payments to partners			**10**	
	11	Repairs and maintenance			**11**	
	12	Bad debts			**12**	
	13	Rent			**13**	
	14	Taxes and licenses			**14**	
	15	Interest			**15**	
	16a	Depreciation *(if required, attach Form 4562)*	**16a**			
	b	Less depreciation reported elsewhere on return	**16b**		**16c**	
	17	Depletion (**Do not** deduct oil and gas depletion.)			**17**	
	18	Retirement plans, etc.			**18**	
	19	Employee benefit programs			**19**	
	20	Other deductions *(attach statement)*			**20**	
	21	**Total deductions.** Add the amounts shown in the far right column for lines 9 through 20			**21**	
	22	**Ordinary business income (loss)** from trade or business activities. Subtract line 21 from line 8			**22**	

Form **8865** (2006)

Figure H.20 Form 8865 — Return of a U.S. Person With Respect to Certain Foreign Partnerships, Page 2

Form 8865 (2006) Page 3

Schedule D **Capital Gains and Losses**

Part I **Short-Term Capital Gains and Losses—Assets Held One Year or Less**

	(a) Description of property (e.g., 100 shares of "Z" Co.)	(b) Date acquired (month, day, year)	(c) Date sold (month, day, year)	(d) Sales price (see instructions)	(e) Cost or other basis (see instructions)	(f) Gain or (loss) Subtract (e) from (d)
1						

2	Short-term capital gain from installment sales from Form 6252, line 26 or 37	2	
3	Short-term capital gain (loss) from like-kind exchanges from Form 8824	3	
4	Partnership's share of net short-term capital gain (loss), including specially allocated short-term capital gains (losses), from other partnerships, estates, and trusts	4	
5	**Net short-term capital gain or (loss).** Combine lines 1 through 4 in column (f). Enter here and on Form 8865, Schedule K, line 8 or 11	5	

Part II **Long-Term Capital Gains and Losses—Assets Held More Than One Year**

	(a) Description of property (e.g., 100 shares of "Z" Co.)	(b) Date acquired (month, day, year)	(c) Date sold (month, day, year)	(d) Sales price (see instructions)	(e) Cost or other basis (see instructions)	(f) Gain or (loss) Subtract (e) from (d)
6						

7	Long-term capital gain from installment sales from Form 6252, line 26 or 37	7	
8	Long-term capital gain (loss) from like-kind exchanges from Form 8824.	8	
9	Partnership's share of net long-term capital gain (loss), including specially allocated long-term capital gains (losses), from other partnerships, estates, and trusts.	9	
10	Capital gain distributions	10	
11	**Net long-term capital gain or (loss).** Combine lines 6 through 10 in column (f). Enter here and on Form 8865, Schedule K, line 9a or 11	11	

Form **8865** (2006)

Figure H.21 Form 8865 — Return of a U.S. Person With Respect to Certain Foreign Partnerships, Page 3

Form 8865 (2006) Page 4

Schedule K — Partners' Distributive Share Items

			Total amount
Income (Loss)	1 Ordinary business income (loss) (page 2, line 22)	1	
	2 Net rental real estate income (loss) *(attach Form 8825)*	2	
	3a Other gross rental income (loss) — 3a		
	b Expenses from other rental activities *(attach statement)* — 3b		
	c Other net rental income (loss). Subtract line 3b from line 3a	3c	
	4 Guaranteed payments	4	
	5 Interest income	5	
	6 Dividends: a Ordinary dividends	6a	
	b Qualified dividends — 6b		
	7 Royalties	7	
	8 Net short-term capital gain (loss)	8	
	9a Net long-term capital gain (loss)	9a	
	b Collectibles (28%) gain (loss) — 9b		
	c Unrecaptured section 1250 gain *(attach statement)* — 9c		
	10 Net section 1231 gain (loss) *(attach Form 4797)*	10	
	11 Other income (loss) *(see instructions)* Type ▶	11	
Deductions	12 Section 179 deduction *(attach Form 4562)*	12	
	13a Contributions	13a	
	b Investment interest expense	13b	
	c Section 59(e)(2) expenditures: (1) Type ▶ (2) Amount ▶	13c(2)	
	d Other deductions *(see instructions)* Type ▶	13d	
Self-Employment	14a Net earnings (loss) from self-employment	14a	
	b Gross farming or fishing income	14b	
	c Gross nonfarm income	14c	
Credits	15a Low-income housing credit (section 42(j)(5))	15a	
	b Low-income housing credit (other)	15b	
	c Qualified rehabilitation expenditures (rental real estate) *(attach Form 3468)*	15c	
	d Other rental real estate credits (see instructions) Type ▶	15d	
	e Other rental credits (see instructions) Type ▶	15e	
	f Other credits *(see instructions)* Type ▶	15f	
Foreign Transactions	16a Name of country or U.S. possession ▶		
	b Gross income from all sources	16b	
	c Gross income sourced at partner level	16c	
	Foreign gross income sourced at partnership level		
	d Passive ▶ e Listed categories *(attach statement)* ▶ f General limitation ▶	16f	
	Deductions allocated and apportioned at partner level		
	g Interest expense ▶ h Other ▶	16h	
	Deductions allocated and apportioned at partnership level to foreign source income		
	i Passive ▶ j Listed categories *(attach statement)* ▶ k General limitation ▶	16k	
	l Total foreign taxes (check one): ▶ ☐ Paid ☐ Accrued	16l	
	m Reduction in taxes available for credit *(attach statement)*	16m	
	n Other foreign tax information *(attach statement)*		
Alternative Minimum Tax (AMT) Items	17a Post-1986 depreciation adjustment	17a	
	b Adjusted gain or loss	17b	
	c Depletion (other than oil and gas)	17c	
	d Oil, gas, and geothermal properties—gross income	17d	
	e Oil, gas, and geothermal properties—deductions	17e	
	f Other AMT items *(attach statement)*	17f	
Other Information	18a Tax-exempt interest income	18a	
	b Other tax-exempt income	18b	
	c Nondeductible expenses	18c	
	19a Distributions of cash and marketable securities	19a	
	b Distributions of other property	19b	
	20a Investment income	20a	
	b Investment expenses	20b	
	c Other items and amounts *(attach statement)*		

Form **8865** (2006)

Figure H.22 Form 8865 — Return of a U.S. Person With Respect to Certain Foreign Partnerships, Page 4

Form 8865 (2006) Page **5**

Schedule L **Balance Sheets per Books.** (Not required if Item G9, page 1, is answered "Yes.")

Assets	Beginning of tax year		End of tax year	
	(a)	**(b)**	**(c)**	**(d)**
1 Cash				
2a Trade notes and accounts receivable				
b Less allowance for bad debts				
3 Inventories				
4 U.S. government obligations				
5 Tax-exempt securities				
6 Other current assets *(attach statement)*				
7 Mortgage and real estate loans				
8 Other investments *(attach statement)*				
9a Buildings and other depreciable assets				
b Less accumulated depreciation				
10a Depletable assets				
b Less accumulated depletion				
11 Land (net of any amortization)				
12a Intangible assets (amortizable only)				
b Less accumulated amortization				
13 Other assets *(attach statement)*				
14 **Total** assets				
Liabilities and Capital				
15 Accounts payable				
16 Mortgages, notes, bonds payable in less than 1 year				
17 Other current liabilities *(attach statement)*				
18 All nonrecourse loans				
19 Mortgages, notes, bonds payable in 1 year or more				
20 Other liabilities *(attach statement)*				
21 Partners' capital accounts				
22 **Total** liabilities and capital				

Form **8865** (2006)

Figure H.23 Form 8865 — Return of a U.S. Person With Respect to Certain Foreign Partnerships, Page 5

Form 8865 (2006) Page 6

Schedule M **Balance Sheets for Interest Allocation**

	(a) Beginning of tax year	(b) End of tax year
1 Total U.S. assets		
2 Total foreign assets:		
a Passive income category		
b Listed categories *(attach statement)*		
c General limitation income category		

Schedule M-1 **Reconciliation of Income (Loss) per Books With Income (Loss) per Return.** (Not required if Item G9, page 1, is answered "Yes.")

1 Net income (loss) per books		6 Income recorded on books this year not included on Schedule K, lines 1 through 11 (itemize):	
2 Income included on Schedule K, lines 1, 2, 3c, 5, 6a, 7, 8, 9a, 10, and 11 not recorded on books this year (itemize):		a Tax-exempt interest $	
3 Guaranteed payments (other than health insurance)		7 Deductions included on Schedule K, lines 1 through 13d, and 16l not charged against book income this year (itemize):	
4 Expenses recorded on books this year not included on Schedule K, lines 1 through 13d, and 16l (itemize):		a Depreciation $	
a Depreciation $			
b Travel and entertainment $		8 Add lines 6 and 7	
5 Add lines 1 through 4		9 Income (loss). Subtract line 8 from line 5	

Schedule M-2 **Analysis of Partners' Capital Accounts.** (Not required if Item G9, page 1, is answered "Yes.")

1 Balance at beginning of year		6 Distributions: a Cash	
2 Capital contributed:		b Property	
a Cash		7 Other decreases (itemize):	
b Property			
3 Net income (loss) per books			
4 Other increases (itemize):			
		8 Add lines 6 and 7	
5 Add lines 1 through 4		9 Balance at end of year. Subtract line 8 from line 5	

Form **8865** (2006)

Figure H.24 Form 8865 — Return of a U.S. Person With Respect to Certain Foreign Partnerships, Page 6

Form 8865 (2006) Page **7**

Schedule N **Transactions Between Controlled Foreign Partnership and Partners or Other Related Entities**

Important: Complete a separate Form 8865 and Schedule N for each controlled foreign partnership. Enter the totals for each type of transaction that occurred between the foreign partnership and the persons listed in columns (a) through (d).

Transactions of foreign partnership	**(a)** U.S. person filing this return	**(b)** Any domestic corporation or partnership controlling or controlled by the U.S. person filing this return	**(c)** Any other foreign corporation or partnership controlling or controlled by the U.S. person filing this return	**(d)** Any U.S. person with a 10% or more direct interest in the controlled foreign partnership (other than the U.S. person filing this return)
1 Sales of inventory . . .				
2 Sales of property rights (patents, trademarks, etc.)				
3 Compensation received for technical, managerial, engineering, construction, or like services				
4 Commissions received .				
5 Rents, royalties, and license fees received . .				
6 Distributions received . .				
7 Interest received . . .				
8 Other				
9 Add lines 1 through 8 . .				
10 Purchases of inventory .				
11 Purchases of tangible property other than inventory				
12 Purchases of property rights (patents, trademarks, etc.) . . .				
13 Compensation paid for technical, managerial, engineering, construction, or like services				
14 Commissions paid . . .				
15 Rents, royalties, and license fees paid . . .				
16 Distributions paid . . .				
17 Interest paid				
18 Other				
19 Add lines 10 through 18 .				
20 Amounts borrowed (enter the maximum loan balance during the year)—see instructions . . .				
21 Amounts loaned (enter the maximum loan balance during the year)—see instructions				

Form **8865** (2006)

Figure H.25 Form 8865 — Return of a U.S. Person With Respect to Certain Foreign Partnerships, Page 7

Figures H.26 and H.27 show Form 8858 — Information Return of U.S. Persons With Respect to Foreign Disregarded Entities (2 pages).

Form **8858** (December 2004) Department of the Treasury Internal Revenue Service

Information Return of U.S. Persons With Respect To Foreign Disregarded Entities

▶ **See separate instructions.**

Information furnished for the foreign disregarded entity's annual accounting period (see instructions) beginning , 20 , and ending , 20

OMB No. 1545-1910

Attachment Sequence No. **140**

Name of person filing this return | **Filer's identifying number**

Number, street, and room or suite no. (or P.O. box number if mail is not delivered to street address)

City or town, state, and ZIP code

Filer's tax year beginning , 20 , and ending , 20

Important: *Fill in all applicable lines and schedules. All information* ***must*** *be in English. All amounts* ***must*** *be stated in U.S. dollars unless otherwise indicated.*

1a Name and address of foreign disregarded entity | **b** U.S. identifying number, if any

c Country(ies) under whose laws organized and entity type under local tax law | **d** Date(s) of organization | **e** Effective date as foreign disregarded entity

f If benefits under a U.S. tax treaty were claimed with respect to income of the foreign disregarded entity, enter the treaty and article number | **g** Country in which principal business activity is conducted | **h** Principal business activity | **i** Functional currency

2 Provide the following information for the foreign disregarded entity's accounting period stated above.

a Name, address, and identifying number of branch office or agent (if any) in the United States | **b** Name and address (including corporate department, if applicable) of person(s) with custody of the books and records of the foreign disregarded entity, and the location of such books and records, if different

3 For the **tax owner** of the foreign disregarded entity (if different from the filer) provide the following:

a Name and address | **b** Annual accounting period covered by the return (see instructions) | **c** U.S. identifying number, if any | **d** Country under whose laws organized | **e** Functional currency

4 For the **direct owner** of the foreign disregarded entity (if different from the tax owner) provide the following:

a Name and address | **b** Country under whose laws organized | **c** U.S. identifying number, if any | **d** Functional currency

5 Attach an organizational chart that identifies the name, placement, percentage of ownership, tax classification, and country of organization of all entities in the chain of ownership between the tax owner and the foreign disregarded entity, and the chain of ownership between the foreign disregarded entity and each entity in which the foreign disregarded entity has a 10% or more direct or indirect interest. See instructions.

Schedule C **Income Statement** (see instructions)

Important: *Report all information in functional currency in accordance with U.S. GAAP. Also, report each amount in U.S. dollars translated from functional currency (using GAAP translation rules or the average exchange rate determined under section 989(b)). If the functional currency is the U.S. dollar, complete only the U.S. Dollars column. See instructions for special rules for foreign disregarded entities that use DASTM.*

If you are using the average exchange rate (determined under section 989(b)), check the following box . . . . ☐

			Functional Currency	U.S. Dollars
1	Gross receipts or sales (net of returns and allowances)	1		
2	Cost of goods sold	2		
3	Gross profit (subtract line 2 from line 1)	3		
4	Other income	4		
5	Total income (add lines 3 and 4)	5		
6	Total deductions	6		
7	Other adjustments	7		
8	Net income (loss) per books	8		

For Paperwork Reduction Act Notice, see the separate instructions. Cat. No. 21457L Form **8858** (12-2004)

Figure H.26 Form 8858 — Information Return of U.S. Persons With Respect to Foreign Disregarded Entities, Page 1

Form 8858 (12-2004) Page 2

Schedule C-1 Section 987 Gain or Loss Information

			(a) Amount stated in functional currency of foreign disregarded entity	(b) Amount stated in functional currency of recipient
1	Remittances from the foreign disregarded entity	1		
2	Section 987 gain (loss) of recipient	2		

		Yes	No
3	Were all remittances from the foreign disregarded entity treated as made to the direct owner?		
4	Did the tax owner change its method of accounting for section 987 gain or loss with respect to remittances from the foreign disregarded entity during the tax year?		

Schedule F Balance Sheet

Important: *Report all amounts in U.S. dollars computed in functional currency and translated into U.S. dollars in accordance with U.S. GAAP. See instructions for an exception for foreign disregarded entities that use DASTM.*

	Assets		(a) Beginning of annual accounting period	(b) End of annual accounting period
1	Cash and other current assets	1		
2	Other assets	2		
3	Total assets	3		
	Liabilities and Owner's Equity			
4	Liabilities	4		
5	Owner's equity	5		
6	Total liabilities and owner's equity	6		

Schedule G Other Information

		Yes	No
1	During the tax year, did the foreign disregarded entity own an interest in any trust?		
2	During the tax year, did the foreign disregarded entity own at least a 10% interest, directly or indirectly, in any foreign partnership?		
3	*Answer the following question only if the foreign disregarded entity made its election to be treated as disregarded from its owner during the tax year:* Did the tax owner claim a loss with respect to stock or debt of the foreign disregarded entity as a result of the election?		
4	*Answer the following question only if the foreign disregarded entity is owned directly or indirectly by a domestic corporation and the foreign disregarded entity incurred a net operating loss for the tax year:* Is the foreign disregarded entity a separate unit as defined in Regulations sections 1.1503-2(c)(3) and (4)? (If yes, see the instructions)		
5	*Answer the following question only if the tax owner of the foreign disregarded entity is a controlled foreign corporation (CFC):* Were there any intracompany transactions between the foreign disregarded entity and the CFC or any other branch of the CFC during the tax year, in which the foreign disregarded entity acted as a manufacturing, selling, or purchasing branch?		

Schedule H Current Earnings and Profits or Taxable Income (see instructions)

Important: *Enter the amounts on lines 1 through 6 in functional currency.*

1	Current year net income or (loss) per foreign books of account	1	
2	Total net additions	2	
3	Total net subtractions	3	
4	Current earnings and profits (or taxable income—see instructions) (line 1 plus line 2 minus line 3)	4	
5	DASTM gain or loss (if applicable)	5	
6	Combine lines 4 and 5	6	
7	Current earnings and profits (or taxable income) in U.S. dollars (line 6 translated at the average exchange rate determined under section 989(b) and the related regulations (see instructions))	7	
	Enter exchange rate used for line 7 ▶		

Printed on recycled paper

Form **8858** (12-2004)

Figure H.27 Form 8858 — Information Return of U.S. Persons With Respect to Foreign Disregarded Entities, Page 2

Figures H.28 through H.31 show Form 5713 — International Boycott Report (4 pages).

Form **5713** (Rev. December 2004) Department of the Treasury Internal Revenue Service

International Boycott Report

For tax year beginning ...., 20 ...., and ending ...., 20 .....

▶ Controlled groups, see page 3 of instructions.

OMB No. 1545-0216 | Attachment Sequence No. 123 | File in Duplicate (See Instructions)

Name | Identifying number

Number, street, and room or suite no. (If a P.O. box, see page 2 of instructions.)

City or town, state, and ZIP code

Address of service center where your tax return is filed

Type of filer (check one): ☐ Individual ☐ Partnership ☐ Corporation ☐ Trust ☐ Estate ☐ Other

1 **Individuals**—Enter adjusted gross income from your tax return (see page 2 of instructions)

2 **Partnerships and corporations:**

a Partnerships—Enter each partner's name and identifying number.

b Corporations—Enter the name and employer identification number of each member of the controlled group (as defined in section 993(a)(3)). Do not list members included in the consolidated return; instead, attach a copy of Form 851. List all other members of the controlled group not included in the consolidated return.

If you list any corporations below or if you attach Form 851, you must designate a common tax year. Enter on line 4b the name and employer identification number of the corporation whose tax year is designated.

Name	Identifying number

If more space is needed, attach additional sheets and check this box . . . . . ▶ ☐

	Code	Description
c Enter principal business activity code and description (see instructions)		
d IC-DISCs—Enter principal product or service code and description (see instructions)		

3 **Partnerships**—Each partnership filing Form 5713 must give the following information:

a Partnership's total assets (see instructions) . . . . .

b Partnership's ordinary income (see instructions) . . . . .

4 **Corporations**—Each corporation filing Form 5713 must give the following information:

a Type of form filed (Form 1120, 1120-F, 1120-FSC, 1120-IC-DISC, 1120-L, 1120-PC, etc.)

b Common tax year election (see page 2 of instructions)

(1) Name of corporation ▶

(2) Employer identification number . . . . .

(3) Common tax year beginning ...., 20 ...., and ending ...., 20 .....

c Corporations filing this form enter:

(1) Total assets (see instructions) . . . . .

(2) Taxable income before net operating loss and special deductions (see instructions) . .

5 **Estates or trusts**—Enter total income (Form 1041, page 1) . . . . .

6 Enter the total amount (before reduction for boycott participation or cooperation) of the following tax benefits (see instructions):

a Foreign tax credit . . . . .

b Deferral of earnings of controlled foreign corporations . . . . .

c Deferral of IC-DISC income . . . . .

d FSC exempt foreign trade income . . . . .

e Foreign trade income qualifying for the extraterritorial income exclusion . . . . .

Please Sign Here Under penalties of perjury, I declare that I have examined this report, including accompanying schedules and statements, and to the best of my knowledge and belief, it is true, correct, and complete.

▶ Signature | Date | ▶ Title

For Paperwork Reduction Act Notice, see page 4 of the separate instructions. Cat. No. 12030E Form **5713** (Rev. 12-2004)

Figure H.28 Form 5713 — International Boycott Report, Page 1

Form 5713 (Rev. 12-2004) Page 2

		Yes	No
7a	Are you a U.S. shareholder (as defined in section 951(b)) of any foreign corporation (including a FSC that does not use the administrative pricing rules) that had operations reportable under section 999(a)?		
b	If the answer to question 7a is "Yes," is any foreign corporation a controlled foreign corporation (as defined in section 957(a))?		
c	Do you own any stock of an IC–DISC?.		
d	Do you claim any foreign tax credit?		
e	Do you control (within the meaning of section 304(c)) any corporation (other than a corporation included in this report) that has operations reportable under section 999(a)?		
	If "Yes," did that corporation participate in or cooperate with an international boycott at any time during its tax year that ends with or within your tax year?		
f	Are you controlled (within the meaning of section 304(c)) by any person (other than a person included in this report) who has operations reportable under section 999(a)?		
	If "Yes," did that person participate in or cooperate with an international boycott at any time during its tax year that ends with or within your tax year?.		
g	Are you treated under section 671 as the owner of a trust that has reportable operations under section 999(a)?		
h	Are you a partner in a partnership that has reportable operations under section 999(a)?		
i	Are you a foreign sales corporation (FSC) (as defined in section 922(a), as in effect before its repeal)?		
j	Are you excluding extraterritorial income (defined in section 114(e)) from gross income?		

Part I **Operations in or Related to a Boycotting Country** (See instructions beginning on page 3.)

		Yes	No
8	**Boycott of Israel**—Did you have any operations in or related to any country (or with the government, a company, or a national of that country) associated in carrying out the boycott of Israel which is on the list maintained by the Secretary of the Treasury under section 999(a)(3)? (See **Boycotting Countries** on page 2 of the instructions.).		

If "Yes," complete the following table. If more space is needed, attach additional sheets using the exact format and check this box ▶ ☐

	Name of country (1)	Identifying number of person having operations (2)	Principal business activity: Code (3)	Principal business activity: Description (4)	IC-DISCs only—Enter product code (5)
a					
b					
c					
d					
e					
f					
g					
h					
i					
j					
k					
l					
m					
n					
o					

Form **5713** (Rev. 12-2004)

Figure H.29 Form 5713 — International Boycott Report, Page 2

Form 5713 (Rev. 12-2004) Page **3**

9 Nonlisted countries boycotting Israel—Did you have operations in any nonlisted country which you know or have reason to know requires participation in or cooperation with an international boycott directed against Israel? **Yes** **No**

If "Yes," complete the following table. If more space is needed, attach additional sheets using the exact format and check this box . . . ▶ ☐

	Name of country (1)	Identifying number of person having operations (2)	Principal business activity: Code (3)	Principal business activity: Description (4)	IC-DISCs only—Enter product code (5)
a					
b					
c					
d					
e					
f					
g					
h					

10 Boycotts other than the boycott of Israel—Did you have operations in any other country which you know or have reason to know requires participation in or cooperation with an international boycott other than the boycott of Israel? **Yes** **No**

If "Yes," complete the following table. If more space is needed, attach additional sheets using the exact format and check this box . . . ▶ ☐

	Name of country (1)	Identifying number of person having operations (2)	Principal business activity: Code (3)	Principal business activity: Description (4)	IC-DISCs only—Enter product code (5)
a					
b					
c					
d					
e					
f					
g					
h					

Yes **No**

11 Were you requested to participate in or cooperate with an international boycott? . . .

If "Yes," attach a copy (in English) of any and all such requests received during your tax year. If the request was in a form other than a written request, attach a separate sheet explaining the nature and form of any and all such requests. (See page 4 of instructions.)

12 Did you participate in or cooperate with an international boycott?. . . .

If "Yes," attach a copy (in English) of any and all boycott clauses agreed to, and attach a general statement of the agreement. If the agreement was in a form other than a written agreement, attach a separate sheet explaining the nature and form of any and all such agreements. (See page 4 of instructions.)

Note: *If the answer to either question 11 or 12 is "Yes," you must complete the rest of Form 5713. If you answered "Yes" to question 12, you must complete Schedules A and C or B and C (Form 5713).*

Form **5713** (Rev. 12-2004)

Figure H.30 Form 5713 — International Boycott Report, Page 3

Form 5713 (Rev. 12-2004) Page 4

Part II **Requests for and Acts of Participation in or Cooperation With an International Boycott**

	Requests Yes	Requests No	Agreements Yes	Agreements No
13a Did you receive requests to enter into, or did you enter into, any agreement (see page 4 of instructions):				
(1) As a condition of doing business directly or indirectly within a country or with the government, a company, or a national of a country to—				
(a) Refrain from doing business with or in a country which is the object of an international boycott or with the government, companies, or nationals of that country?				
(b) Refrain from doing business with any U.S. person engaged in trade in a country which is the object of an international boycott or with the government, companies, or nationals of that country?				
(c) Refrain from doing business with any company whose ownership or management is made up, in whole or in part, of individuals of a particular nationality, race, or religion, or to remove (or refrain from selecting) corporate directors who are individuals of a particular nationality, race, or religion?				
(d) Refrain from employing individuals of a particular nationality, race, or religion?				
(2) As a condition of the sale of a product to the government, a company, or a national of a country, to refrain from shipping or insuring products on a carrier owned, leased, or operated by a person who does not participate in or cooperate with an international boycott?				

b Requests and agreements—If the answer to any part of 13a is "Yes," complete the following table. If more space is needed, attach additional sheets using the exact format and check this box . . . . ▶ ☐

	Name of country (1)	Identifying number of person receiving the request or having the agreement (2)	Principal business activity: Code (3)	Principal business activity: Description (4)	IC-DISCs only—Enter product code (5)	Number of requests: Total (6)	Number of requests: Code (7)	Number of agreements: Total (8)	Number of agreements: Code (9)
a									
b									
c									
d									
e									
f									
g									
h									
i									
j									
k									
l									
m									
n									
o									
p									

(Type of cooperation or participation: columns (6)–(9))

Printed on recycled paper   Form **5713** (Rev. 12-2004)

Figure H.31 Form 5713 — International Boycott Report, Page 4

Figures H.32 through H.33 show Form 8873 — Extraterritorial Income Exclusion (2 pages).

Form **8873** — **Extraterritorial Income Exclusion**

Department of the Treasury
Internal Revenue Service

▶ Attach to your tax return.
▶ See separate instructions.

OMB No. 1545-1722
2006
Attachment Sequence No. 126

Name(s) as shown on return | Identifying number

Part I Elections and Other Information

1 Check the box if you are electing under section 942(a)(3) to exclude a portion of your gross receipts from foreign trading gross receipts on line 15. Attach a schedule indicating which receipts are being excluded . . . ▶ ☐

2 Check the box if you are electing to apply the extraterritorial income exclusion provisions to certain transactions involving a FSC (see instructions). Attach a schedule listing the affected transactions . . . ▶ ☐

3 Check the box if the taxpayer is a foreign corporation electing to be treated as a domestic corporation (see instructions) . . ▶ ☐

4a Are you excepted from the foreign economic process requirements because your foreign trading gross receipts are $5 million or less? . . . ▶ ☐ Yes ☐ No

b If "No," check the applicable box to indicate how you met the foreign economic process requirements:
(1) ☐ You met the 50% foreign direct cost test (see instructions).
(2) ☐ You met the alternative 85% foreign direct cost test (see instructions).

5 See instructions before completing lines 5a through 5c. **Note:** *For transactions for which the exclusion is determined using the foreign sale and leasing income method (i.e., line 44 equals line 45), complete only lines 5a and 5c(1).*

a Business activity code ______ b Product or product line ______

c Check the applicable box to indicate the basis of your reporting:
(1) Transaction-by-transaction:
(a) ☐ Aggregate on Form 8873 (b) ☐ Aggregate on tabular schedule (c) ☐ Tabular schedule of transactions
(2) ☐ Group of transactions

Part II Foreign Trade Income and Foreign Sale and Leasing Income

		Line	(a) Foreign Trade Income	(b) Foreign Sale and Leasing Income
	Caution: *If a related person is also eligible for an extraterritorial income exclusion, see* ***Excluded property*** *in the instructions.*			
6	Sale, exchange, or other disposition of qualifying foreign trade property	6		
7	Enter the amount from line 6, column (a), attributable to the sale of property formerly leased or rented for use by the lessee outside the United States	7		
8	Lease or rental of qualifying foreign trade property for use by the lessee outside the United States. Enter the same amount in both columns	8		
9	Services related and subsidiary to the sale, exchange, or other disposition of qualifying foreign trade property	9		
10	Enter the amount from line 9, column (a), attributable to the sale of property formerly leased or rented for use by the lessee outside the United States	10		
11	Services related and subsidiary to the lease of qualifying foreign trade property for use by the lessee outside the United States. Enter the same amount in both columns	11		
12	Engineering or architectural services for construction projects outside the United States	12		
13	Managerial services provided to unrelated persons (see instructions)	13		
14	Enter the sum of the amounts from lines 6, 9, 12, and 13 of column (a) attributable to foreign economic processes. **Do not** include any amounts already included on lines 7, 8, 10, or 11 in column (b)	14		
15	**Foreign trading gross receipts.** Add lines 6 through 13 in column (a)	15		
16	Add lines 7 through 14 in column (b)	16		
17	**Cost of goods sold:**			
a	Inventory at beginning of year	17a		
b	Purchases	17b		
c	Cost of labor	17c		
d	Additional section 263A costs (attach schedule)	17d		
e	Other costs (attach schedule)	17e		
f	Total. Add lines 17a through 17e	17f		
g	Inventory at end of year	17g		
h	Subtract line 17g from line 17f	17h		
18	In column (a), subtract line 17h from line 15. In column (b), subtract line 17h from line 16	18		
19	Other expenses and deductions (see instructions) (attach schedule)	19		
20	**Foreign trade income.** In column (a), subtract line 19 from line 18. If -0- or less, stop here. You do not qualify for the exclusion	20		
21	**Foreign sale and leasing income.** In column (b), subtract line 19 from line 18	21		

For Paperwork Reduction Act Notice, see instructions. Cat. No. 30732F Form **8873** (2006)

Figure H.32 Form 8873 — Extraterritorial Income Exclusion, Page 1

Form 8873 (2006) Page 2

Part III **Marginal Costing** (**Note:** *If you are **not** using Marginal Costing, skip Part III and go to Part IV*)

Section A — Foreign Trade Income Using Marginal Costing Method

22	Foreign trading gross receipts. Enter the amount from line 15		22
23	Costs and expenses allocable to the amount reported on line 22:		
a	Cost of direct material attributable to property sold	23a	
b	Cost of direct labor attributable to property sold	23b	
c	Add lines 23a and 23b		23c
24	Subtract line 23c from line 22		24
25	Worldwide gross receipts from sales of the product or product line		25
26	Costs and expenses allocable to the amount reported on line 25:		
a	Cost of goods sold attributable to property sold	26a	
b	Other expenses and deductions attributable to gross income	26b	
c	Add lines 26a and 26b		26c
27	Subtract line 26c from line 25. (**Note:** *If -0- or less, stop here. You may not use Part III to determine your qualifying foreign trade income. Go to line 37.*)		27
28	Overall profit percentage. Divide line 27 by line 25. Carry the result to at least three decimal places		28
29	Overall profit percentage limitation. Multiply line 22 by line 28		29
30	**Foreign trade income using marginal costing.** Enter the **smaller** of line 24 or line 29		30

Section B — 15% of Foreign Trade Income Method

31	Multiply line 30 by 15% (.15)	31
32	**Foreign trade income using full costing.** Enter the amount from line 20	32
33	Enter the **smaller** of line 31 or line 32	33

Section C — 1.2% of Foreign Trading Gross Receipts Method

34	Multiply line 22 by 1.2% (.012)	34
35	Multiply line 30 by 30% (.30)	35
36	Enter the **smallest** of lines 32, 34, or 35	36

Part IV **Extraterritorial Income Exclusion (Net of Disallowed Deductions)**

37	Enter your foreign trade income from line 20		37
38	Multiply line 37 by 15% (.15)		38
39	Enter your foreign trading gross receipts from line 15	39	
40	Multiply line 39 by 1.2% (.012)	40	
41	Multiply line 38 by 2.0	41	
42	Enter the **smaller** of line 40 or line 41		42
43	Enter your foreign sale and leasing income from line 21		43
44	Multiply line 43 by 30% (.30)		44
45	Enter the **greatest** of lines 33, 36, 38, 42, or 44. If you are using the alternative computation, see instructions for the amount to enter		45
	Note: *If you do not have a reduction for international boycott operations, illegal bribes, kickbacks, etc. (see the instructions for line 50), skip lines 46 through 51 and enter on line 52 the amount from line 45.*		
46	If line 44 equals line 45, divide the amount on line 45 by the amount on line 43. Otherwise, divide the amount on line 45 by the amount on line 37. Carry the result to at least three decimal places	46	
47	If line 44 equals line 45, enter the amount from line 19, column (b). Otherwise, enter the amount from line 19, column (a)	47	
48	Multiply line 46 by line 47		48
49	Add lines 45 and 48		49
50	Reduction for international boycott operations, illegal bribes, kickbacks, etc. (see instructions)		50
51	**Qualifying foreign trade income.** Subtract line 50 from line 49. If -0- or less, stop here. You do not qualify for the exclusion		51
52	Subtract line 48 from line 51		52
53a	Enter the amount from line 52 that is attributable to 100% transactions (see instructions)		53a
b	Multiply the amount from line 52 that is attributable to 80% transactions (see instructions) by 80% (0.80) and enter the result		53b
c	Multiply the amount from line 52 that is attributable to 60% transactions (see instructions) by 60% (0.60) and enter the result		53c
54	**Extraterritorial income exclusion (net of disallowed deductions).** Add lines 53a through 53c. Enter the result here and include it on the "other deductions" line of your tax return or schedule (see instructions)		54

Form **8873** (2006)

Figure H.33 Form 8873 — Extraterritorial Income Exclusion, Page 2

H.3 Tax Forms for Chapter 5

Figure H.34 shows Form 1099 – Miscellaneous Income (1 page).

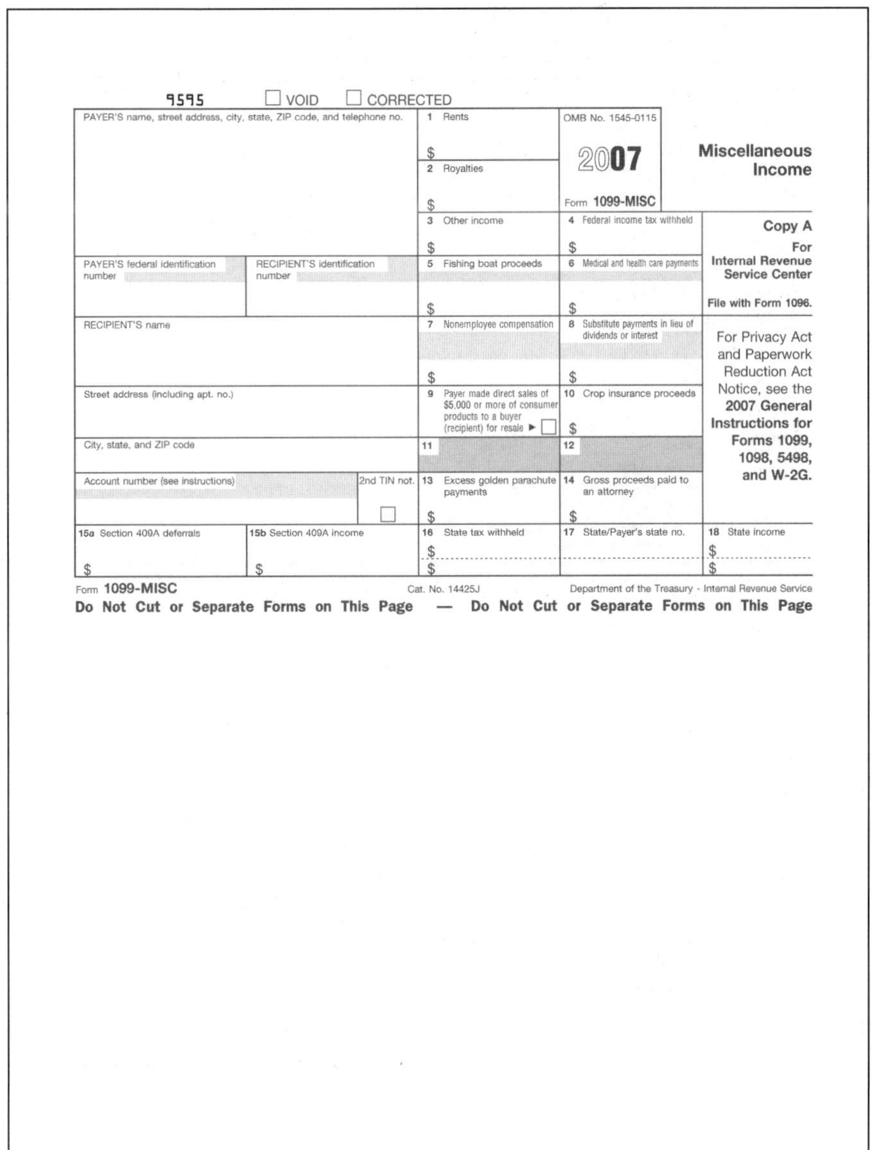

9595 ☐ VOID ☐ CORRECTED

PAYER'S name, street address, city, state, ZIP code, and telephone no.

1 Rents $

2 Royalties $

OMB No. 1545-0115

2007

Form 1099-MISC

Miscellaneous Income

3 Other income $

4 Federal income tax withheld $

Copy A For Internal Revenue Service Center

File with Form 1096.

PAYER'S federal identification number

RECIPIENT'S identification number

5 Fishing boat proceeds $

6 Medical and health care payments $

RECIPIENT'S name

7 Nonemployee compensation $

8 Substitute payments in lieu of dividends or interest $

For Privacy Act and Paperwork Reduction Act Notice, see the **2007 General Instructions for Forms 1099, 1098, 5498, and W-2G.**

Street address (including apt. no.)

9 Payer made direct sales of $5,000 or more of consumer products to a buyer (recipient) for resale ► ☐

10 Crop insurance proceeds $

City, state, and ZIP code

11

12

Account number (see instructions)

2nd TIN not. ☐

13 Excess golden parachute payments $

14 Gross proceeds paid to an attorney $

15a Section 409A deferrals $

15b Section 409A income $

16 State tax withheld $ $

17 State/Payer's state no.

18 State income $ $

Form **1099-MISC** Cat. No. 14425J Department of the Treasury - Internal Revenue Service

Do Not Cut or Separate Forms on This Page — Do Not Cut or Separate Forms on This Page

Figure H.34 Form 1099 — Miscellaneous Income

Figure H.35 shows Form W-9 — Request for Taxpayer Identification Number and Certification (1 page).

Form **W-9**
(Rev. November 2005)
Department of the Treasury
Internal Revenue Service

Request for Taxpayer Identification Number and Certification

Give form to the requester. Do not send to the IRS.

Print or type
See Specific Instructions on page 2.

Name (as shown on your income tax return)

Business name, if different from above

Check appropriate box: ☐ Individual/ Sole proprietor ☐ Corporation ☐ Partnership ☐ Other ▶ .... ☐ Exempt from backup withholding

Address (number, street, and apt. or suite no.) | Requester's name and address (optional)

City, state, and ZIP code

List account number(s) here (optional)

Part I **Taxpayer Identification Number (TIN)**

Enter your TIN in the appropriate box. The TIN provided must match the name given on Line 1 to avoid backup withholding. For individuals, this is your social security number (SSN). However, for a resident alien, sole proprietor, or disregarded entity, see the Part I instructions on page 3. For other entities, it is your employer identification number (EIN). If you do not have a number, see *How to get a TIN* on page 3.

Note. If the account is in more than one name, see the chart on page 4 for guidelines on whose number to enter.

Social security number

or

Employer identification number

Part II **Certification**

Under penalties of perjury, I certify that:

1. The number shown on this form is my correct taxpayer identification number (or I am waiting for a number to be issued to me), and
2. I am not subject to backup withholding because: (a) I am exempt from backup withholding, or (b) I have not been notified by the Internal Revenue Service (IRS) that I am subject to backup withholding as a result of a failure to report all interest or dividends, or (c) the IRS has notified me that I am no longer subject to backup withholding, and
3. I am a U.S. person (including a U.S. resident alien).

Certification instructions. You must cross out item 2 above if you have been notified by the IRS that you are currently subject to backup withholding because you have failed to report all interest and dividends on your tax return. For real estate transactions, item 2 does not apply. For mortgage interest paid, acquisition or abandonment of secured property, cancellation of debt, contributions to an individual retirement arrangement (IRA), and generally, payments other than interest and dividends, you are not required to sign the Certification, but you must provide your correct TIN. (See the instructions on page 4.)

Sign Here | **Signature of U.S. person ▶** | **Date ▶**

Purpose of Form

A person who is required to file an information return with the IRS, must obtain your correct taxpayer identification number (TIN) to report, for example, income paid to you, real estate transactions, mortgage interest you paid, acquisition or abandonment of secured property, cancellation of debt, or contributions you made to an IRA.

U.S. person. Use Form W-9 only if you are a U.S. person (including a resident alien), to provide your correct TIN to the person requesting it (the requester) and, when applicable, to:

1. Certify that the TIN you are giving is correct (or you are waiting for a number to be issued),
2. Certify that you are not subject to backup withholding, or
3. Claim exemption from backup withholding if you are a U.S. exempt payee.

In 3 above, if applicable, you are also certifying that as a U.S. person, your allocable share of any partnership income from a U.S. trade or business is not subject to the withholding tax on foreign partners' share of effectively connected income.

Note. If a requester gives you a form other than Form W-9 to request your TIN, you must use the requester's form if it is substantially similar to this Form W-9.

For federal tax purposes, you are considered a person if you are:

- An individual who is a citizen or resident of the United States,
- A partnership, corporation, company, or association created or organized in the United States or under the laws of the United States, or
- Any estate (other than a foreign estate) or trust. See Regulations sections 301.7701-6(a) and 7(a) for additional information.

Special rules for partnerships. Partnerships that conduct a trade or business in the United States are generally required to pay a withholding tax on any foreign partners' share of income from such business. Further, in certain cases where a Form W-9 has not been received, a partnership is required to presume that a partner is a foreign person, and pay the withholding tax. Therefore, if you are a U.S. person that is a partner in a partnership conducting a trade or business in the United States, provide Form W-9 to the partnership to establish your U.S. status and avoid withholding on your share of partnership income.

The person who gives Form W-9 to the partnership for purposes of establishing its U.S. status and avoiding withholding on its allocable share of net income from the partnership conducting a trade or business in the United States is in the following cases:

- The U.S. owner of a disregarded entity and not the entity,

Cat. No. 10231X   Form **W-9** (Rev. 11-2005)

Figure H.35 Form W-9 — Request for Taxpayer Identification Number and Certification

Figure H.36 shows Form 1042 — Annual Withholding Tax Return for U.S. Source Income of Foreign Persons (1 page).

Form **1042**
Department of the Treasury
Internal Revenue Service

Annual Withholding Tax Return for U.S. Source Income of Foreign Persons
▶ **See instructions.**

OMB No. 1545-0096
2006

If this is an amended return, check here . . . . . ▶ ☐

Name of withholding agent	Employer identification number	For IRS Use Only	
		CC	FD
Number, street, and room or suite no. (if a P.O. box, see instructions)		RD	FF
		CAF	FP
City or town, province or state, and country (including postal code)		CR	I
		EDC	SIC

If you will not be liable for returns in the future, check here ▶ ☐ Enter date final income paid ▶ ....
Check here if you made quarter-monthly deposits using the 90% rule (see **Deposit Requirements** in the instructions) . . . ▶ ☐
Check if you are a: QI/Withholding foreign partnership or trust ☐ NQI/Flow-through entity ☐ (See instructions.)

Record of Federal Tax Liability (Do not show federal tax deposits here.)

Line No.	Period ending		Tax liability for period (including any taxes assumed on Form(s) 1000)	Line No.	Period ending		Tax liability for period (including any taxes assumed on Form(s) 1000)	Line No.	Period ending		Tax liability for period (including any taxes assumed on Form(s) 1000)
1		7		21		7		41		7	
2	Jan.	15		22	May	15		42	Sept.	15	
3		22		23		22		43		22	
4		31		24		31		44		30	
5	Jan. total			25	May total			45	Sept. total		
6		7		26		7		46		7	
7	Feb.	15		27	June	15		47	Oct.	15	
8		22		28		22		48		22	
9		28		29		30		49		31	
10	Feb. total			30	June total			50	Oct. total		
11		7		31		7		51		7	
12	Mar.	15		32	July	15		52	Nov.	15	
13		22		33		22		53		22	
14		31		34		31		54		30	
15	Mar. total			35	July total			55	Nov. total		
16		7		36		7		56		7	
17	Apr.	15		37	Aug.	15		57	Dec.	15	
18		22		38		22		58		22	
19		30		39		31		59		31	
20	Apr. total			40	Aug. total			60	Dec. total		

61 No. of Forms 1042-S filed: **a** On magnetic media .... **b** On paper .... **c** Electronically ....
62 For **all** Form(s) 1042-S and 1000: **a** Gross income paid **b** Taxes withheld or assumed
63a Total tax liability (add monthly total lines from above) 63a
b Adjustments (see instructions) 63b
c Total **net tax** liability (combine lines 63a and 63b) . . . . ▶ 63c
64 Total paid by federal tax deposit coupons or by electronic funds transfer (or with a request for an extension of time to file) for 2006 64
65 Enter overpayment applied as a credit from 2005 Form 1042 . 65
66 Credit for amounts withheld by other withholding agents (see inst.) 66
67 **Total payments.** Add lines 64 through 66 . . . . ▶ 67
68 If line 63c is larger than line 67, enter **balance due** here 68
69 If line 67 is larger than line 63c, enter **overpayment** here 69
70 Penalty for failure to deposit tax when due. Also include on line 68 or line 69 (see instructions) 70
71 Apply overpayment on line 69 to (check one): ☐ **Credit on 2007 Form 1042 or** ☐ **Refund**

Third Party Designee Do you want to allow another person to discuss this return with the IRS (see page 4)? ☐ **Yes.** Complete the following. ☐ **No**
Designee's name ▶ Phone no. ▶ Personal identification number (PIN) ▶

Sign Here Under penalties of perjury, I declare that I have examined this return, including accompanying schedules and statements, and to the best of my knowledge and belief, it is true, correct, and complete. Declaration of preparer (other than withholding agent) is based on all information of which preparer has any knowledge.
Your signature ▶ Date Capacity in which acting ▶
Daytime phone number ▶

Paid Preparer's Use Only Preparer's signature ▶ Date Check if self-employed ▶ ☐ Preparer's SSN or PTIN
Firm's name (or yours if self-employed), address, and ZIP code ▶ EIN ▶
Phone no.

For Privacy Act and Paperwork Reduction Act Notice, see the instructions. Cat. No. 11384V Form **1042** (2006)

Figure H.36 Form 1042 — Annual Withholding Tax Return for U.S. Source Income of Foreign Persons

H.4 Tax Forms for Chapter 7

Figures H.37 through H.39 show Form 941 — Employer's Quarterly Federal Tax Return (3 pages).

Form **941 for 2007: Employer's QUARTERLY Federal Tax Return** 990107
(Rev. January 2007) Department of the Treasury — Internal Revenue Service OMB No. 1545-0029

(EIN) Employer identification number ☐☐ – ☐☐☐☐☐☐☐

Name (*not your trade name*)

Trade name (*if any*)

Address — Number, Street, Suite or room number; City, State, ZIP code

Report for this Quarter of 2007 (Check one.)
☐ 1: January, February, March
☐ 2: April, May, June
☐ 3: July, August, September
☐ 4: October, November, December

Read the separate instructions before you fill out this form. Please type or print within the boxes.

Part 1: Answer these questions for this quarter.

1 **Number of employees who received wages, tips, or other compensation for the pay period including:** ***Mar. 12*** **(Quarter 1),** ***June 12*** **(Quarter 2),** ***Sept. 12*** **(Quarter 3),** ***Dec. 12*** **(Quarter 4)** . . . 1

2 **Wages, tips, and other compensation** . . . 2

3 **Total income tax withheld from wages, tips, and other compensation** . . . 3

4 **If no wages, tips, and other compensation are subject to social security or Medicare tax** . . ☐ Check and go to line 6.

5 **Taxable social security and Medicare wages and tips:**

	Column 1		Column 2
5a **Taxable social security wages**	.	× .124 =	.
5b **Taxable social security tips**	.	× .124 =	.
5c **Taxable Medicare wages & tips**	.	× .029 =	.

5d **Total social security and Medicare taxes** (*Column 2*, lines 5a + 5b + 5c = line 5d) . . 5d

6 **Total taxes before adjustments** (lines 3 + 5d = line 6) . . . 6

7 **TAX ADJUSTMENTS** (Read the instructions for line 7 before completing lines 7a through 7h.):

7a **Current quarter's fractions of cents** . . .

7b **Current quarter's sick pay** . . .

7c **Current quarter's adjustments for tips and group-term life insurance**

7d **Current year's income tax withholding** (attach Form 941c) . . .

7e **Prior quarters' social security and Medicare taxes** (attach Form 941c)

7f **Special additions to federal income tax** (attach Form 941c) . . .

7g **Special additions to social security and Medicare** (attach Form 941c)

7h **TOTAL ADJUSTMENTS** (Combine all amounts: lines 7a through 7g.) . . . 7h

8 **Total taxes after adjustments** (Combine lines 6 and 7h.) . . . 8

9 **Advance earned income credit (EIC) payments made to employees** . . . 9

10 **Total taxes after adjustment for advance EIC** (line 8 – line 9 = line 10) . . . 10

11 **Total deposits for this quarter, including overpayment applied from a prior quarter** . . . 11

12 **Balance due** (If line 10 is more than line 11, write the difference here.) . . . 12
Follow the Instructions for Form 941-V, Payment Voucher.

13 **Overpayment** (If line 11 is more than line 10, write the difference here.) . Check one ☐ Apply to next return. ☐ Send a refund.

▶ You **MUST** fill out both pages of this form and **SIGN** it.

Next ➔

For Privacy Act and Paperwork Reduction Act Notice, see the back of the Payment Voucher. Cat. No. 17001Z Form **941** (Rev. 1-2007)

Figure H.37 Form 941 — Employer's Quarterly Federal Tax Return, Page 1

990207

Name *(not your trade name)* | Employer identification number (EIN)

Part 2: Tell us about your deposit schedule and tax liability for this quarter.

If you are unsure about whether you are a monthly schedule depositor or a semiweekly schedule depositor, see *Pub. 15 (Circular E)*, section 11.

14 ☐☐ **Write the state abbreviation for the state where you made your deposits** OR **write "MU" if you made your deposits in *multiple* states.**

15 **Check one:** ☐ **Line 10 is less than $2,500.** Go to Part 3.

☐ **You were a monthly schedule depositor for the entire quarter. Fill out your tax liability for each month.** Then go to Part 3.

Tax liability: Month 1 ______ .

Month 2 ______ .

Month 3 ______ .

Total liability for quarter ______ . **Total must equal line 10.**

☐ **You were a semiweekly schedule depositor for any part of this quarter.** Fill out *Schedule B (Form 941): Report of Tax Liability for Semiweekly Schedule Depositors,* and attach it to this form.

Part 3: Tell us about your business. If a question does NOT apply to your business, leave it blank.

16 **If your business has closed or you stopped paying wages** . . . . ☐ Check here, and

enter the final date you paid wages ___ / ___ / ___ .

17 **If you are a seasonal employer and you do not have to file a return for every quarter of the year** . . ☐ Check here.

Part 4: May we speak with your third-party designee?

Do you want to allow an employee, a paid tax preparer, or another person to discuss this return with the IRS? (See the instructions for details.)

☐ Yes. Designee's name ______

Select a 5-digit Personal Identification Number (PIN) to use when talking to IRS. ☐☐☐☐☐

☐ No.

Part 5: Sign here. You MUST fill out both pages of this form and SIGN it.

Under penalties of perjury, I declare that I have examined this return, including accompanying schedules and statements, and to the best of my knowledge and belief, it is true, correct, and complete.

X **Sign your name here** ______

Print your name here ______

Print your title here ______

Date ___ / ___ / ___

Best daytime phone ( ) –

Part 6: For paid preparers only *(optional)*

Paid Preparer's Signature ______

Firm's name ______

Address ______ EIN ______

ZIP code ______

Date ___ / ___ / ___ Phone ( ) – SSN/PTIN ______

☐ Check if you are self-employed.

Page **2** Form **941** (Rev. 1-2007)

Figure H.38 Form 941 — Employer's Quarterly Federal Tax Return, Page 2

Form 941-V, Payment Voucher

Purpose of Form

Complete Form 941-V, Payment Voucher, if you are making a payment with Form 941, Employer's QUARTERLY Federal Tax Return. We will use the completed voucher to credit your payment more promptly and accurately, and to improve our service to you.

If you have your return prepared by a third party and make a payment with that return, please provide this payment voucher to the return preparer.

Making Payments With Form 941

Make your payment with Form 941 **only if:**

- Your net taxes for the quarter (line 10 on Form 941) are less than $2,500 and you are paying in full with a timely filed return or
- You are a monthly schedule depositor making a payment in accordance with the Accuracy of Deposits Rule. (See section 11 of Pub. 15 (Circular E), Employer's Tax Guide, for details.) In this case, the amount of your payment may be $2,500 or more.

Otherwise, you must deposit your taxes at an authorized financial institution or by electronic funds transfer. (See section 11 of Pub. 15 (Circular E) for deposit instructions.) Do not use Form 941-V to make federal tax deposits.

Caution. *If you pay amounts with Form 941 that should have been deposited, you may be subject to a penalty. See* Deposit Penalties *in section 11 of Pub. 15 (Circular E).*

Specific Instructions

Box 1—Employer identification number (EIN). If you do not have an EIN, apply for one on Form SS-4, Application for Employer Identification Number, and write "Applied For" and the date you applied in this entry space.

Box 2—Amount paid. Enter the amount paid with Form 941.

Box 3—Tax period. Darken the capsule identifying the quarter for which the payment is made. Darken only one capsule.

Box 4—Name and address. Enter your name and address as shown on Form 941.

- Enclose your check or money order made payable to the "United States Treasury." Be sure also to enter your EIN, "Form 941," and the tax period on your check or money order. Do not send cash. Please do not staple Form 941-V or your payment to the return (or to each other).
- Detach Form 941-V and send it with your payment and Form 941 to the address provided in the Instructions for Form 941.

Note. You must also complete the entity information above Part 1 on Form 941.

▼ Detach Here and Mail With Your Payment and Tax Return. ▼

Form **941-V** | **Payment Voucher** | OMB No. 1545-0029

Department of the Treasury Internal Revenue Service | ► Do not staple or attach this voucher to your payment. | **2007**

1 Enter your employer identification number (EIN).		2 **Enter the amount of your payment.** ►	Dollars	Cents
3 Tax period		4 Enter your business name (individual name if sole proprietor).		
○ 1st Quarter	○ 3rd Quarter	Enter your address.		
○ 2nd Quarter	○ 4th Quarter	Enter your city, state, and ZIP code.		

Figure H.39 Form 941 — Employer's Quarterly Federal Tax Return, Page 3

Figures H.40 through H.42 show Form 940 — Employer's Annual Federal Unemployment (FUTA) Tax Return (3 pages).

Form **940 for 2006: Employer's Annual Federal Unemployment (FUTA) Tax Return** 850106

Department of the Treasury — Internal Revenue Service

OMB No. 1545-0028

(EIN) Employer identification number ☐☐ – ☐☐☐☐☐☐☐

Name *(not your trade name)*

Trade name *(if any)*

Address Number Street Suite or room number

City State ZIP code

Type of Return (Check all that apply.)

☐ **a.** Amended

☐ **b.** Successor employer

☐ **c.** No payments to employees in 2006

☐ **d.** Final: Business closed or stopped paying wages

Read the separate instructions before you fill out this form. Please type or print within the boxes.

Part 1: Tell us about your return. If any line does NOT apply, leave it blank.

1 **If you were required to pay your state unemployment tax in ...**

1a **One state only,** write the state abbreviation . . . . 1a ☐☐

- OR -

1b **More than one state** (You are a multi-state employer) . . . . 1b ☐ Check here. Fill out Schedule A.

2

Part 2: Determine your FUTA tax before adjustments for 2006. If any line does NOT apply, leave it blank.

3 **Total payments to all employees** . . . . 3 ______ .

4 **Payments exempt from FUTA tax** . . . . 4 ______ .

Check all that apply: 4a ☐ Fringe benefits 4c ☐ Retirement/Pension 4e ☐ Other
4b ☐ Group term life insurance 4d ☐ Dependent care

5 **Total of payments made to each employee in excess of $7,000** . . . . 5 ______ .

6 **Subtotal** (line 4 + line 5 = line 6) . . . . 6 ______ .

7 **Total taxable FUTA wages** (line 3 – line 6 = line 7) . . . . 7 ______ .

8 **FUTA tax before adjustments** (line 7 × .008 = line 8) . . . . 8 ______ .

Part 3: Determine your adjustments. If any line does NOT apply, leave it blank.

9 **If ALL of the taxable FUTA wages you paid were excluded from state unemployment tax, multiply line 7 by .054** (line 7 × .054 = line 9). Then go to line 12 . . . . 9 ______ .

10 **If SOME of the taxable FUTA wages you paid were excluded from state unemployment tax, OR you paid ANY state unemployment tax late** (after the due date for filing Form 940), fill out the worksheet in the instructions. Enter the amount from line 7 of the worksheet onto line 10 . . 10 ______ .

11

Part 4: Determine your FUTA tax and balance due or overpayment for 2006. If any line does NOT apply, leave it blank.

12 **Total FUTA tax after adjustments** (lines 8 + 9 + 10 = line 12) . . . . 12 ______ .

13 **FUTA tax deposited for the year, including any payment applied from a prior year** . . . . 13 ______ .

14 **Balance due** (If line 12 is more than line 13, enter the difference on line 14.)

- If line 14 is more than $500, you must deposit your tax.
- If line 14 is $500 or less and you pay by check, make your check payable to the United States Treasury and write your EIN, *Form 940,* and *2006* on the check . . . . 14 ______ .

15 **Overpayment** (If line 13 is more than line 12, enter the difference on line 15 and check a box below.) . . . . 15 ______ .

Check one ☐ Apply to next return.
☐ Send a refund.

▶ You **MUST** fill out both pages of this form and **SIGN** it.

Next ➔

For Privacy Act and Paperwork Reduction Act Notice, see the back of Form 940-V, Payment Voucher. Cat. No. 11234O Form **940** (2006)

Figure H.40 Form 940 — Employer's Annual Federal Unemployment (FUTA) Tax Return, Page 1

850206

Name *(not your trade name)* | **Employer identification number (EIN)**

Part 5: Report your FUTA tax liability by quarter only if line 12 is more than $500. If not, go to Part 6.

16 **Report the amount of your FUTA tax liability for each quarter; do NOT enter the amount you deposited. If you had no liability for a quarter, leave the line blank.**

16a **1st quarter** (January 1 – March 31) . . . . **16a** [.]

16b **2nd quarter** (April 1 – June 30) . . . . **16b** [.]

16c **3rd quarter** (July 1 – September 30) . . . . **16c** [.]

16d **4th quarter** (October 1 – December 31) . . . . **16d** [.]

17 **Total tax liability for the year** (lines 16a + 16b + 16c + 16d = line 17) **17** [.] **Total must equal line 12.**

Part 6: May we speak with your third-party designee?

Do you want to allow an employee, a paid tax preparer, or another person to discuss this return with the IRS? See the instructions for details.

☐ **Yes.** Designee's name

Select a 5-digit Personal Identification Number (PIN) to use when talking to IRS ☐☐☐☐☐

☐ **No.**

Part 7: Sign here.

You MUST fill out both pages of this form and SIGN it.

Under penalties of perjury, I declare that I have examined this return, including accompanying schedules and statements, and to the best of my knowledge and belief, it is true, correct, and complete, and that no part of any payment made to a state unemployment fund claimed as a credit was, or is to be, deducted from the payments made to employees.

X Sign your name here

Print your name here

Print your title here

Date / /

Best daytime phone ( ) –

Part 8: For PAID preparers only (optional)

If you were paid to prepare this return and are not an employee of the business that is filing this return, you may choose to fill out Part 8.

Paid Preparer's name

Preparer's SSN/PTIN

Paid Preparer's signature

Date / /

☐ Check if you are self-employed.

Firm's name

Firm's EIN

Street address

City

State

ZIP code

Page **2** Form **940** (2006)

Figure H.41 Form 940 — Employer's Annual Federal Unemployment (FUTA) Tax Return, Page 2

Form 940-V, Payment Voucher

What Is Form 940-V?

Form 940-V is a transmittal form for your check or money order. Using Form 940-V allows us to process your payment more accurately and efficiently. If you have any balance due of $500 or less on your 2006 Form 940, fill out Form 940-V and send it with your check or money order.

Note. If your balance is more than $500, see *When Must You Deposit Your FUTA Tax?* in the Instructions for Form 940.

How Do You Fill Out Form 940-V?

Type or print clearly.

Box 1. Enter your employer identification number (EIN). Do not enter your social security number (SSN).

Box 2. Enter the amount of your payment. Be sure to put dollars and cents in the appropriate spaces.

Box 3. Enter your business name and complete address exactly as they appear on your Form 940.

How Should You Prepare Your Payment?

- Make your check or money order payable to the *United States Treasury.* Do not send cash.
- On the memo line of your check or money order, write:
  - — your EIN,
  - — Form 940, and
  - — 2006.
- Carefully detach Form 940-V along the dotted line.
- Do not staple your payment to the voucher.
- Mail your 2006 Form 940, your payment, and Form 940-V in the envelope that came with your 2006 Form 940 instruction booklet. If you do not have that envelope, use the table in the Instructions for Form 940 to find the mailing address.

▼ **Detach Here and Mail With Your Payment and Tax Return.** ▼

Form **940-V** Department of the Treasury Internal Revenue Service	**Payment Voucher** ► **Do not staple or attach this voucher to your payment.**		OMB No. 1545-0028 **2006**
1 Enter your employer identification number (EIN).	**2** **Enter the amount of your payment.** ►	Dollars	Cents
	3 Enter your business name (individual name if sole proprietor). Enter your address. Enter your city, state, and ZIP code.		

Figure H.42 Form 940 — Employer's Annual Federal Unemployment (FUTA) Tax Return, Page 3

Figures H.43 and H.44 show a State Unemployment Tax Return (SUTA) for the State of New York, (2 pages). All states have similar returns.

NYS-45-MN (7/06) **Quarterly Combined Withholding, Wage Reporting, And Unemployment Insurance Return**

40629414

Reference these numbers in all correspondence:

UI Employer registration number

Withholding identification number

Employer legal name:

Mark an *X* in only **one** box to indicate the quarter (a separate return must be completed for each quarter) and enter the tax year.

Jan 1 - Mar 31 (1) | Apr 1 - Jun 30 (2) | July 1 - Sep 30 (3) | Oct 1 - Dec 31 (4) | Tax year Y Y

If **seasonal employer,** mark an *X* in the box.......

For office use only: Postmark; Received date; UI SK; AI; SI; WT SK

Number of employees
Enter the number of full-time and part-time covered employees who worked during or received pay for the week that includes the **12th** day of each month.

a. First month	b. Second month	c. Third month

Part A - Unemployment insurance (UI) information

1. Total remuneration paid this quarter 00
2. Remuneration paid this quarter to each employee in excess of $8,500 since January 1 00
3. Wages subject to contribution *(subtract line 2 from line 1)* 00
4. UI contributions due — Enter your Tax rate ☐ . ☐ %
5. Re-employment service fund *(multiply line 3 x .00075)* ....
6. UI previously underpaid with interest
7. Total of lines 4, 5, and 6 ....
8. Enter UI previously overpaid.....
9. **Total UI amounts due** *(if line 7 is greater than line 8, enter difference)* ......
10. Total UI overpaid *(if line 8 is greater than line 7, enter difference and mark box 11 below)* * ....
11. Apply to outstanding liabilities and/or refund .... ☐

Part B - Withholding tax (WT) information

12. New York State tax withheld ....
13. New York City tax withheld ....
14. Yonkers tax withheld ....
15. Total tax withheld *(add lines 12, 13, and 14)* ....
16. WT credit from **previous quarter's** return *(see instr.)* ......
17. Form NYS-1 payments made for quarter ....
18. Total payments *(add lines 16 and 17)* ....
19. **Total WT amount due** *(if line 15 is greater than line 18, enter difference)* ......
20. Total WT overpaid *(if line 18 is greater than line 15, enter difference here and mark an X in 20a or 20b)* * .....

20a. Apply to outstanding liabilities and/or refund ...... ☐ **or** 20b. Credit to next quarter withholding tax .... ☐

21. **Total payment due** *(add lines **9** and **19**; make one remittance payable to* **NYS Employment Taxes***)* ....

*** An overpayment of either tax cannot be used to offset the amount due on the other tax.**
Complete Parts D and E on back of form, if required. This is a scannable form; please file the original.

Part C – Employee wage and withholding information

Quarterly employee/payee wage reporting information *(if more than five employees or if reporting other wages,* ***do not*** *make entries in this section; complete Form NYS-45-ATT.* ***Do not*** *use negative numbers; see instructions)*

Annual wage and withholding totals — If this return is for the 4th quarter or the last return you will be filing for the calendar year, complete columns d and e.

a Social security number	b Last name, first name, middle initial	c UI total remuneration/gross wages paid this quarter	d Gross wages or distribution *(see instructions)*	e Total tax withheld
Totals *(column c must equal remuneration on line 1; see instructions for exceptions)*				

Sign your return: I certify that the information on this return and any attachments is to the best of my knowledge and belief true, correct, and complete.

Taxpayer's signature	Signer's name *(please print)*	Title

Date | Telephone number

Figure H.43 Form NYS-45-MN, Page 1 (Source: www.tax.state.ny.us/pdf/2006/fillin/wt/nys45mn_706_fill_in.pdf)

Withholding identification number

40629421

Part D - Form NYS-1 corrections/additions

Use Part D **only** for corrections/additions for the quarter being reported in Part B of **this** return. To correct original withholding information reported on Form(s) NYS-1, complete columns a, b, c, and d. To report additional withholding information not previously submitted on Form(s) NYS-1, complete **only** columns c and d. Lines 12 through 15 on the front of this return **must** reflect these corrections/additions.

a **Original** last payroll date reported on Form NYS-1, line A (MMDD)	b **Original** total withheld reported on Form NYS-1, line 4	c **Correct** last payroll date (MMDD)	d **Correct** total withheld

Part E - Change of business information

22. Enter below the address at which you want to receive this form if different from the preprinted address.

Taxpayer's trade name

c/o: ☐ attn: ☐ *(if applicable, mark* ***either*** *box* ***and*** *enter name)*

Number and street or PO box

City | State | ZIP code

If the above address is for your paid preparer, mark this box and the c/o box, and enter preparer's name on the second line above ☐

23. If you **permanently ceased paying wages**, enter the date (MMDDYY) of the final payroll *(see* Note *below)*

24. Did you sell or transfer all or part of your business? ☐ Yes ☐ No

If *Yes*, indicate if sale or transfer was in ☐ Whole or ☐ Part

Note: Complete Form DTF-95, *Business Tax Account Update*, to report changes in federal identification number/withholding ID number, ownership, business name, business activity, telephone number, owner/officer/partner/responsible person information, or changes that affect any other tax administered by the NYS Tax Department. For questions regarding additional changes to your unemployment insurance account, call the Department of Labor at (518) 485-8589 or 1 888 899-8810.

If you are using a paid preparer or a payroll service, the section below must be completed.

Paid preparer's use	Preparer's signature	Telephone number ( )	Date	Mark an *X* if self-employed ☐	Preparer's SSN or PTIN
	Preparer's firm name *(or yours, if self-employed)*	Address		Preparer's EIN	

Payroll service name	Payroll service's EIN

Checklist for mailing:
- **File original return and keep a copy for your records.**
- **Complete lines 9 and 19 to ensure proper credit of payment.**
- **Enter your withholding ID number on your remittance.**
- **Make remittance payable to *NYS Employment Taxes*.**
- **Enter your telephone number in boxes below your signature.**

Need help or forms? Call 1 877 698-2910.

Mail to:
NYS EMPLOYMENT TAXES
PO BOX 4119
BINGHAMTON NY 13902-4119

NYS-45-MN (7/06) (back)

Figure H.44 Form NYS-45-MN, Page 2 (Source: www.tax.state.ny.us/pdf/2006/fillin/wt/nys45mn_706_fill_in.pdf)

Figure H.45 shows Form W-2 — Wage and Tax Statement (1 page).

22222 | Void ☐ | a Employee's social security number | For Official Use Only ► OMB No. 1545-0008

b Employer identification number (EIN)	1 Wages, tips, other compensation	2 Federal income tax withheld
c Employer's name, address, and ZIP code	3 Social security wages	4 Social security tax withheld
	5 Medicare wages and tips	6 Medicare tax withheld
	7 Social security tips	8 Allocated tips
d Control number	9 Advance EIC payment	10 Dependent care benefits
e Employee's first name and initial / Last name / Suff.	11 Nonqualified plans	12a See instructions for box 12
	13 Statutory employee ☐ Retirement plan ☐ Third-party sick pay ☐	12b
	14 Other	12c
f Employee's address and ZIP code		12d

15 State	Employer's state ID number	16 State wages, tips, etc.	17 State income tax	18 Local wages, tips, etc.	19 Local income tax	20 Locality name

Form **W-2** **Wage and Tax Statement** **2007**

Department of the Treasury—Internal Revenue Service

For Privacy Act and Paperwork Reduction Act Notice, see back of Copy D.

Copy A For Social Security Administration — Send this entire page with Form W-3 to the Social Security Administration; photocopies are **not** acceptable.

Cat. No. 10134D

Do Not Cut, Fold, or Staple Forms on This Page — Do Not Cut, Fold, or Staple Forms on This Page

Figure H.45 Form W-2 — Wage and Tax Statement (Source: www.tax.state.ny.us/pdf/2006/fillin/wt/nys45mn_706_fill_in.pdf)

Figure H.46 shows Form W-3 — Transmittal of Wage and Tax Statements (1 page).

DO NOT STAPLE

33333	a Control number	For Official Use Only ▶ OMB No. 1545-0008	
b Kind of Payer ▶ 941 ☐ Military ☐ 943 ☐ 944 ☐ CT-1 ☐ Hshld. emp. ☐ Medicare govt. emp. ☐ Third-party sick pay ☐		1 Wages, tips, other compensation	2 Federal income tax withheld
		3 Social security wages	4 Social security tax withheld
c Total number of Forms W-2	d Establishment number	5 Medicare wages and tips	6 Medicare tax withheld
e Employer identification number (EIN)		7 Social security tips	8 Allocated tips
f Employer's name		9 Advance EIC payments	10 Dependent care benefits
		11 Nonqualified plans	12 Deferred compensation
		13 For third-party sick pay use only	
g Employer's address and ZIP code		14 Income tax withheld by payer of third-party sick pay	
h Other EIN used this year			
15 State	Employer's state ID number	16 State wages, tips, etc.	17 State income tax
		18 Local wages, tips, etc.	19 Local income tax
Contact person		Telephone number ( )	For Official Use Only
Email address		Fax number ( )	

Under penalties of perjury, I declare that I have examined this return and accompanying documents, and, to the best of my knowledge and belief, they are true, correct, and complete.

Signature ▶ Title ▶ Date ▶

Form **W-3 Transmittal of Wage and Tax Statements** **2007** Department of the Treasury Internal Revenue Service

Send this entire page with the entire Copy A page of Form(s) W-2 to the Social Security Administration. Photocopies are not acceptable.

Do not send any payment (cash, checks, money orders, etc.) with Forms W-2 and W-3.

What's New

Relocation of form ID on Form W-3. For consistency with the revisions to Form W-2, we relocated the form ID number ("33333") to the top left corner of Form W-3.

Reminder

Separate instructions. See the 2007 Instructions for Forms W-2 and W-3 for information on completing this form.

Purpose of Form

Use Form W-3 to transmit Copy A of Form(s) W-2, Wage and Tax Statement. Make a copy of Form W-3 and keep it with Copy D (For Employer) of Form(s) W-2 for your records. Use Form W-3 for the correct year. **File Form W-3 even if only one Form W-2 is being filed.** If you are filing Form(s) W-2 electronically, **do not** file Form W-3.

When To File

File Form W-3 with Copy A of Form(s) W-2 by February 29, 2008.

Where To File

Send this entire page with the entire Copy A page of Form(s) W-2 to:

Social Security Administration
Data Operations Center
Wilkes-Barre, PA 18769-0001

Note. If you use "Certified Mail" to file, change the ZIP code to "18769-0002." If you use an IRS-approved private delivery service, add "ATTN: W-2 Process, 1150 E. Mountain Dr." to the address and change the ZIP code to "18702-7997." See Publication 15 (Circular E), Employer's Tax Guide, for a list of IRS-approved private delivery services.

For Privacy Act and Paperwork Reduction Act Notice, see the back of Copy D of Form W-2.

Cat. No. 10159Y

Figure H.46 Form W-3 — Transmittal of Wage and Tax Statements

H.5 Tax Forms for Chapter 10

Figure H.47 shows Form 8903 — Domestic Production Activities Deduction (1 page).

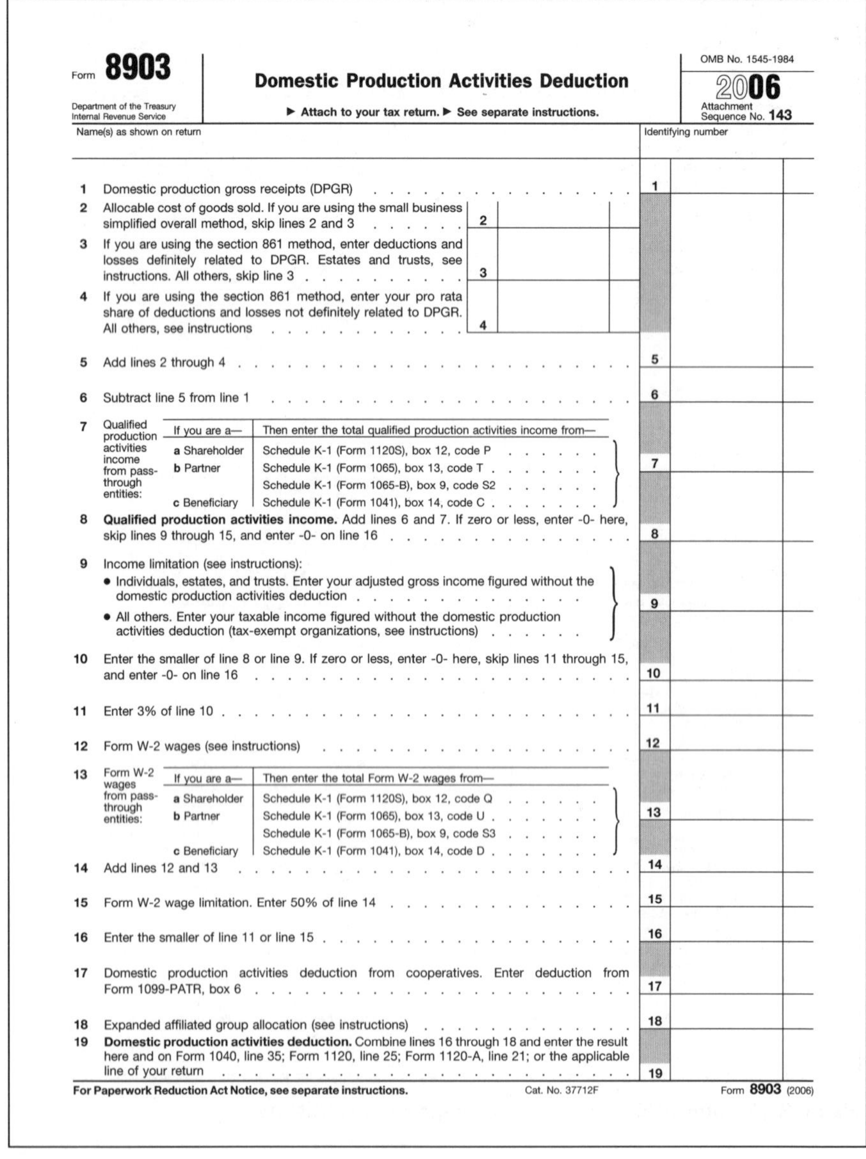

Form **8903**

Department of the Treasury
Internal Revenue Service

Domestic Production Activities Deduction

► Attach to your tax return. ► See separate instructions.

OMB No. 1545-1984

2006

Attachment Sequence No. **143**

Name(s) as shown on return | Identifying number

1 Domestic production gross receipts (DPGR) 1

2 Allocable cost of goods sold. If you are using the small business simplified overall method, skip lines 2 and 3 2

3 If you are using the section 861 method, enter deductions and losses definitely related to DPGR. Estates and trusts, see instructions. All others, skip line 3 3

4 If you are using the section 861 method, enter your pro rata share of deductions and losses not definitely related to DPGR. All others, see instructions 4

5 Add lines 2 through 4 5

6 Subtract line 5 from line 1 6

7 Qualified production activities income from pass-through entities:

If you are a—	Then enter the total qualified production activities income from—
a Shareholder	Schedule K-1 (Form 1120S), box 12, code P
b Partner	Schedule K-1 (Form 1065), box 13, code T
	Schedule K-1 (Form 1065-B), box 9, code S2
c Beneficiary	Schedule K-1 (Form 1041), box 14, code C

7

8 **Qualified production activities income.** Add lines 6 and 7. If zero or less, enter -0- here, skip lines 9 through 15, and enter -0- on line 16 8

9 Income limitation (see instructions):
- Individuals, estates, and trusts. Enter your adjusted gross income figured without the domestic production activities deduction . . . . .
- All others. Enter your taxable income figured without the domestic production activities deduction (tax-exempt organizations, see instructions) . . . . .

9

10 Enter the smaller of line 8 or line 9. If zero or less, enter -0- here, skip lines 11 through 15, and enter -0- on line 16 10

11 Enter 3% of line 10 11

12 Form W-2 wages (see instructions) 12

13 Form W-2 wages from pass-through entities:

If you are a—	Then enter the total Form W-2 wages from—
a Shareholder	Schedule K-1 (Form 1120S), box 12, code Q
b Partner	Schedule K-1 (Form 1065), box 13, code U
	Schedule K-1 (Form 1065-B), box 9, code S3
c Beneficiary	Schedule K-1 (Form 1041), box 14, code D

13

14 Add lines 12 and 13 14

15 Form W-2 wage limitation. Enter 50% of line 14 15

16 Enter the smaller of line 11 or line 15 16

17 Domestic production activities deduction from cooperatives. Enter deduction from Form 1099-PATR, box 6 17

18 Expanded affiliated group allocation (see instructions) 18

19 **Domestic production activities deduction.** Combine lines 16 through 18 and enter the result here and on Form 1040, line 35; Form 1120, line 25; Form 1120-A, line 21; or the applicable line of your return 19

For Paperwork Reduction Act Notice, see separate instructions. Cat. No. 37712F Form **8903** (2006)

Figure H.47 Form 8903 — Domestic Production Activities Deduction

Figures H.48 and H.49 show Form 6765 – Credit for Increasing Research Activities (2 pages).

Form **6765** — **Credit for Increasing Research Activities**

► Attach to your tax return.

Department of the Treasury
Internal Revenue Service

OMB No. 1545-0619
2006
Attachment Sequence No. 81

Name(s) shown on return | Identifying number

Section A—Regular Credit. Skip this section and go to Section B if you are electing or previously elected (and are not revoking) the alternative incremental credit.

1	Certain amounts paid or incurred to energy consortia (see instructions)		1
2	Basic research payments to qualified organizations (see instructions)	2	
3	Qualified organization base period amount	3	
4	Subtract line 3 from line 2. If zero or less, enter -0-		4
5	Wages for qualified services (do not include wages used in figuring the work opportunity credit)	5	
6	Cost of supplies	6	
7	Rental or lease costs of computers (see instructions)	7	
8	Enter the applicable percentage of contract research expenses (see instructions)	8	
9	Total qualified research expenses. Add lines 5 through 8	9	
10	Enter fixed-base percentage, but not more than 16% (see instructions)	10 %	
11	Enter average annual gross receipts (see instructions)	11	
12	Multiply line 11 by the percentage on line 10	12	
13	Subtract line 12 from line 9. If zero or less, enter -0-	13	
14	Multiply line 9 by 50% (.50)	14	
15	Enter the **smaller** of line 13 or line 14		15
16	Add lines 1, 4, and 15		16
17a	Are you electing the reduced credit under Section 280C? ► Yes ☐ No ☐ If "Yes," **and** you are not electing the alternative simplified credit in Section C, multiply line 16 by 13% (.13). If "No," **or** you are electing the alternative simplified credit in Section C, multiply line 16 by 20% (.20). Also, see the instructions for the schedule that must be attached if you checked "No." Members of controlled groups or businesses under common control: see instructions for the schedule that must be attached		17a
b	If your tax year ended after December 31, 2006, and you are electing the alternative simplified credit in Section C, multiply line 17a by the applicable 2006 percentage (see instructions)		17b

Section B—Alternative Incremental Credit. Skip this section if you completed Section A.

18	Certain amounts paid or incurred to energy consortia (see the line 1 instructions)		18
19	Basic research payments to qualified organizations (see the line 2 instructions)	19	
20	Qualified organization base period amount (see the line 3 instructions)	20	
21	Subtract line 20 from line 19. If zero or less, enter -0-		21
22	Add lines 18 and 21		22
23	Multiply line 22 by 20% (.20)		23
24	Wages for qualified services (do not include wages used in figuring the work opportunity credit)	24	
25	Cost of supplies	25	
26	Rental or lease costs of computers (see the line 7 instructions)	26	
27	Enter the applicable percentage of contract research expenses (see the line 8 instructions)	27	
28	Total qualified research expenses. Add lines 24 through 27	28	
29	Enter average annual gross receipts (see the line 11 instructions)	29	
30	Multiply line 29 by 1% (.01)	30	
31	Subtract line 30 from line 28. If zero or less, enter -0-	31	
32	Multiply line 29 by 1.5% (.015)	32	
33	Subtract line 32 from line 28. If zero or less, enter -0-	33	
34	Subtract line 33 from line 31	34	
35	Multiply line 29 by 2% (.02)	35	
36	Subtract line 35 from line 28. If zero or less, enter -0-	36	
37	Subtract line 36 from line 33	37	

For Paperwork Reduction Act Notice, see instructions. Cat. No. 13700H Form **6765** (2006)

Figure H.48 Form 6765 Credit for Increasing Research Activities, Page 1

Form 6765 (2006) Page **2**

Section B—Alternative Incremental Credit *(continued)*

38	Multiply line 34 by 2.65% (.0265) (for a tax year ending after December 31, 2006, see instructions for percentage)	**38**	
39	Multiply line 37 by 3.2% (.032) (for a tax year ending after December 31, 2006, see instructions for percentage)	**39**	
40	Multiply line 36 by 3.75% (.0375) (for a tax year ending after December 31, 2006, see instructions for percentage)	**40**	
41	Add lines 23, 38, 39, and 40	**41**	
42a	Are you electing the reduced credit under Section 280C? ▶ Yes ☐ No ☐ If "Yes," **and** you are not electing the alternative simplified credit in Section C, multiply line 41 by 65% (.65). If "No," **or** you are electing the alternative simplified credit in Section C, enter the amount from line 41. Also, see the line 17a instructions for the schedule that must be attached if you checked "No." Members of controlled groups or businesses under common control: see instructions for the schedule that must be attached	**42a**	
b	If your tax year ended after December 31, 2006, and you are electing the alternative simplified credit in Section C, multiply line 42a by the applicable 2006 percentage (see instructions)	**42b**	

Section C—Alternative Simplified Credit (for tax years ending after December 31, 2006). Also complete Section A or B.

43	Certain amounts paid or incurred to energy consortia (see the line 1 instructions)			**43**	
44	Basic research payments to qualified organizations (see the line 2 instructions)	**44**			
45	Qualified organization base period amount (see the line 3 instructions)	**45**			
46	Subtract line 45 from line 44. If zero or less, enter -0-			**46**	
47	Add lines 43 and 46			**47**	
48	Multiply line 47 by 20% (.20)			**48**	
49	Wages for qualified services (do not include wages used in figuring the work opportunity credit)	**49**			
50	Cost of supplies	**50**			
51	Rental or lease costs of computers (see the line 7 instructions)	**51**			
52	Enter the applicable percentage of contract research expenses (see the line 8 instructions)	**52**			
53	Total qualified research expenses. Add lines 49 through 52	**53**			
54	Enter your total qualified research expenses for the prior 3 tax years. If you had no qualified research expenses in any one of those years, skip lines 55 and 56	**54**			
55	Divide line 54 by 6.0	**55**			
56	Subtract line 55 from line 53. If zero or less, enter -0-	**56**			
57	Multiply line 56 by 12% (.12). If you skipped lines 55 and 56, multiply line 53 by 6% (.06)			**57**	
58	Add lines 48 and 57			**58**	
59	Multiply line 58 by the applicable 2007 percentage (see instructions)			**59**	
60	Add line 17b or line 42b (whichever applies) and line 59			**60**	
61	Are you electing the reduced credit under Section 280C? ▶ Yes ☐ No ☐ If "Yes," multiply line 60 by 65% (.65). If "No," enter the amount from line 60 and see the line 17a instructions for the schedule that must be attached. Members of controlled groups or businesses under common control: see instructions for the schedule that must be attached			**61**	

Section D—Summary

62	Credit for increasing research activities from partnerships, S corporations, estates, and trusts	**62**	
63	If you did not complete Section C, add line 17a or line 42a (whichever applies) to line 62. If you completed Section C, add lines 61 and 62. Estates and trusts go to line 64; partnerships and S corporations, report this amount on Schedule K; all others, report this amount on line 1d of Form 3800	**63**	
64	Amount allocated to beneficiaries of the estate or trust (see instructions)	**64**	
65	Estates and trusts: subtract line 64 from line 63. Report the credit on line 1d of Form 3800	**65**	

Form **6765** (2006)

Figure H.49 Form 6765 Credit for Increasing Research Activities, Page 2

H.6 Tax Forms for Chapter 11

Figure H.50 shows a Property Tax Return for the State of California. It involves natural gas pipeline property and is entitled: Property Statement – Intercounty Pipelines – Natural Gas Pipelines (1 page).

BOE-517-PG (S1F) REV. 15 (12-06)
PROPERTY STATEMENT — INTERCOUNTY PIPELINES — NATURAL GAS PIPELINES

STATE OF CALIFORNIA
BOARD OF EQUALIZATION
2007

DECLARATION OF COSTS AND OTHER RELATED PROPERTY INFORMATION AS OF 12:01 A.M., JANUARY 1, 2007

This statement must be completed, signed, and filed with the Valuation Division, Board of Equalization, PO Box 942879, Sacramento, California 94279-0061, by March 1, 2007. Omit cents; round to the nearest dollar.

NAME, STREET, CITY, STATE and ZIP CODE

OFFICIAL REQUEST
This request is made in accordance with section 826 of the Revenue and Taxation Code. This property statement must be completed according to the instructions and filed with the Board of Equalization on or before March 1, 2007. If you do not file this statement, you may be subject to the penalty provided in section 830 of the Revenue and Taxation Code. Attached schedules are considered to be part of the statement. THIS STATEMENT IS SUBJECT TO AUDIT.

MAKE NECESSARY CORRECTIONS TO ADDRESS LABEL

☐ Indicate if above is a change of name and/or address.

THIS STATEMENT SHALL CONSIST OF:	SUBMITTED HEREWITH	DATE TO BE SUBMITTED	N/A
(1) Dollar-Age Detail Report			
a. Fixed Equipment — BOE-533-PF			
b. Continuous Pipeline — BOE-533-PP			
c. Pipeline Mileage Report — BOE-575-P			
(2) BOE-517-PC Schedules:			
a. Comparative Balance Sheet			
b. Plant and Equipment			
c. Revenues and Expenses & Rental Expense			
d. Stmts. of Income and Retained Earnings			
h. Construction Work In Progress			
i. Pipeline Statistics			
(3) Schedule of Intangible Information — BOE-529-I			
(4) Other information as Requested:			
a. Annual Report to Federal Agencies			
b. Annual Report to State Agencies			
c. Form 10K			
d. Shareholders Report — 3 copies			
e. Supplemental Information			

NAME AND ADDRESS OF PERSON TO WHOM CORRESPONDENCE REGARDING AUDIT SHOULD BE ADDRESSED:

NAME

MAILING ADDRESS *(city, state, and zip code)* | TELEPHONE NUMBER ( )

LOCATION OF ACCOUNTING RECORDS:

NAME OF AUTHORIZED REPRESENTATIVE *(if applicable)* (BOE-892, *Statement of Authorization, must be filed annually)*

ADDRESS *(street, city, state, and zip code)* | DAYTIME TELEPHONE NUMBER ( )

CERTIFICATION

I certify (or declare) under penalty of perjury under the laws of the State of California that I have examined this Property Statement, including accompanying schedules and statements, and to the best of my knowledge and belief it is true, correct, and complete and covers all property required to be reported which is owned, claimed, possessed, controlled, or managed by the person named in the statement at 12:01 a.m. on January 1, 2007. If prepared by a person other than the taxpayer, this declaration is based on all information of which preparer has knowledge.

FULL LEGAL NAME IF INCORPORATED

FOR OFFICIAL USE ONLY

SIGNATURE OF OWNER, PARTNER, OFFICER, OR AUTHORIZED AGENT | DATE 2007

PRINTED NAME OF SIGNATORY | TITLE

SIGNATURE AND ADDRESS OF PREPARER OTHER THAN TAXPAYER | DATE 2007

Figure H.50 Property Tax Form (Source: www.boe.ca.gov/proptaxes/pdf/boe517pg.pdf)

H.7 Tax Forms for Chapter 12

Figure H.51 shows Form 26140, a Sales and Use Tax Return for the State of Texas (1 page).

01-117 (Rev.5-06/29) TEXAS SALES AND USE TAX RETURN HHH

a. 26140 • Do not fold, staple or paper clip • Write only in white areas.

l. OUT OF BUSINESS DATE DO NOT ENTER UNLESS no longer in business.

c. Taxpayer number

d. Filing period

g. Due date

f. Outlet no./location

k. Outlet address (Do not use a P.O. box address)

Taxpayer name and mailing address

	DOLLARS	CENTS
1. TOTAL SALES (Whole dollars only)		
2. TAXABLE SALES (Whole dollars only)		
3. TAXABLE PURCHASES + (Whole dollars only)		
4. Total amount subject to tax = (Item 2 plus Item 3)		
5. Tax due - Multiply Item 4 by the combined tax rate (Include state & local)		
6. TIMELY FILING DISCOUNT -		
7. Prior payments -		
8. Net tax due = (Subtract Items 6 and 7 from Item 5.)		
9. Penalty & interest + (See instructions)		
10. TOTAL AMOUNT DUE AND PAYABLE = (Item 8 plus Item 9)		

I declare that the information in this document and any attachments is true and correct to the best of my knowledge and belief.

sign here: Taxpayer or duly authorized agent

Date | Daytime phone (Area code & no.)

Blacken this box if out of business or address has changed.

PLEASE DETACH AND RETURN TOP PORTION ONLY

01-117 (Rev.5-06/29)

TEXAS SALES AND USE TAX RETURN - SHORT FORM

WHO MAY FILE THE SHORT FORM - You may file the short form if you meet ALL of the following criteria:

- your business has a single location (just one outlet) in Texas;
- you report applicable local taxes only to the entities (city, transit authority, county, or special purpose district) in which your business is located;
- you do not ship or deliver taxable items outside the transit authority in which your business is located;
- you do not prepay your state and local taxes;
- you do not have a credit to take on this return for taxes you paid in error on your purchases; and
- you do not have customs broker refunds to report.

You must file the long form (Form 01-114) if any of these statements do not apply to your business. You must file a long form if you are responsible for out-of-state use tax and have no in-state locations.

If you have a credit to take on this return for taxes you paid in error or customs broker refunds to report, you are required to complete Form 01-114 Sales and Use Tax Return and Form 01-148 Texas Sales and Use Tax Return Credits and Customs Broker Schedule.

WHEN TO FILE - Returns must be filed or postmarked on or before the 20th day of the month following the end of each reporting period. If the due date falls on a Saturday, Sunday or legal holiday, the next business day will be the due date.

BUSINESS CHANGES - Blacken the box to the right of the signature line if you are out of business or if your mailing or outlet address has changed. These changes may also be made via voice mail by calling 1-800-224-1844.

INSTRUCTIONS FOR FILING AN AMENDED TEXAS SALES AND USE TAX RETURN -

1) Make a copy of the original return you filed or download a blank return from our website at www.window.state.tx.us/taxinfo/taxforms.html.
2) Write "AMENDED RETURN" on the top of the form.
3) If you're using a copy of your original return, cross out the amounts that are wrong and write in the correct amounts. If you're using a blank return, enter the amounts as they should have appeared on the original return.
4) Sign and date the return.

If the amended return shows you underpaid your taxes, please send the additional tax due plus any penalties and interest that may apply.

WHOM TO CONTACT FOR ASSISTANCE - If you have any questions regarding sales tax, you may contact the Texas State Comptroller's field office in your area or call 1-800-252-5555, toll free, nationwide. The Austin number is 512/463-4600.

GENERAL INSTRUCTIONS

- Please do not write in shaded areas.
- If any preprinted information on this return is incorrect, OR if you do not qualify to file this return, contact the Comptroller's office.
- Do not leave Items 1, 2, 3 or 4 blank. Enter "0" if the amount is zero.
- You must file a return even if you had no sales.
- If any amounts entered are negative, bracket them as follows: <XX,XXX.XX>.
- If hand printing, please enter all numbers within the boxes, as shown. USE BLACK INK. 0 1 2 3 4 5 6 7 8 9
- If typing, numbers may be typed consecutively. 0123456789

Instructions continued on back.

File Texas Style with WebFile!
www.window.state.tx.us

Have this form available when you file your short form electronically using WebFile. Payment options are credit card or web electronic fund transfer. No-tax-due filing is also available through TeleFile at 1-888-4FILING (1-888-434-5464).

You have certain rights under Ch. 559, Government Code, to review, request, and correct information we have on file about you. Contact us at the address or toll-free number listed on this form.

Figure H.51 Form 26140 — Texas Sales and Use Tax Return
(Source: www.window.state.tx.us/taxinfo/taxForms/01-117.pdf)

I Glossary

ABAP4 SAP's programming language.

Access Sequence A code used in a pricing or tax procedure that determines the order in which steps in the procedure are executed.

Apportionment Used in all aspects of tax but most heavily for dividing the tax liability between states for corporations doing business in more than one state. Apportionment is basically the act of allocating taxable income usually based on the ratio of total assets, sales, or employees in a location to those in the total United States.

ASUG The America's SAP User Group. A group of SAP users from all disciplines that meet often for the purpose of education and influencing the direction of SAP software.

Backup withholding Withholding required from certain vendor payments either for 1099 or 1042 vendors. Backup withholding is generally required when the vendor has not adequately provided tax ID information to the payer.

Condition record Condition records are subordinate to condition types and contain information in a defined format that relate to the subject of the condition type. They can be thought of as a row of information in a table.

Condition technique SAP uses the condition technique as a tool to build pricing and tax procedures. It takes advantage of condition types and condition records to build formulas for calculations.

Condition type SAP software defines condition types for various purposes. A condition type is a code designed to categorize multiple condition records relating to a given subject.

DART SAP's Data Retention Tool. DART is used in a variety of ways, but it was created to extract data from ECC so tax departments can respond to federal tax audits.

Data element A single bit of information required for tax reporting. It can be best related to a required field in a table. In the fixed asset area, an examples of data elements include asset acquisition data, asset cost, asset useful life, and so on.

Direct taxes Taxes that are levied and paid on a taxpayer who in turn files directly with the tax jurisdiction. Corporate income tax is an example of a direct tax.

Domestic manufacturing deduction A statute giving companies a tax deduction for manufacturing activities performed in the United States.

ECC ECC replaced R/3 as the name for SAP's core ERP suite. SAP literature refers to ECC as both ERP Core Component and ERP Central Component.

Embedded software Software that is built-in to an asset but can be handled differently from the remaining asset cost for property tax purposes in some tax juridictions.

Extended withholding An advanced tax withholding application that is capable of backup and NRA withholding and in addition tracks payments for 1099 and 1042 compliance.

Form 1042 The IRS form used to report certain payments to foreign vendors and related nonresident alien withholding.

Form 1099 The IRS form required to be sent usually to noncorporate vendors to report total transactions with the vendor for a tax year.

Form 1120 The IRS form used to report corporate income and the associated tax liability.

Form 940 An annual return used to report and remit a corporation's federal unemployment insurance liability.

Form 941 The primary quarterly payroll tax return used to report wages, withholding, and social security of employees for the quarter.

Form W-2 The annual IRS form that reports an employee's wages, withholding, and social security for the year.

Form W-9 An IRS form providing a tax ID number and attesting to the fact that the number is really yours.

IDR Information Document Request. The IRS often requests information during the audit process. The IDR is the official form used to request the information.

IMG Implementation Guide. SAP software is constructed with two working sides: the application side and the Implementation Guide. The IMG is where the system configuration is done.

Indirect taxes Taxes that are collected by a business entity from other parties in the course of business and later remitted to the taxing authorities. Sales and use tax is an example of an indirect tax.

NetWeaver SAP's suite of applications that sits on top of ECC and provides a means to connect data from all parts of the system. NetWeaver components include BI (Business Intelligence), KM (Knowledge Management), MD (Master Data Management), an enterprise portal, and various other technical tools.

NRA withholding Withholding required for certain payments to nonresident aliens.

Pricing procedure A combination of condition types, condition records, and access sequences used to determine a product's price.

R&D tax credit A credit allowed against an entity's income tax liability for research and development expenditures.

R/3 SAP's client server ERP system with three-layer architecture. R/3 was released in the 1990s and was the predominate SAP offering until ECC was released.

Report Painter An SAP report or query generation tool. Report Painter uses libraries built on summary tables as its source of data. It is a user-friendly tool that is capable of better formatting and totalling then SAP Query.

Report Writer An SAP report or query generation tool. Report Writer has a more technical slant then Report Painter but also uses libraries and summary tables. Report Writer is not as user friendly as Report Painter or SAP Query but allows technical people the freedom of better contolling the code. The advantage of controlling the code, while good for technical programmers, requires more details for nonexperienced users.

Rev. Proc 98–25 The IRS Revenue Procedure that governs the retention of electronic books and records.

RFC Remote Function Call. A means of communicating with a program outside or inside the SAP system.

RVAXUD RVAXUD is the newer U.S. pricing procedure designed so an entire document can be read prior to assigning a tax rate. It was designed to handle more complex tax calculations such as max tax calculations.

RVAXUS The older U.S. pricing procedure designed to pass information to an external tax system one line at a time.

Sabrix A third-party sales and use tax software vendor.

SAP The name of the corporation located in Walldorf, Germany that created the R/2, R/3, and ECC ERP software systems. The name stands for Systems, Applications, and Products in data processing.

SAP Query An SAP report or query generation tool. SAP Query makes use of InfoSets to combine data from different tables as its source of data. It is very user friendly but not capable of sophisticated data mining or formatting.

Solution Manager SAP's project management tool. Solution Manager can be used to control many aspects of an implementation's progress.

Structured data The term given to electronic data in database form that is easily stored and queried. DART extracts are defined as structured data.

SUTA reports A tax return used to report quarterly employee earnings for state unemployment tax purposes. The format changes from state to state.

Tax data matrix A listing of tax data elements. The tax data matrix is a comprehensive way of identifying all the information required to be captured during an implementation.

Tax integration The process of working with an ECC system for the purpose of improving functionality from a tax point of view.

Tax procedure A combination of condition types, condition records, and access sequences used to determine a tax rate and amount.

Tax Reporter SAP's payroll tax reporting tool included in the HR module.

TAXUS A U.S. tax procedure for calculating sales and use tax within ECC. It makes use of tax codes but does not use jurisdiction codes.

TAXUSJ A U.S. tax procedure for calculating sales and use tax within ECC. It uses jurisdiction codes so tax can be tracked by location.

TAXUSX A U.S. tax procedure used with an external third-party bolt-on tax software product.

Taxware A third-party sales and use tax software vendor.

Transfer pricing Arm's length markup required by the United States and other countries for intercompany cross border transactions.

Unstructured data Data with variable formats. Unstructured data is not easily stored and not easily queried. Electronic spreadsheets, emails, and Word documents are all examples of unstructured data.

Vertex A third-party sales and use tax software vendor.

WRICEF The various types of development requirements during an implementation. Stands for Workflows, Reports, Interfaces, Conversions, Enhancements, and Forms.

J About the Author

Michael E. Scott is a senior managing consultant with IBM and a member of the Global Business Services SAP implementation team. He has been involved with tax and SAP work for over nine years and co-led the development of the DART and tax integration practices for PricewaterhouseCoopers.

As a leader in the industry, Michael has been a speaker referencing tax issues at ASUG events on numerous occasions, including annual ASUG conventions. Teaching at two universities increased Mr. Scott's skill in communicating effectively with students primarily unfamiliar with course subject matter. Michael has on multiple occasions instructed computer audit specialists from the Internal Revenue Service about SAP and DART, and trained SAP's clients on DART. He holds a master's degree in Accounting from Brigham Young University as well as a CPA and a CMA.

In his free time, he enjoys reading, writing, oil painting, and almost anything that includes a ball. Fishing, hiking, and camping are his ultimate relaxation activities. In case life isn't busy enough, Michael has taken up endurance racing with his favorite Arab mare, Kalilah. He lives with his family at the foot of the Wind River Mountain Range in Wyoming.

Index

H

I

J

K

L

M

N

O

P

Q

R

S

T

U

V

W

Z